Milcah Martha Moore's Book

Milcah Martha Moore's Book

A Commonplace Book from Revolutionary America

Edited by
Catherine La Courreye Blecki
and
Karin A. Wulf

The Pennsylvania State University Press
University Park, Pennsylvania

Library of Congress Cataloging-in-Publication Data

Milcah Martha Moore's book : a commonplace book from revolutionary America /
    edited by Catherine La Courreye Blecki and Karin A. Wulf.

    p.   cm.
    Includes bibliographical references and indexes
    ISBN 0-271-01690-6 (cloth : alk. paper)
    ISBN 0-271-01691-4 (pbk. : alk. paper)
    1. American literature—Colonial period, ca. 1600–1775. 2. Philadelphia
(Pa.)—Intellectual life—18th century—Sources. 3. Moore, Milcah Martha,
1740–1829—Friends and Associates. 4. American literature—Revolutionary
period, 1775–1783. 5. American literature—Pennsylvania—Philadelphia.
6. American literature—Women authors. 7. Commonplace books. I. Blecki,
Catherine L. (Catherine La Courreye), 1939– . II. Wulf, Karin A., 1964– .
PS530.M46   1997
810.8′002–dc21
                                                96-37555
                                                 CIP

It is the policy of The Pennsylvania State University Press to use acid-free paper
for the first printing of all clothbound books. Publications on uncoated stock
satisfy the minimum requirements of American National Standard for Information
Sciences—Permanence of Paper for Printed Library Materials, ANSI Z39.48-1992.

For Sarah A. G. Smith
in recognition of her many contributions.

CONTENTS

LIST OF ILLUSTRATIONS

PREFACE

Throughout her long life, Milcah Martha (Hill) Moore (1740–1829) loved the written word. Her legacy is her correspondence, her printed *Miscellanies, Moral and Instructive* (1787–1829), and three common-place books.[1] One of them, entitled "Martha Moore's Book" in Moore's own handwriting, is being published here for the first time as *Milcah Martha Moore's Book*. Within *Moore's Book* is a treasure of American literary documents—poems and prose by American women writers—previously unknown or thought to be lost and that reflect the eighteenth-century debate over the American Revolutionary War.

The first extant letter from Milcah Martha Hill's hand was written in 1748, when she was just eight years old and living with her parents on the island of Madeira. Addressed to her sisters in America, the letter conveys a prescient understanding of the place that the reading and transcribing of verse would play in her adult life. She requested that her sister Rachel send "some verses" and then reminded Rachel, "pray don't forget next time to send them." In exchange, "I now send you some verses but a great many of them are wrote so bad I am asham'd of them." It was not her handwriting, but the technology of writing that had failed her. Never one to be daunted by such a pedestrian problem, she explained that "I cant mend my pens myself but I will learn that I may have a good pen when I want one."[2]

Hill overcame the problem of the pen to assume a lifelong habit of exchanging and conserving verse. Four years after writing this letter Hill left Madeira for Philadelphia, where she joined her sisters in

1. Commonplace books are manuscript collections of prose and poetry usually transcribed by one person and usually from printed sources. See Catherine La Courreye Blecki's introduction, "Reading *Moore's Book*: Manuscript vs. Print Culture and the Development of Early American Literature," for a detailed definition.

2. Milcah Hill to her sisters, Madeira, May 17, 1748; Edward Wanton Smith Collection, Quaker Collection, Haverford College Library, Haverford, Pa. (hereafter EWS).

1752, and eventually married Dr. Charles Moore in 1767.[3] Residing in the Delaware Valley among an elite group of Quakers (Society of Friends), she lived through the turbulence of the late eighteenth century, including the American Revolution. Yet the constancy of reading and writing throughout her life is remarkable. *Moore's Book* is no accidental collection. When Moore began compiling this manuscript, she had a clear purpose in mind: to collect a body of work by her friends and family, particularly the women among her circle who were writers. Moore preserved three significant collections of manuscripts written by women: that of Susanna Wright (1697–1784), a friend; Hannah Griffitts (1727–1817), a cousin; and Elizabeth Graeme Fergusson (1737–1801), another friend. Moore's commonplace book contains the only known copies of many of Wright's and Griffitts's poems and Elizabeth Graeme Fergusson's travel journal to England in 1764. For these women, the handwritten manuscript, circulated among friends and family, was their preferred form of publication.[4] Of the 126 entries in the manuscript, women wrote about 100 pieces of prose or poetry.[5]

Moore's Book also reflects the multi-faceted culture of Philadelphia during the late eighteenth century. Although most of the manuscript was attributed to women, it also includes prose and poetry by at least

3. See John J. Smith, ed. *Letters of Doctor Richard Hill and His Children* (Philadelphia, 1854), 75–89, 195.

4. Wright and Griffitts did not seek publication for their poetry in print form, though both circulated their poetry freely among Quakers. A few of Griffitts's poems were reprinted in colonial newspapers, probably without her permission, including: "The female Patriots," *Pennsylvania Chronicle* (December 18–25, 1769): 372; and "To David Rittenhouse," *Pennsylvania Evening Post* (December 2, 1777): 562. Some of Elizabeth Graeme Fergusson's poems were also printed in colonial magazines. See Martha C. Slotten, "Elizabeth Graeme Fergusson, a Poet in 'The Athens of North America,'" *Pennsylvania Magazine of History and Biography* (hereafter *PMHB*) 108 (1984): 268n. Her exchange of poems with Nathaniel Evans appears in his *Poems on Several Occasions* (Philadelphia, 1772).

5. There are some entries that are anonymous or pseudonymous that we have been unable to identify whether the writer was a man or a woman. Moore was careful to attribute each entry by noting the author's name, pseudonym, or initials. None of the entries in *Moore's Book* appear to be written by her. After searching the Edward Wanton Smith Collection (EWS) at Haverford College Library in Pennsylvania and the relevant collections at the Historical Society of Pennsylvania (hereafter HSP), no poems written by Moore were found, except the poem written on the death of her husband, Charles, in 1801.

thirteen other authors who were either men or unidentified: letters and poems by noted intellectuals and prominent colonials, Quaker and non-Quaker, and people from many sides of the debate over the American Revolution, including Benjamin Franklin (1706–90), Patrick Henry (1736–99), Timothy Matlack (1736–1829), a Quaker disowned for being a revolutionary, Samuel Fothergill (1715–72), a British traveling Quaker minister, and Jonathan Odell (1736–1818), an Anglican loyalist. Some of these entries are not unique to this manuscript but come from material that was widely circulated in hand-written manuscript and in print, and reflect Moore's interest in public, especially political, issues.

Although there are significant passages of prose in *Moore's Book* (letters, a journal, and other brief prose pieces), the dominant literary genre is poetry. Following the example of other eighteenth-century educated people, particularly the English, Americans used verse to both communicate and entertain. Colonial almanacs and literary magazines always included poetry on contemplative, political, or comic themes. Verse played a particularly prominent role in the epistolary correspondence of early Americans. They sent poems to celebrate a birthday or to express their condolences after a friend's or relative's death or to express their own grief. They wrote poems as a form of intellectual exercise, challenging one another to respond in kind or to make revisions. Quakers celebrated with poetry the arrival of ministers from England or the return of public Friends from ministering travels. Americans wrote poems to support or castigate politicians at home and abroad and to express their connections with England or their emerging sense of political and independent cultural control. Each of these types of verse is represented in *Moore's Book* along with meditations, exchanges of poems between women, and a paraphrase of a Quaker testimony, which are particular to Moore's taste as the compiler of this commonplace book.[6]

6. Recorded in J. A. Leo Lemay, ed., *A Calendar of American Poetry in the Colonial Newspapers and Magazines and in the Major English Magazines Through 1765* (Worcester, Mass.: American Antiquarian Society, 1972), similar types of verse include: acrostics, biblical paraphrase, birthday verse, *carpe diem*, complimentary verse, various kinds of poetry on the "war of the sexes," death, dreams, elegies, epithalamium, epistolary poems, epitaphs, and "mock epitaph," friendship, pair of poems, political [poetry], Quakers, retirement theme, riddle[s], satire, Stamp Act, Tea, "*vers de société*."

The Manuscript

Moore's hand-written manuscript is located in the Edward Wanton Smith Collection in the Quaker Collection Library, Haverford College, Pennsylvania. It was found among the papers of Daniel B. Smith (1792–1888) and donated to Haverford College by Smith's great-great-granddaughter, Sarah A. G. Smith, in 1966. Daniel Smith's grandmother was Moore's sister, Margaret Hill Morris.

Originally the volume was bound in calfskin, but about 1969 it was rebound in sheepskin.[7] Measuring 7 × 9 inches, the volume has 132 leaves, with entries on both sides of the page. The text is in excellent condition; there are no torn pages or holes leaving illegible words. Milcah Martha Moore is the only transcriber. Her handwriting is very clear and regular; thus, there are few problems in legibility, except for the gradual fading of the ink in some places that makes it difficult to distinguish a comma from a period. The following biographies briefly summarize the lives of Moore and the three women who were the main contributors to her book: Susanna Wright, Hannah Griffitts, and Elizabeth Graeme Fergusson.

Milcah Martha Hill Moore

Milcah Martha Hill Moore (1740–1829) was the daughter of Dr. Richard Hill and Deborah Moore Hill. "Patty," or "Patsy," as she was known to her family and friends, was born on the island of Madeira, but lived primarily in the Delaware Valley, moving between urban and rural Philadelphia County and Burlington, New Jersey. A descendant of Thomas and Mary Lloyd (who arrived in Philadelphia from Wales in 1683[8]), she belonged to an elite network of related Quaker families (see Abbreviated Lloyd Genealogy, p. 17). In 1767 she mar-

---

7. In the binding process, four leaves were misbound, but they have been printed in the proper order in this edition. The book was foliated by Moore or another owner in the upper right-hand corner of the recto-side of each leaf, except for the leaf after *MMMB* 103 recto, which is blank.

8. See Jean R. Soderlund, ed., *William Penn and the Founding of Pennsylvania, 1680–1684: A Documentary History* (Philadelphia: University of Pennsylvania Press, 1983), 376n.

ried a cousin, Dr. Charles Moore. Earlier (1747) her older sister Hannah Hill Moore also married a cousin, Samuel Preston Moore, brother of Charles. Ordinarily, Quakers did not allow marriage between cousins. But while Hannah and Samuel were allowed to remain in the Society of Friends after their marriage, Milcah and Charles were not. Friends and family considered them a happy, devoted couple, but their estrangement from Quakerism was painful for both of them and for their families.[9] The Moores had no children.

Long a keeper of commonplace books and quoted material on loose sheets of paper, Moore published a collection in 1787, entitled *Miscellanies, Moral and Instructive* (1787–1829), for use in schools. Her *Miscellanies* went through many editions and were published in Philadelphia, Burlington (New Jersey), London, and Dublin.[10] The volume was used at various Quaker schools, including Westtown. Moore donated the proceeds from the *Miscellanies* to endow her school for indigent girls, and she also left a fund to educate the poor children of her community in Montgomery, Pennsylvania.[11]

After Charles Moore died in 1801, his widow resumed her membership in the Quaker faith and retired to share a home with her sister

9. For evidence of this estrangment, see Samuel Preston Moore and Hannah Moore to the Monthly Meeting of Friends at West River, September 9, 1747; Milcah Martha Moore to George Dillwyn, Montgomery, December 7, 1780, in J. J. Smith, *Letters of Doctor Richard Hill*, 242–43; Milcah Martha Moore to Hannah Moore [May 1784?]; and "The Happy Union," all in EWS.

10. Many editions of *Miscellanies, Moral and Instructive* were printed (and reprinted) on both sides of the Atlantic. Our search of the *Research Libraries Information Network* (RLIN), the *Eighteenth-century Short-Title Catalogue* (ESTC), and *The National Index of American Imprints* yielded approximately fifteen publications of *Miscellanies*. What follows is an abridged list of the publications, by publisher, city, and date.

The first publication was by Joseph James, in Philadelphia, 1787; it was reprinted in London by James Philips that same year. J. Jones reprinted the Philadelphia edition in Dublin in 1789. Publisher Isaac Neale printed the "Second Edition" in Burlington, New Jersey, in 1792, and again with his partner Kammerer in June 1796. Editions were reprinted in other American cities: Boston, by Spotswood in 1795; Baltimore, by Warner and Hanna in 1807; and Philadelphia, by Edmund Morris in 1829, the year of Moore's death.

11. See J. J. Smith, *Letters of Doctor Richard Hill*, 202–93. Will of Milcah Martha Moore with codicil, dated February 12, 1828, in Robinson-Wood Papers, Box 2:6, Newport Historical Society, Newport, Rhode Island.

Margaret Morris in Burlington. Milcah Martha Hill Moore died in Burlington, New Jersey, in 1829.

Susanna Wright

Born in 1697, Susanna Wright lived in her native England until her late teens when she migrated with her parents and siblings to Chester County, Pennsylvania.[12] In the late 1720s she, her widowed father, and her brother James, settled in frontier Lancaster County. There the Wrights continued to be active in Quaker Meeting and in provincial politics. Despite their frontier residence, the Wrights formed long-lasting friendships with Philadelphians, including other Quaker elites such as the Logan and Norris families and colonial luminaries such as Benjamin Franklin. Susanna Wright read widely and exchanged books and correspondence, including poetry, with friends and relatives. She was interested in literature, medicine, and law, acting as secretary or deputy prothonotary for Lancaster magistrate Samuel Blunston. Contemporary accounts suggest that while she could not serve in the legislature, as did her father and brother, she actively campaigned for political candidates.

Susanna Wright never married, but when Blunston died in the 1740s, he left her a life interest in his estate at Hempfield. Wright lived in this home for the majority of her adult life, composing poetry and engaging in horticulture and the raising silkworms. Samples of her silk were presented to the royal family in London by silk-production promoter Franklin.[13]

Susanna Wright died at her home in 1785 at age eighty-nine. She was remembered by Benjamin Rush as the famous "Suzey Wright, a lady . . . celebrated Above half a century for her wit, good Sense & valuable improvements of mind."[14]

12. John and Patience Wright were received by the Chester Monthly Meeting in 1714, according to the minutes for the Chester Monthly Meeting for 1714. Some sources suggest that Susanna did not join the family until several years later, instead remaining in England for schooling.

13. "Benjamin Franklin in Lancaster Country," *Journal of the Lancaster Country Historical Society* 61 (1957): 4–5.

14. Lyman Butterfield, "Dr. Benjamin Rush's Journal of a Trip to Carlisle in 1784," *PMHB* 74 (1950): 443–56. Biographical information on Susanna Wright is drawn

Hannah Griffitts

Born in 1727, Hannah Griffitts lived in Philadelphia for all of her long life. Griffitts was the daughter of Thomas and Mary Norris Griffitts, and belonged to the same extended Quaker family as Milcah Moore. Her grandmother and Moore were sisters, making Griffitts and Moore second cousins. Hannah Griffitts never married; instead she devoted her life to poetry. Her efforts were encouraged by Susanna Wright, with whom she exchanged letters and poems.[15] Griffitts took the pseudonym "Fidelia," possibly to indicate her faithfulness to the single life and her commitment to the Quaker faith and community.

Griffitts spent most of her life either being cared for or caring for other female relatives, most of them also unmarried. After her parents' deaths in the late 1740s, she lived with her cousins at the Norris mansion called Fairhill. She was very attached to her aunt Elizabeth Norris, also a spinster. In the early 1770s Griffitts took in this aunt, whom she tended for almost ten years. Then Griffitts cared for her spinster sister Mary, who died in the 1790s. Other relations then began helping to care for Griffitts, bringing her supplies, helping keep her household in order, visiting often, and writing letters to her. Her extensive and affectionate kinship network included Mary Norris Dickinson, a niece and the wife of John Dickinson, author of *Letters from a Farmer in Pennsylvania* (1768) and a prominent politician. Another niece, Deborah Logan, wrote an account of Griffitts's death in 1817; Griffitts was ninety years of age.[16]

Elizabeth Graeme Fergusson

Elizabeth Graeme Fergusson (1737–1801) was born into Philadelphia's Anglican gentry. Her father, Dr. Thomas Graeme, held a vari-

---

from Karin Wulf, "A Marginal Independence: Unmarried Women in Colonial Philadelphia" (Ph.D. diss., The Johns Hopkins University, Baltimore, 1993), 211–15; see also "The Early Silk Industry in Lancaster County," *Lancaster County Historical Society Papers* 23 (1919): 27–37.

15. Their exchange of poems and letters is described in Karin Wulf's introduction, "*Milcah Martha Moore's Book*: Documenting Culture and Connection in the Revolutionary Era," and Catherine Blecki's introduction, "Reading *Moore's Book*."

16. See Wulf, "A Marginal Independence," chap. 6, for examples of Griffitts's dependence on supplies from relations, and her letter to Milcah Martha More, March 30, 1799; see Deborah Norris Logan account of Hannah Griffitts's death, EWS.

ety of political offices in Pennsylvania, and her mother, Ann Diggs Graeme, was the stepdaughter of Governor William Keith. The family divided their time between a home in Philadelphia and a country estate in Horsham. Graeme Park, located about twenty miles north of Philadelphia, has been restored and is now open to the public. Elizabeth Graeme Fergusson was one of colonial Philadelphia's best-known literary figures. Her work was published in literary magazines from the late 1780s into the 1790s, but well before then her reputation was secured as a person of virtue and talent, "luminous" in her display of "knowledge and eloquence."[17] She invited friends, many from among the circle of elite communicants at Christ Church, to literary attic evenings. She wrote prodigiously and corresponded with other poets and writers, including Annis Boudinot Stockton, Anglican minister Jacob Duché, Nathaniel Evans, and Dr. Benjamin Rush. After an early and unsatisfactory relationship with William Franklin, son of Benjamin Franklin and the future royal governor of New Jersey, Elizabeth Graeme secretly married Henry Hugh Fergusson in 1772. Although not much is known of Henry Fergusson's background, his loyalism during the American Revolution caused Graeme Park to be seized by the Patriots. However, she never saw her husband after 1779. She spent the latter years of her life on her farm with a female friend "who had been a companion of her youth," probably Eliza Stedman. Fergusson died on February 23, 1801, "at the house of Seneca Lukins, a member of the Society of Friends near Graeme Park. Her body was interred, agreeably to her request by the side of her parents in the enclosure of Christ Church, in Philadelphia."[18]

17. "Account of the Life and Character of Mrs. Elizabeth Ferguson," *Port Folio* 1 (June 1809): 523.
18. Ibid., 527.

ACKNOWLEDGMENTS

We thank John Van Horne, Librarian of the Library Company of Philadelphia, for his generous assistance and careful readings of the full manuscript; Elisabeth Potts Brown, Diana Franzusoff Peterson, Diane Rofini, Ann W. Upton, and especially Emma Lapsansky of the Quaker Collection at Haverford College for all their help and encouragement; the staff of the Library Company of Philadelphia; and the Historical Society of Pennsylvania, especially their manuscript and archives curator, Linda Stanley. David Shields and Carla Mulford read our original proposal for Penn State Press and have been the best kind of critical readers: encouraging, and with a keen eye for the opportunities and potential of Moore's commonplace book. Their suggestions and questions made our work better. For her time and energy in reading parts of the text, and her helpful research tips, we thank Lorett Treese. Anne Ousterhout shared information about Elizabeth Graeme Fergusson; Ann Cline Kelley helped in our search for "M. Morris."

Karin Wulf wishes to thank Robert Calhoon, Alison Games, Julie Hardwick, Susan Klepp, Carolyn Lawes, Stephen Lofgren, Robert Olwell, and the members of the Friends Historical Association, particularly Jerry Frost, for their comments and suggestions. She also thanks Jim Green and David Shields for sharing their perspectives on early American literary culture. A Gest Fellowship from the Quaker collection at Haverford College and an Andrew W. Mellon Fellowship from the Library Company of Philadelphia provided her with much appreciated support for this project.

Catherine Blecki thanks her colleagues who read and commented on her literary essay: Professors John Engell, Elsie Leach, and Susan Shillinglaw. Graduate students Megan Hodges and Rebecca Webb did outstanding work in team-proofing the manuscript and double-checking the accuracy of annotations. San Jose State University, especially Dean of Humanities and Arts John K. Crane, sustained the project with financial aid in the form of several grants, while a Gest Fellowship from the Quaker Collection, Haverford College, provided needed support for three weeks research during the summer of 1996. She could not have finished the book without her husband David's enthusiasm for the project as well as his culinary and computer skills.

Both editors wish to thank Peter J. Potter and the staff of Penn State Press for their professional and personal help in bringing our manuscript to publication.

Sarah A. G. Smith contributed Milcah Martha Moore's commonplace book to the Quaker Collection at Haverford College, along with a collection of family letters and other materials. She has been a tireless supporter of this project, sending us research hints as well as her reconstruction of her family histories. Her commitment, not just to the history of her family, but to early American and Quaker history more broadly, has been a source of inspiration for us and for many other scholars.

LIST OF ABBREVIATIONS

DAB	*Dictionary of American Biography*. Edited by Allen Johnson. 10 vols. New York: Scribner, 1928–36.
DNB	*Dictionary of National Biography*. Edited by Leslie Stephen and Sidney Lee, et. al. 63 vols. London: Oxford University Press, 1885–1900.
EAL	*Early American Literature*
EWS	Edward Wanton Smith Collection, Haverford College Library, Haverford, Pennsylvania.
HSP	Historical Society of Pennsylvania, Philadelphia, Pennsylvania.
LCP	Library Company of Philadelphia, Philadelphia, Pennsylvania.
MMMB	*Milcah Martha Moore's Book*
OCCL	*Oxford Companion to Classical Literature*. Edited by Paul Harvey. Oxford: Clarendon Press, 1937.
OCEL, 3d	*Oxford Companion to English Literature*. 3d edition. Edited by Paul Harvey. Oxford: Clarendon Press, 1946.
OCEL, 5th	*Oxford Companion to English Literature*. 5th edition. Edited by Margaret Drabble. Oxford: Oxford University Press, 1987.
OED	*Oxford English Dictionary*. 2d ed. Edited by J. A. Simpson and E. S. C. Weiner. Oxford: Clarendon Press, 1982.
PMHB	*Pennsylvania Magazine of History and Biography*
QC	Quaker Collection, Haverford College Library, Haverford, Pennsylvania.
WMQ	*William and Mary Quarterly*

Notes on the Text

As editors, we have sought to retain the integrity of this historical document by preserving Milcah Martha Moore's ordering of its contents. In this edition, a number has been assigned to each poem or prose entry. We have provided a table of contents, listing the numbered entries in the book. Moore did not number the lines of the poems; we have added line numbers for the convenience of the reader.

Our basic textual methodology generally follows the "middle way" of Mary-Jo Kline in *A Guide to Documentary Editing* (Baltimore: Johns Hopkins University Press [1987], 121–22). This methodology maintains the eighteenth-century character of the text as Moore transcribed it with as few modifications as possible, while offering a readable text for twentieth-century students and scholars. Eighteenth-century spelling, capitalization, and punctuation have been retained. Changes to accidentals like punctuation that may be significant have been placed in brackets. We have retained the spelling inconsistencies of the original; thus, "veil" will also appear sometimes as "viel."

Eighteenth-century names sometimes varied in spelling; thus, E. G. Fergusson usually has two esses ("ss"), but sometimes only one ess ("s"). When someone quotes "Ferguson" with one ess, then we follow the form in the quotation. The name of her friend, Elizabeth Stedman, is also spelled sometimes as "Steadman." In prose, eighteenth-century writers used more commas and colons than periods. We have followed their practice, except in a few cases that seemed confusing to twentieth-century readers; when this happened, we enclosed modern punctuation in brackets. Some paragraphs do not end in any punctuation. Moore often finished a paragraph of prose with a flourish rather than punctuation. Basically, all editor's additions or minor corrections appear in brackets.

Moore's original vertical flourishes for triple rhymes have been retained in the text; most of her many horizontal flourishes have been deleted for reasons of page composition and space. A few have been retained, however, for aesthetic purposes.

The following changes to Moore's original text have been made discretely:

1. The thorn "y" has been replaced by "th"; the long "s" in script with the modern "s."
2. Superscript characters are lowered to the line of type and the resulting abbreviations have been kept unless they may be obscure to the modern reader, such as "oppo." for "opportunity" on page 192. In such cases, which are very few, the changes are bracketed.
3. Moore's practice of writing the first word of the following page at the bottom of a page in order to prompt a reader or reciter has not been adopted in this edition.
4. In some cases authorial attributions or dates were noted only at the bottom of the poem or prose piece. We have moved these to the top of the work for ease of reading and for consistency.
5. Moore's marginal notes have been preserved, although not, of course, in the exact order of their appearance in her commonplace book. These comments are placed at the end of a poem or prose piece and are identified as marginal notes. In some cases they were accompanied, as they are in the edition, by an asterisk. In a very few cases Moore recorded the last stanza of a poem in the margin. In these cases we have moved this last stanza to the end of the poem without comment.
6. The editors' line numbering appears to the right of each selection. In one case, "To the Memory of Sally Norris" (*MMMB* 47), Moore also numbered the stanzas. Her numbering appears to the left, as it did in her commonplace book.

The aim of providing annotations is to supply brief explanatory historical and literary information. Obscure words, for example, not found in standard dictionaries such as *The American Heritage Dictionary* or *Webster's Collegiate Dictionary*, are defined here. Frequently cited sources are noted in the list of short titles and abbreviations. Some footnotes do not have citations because they are summaries of historical events that are common knowledge and mythological allusions that can be readily looked up in a classical dictionary.

MILCAH MARTHA MOORE'S BOOK

Documenting Culture and
Connection in the Revolutionary Era

Karin A. Wulf

Milcah Martha Moore's Book is a twentieth-century edition of an eighteenth-century book that was never in print, but that nonetheless circulated among an audience of readers. An intimate, handwritten publication, the book is a collection of poetry and prose by at least sixteen different authors, collected, organized, and transcribed by Milcah Martha Moore (1740–1829) of Philadelphia. In a sense this commonplace book is a kind of literary diary, but it is also a documentary testament to the significance of women's literacy for forming relationships and expressing sentiments on subjects ranging from politics and war to marriage and housework, and to the complexity of the Quaker culture of the eighteenth-century Delaware Valley. Compiled during the middle years of the American Revolution, the book is also a vivid depiction of the war's impact on people and property, and provides a record of contested allegiances during a time of crisis.

Opening Milcah Martha Moore's commonplace book for the first time, contemporary readers might imagine themselves not as alien to the subjects and style of the writing Moore preserved but as part of her intended audience. If it is harder for the modern reader to find Moore's book as accessible as did the author's contemporaries, it is nonetheless possible to recapture many aspects of the eighteenth-century culture shared by Moore and her original audience. The friends and family members with whom Moore shared her book would have known the full cast of characters represented in the book, ranging from cousins who authored some poetry to the royal family referenced in a number of pieces. They would have understood the jests, the sly allusions, and the biblical citations. They would have found the language, the style of verse, and the topics familiar. The modern reader may be more immediately engaged by subjects less obvious to Moore and her readers, such as the significance of women's writing in the eighteenth century, and the historical and literary environments in which Moore compiled the poetry and prose that forms her commonplace book.

By learning more about the specific historical and literary contexts in which the book was produced, we can appreciate more fully the authors, their subjects, their styles of expression, and their culture. Moore's commonplace book was written by a woman who found poetical expression specifically, and writing generally, a comfortable mode of expression and education. From her youth on the Atlantic island of Madeira to her adult years in Philadelphia, Moore used long letters and verse collections to communicate with friends and kin. This book, then, is part of a long conversation conducted in letters and verse among Moore's circle of family and friends. The book is also representative of a specific historical experience. That Moore was able to produce such a document reflects her education, her commitment to writing, and the leisure she was afforded by modest wealth, a supportive husband, and the lack of her own children. The works Moore selected represent her experience as a woman, a Quaker, a member of an extensive kin network that included many of the most politically and economically powerful people in the Delaware Valley, and a Loyalist during the years of the American Revolution.

To open *Moore's Book* is to open a window into the eighteenth century. Readers see the reality of high mortality through the deaths of dear friends and relations, including many young children. We see the experiences of Moore's privileged circle through their literacy, their education and comfortable economic circumstances, which afforded

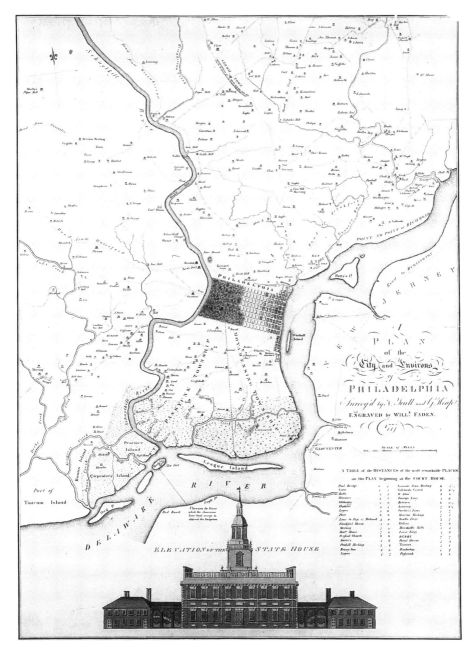

Fig. 1.   Delaware Valley, 1777. Courtesy, Library Company of Philadelphia,
Philadelphia, Pennsylvania.

them travel and leisure. We see the complexity of Quaker politics through the challenge of the American Revolution and the attempts of Quakers to remain passive and neutral in a revolutionary and wartime environment that demanded loyalty to one side or the other. Moore's commonplace book, however, does not provide a clear, unobstructed view of the totality of eighteenth-century life. What it is instead is a particular view, a vista bounded by the socioeconomic, geographic, religious, political, and educational circumstances of Moore, the authors whose works she copied, and the subjects whose experiences they documented.

This introductory essay looks at Milcah Martha Moore's world as revealed through her commonplace book: her family and friends; her Quaker background, childhood, and marriage; the significance of writing and reading, particularly for women in early America; and the dramatic events of the American Revolution. Exploring first Moore's Quaker heritage, then the place of her commonplace book within the development of women's literary culture in the Delaware Valley, it is clear that Moore's familial and kinship connections were important aspects of how her commonplace book was formed and organized. For example, Quaker ideas and beliefs are central to much of the poetry and prose included in Moore's commonplace book (a topic dealt with at greater length in Catherine Blecki's introduction). In addition, Moore's relationships with the three women whose work forms the core of the commonplace book, Susanna Wright (1697–1784), Hannah Griffitts (1727–1817), and Elizabeth Graeme Fergusson (1737–1801), help illuminate their works' inclusion in the volume. Turning then to the Revolutionary War context of the book's compilation, it is clear that the events of the 1760s and 1770s, and Moore's particular situation as a Quaker in the Delaware Valley, helped shape her choices of inclusion. At the same time, the range of material she included helps illuminate the complexity of Quakers' position during the Revolutionary years. Examining each of these facets of Moore's world demonstrates that, while her commonplace book is an extraordinary document, it was as well the product of her interests, talents, background, and opportunities. Moore's commonplace book is unique, but it also represents a broader context of literary and historical developments.[1]

1. Another excellent example of the way in which the analysis of women's writing can reveal much about eighteenth-century culture is explained in Elaine Forman

Milcah Moore's Quaker Heritage

Moore's commonplace book demonstrates the strength and extent of networks of association among colonial Americans. Early Americans, particularly the elite, prized human connections created by blood, marriage, religious affinity, or economic partnership. They expressed their relationships to others in these terms: How might they know of someone? To whom was this person related? With whom did they do business, or with whom did they worship? Through her choice of authors and subjects, Milcah Martha Moore's commonplace book celebrates the connections of kinship, friendship, religion, and sympathy. Thus, to understand the context in which she compiled the book, it is essential to understand her family background, her Quaker roots, and her life in Philadelphia.

We often think of America as a place where people from around the world were drawn by the promise of economic betterment. For the family of Richard Hill, America provided opportunity with one hand and took it away with the other. Richard Hill, Milcah Moore's father, was a second-generation native Marylander. His grandfather had received a modest tract of land (one hundred acres) on the Eastern Shore from Lord Baltimore and settled there in 1673. A sure sign of the Hills' success was their marriages with the Lloyds of Philadelphia. In 1703 Richard's uncle, also named Richard, became the second husband of Hannah Lloyd Delavel Hill, daughter of Thomas Lloyd. In 1726, the younger Richard Hill confirmed this connection by marrying Deborah Moore of Annapolis, a granddaughter of Thomas Lloyd. Thomas Lloyd was the most powerful force in Pennsylvania during the colony's earliest years. Arriving in Pennsylvania in 1683 from his ancestral home of Dolobran in Montgomeryshire, Wales, Lloyd quickly became an important merchant and politician. William Penn appointed Lloyd acting governor of the province in 1684, a post he retained until he died in 1694. Thomas Lloyd's wife, Mary Jones Lloyd, died soon after their arrival in Philadelphia and is said to have been the first person buried in Philadelphia's Friends Burial Ground.[2] The

---

Crane's work on the diary of Elizabeth Drinker (1735–1807). See especially Crane, "The World of Elizabeth Drinker," *PMHB* 107 (1983): 3–28; idem, *Diary of Elizabeth Drinker.*

2. See Soderlund, *William Penn*, 376n.

intermarriage among the Lloyd relations continued on down to Milcah Martha Hill's 1767 marriage to her cousin Charles Moore. The dizzying combination of blood and marriage connections made spouses and in-laws of cousins, aunts, and uncles. These connections were important for kinship and business reasons.

While the Hills prospered by their connection to the Lloyds—and indeed it was extremely important to them—Richard Hill's business was not consistently prosperous. In 1739 a combination of debts and the desire to avoid his creditors led Hill to resettle far from Maryland, in the port town of Funchal on the island of Madeira off the west coast of Africa.[3] Six of the nine Hill children were sent to Philadelphia in the care of their sixteen-year-old sister Hannah Hill, recently married to their cousin Samuel Preston Moore. Two of the Hill daughters, Mary and Harriet, accompanied their parents to the Spanish island; a third, Deborah, eventually joined them; and a fourth daughter, Milcah Martha, was born there in 1740. The separation of the family turned out to have long-term consequences, for, with the exception of Milcah Martha, the Madeira-bound sisters never returned to America. Mary, Harriet, and Deborah all married and settled in England, while the rest of the family either grew up in or returned to Philadelphia.

Although he remained troubled by debts in America, Richard Hill established a modestly successful trading business on Madeira. By 1744 Hill recounted commissions on sales above £30,000, and on trading ventures to Virginia, Philadelphia, New York, London, Liverpool,

3. Madeira was the center of a trading network between Africa, Europe, the Caribbean, and the Americas and is located off the coasts of Portugal and northwest Africa. Though small in size, Madeira, like the other Atlantic islands, attracted sailors in search of resupply, as well as traders interested in sugar and then wine, which became the island's staple products. By 1700 shipments from the American colonies, including wheat from Pennsylvania, were imported to the island. Pennsylvania and Virginia became favorite destinations for Madeira wine, as merchants ever more successfully marketed that product to the colonists. See T. Bentley Duncan, *Atlantic Islands: Madeira, the Azores and Cape Verdes in Seventeenth-Century Commerce and Navigation* (Chicago: University of Chicago Press, 1972), 46, 70, 153.

Madeira was first settled as a province of Portugal in the fifteenth century, and by 1760 its population exceeded 60,000. English settlers dominated the merchant community. Funchal was the only town and viable port on the 286-square-mile island. See Desmond Gregory, *The Beneficent Usurpers: A History of the British in Madeira* (London: Associated University Presses, 1988), 18–22.

and Boston.[4] At that time he thought he might be successful enough to settle his debts in America and generate enough money for his children's independence.[5] Bad fortune struck, however, when expected cargoes were lost at sea. Although he never made enough money to allow him both to pay his creditors and to leave what he considered sufficient fortune to his daughters and sons, Richard Hill's business did grow, especially after a son and three sons-in-law joined him in partnership.[6] Hill finally returned to America in 1754 to visit family and solicit trading business. When he died in 1757 he left a thriving business for the other partners to share.[7]

Students of early American history may be startled to discover how far flung were the members of Milcah Martha Moore's family. We often think of European-American colonists as rooted in the American soil. Arriving from disparate European locations, the popular conception holds, they planted here and flourished. For many who voluntarily immigrated to North America, this is a fair description. New Englanders, for example, tended to live long lives and maintain strong familial ties to particular areas. Milcah Moore's life, by contrast, began on the island of Madeira, where her American-born parents emigrated. She and some of her sisters ended up in Philadelphia, but others scattered to England, the homeland of their grandparents. Although separated by great distance, the Hill family remained extremely close, sending letters by every available conveyance.[8]

4. See Richard Hill to Samuel Preston Moore, Madeira, September 15, 1744, in J. J. Smith, *Letters of Doctor Richard Hill*, 36–38.

5. See Richard Hill to Hannah Moore, Madeira, August 29, 1752, in J. J. Smith, *Letters of Doctor Richard Hill*, 82–83. See also Deborah Hill's comments on Richard Hill's estimations about the size fortune he needed to return to America: Deborah Hill to Hannah Moore, Madeira, August 23, 1750, in J. J. Smith, *Letters of Doctor Richard Hill*, 63.

6. See J. J. Smith, *Letters of Doctor Richard Hill*, xv.

7. Richard Hill arrived in Philadelphia in 1754 and set out for a trip to the Chesapeake Bay, partly to procure more business. See Milcah Martha Moore's genealogical notes with dates, Box 5, EWS.

8. A keen concern for all was the health and well-being of the young children left in the care of their older sister Hannah Moore. Deborah and Richard Hill sent to the Moores food items and cloth but most often advice and queries. They also expressed enormous trust and confidence in Hannah and her husband, Samuel Preston Moore. Letters to the family in Philadelphia reiterate their appreciation, and their hopes that the children appreciated, the sister and brother-in-law's care.

Fig. 2.   Dr. Richard Hill's Villa, Madeira. From John Jay Smith, ed., *Letters of Doctor Richard Hill and His Children* (Philadelphia, 1854).

In late 1751, when Milcah Hill was eleven, her mother Deborah died.[9] Deborah Hill had planned to leave Madeira the following spring for a visit with her children in America. Instead, her sister-in-law Mary Moore, who had moved to Madeira to assist the Hills in housekeeping, escorted young Milcah and a brother back to Philadelphia.[10] Hannah Moore opened her house to Milcah as she had to her other sisters. After twelve years on a remote Atlantic island, connected to her siblings only by letters, Milcah Hill entered a house full of sisters and a city full of kin.

By moving to Philadelphia, Milcah joined not only her sisters but entered the center of Quakerism in America. The Hill children were now surrounded by an extended family of elite Quakers in the Quaker capital of the New World. Among their aunts, uncles, cousins, and in-laws were ministers and leading members of the So-

9. Milcah Moore recorded the death of Deborah Hill as December 19, 1751. See genealogical notes, Box 5, EWS.

10. See Richard Hill to Richard Hill Jr., Madeira, October 27, 1751; Richard Hill to Hannah Moore, Madeira, June 15, 1752, both in J. J. Smith, *Letters of Doctor Richard Hill,* 67–68, 74–75.

ciety of Friends (called Quakers or Friends).[11] Philadelphia's Yearly
Meeting was by far the largest and most influential organization of
Quakers in America. Leading Quakers from England and Ireland
regularly visited the city, introducing the children to Quaker luminaries like Samuel Fothergill and Catherine Peyton.[12] The import-
ing, printing, and circulation of a range of Quaker materials, from
epistles sent from meeting to meeting, to memoirs of ministers, to testimonials of prominent Friends made Philadelphia a center of Quaker
literature.[13]

The intensity of this Quaker culture would have been a new experience for the Hills. In Maryland, the place of the Hills' American
origins, Quakers were an important minority and on Madeira they
were a small minority indeed. In Philadelphia in the mid-eighteenth
century, Quakers were not a majority among the population, but
nonetheless remained a culturally dominant force.[14] When William
Penn founded Pennsylvania in the late seventeenth century, English
and Welsh Quakers comprised the majority of the population. By
1750, Quakers were only about one-sixth of the population.[15] Irish
and German immigration as well as the arrival of Presbyterians, Anglicans, and Lutherans made Quakers just one among a number of

11. The Hill's aunt Hannah Hill was a clerk of the Women's Meeting. See Jean R.
Soderlund, "Women's Authority in Pennsylvania and New Jersey Meetings,
1680–1760," *William and Mary Quarterly* [hereafter cited as *WMQ*], 3d ser. 44
(1987): 734. Cousins Israel and James Pemberton served as clerks of the Men's and
Yearly Meetings. Cousin Sarah Morris and brother-in-law George Dillwyn were
ministers.

12. See "An Account of Ministering Friends from Europe who visited America,
1656 to 1793," *Journal of the Friends Historical Society* 10 (1913): 117–32.

13. J. William Frost, "Quaker Books in Colonial Pennsylvania," *Quaker History*
80 (1991): 1–23, concludes that "scholars can still assume members of Philadelphia
yearly Meeting shared a religious literature joining men and women, minister and
laity, city and country members in worship and in daily life."

14. For a discussion of the role of Quakers in seventeenth- and early eighteenth-
century Maryland, see David W. Jordan, "'Gods Candle' within Government: Quakers and Politics in Early Maryland," *WMQ* 3d ser. 39 (1982): 628–54. I find no mention in the secondary literature of Quakers other than the Hills living on Madeira in
the seventeenth and early eighteenth century.

15. See Alan Tully, *William Penn's Legacy: Politics and Social Structure in
Provincial Pennsylvania, 1726–1755* (Baltimore: Johns Hopkins University Press,
1977), 54.

ethnic and religious groups. But the city and its immediate hinterland continued to reflect its Quaker heritage.[16]

Hannah Hill and Samuel Preston Moore made sure that the children in their care were educated and exposed to the richness of Quaker culture, and to Quaker ideals and practices. The tenets of Quakerism included a belief in the inherent ability of every soul to experience the "light [of God] within." There was a dedication to family forms which included endogamy, a very informal and spontaneous worship service, an extensive traveling ministry, and a devotion to pacifism.[17] All Protestants believed in the equality of souls, but Quakers also had a strong tradition of opposing any form of hierarchy. As a religion that developed in England during the upheavals of the mid-seventeenth century, Quakerism included a critique of contemporary social practices. Quaker opposition to using forms of language such as deferential pronouns (such as the "you" and "your" then used to acknowledge social hierarchy; Quakers substituted "thee," "thou," and "thine"), elaborate dress, and taking oaths were all part of their dedication to avoiding hierarchy and hypocrisy.

Another significant aspect of Quakerism that had an important impact on Milcah Martha Moore and other women of her time was its emphasis on the spiritual equality of men and women. The Quakers' most radical social critique was their revisioning of family and gender relations. Quaker ideas about family and gender began with an understanding of the events in the garden of Eden that differed markedly from traditional Christian interpretations, which held that Eve's role in the ultimate mortality of humanity was indicative of woman's innate weakness. If women were weak and inclined to follow the devil, then they needed to be controlled by men. Quakers, on the other hand, believed that one of the lessons to be learned from the Edenic

16. Explaining the continued importance of Quaker ideas in Pennsylvania, Tully writes: "The Quakers remained so entrenched in power in the late colonial years because they continued to have the minds of the people. The Quaker system of politics and the ideology of civil Quakerism continued to have unrivaled persuasive power even in such uncertain times." See Allan Tully, *Forming American Politics: Ideals, Interests and Institutions in Colonial New York and Pennsylvania* (Baltimore: Johns Hopkins University Press, 1994), 309.

17. An excellent introduction to Quaker theology can be found in J. William Frost, *The Quaker Family in Colonial America: A Portrait of the Society of Friends* (New York: St. Martin's Press, 1973), chap. 1.

experience was that before the Fall, men and women were "helps-meet," or equal partners, and that subsequent generations should strive to achieve the state of equality that existed before the Fall, or before mortality and evil were introduced to humans. The marriage between the founder of Quakerism, George Fox, and his wife, Margaret Fell Fox, was the model of an equalitarian union.[18] Some historians have wondered about the dedication of Quaker men and women to attaining those goals of gendered equality.[19] They have questioned the extent to which Quaker notions about equality were affected by the rising wealth and subsequent interest in secular indications of status of many Quaker merchants in the eighteenth century. Quakers, like other colonial Americans, apparently adhered to a gender hierarchy that gave men primary control over economic and political matters.

Yet extensive evidence suggests that Quaker women were not unaffected by the radical implications of their religion's theology, which may have freed them from more traditional ideas about women's sole functions as wives and mothers. For example, Quaker women participated in the ministry in large numbers, traveling extensively throughout Europe and America with the support of their families and their Meetings (the Quaker congregation was called "The Meeting"). In addition, while marriage and motherhood were common phenomena, normative and certainly encouraged, neither role was as central to Quaker ideals of womanhood as it was for other groups' ideals.[20]

18. The best introduction to the differences between Quaker ideas about women and those of other Protestants is Mary Maples Dunn, "Saints and Sisters: Congregational and Quaker Women in the Early Colonial Period," in Janet Wilson James, ed., *Women in American Religion* (Philadelphia: University of Pennsylvania Press, 1980), 27–46. Other excellent works include Phyllis Mack, *Visionary Women: Ecstatic Prophesy in Seventeenth-Century England* (Berkeley and Los Angeles: University of California Press, 1992); and Jacques Tual, "Sexual Equality and Conjugal Harmony: The Way to Celestial Bliss, A View of Early Quaker Matrimony," *Journal of the Friends Historical Society* 55 (1988): 161–74.

19. See Frederick B. Tolles, *Meeting House and Counting House: The Quaker Merchants of Colonial Philadelphia, 1682–1763* (Chapel Hill: University of North Carolina Press, 1948); and Barry Levy, *Quakers and the American Family: British Settlement in the Delaware Valley* (New York: Oxford University Press, 1988).

20. High percentages of Quaker women never married. For example, while only 2.9 percent of all Philadelphians over the age of forty who died before 1775 were single; between 1751 and 1776, 17.6 percent of women among the largely Quaker

Many Quaker women experienced neither marriage nor motherhood, and some married women had no children. Milcah Martha Moore's childlessness was probably related to the high incidence of intermarriage in her family and thus did not represent a choice. But other women did make choices between marriage and singleness, finding the latter more appealing than the former. As Hannah Griffitts wrote to Moore after a life without marriage, "There are many of you wed[d]ed ones who I believe are Placed in your (Proper) Sphere [and] I sincerely wish you encrease of Hap[p]iness in it without envying you one atom . . . everyone is not fitted for the single Life, nor was I ever moulded for the wed[d]ed one."[21] Perhaps because of the equalitarian nature of their theology and their acknowledgement of different forms of female authority, Quaker women may also have been able to participate in a wider range of political activities than women in other colonies. Some of the most tantalizing evidence of women's direct political activity in the colonies concerns Quaker Susanna Wright's campaigning for a candidate for the Pennsylvania Assembly and Quaker minister Catherine Peyton's meeting with the Assemblymen to discuss the prospect of war in the 1750s.[22] Both of these women appear in Moore's commonplace book. Thus the Hill children's exposure to an intensively Quaker culture in Philadelphia gave them access to ideas about women's activities that could challenge broader cultural notions emphasizing women's responsibility for exclusively domestic roles.[23]

Along with inculcating her sisters in Quaker values and culture, Hannah Moore tended to their education. Education was highly

Philadelphia gentry were single at age fifty. See the work of Robert Gough, Susan Klepp, Barry Levy, and Robert Wells presented in Klepp, "Fragmented Knowledge: Questions in Regional Demographic History," *Proceedings of the American Philosophical Society* (June 1989), 232. For a different interpretation of the significance of the role of wife and mother to Quaker ideals of womanhood, see Levy, *Quakers and the American Family*, 193–230.

21. Hannah Griffitts [to Milcah Martha Moore], n.d., EWS.

22. Both women are cited in Tully, *Forming American Politics*, 351, as outstanding examples of Quaker women's activity in politics.

23. These Quaker "options" could be compared with the ideas discussed in Laurel Thatcher Ulrich, *Good Wives: Image and Reality in the Lives of Women in Northern New England, 1650–1750* (New York: Oxford University Press, 1980). An interesting discussion of Quaker women's interest in gender-related issues, and the tensions in Quaker communities about these issues, is Bonnelyn Young Kunze, "'vessells fit

prized by Quakers, as other Protestants, for providing access to the Bible. Although by the 1740s a number of Quaker schools catered to female students, most of the Hill girls were educated privately.[24] Hannah Moore settled on the latter course, perhaps because her mother commended it. "I must approve of thy not sending my dear little girls to school, but having them taught at home under thy own eye," Deborah Hill wrote, "[T]he instruction . . . will ground them in a good hand, which they may keep if they write a copy or two a day."[25] Milcah must have had a fair handwriting and a decent education even before her arrival in Philadelphia, for, even as a young girl, she apparently worked as a copyist for her father's business.[26] This emphasis on copying as a means of improving minds and penmanship was a common educational theme. Girls and boys were often given poetry and prose to copy, and a number of surviving commonplace books were written during school exercises.[27]

Philadelphia during the mid-eighteenth century was a thriving port city with enough population and wealth to support educational institutions such as the Quaker schools and the College of Philadelphia (now the University of Pennsylvania).[28] By 1750 the city's population exceeded 12,000; by the start of the American Revolution it had more than doubled to exceed 33,000.[29] The port attracted merchants and their goods from all over the Atlantic world. The city's physical layout

---

for the masters us[e]': A Transatlantic Community of Religious Women, The Quakers 1675–1753," in Kunze and Dwight D. Brautigam, eds. *Court, Country and Culture: Essays on Early Modern British History in Honor of Perez Zagorin* (Rochester: Rochester University Press, 1992), 177–97.

24. See Nancy Rosenberg, "The Sub-textual Religion: Quakers, the Book, and Public Education in Philadelphia, 1682–1800" (Ph.D. diss., University of Michigan, Ann Arbor, 1991), 339–49.

25. Deborah Hill to Hannah Moore, Madeira, August 23, 1750, in J. J. Smith, *Letters of Doctor Richard Hill*, 63.

26. Ibid.

27. Examples include the Mary Flower, Catherine Haines, and Deborah Haines commonplace books, QC; and the Sarah Sandwith Drinker commonplace books, HSP.

28. A good introduction to Philadelphia's early history can be found in Russell F. Weigley, ed., *Philadelphia: A 300-year History* (New York: W. W. Norton, 1982).

29. For an excellent discussion of the estimation of Philadelphia's population, see Billy G. Smith, *The "Lower Sort": Philadelphia's Laboring People, 1750–1800* (Ithaca: Cornell University Press, 1990), Appendix B.

was also impressive. An early courthouse stood atop city markets sprawling for several blocks along High Street, while the new State-house (now known as Independence Hall) occupied an imposing cor-ner a few blocks away. Street life in the city's center was energized by commercial and political activity.[30]

Milcah Martha Hill's family was well positioned to enjoy these and other benefits available to wealthy Philadelphians. While her own fam-ily was certainly comfortable—but not especially rich—they were part of an extended family with both great material wealth and significant political power. For example, the Hills' cousins, the Norrises, were among the wealthiest and most powerful families in Pennsylvania. Isaac Norris Sr. was the most extensive landowner of his generation, and also served in the Assembly. His son, Isaac Norris Jr., added to those holdings and served as speaker of the Assembly.[31] The Moore cousins into whose family Milcah and Hannah Hill married, by con-trast, while wealthy enough to own a carriage, could not match the fabulous wealth of the Norrises.

Milcah Martha Hill married her cousin, Dr. Charles Moore in 1767, when she was twenty-seven and he was forty-three. Like her, he benefitted from the elite status of his family, as indicated by his medi-cal training. In an era when medical colleges were expanding scien-tific inquiry and the extent of schooling expected for physicians was increasing, the medical profession was an increasingly attractive op-tion for sons from respectable families who nonetheless needed to earn a living or wanted a profession.[32] In 1748 the Quaker Meeting in

30. For an analysis of the hardships of daily life for the majority of Philadelphia's population, see Smith, *The "Lower Sort,"* esp. 7–39.

31. Details about the Norris landholdings can be found in Tolles, *Meeting House and Counting House*, 96–97.

32. Charles Moore was not especially wealthy. Although his family was quite well off, it was his older brother, Dr. Samuel Preston Moore, who seemed to inherit. In 1756, Charles Moore was rated by the tax assessor in Lower Delaware Ward for £30 of property, while Samuel Preston Moore was rated in North Ward at £300. Milcah's mother Deborah Moore Hill noted in a letter of 1751 that she understood Charles Moore was studying "so closely, that I fear he will hurt himself," and that she wished she could "contribute something toward his fitting himself for the painful employ-ment he has fixed on" (Deborah Hill to Hannah Moore, Madeira September 30, 1751, in J. J. Smith, *Letters of Doctor Richard Hill*, 66). Frederick Tolles reported that doc-tors were quite well respected among the Quakers and that "Doctor" was the only title Quakers used (Tolles, *Meeting House and Counting House,* 121).

Philadelphia gave Moore a certificate of removal to the Meeting in Edinburgh, Scotland, where he was traveling with the "design of improving himself in the Practice of Physic."[33] This was the most prestigious medical school in the British empire.[34] In 1751 Moore received a certificate from surgeon Thomas Young, stating that Moore attended Young's lectures on "the Theory and Practice of Midwifery by which Means He had an Opportunity of Seeing and Operating in all the different Sorts of Births."[35] Three years later, his schooling complete, Moore returned to Philadelphia with a medical degree.[36] He was a relatively successful doctor, claiming as his patients many of the members of his and his wife's extended family.[37] In Philadelphia he formed part of a circle of doctors and others interested in science and natural philosophy, joining the American Philosophical Society and the Library Company.[38]

Milcah Martha Hill's marriage to Charles Moore caused their breach with the Society of Friends. This break had nothing to do with marital harmony; they clearly shared a strong bond of affection. Only a year after they married, Charles wrote a poem proclaiming, "I can truly declare, That a happier pair, Is not to be found in the land."[39] They had known each other for many years, as her eldest sister was married to his older brother, and they were cousins. Lineage, however, was precisely the problem. In the 1750s and 1760s the Quakers were in the midst of an important period of reform. Reformers

33. Certificate of removal, Philadelphia, November 28 1748, Box 5, EWS.

34. See Lisa Rosner, "Thistle on the Delaware: Edinburgh Medical Education and Philadelphia Practice, 1800–1825," *Social History of Medicine* 5, no. 1 (1992): 19–42.

35. Certificate of Midwifery, June 21, 1751, signed by Thomas Young, in Rosner, "Thistle on the Delaware."

36. A report from the Edinburgh Yearly Meeting in 1753 reported that Moore had received his degree, and that he was free of financial or marital entanglements. See Box 5, EWS. Moore was only the second American to receive a degree from the University of Edinburgh. See Tolles, *Meeting House and Counting House*, 227.

37. For example, Moore submitted receipts for medical care to cousins Mary Parker Norris (in 1773 and 1775) and Thomas Harrison (in 1759). See Norris Papers, Family Accounts, 6:115 and 7:30; Logan Papers, 21:85, HSP.

38. See Draft of Charles Moore biography prepared for the American Philosophical Society by Whitfield J. Bell, Jr., Box 5, EWS; share no. 593, dated April 5, 1790, Record Book A, LCP; Tolles, *Meeting House and Counting House*, 221.

39. Copy by Milcah Martha Moore dated Philadelphia, May 2, 1769, EWS. See also "The Happy Union," EWS.

wanted to revitalize Quakers' commitment to the original teachings of the founder, George Fox. One area of concern was the prohibition on consanguinity, the marriage of close blood relations. More rigorous enforcement of social and religious requirements meant that substantial members of the Quaker community who failed to comply were disowned at mid-century.[40] This posed a serious dilemma. Quakers in the colonies had long tacitly sanctioned such marriages, and in fact within Moore's family many family members married close kin. For many, these family ties were extremely important to their sense of identity and the Quaker prohibition against marrying non-Quakers was so strong that to marry kin was an obvious solution, especially if potential marriage partners were limited by requirements of social and economic status as well as by religion.

Moore's family was large, extensively intermarried, and almost entirely descendants or relations of Thomas Lloyd.[41] Their connection to Lloyd was a source of tremendous pride, for it linked them to both a distinguished Quaker and Welsh heritage and one of the earliest and most prominent Philadelphians. Generations of Lloyd relations intermarried, in part because elite Quakers often married other elite Quakers. Within that small circle, there was bound to be intermarriage. These connections could be as relatively straightforward as that between Milcah Martha Moore and her husband Charles Moore, who were also both first and second cousins. The Moores' parents were siblings (his father and her mother), and their grandparents were siblings (her mother's mother, and his mother's mother). Thus, also directly related were Charles Moore's parents. His mother Margaret Preston married her first cousin, Richard Moore (brother of Milcah Hill Moore's mother). These connections could be even more com-

---

40. See Jack D. Marietta, *The Reformation of American Quakerism, 1748–1783* (Philadelphia: University of Pennsylvania Press, 1984).

41. The Lloyds had ten children. A number of the daughters married men who became wealthy and prominent. This generation included Isaac and Mary Lloyd Norris, maternal grandparents of Hannah Griffitts; Richard and Hannah Lloyd Delavel Hill; Samuel and Rachel Lloyd Preston, maternal grandparents of Milcah Martha Moore's husband Charles Moore; and Moredcai and Deborah Lloyd Moore, Milcah Moore's maternal grandparents. Thus Milcah Martha Moore and her husband Charles, Hannah Griffitts, Mary Norris Dickinson, and others were all related through their maternal grandparents. For a brief discussion of the significance of Quaker intermarriage among the elites, see Tolles, *Meeting House and Counting House*, 119–21.

Abbreviated Lloyd Genealogy

Thomas Lloyd (1640–1694) and Mary Jones Lloyd (1640?–1683)
(of 10 children)

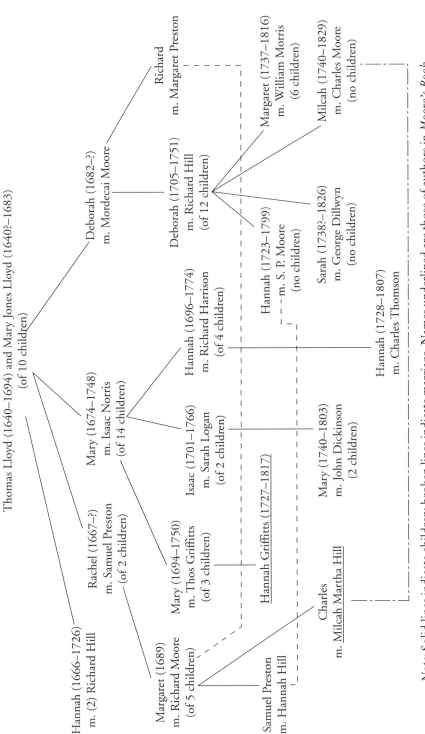

Hannah (1666–1726)
m. (2) Richard Hill

Rachel (1667–?)
m. Samuel Preston
(of 2 children)

Margaret (1689)
m. Richard Moore
(of 5 children)

Mary (1674–1748)
m. Isaac Norris
(of 14 children)

Mary (1694–1750)
m. Thos Griffitts
(of 3 children)

Isaac (1701–1766)
m. Sarah Logan
(of 2 children)

Hannah Griffitts (1727–1817)

Samuel Preston
m. Hannah Hill

Charles
m. Milcah Martha Hill

Mary (1740–1803)
m. John Dickinson
(2 children)

Deborah (1682–?)
m. Mordecai Moore

Richard
m. Margaret Preston

Deborah (1705–1751)
m. Richard Hill
(of 12 children)

Hannah (1696–1774)
m. Richard Harrison
(of 4 children)

Hannah (1723–1799)
– – m. S. P. Moore
(no children)

Sarah (1738?–1826)
m. George Dillwyn
(no children)

Hannah (1728–1807)
m. Charles Thomson

Margaret (1737–1816)
m. William Morris
(6 children)

Milcah (1740–1829)
m. Charles Moore
(no children)

Note: Solid lines indicate children; broken lines indicate marriage. Names underlined are those of authors in *Moore's Book.*

plex and tangled. Eminent Quaker minister Sarah Morris, for example (see *Milcah Martha Moore's Book,* entry no. 85),[42] was related to Milcah Martha Moore's sister Margaret Hill Morris. Margaret Morris's husband William was Sarah Morris's half great-nephew (the grandson of Sarah Morris's father by the first of his four wives).[43] Family members sometimes traced connections through both their maternal and paternal lines. For example, Milcah Moore's father, Dr. Richard Hill, married Deborah Moore, a granddaughter of Thomas Lloyd. Dr. Richard Hill's uncle, also Richard Hill, married Hannah Lloyd, one of Thomas Lloyd's daughters. Thus the two Richard Hills were linked by blood, as uncle and nephew, and by marriage. And thus Milcah Martha Hill Moore's great-aunt's husband was also her own father's uncle!

The density of these connections among elite Delaware Valley Quakers testifies to the importance this group attached to marrying within their own circle of religious and familial connections. Many of these people continued to correspond with members of their family abroad, even generations after migration to America. Various Lloyd descendants, for example, continued to correspond with second and third cousins of great uncles they had never met. They worked on family genealogies, documenting their connections in the old world and described themselves and each other in terms of their relationship to their common ancestor, Thomas Lloyd.[44]

When Milcah Martha Hill and Charles Moore married, they were confirming the significance of these family ties, but because of the recent reforms, the Quaker Meeting could not concur. When Milcah Martha Hill's sister, Hannah, married Charles Moore's brother, Samuel Preston Moore, in 1747, they were reprimanded. They wrote an apologetic, repentant letter to the Meeting and were forgiven. Yet, in 1767, twenty years later, Charles and Milcah Martha Moore were disowned. This meant not only that they were no longer members of

---

42. Hereafter cited as *MMMB* with poem or entry number following (for example, *MMMB* 85).

43. See Robert C. Moon, *The Morris Family of Philadelphia* (Philadelphia, 1898), 1:114–15 and 204–11; *The Friends' Library* (Philadelphia, 1842), 6:478–80.

44. Milcah Martha Moore recorded July 20: "On the 10 Inst: were interred in Frds burying Ground the Remains of Rachel Moore aged 82 years born in Maryland and the last surviving Gd Daughter of the respectable Thos. Lloy" (genealogical notes, Box 5, EWS).

the Quaker Meeting, but that they could not worship with other Friends. This breach was a source of ongoing unease and anxiety for Milcah Moore and the entire family. A spiritual person, she continued to pray and to copy meditations into a diary. She corresponded with close family members about her concerns, describing herself as "an Outcast as to the Society," and referring to her "misspent life," and her "great unworthyness."[45] To her brother-in-law and minister George Dillwyn, she trusted her "Cries in a Time of deep [religious] Exercise."[46] After Charles Moore died in 1801, Milcah Martha Moore rejoined the Quaker Meeting.[47] The Moores long, formal estrangement from the Society of Friends might have been an additional reason for Milcah Moore's determined attachment to her kin. Having lost one source of connection, she strengthened others.

Perhaps another reason that Milcah Martha Moore and others in her family were so devoted to both close and distant kin was the prevalence of death. Certainly eighteenth-century nuclear families regularly sustained grievous losses almost unimagineable by late twentieth-century standards, and extended kin often provided support and material comfort after the death of parents, children, spouses, or siblings. The presence of epidemic diseases such as smallpox and yellow fever, as well as a dangerous environment, especially for infants, meant that infants, older children, and adults were all at risk.[48] Of Milcah Martha Moore's twelve siblings, two died as infants. Many of her married sisters had no children, but those who did experienced the loss of infants. Rachel Hill Wells (1714–96) had twelve children; at least five died in infancy. Margaret Hill Morris (1737–1816) had six children before her husband died in 1766, just eight years after they

---

45. Hannah Moore to Milcah Moore, n.d. [1769]; Unknown [George Dillwyn?] to Milcah Moore, n.d. [1769]; Milcah Moore to Hannah Moore ("I have long been an outcast"), n.d. [1778], EWS.

46. See Milcah Moore to George Dillwyn, September 1778, EWS.

47. See Milcah Moore's certificate of removal from New Jersey to Philadelphia, 1801, Box 5, EWS.

48. The effects of disease and poor sanitation, as well as other health hazards and birth rates, are treated in Billy Smith, *The "Lower Sort,"* 41–62. A consideration of the demographic study of Philadelphia, as well as a documentary history of public health records through the mid-nineteenth century, is Susan E. Klepp, *The Swift Progress of Population: A Documentary and Bibliographic Study of Philadelphia's Growth, 1642–1859* (Philadelphia: American Philosophical Society, 1991).

married; he was thirty-one.[49] Two of their children died as infants. These tragedies were marked with both grief and resolve.[50] Other family members often stepped in with assisstance, as when Milcah Martha and Charles Moore helped Margaret Morris with the education of her fatherless children.

By all accounts the Moores had a happy marriage, but they had no children. Before the Revolution they lived primarily in Philadelphia, where Charles served as clerk of the Pennsylvania Assembly for almost twenty years until resigning in early 1776.[51] He also began serving as an attending physician at the Pennsylvania Hospital in 1773. The Moores also took in the young children of family and friends to apprentice in medicine, eliciting praise from the children's parents and a sense of satisfaction in themselves for guiding these youths.[52] During the Revolution, the Moores retired to a country home in Montgomery (later part of Montgomery County), north of Philadelphia.

In her later life Milcah Martha Moore displayed the same inclination toward reading and writing that had fueled her compilation of the commonplace book. She expanded her audience from the intimacy of the commonplace book to a broader public. In Montgomery during the 1780s, Moore opened a school for girls. As she explained her motivations, "My Heart . . . [had] yearnd towards the poor little neglected Children up & down about our Neighborhood—I mentioned to my d[ea]r Husband . . . that I thought it would be required of me to keep School for the girls." As with most ventures, she consulted her sisters, thought about her spiritual preparation for such an undertaking, and plunged in. She opened the school, she wrote, "belieiving that

49. See J. J. Smith, *Letters of Doctor Richard Hill*, xlii–xliii. See *MMMB* 36, on the death of William Morris Jr..

50. Moore included a large number of poems on death in her commonplace book, including those memorializing relatives, friends, prominent Quakers, and English royalty.

51. Bell, draft of biography of Charles Moore, Box 5, EWS, 2.

52. The Moore's nephew, Margaret Morris's son John, was determined to study medicine rather than another profession. He also insisted on apprenticing with his uncle, Charles Moore. For Margaret Morris and Milcah Martha Moore's letters on this subject, see J. J. Smith, *Letters of Doctor Richard Hill*, 363, 399, 401, and 404–12. For others who asked the Moore's to apprentice their children, see Milcah Martha Moore to Hannah Moore [May 1784?], about the son of David Sands, EWS; and Samuel Emlen to Charles Moore, in reference to the education of his son, Philadelphia, December 6, 1799, EWS.

Fig. 3.   Milcah Martha Moore's sister, Margaret Hill Morris, age seventy-nine.
Moore lived with Margaret after the death of her husband, Charles Moore. Private
collection.

it will be a School for my self to learn in as well as others."[53] Although little is known about the duration of the school, the few accounts that do remain suggest that Moore had good success with her students. In the late 1780s she published a collection of well-known (mostly English) poetry titled *Miscellanies, Moral and Instructive*. It was intended to be used as a school textbook. Moore inscribed a copy of the first edition to the Library Company of Philadelphia in June 1787.[54] She was obviously proud of the book, which then went through many editions. These ventures typified Moore's approach to reading and writing.

Moore's Commonplace Book and Women's Literary Culture

Writing was a constant in Milcah Moore's life. She appreciated a variety of styles of writing, from spiritual Quaker documents such as testimonials and ministers' memoirs to quite secular amusements such as those printed in English and colonial literary magazines. But whether she was reading, writing, or copying religious expressions or "trifles," Moore used them as a way of communicating with family and friends near and far. From the time she was a young girl, she sent her correspondents prose and poetry. In her commonplace book, Moore was documenting her affiliations as much as she was conserving a body of work and copying other significant writings. These works knitted Milcah Moore and her circle closer together. Whether she was corresponding with someone across the Atlantic or simply across the Delaware River, the words she wrote reinforced bonds of intimacy and common knowledge.[55]

53. Milcah Martha Moore notes, Box 5, EWS. Accounts of the school include a list of students, their tuition, and a list of donors. The donors included Elizabeth Graeme Fergusson, who donated a modest fifteen shillings to the school in 1786.

54. For additional information on Moore's *Miscellanies*, see pages 69–76.

55. For another example of the role of a commonplace book in reflecting the experiences of its author, see Carla Mulford, "Political Poetics: Annis Boudinot Stockton and Middle Atlantic Women's Culture," *New Jersey History* 111 (Spring–Summer 1993): 67–110. A fascinating account of the role of reading, writing, and letters in simultaneously creating and reinforcing family connections can be found in Stella

Moore's work in preserving connections through writings such as those that appear in the commonplace book is both specific to her family's experiences and values and part of a wider culture of manuscript communication with roots in both the Quaker and emerging Anglo-American elite traditions. Manuscript materials, of course, long predated printing technology, but even after the printing revolution manuscripts continued to have an important place. Historians and literary scholars are beginning to discover that publication in print was not necessarily the sole hallmark of literary achievement.[56] Merit was found in manuscripts as well. Quakers had long made use of circulating manuscripts. Manuscripts made Quaker ideas, developments, and experiences accessible to members of the Society of Friends separated by the Atlantic. Epistles from meeting to meeting, for example, from the London Yearly Women's Meeting to the Philadelphia Yearly Women's Meeting, were often sent in manuscript rather than printed form and then read aloud, thus furthering distribution. Ministers' accounts of their travels often circulated in manuscript. Friends shared with one another their manuscript diaries of spiritual thoughts and experiences. Letters were read over and over to groups large and small. Sometimes these circulated writings would end up in print, but most often not.

The circulation of manuscript materials intersected with the rise of another form of literary and intellectual interaction, the salon. Salons appeared in early modern Europe, particularly in France but also in England and other places, as venues for male and female intellectuals to gather. The purpose of a salon was to provide an available space for the inspiration, discussion, circulation, and presentation of *belles lettres*—that literature created for the purpose of pleasurable reading rather than strictly educational or religious instruction.[57] Manuscript literature was particularly well suited for the intimate setting of the salons. Unlike printed works, which could be circulated and read more widely, manuscript material might be circulated and read only to a select gathering. Often held in the home of a wealthy female member of

Tillyard, *Aristocrats: Caroline, Emily, Louisa and Sarah Lennox, 1740–1832* (New York: Farrar, Straus and Giroux, 1994), 84–94 and 212–23.

56. See pages 59–60 n.1.

57. See David S. Shields, "British-American Belles Lettres," in Sacvan Bercovitch, gen. ed., *The Cambridge History of American Literature*, I, *1500–1820* (New York: Cambridge University Press, 1994), 307–43.

the literati, salons welcomed and promoted aspiring writers as well as more established authors. These gatherings often took on political significance in several ways. Some women selectively invited salon personnel to reflect and promote particular political agendas. Salons also became highly politicized as their opponents attacked women's participation as emblematic of society run amok: French revolutionaries argued, for example, that the female-led salon was an especially egregious example of the decadence and disorder associated with the *ancien regime*.[58]

In early America, the circulation of manuscripts and the formation of a salon culture proceeded at a slower pace. Although evidence suggests that by the early nineteenth century American women became interested in emulating some aspects of the French model,[59] throughout the pre-Revolutionary era American literary culture was more loosely organized and less explicitly political. Prose and verse were a vernacular colonial political discourse, used in publications such as broadsides and newspapers to clarify political arguments and persuade readers. In private correspondence prose and verse were used to articulate more subtle political intentions.[60] Organized groups of

58. See Claude Dulong, "From Conversation to Creation," in Natalie Zemon Davis and Arlette Farge, *A History of Women: Renaissance and Enlightenment Paradoxes* (Cambridge: Belknap Press of Harvard University Press, 1993), 3:395–419; Joan Landes, *Women and the Public Sphere in the Age of the French Revolution* (Ithaca: Cornell University Press, 1988), 17–65.

59. The work of Carla Mulford, David Shields, Susan Stabile, and Fredrika Teute has developed this theme. See, for example, Mulford's introduction to *Only for the Eye of a Friend: The Poems of Annis Boudinot Stockton* (Charlottesville: University of Virginia Press, 1995); Susan Stabile. "American Women Writers of the Middle Colonies, 1770–1820" (Ph.D. diss., University of Deleware, 1996); and David Shields and Fredrika J. Teute, "The Republican Court and the Historiography of a Woman's Domain in the Public Sphere" (Paper presented, Society for the History of the Early American Republic, 1995). Shields's *Civil Tongues and Polite Letters in British America* (Chapel Hill: University of North Carolina Press, 1997) provides an essential context for the gendered dimensions of polite, political discourse in that era.

60. In *Oracles of Empire: Poetry, Politics, and Commerce in British America, 1690–1750* (Chicago: University of Chicago Press, 1990), David Shields argues that an understanding of commercial empire and American's role in that empire, was worked out through poetry, a favorite mode of expression and communication for key political and mercantile colonials. See also William C. Dowling, *Poetry and Ideology in Revolutionary Connecticut* (Athens: University of Georgia, 1990); Christopher Grasso, "Print, Poetry, and Politics: John Trumbull and the Transformation of

readers were less common, less formal, and less political than the French salon model.[61] Perhaps the best known literary salon in colonial America was that of Elizabeth Graeme Fergusson. Held in an upstairs room of her family home at Graeme Park, north of Philadelphia, the evenings brought together some of the Delaware Valley's most self-consciously cosmopolitan members of the young elite. This heterosocial group, comprised for the most part of members of the Anglican rather than Quaker elite, devoted themselves to appreciating cosmopolitan British literary styles. Fergusson's close friend and fellow lover of literature Annis Boudinot Stockton also gathered a salon at her home in New Jersey, where she demonstrated her affection for the British literary greats by replicating at Morven a version of Alexander Pope's gardens at Twickenham (arguably the center of cosmopolitan literary culture).[62]

Milcah Martha Moore's Book, while related to these broader traditions of manuscript circulation and women's literary and intellectual engagement, owes more to the specifically Quaker traditions that encouraged literacy for women and created a circulating library of Quaker materials. While some of Moore's commonplace book is devoted to subjects of purely political or social interest, deep reflection on the values of friendship, the need for resignation to God's will, and the importance of humility mark the volume as less belle lettristic, more spiritual and instructional, and more closely tied to their interests in marking and maintaining connections.[63] Quakers looked to the circulation of various manuscript materials for spreading inspirational materials among a broad constituency. In a 1768 letter to a cousin, Hannah Harrison commented on the many uses of shared journals, noting that extracts of Quaker epistles and ministers' traveling accounts could be instructive and comforting. As to "my Journal and your Request, As Occassion offers you shall have extracts," Harrison wrote, but for the time being and "In answer to what you say about

Public Discourse in Revolutionary America," *Early American Literature* [hereafter cited as *EAL*] 30 (1995): 5–31; and E. Thomson Shields, Jr., "'A Modern Poem' by the Mecklenburg Censor: Politics and Satire in Revolutionary North Carolina," *EAL* 29 (1994): 205–32.

61. See an account of early literary clubs in Shields, "British-American Belles Lettres."

62. See Mulford, "*Only for the Eye of a Friend*".

63. See pages 81–85, 93–94.

Aunt Hester, I copy page the 20th." These passages, read to another friend, "had the desired Effect, And comforted her in the best Sense." Journals could also provide entertainment for a close circle of kin and Friends. In the same letter offering comforting extracts from her own journal, Harrison noted that she had "by Accident" taken possession of a journal "without [the author's] consent." She would pass it along as soon as she received his permission to do so, for it contained "Most surprising, and Entertaining Anecdotes."[64]

Even in entertainment Quakers stressed instruction. After reading a manuscript copy of Benjamin Franklin's autobiography, Quaker merchant Abel James urged Franklin to publish it immediately. He wrote, "The influence writings under that class have on the minds of youth is very great, and has nowhere appeared to me so plain as in our public friends [Quaker ministers'] journals."[65] A revealing exchange took place in 1771 between prominent Quaker and founding member of the Library Company of Burlington Samuel Allinson and a fellow Burlington devotee of literature, Susannah Hopkins. In the midst of a book exchange, Allinson and Hopkins discussed the relative merits of prose and poetry, with specific reference to the instructional merit of each literary form. Allinson proposed, "it is from Sober Truths delivered in prose . . . our best Hopes of present & future Peace depend . . . . Poetry [while] a pretty kind of play thing to amuse . . . is, I believe, not always Void of Instructional Use."[66] Hopkins replied in kind, stressing that "Prose is the stile which seems best adapted to reach the understanding & convince the Judgement, and is the dress is which Truth appears in its most native Simplicity & Beauty." Yet she also commented much more extensively on the meditative and spiritual value of some poetry Allinson sent to her.[67]

---

64. Hannah Harrison to [William Dillwyn?], Somerville, December 20, 1768, Robert R. Logan Collection, HSP.

65. Abel James to Benjamin Franklin, as quoted in Tolles, *Meeting House and Counting House*, 61.

66. Samuel Allinson to Susannah Hopkins, Burlington, October 18, 1771, Letter-book of Samuel Allinson, QC. For Samuel Allinson's intellectual and religious activities, see Archives of the Library Company of Burlington, Book Borrower Records, Burlington, N.J., vol. 1; Amelia Mott Gummere, "Friends in Burlington," *PMHB* 8 (1884): 165–66.

67. She commented most extensively on poems "especially Young upon the last Day & that to the Memory of Emma," noting that through them "I saw & mourn'd that in Death we are separated from our greatest worldly comfort, the reflection of

The women whose work dominates Milcah Moore's commonplace book were known to their circles of family and friends for both the poetry and prose they authored and circulated. Moore, Hannah Griffitts, Susanna Wright, and Elizabeth Graeme Fergusson were each acclaimed for their literary accomplishments. Although exchanging writing was almost ubiquitous among their acquaintances, and certainly among others of their socioeconomic and educational background, these four were acknowledged to have special talent and intelligence. They were not "famous" in the sense that celebrities achieve fame today, nor were they known publicly in the same way that Benjamin Franklin achieved recognition throughout the American colonies and abroad.[68] Instead, they were each known to a wide circle of family, friends, and associates for their facility with the pen. Some did publish under pseudonyms, but this was rare before the 1780s.

Their circles did not accord each the same level of recognition; each of the four women whose work dominates the commonplace book was known for particular aspects of her talents. Susanna Wright, the eldest of the four and the one who wrote in the earliest period, was acknowledged by Griffitts's and Moore's generation as a kind of elder stateswoman. Acknowledged as extremely pious as well as an important intellectual among the early generation of Quaker elites, Wright was also a close family friend of Griffitts's and Moore's older relatives. Elizabeth Graeme Fergusson was by far the most cosmopolitan of the group. She traveled abroad, and her writing reflected the widest variety and most secular of literary fashions. Hannah Griffitts was known primarily for her memorial poetry, but also for her satires.

---

the Mind upon such subjects as those are often useful " ("Sucky Hopkins to SA in answer" Burlington, N.J., October 10, 1771, Commonplace Book of Samuel Allinson, QC).

68. In *Letters of the Republic: Publication and the Public Sphere in Eighteenth-Century America* (Cambridge. Mass.: Harvard University Press, 1990), 73–96, Michael Warner argues that Benjamin Franklin's relationship to print, as a printer, writer, and politician, was central to his public persona. In an era of an emerging public sphere, where, as Jürgen Habermas has argued, a civil society mediates between the governing and the governed through discourse (primarily printed material), Franklin both created his own relationship to the public world through print at the same time he was creating this public world through printing. This is very different from the way in which Moore and other women in the commonplace book positioned themselves in relationship to texts.

She was a devout Quaker, and friends and neighbors treasured her writings.[69]

Milcah Moore's family long recognized her gifts of letter-writing and collecting verse and prose. As noted in the Preface, her earliest known correspondence from Madeira to her sisters in Philadelphia included "some verses." In 1778 Margaret Hill Morris neatly summarized the family's reaction to Moore's correspondence. In a letter expressing the hope that Moore (known to her intimates as "Patty" or "Patsy") did not share received letters with anyone else, Morris wrote that she did not show Moore's letters to others except in particular circumstances. "When there's a pleasant passage," she wrote,

> or witty remark in them, I read it for the benefit of our little circle, and then there's a sort of exclamation—oh! children when will you be able to write such a letter, and the daughter gravely replies, if we were to have as much practice as aunt P., we should know how to write letters; yes, but not such a letter as this, and then I display it, as if it was any merit to me (who am such a scribbler), that my sweet Patty writes such a fair hand.[70]

Moore's collections of verse and prose also traveled a circuit of kin and friends eager to copy from them. This movement of literary material was a regular feature of correspondence, as an undated letter to Hannah Moore makes clear. Milcah Moore wrote to her older sister to discuss the character of a mutual acquaintance, to muse about the younger Moores' continued estrangement from the Society of Friends, and to pass along news of family health. But she opened with a discussion of commonplace books. "I'm glad thou likes the Book

69. Grateful acknowledgements to Griffitts can be found sprinkled through a variety of letters collections. For one example of the importance of Griffitts's memorial poetry, see the note by Anna Bloodgood attached to a sample of Griffitts's work, which reads, "On the death of my near & Dear by Cousin Hannah Griffith Beautiful Poetry sent by her at their Respective Deaths. & preserved with care by me" (Mrs. Philip Livingston Poe Collection, folder 2, HSP).

70. Margaret Morris to Milcah Martha Moore, Burlington, N.J., March 9, 1778, in J. J. Smith, *Letters of Doctor Richard Hill*, 239. More historians and literary scholars are looking to letter writing, in addition to printed materials, as an important aspect of the creation of literary culture in the eighteenth century. See, for example, Bruce Redford, *The Converse of the Pen: Acts of Intimacy in the Eighteenth-Century Familiar Letter* (Chicago: University of Chicago Press, 1986).

that Prisey took down," she wrote, "but wish she cou'd have staid to write what thou want her to copy [from another book], which wou'd have been better worth thy reading."[71]

Moore's, Wright's, Griffitts's and Fergusson's circles of correspondents, family, friends, and associates were not identical, but overlapped a good deal. They moved in *interlocking* circles of family and kin, connected by birth, education, religion, socioeconomic status and affinity. They did not socialize solely because they found that they enjoyed one another's company, but also because a plethora of circumstances brought them together. Only then did they discover mutual interests in reading and writing poetry and prose. Only after initial connections were formed did these women find that these mutual interests could form the basis of communicating with one another, and the medium through which friendships based on intellectual sympathies could be built.[72]

In important ways these relationships among women mirrored the more formal institutions that became so popular among men with mutual intellectual interests. The American Philosophical Society, the less formal Junto, and the Philadelphia Medical Society, were all formed in the late colonial era to foster communication and enhance knowledge among a circle of Philadelphia men that included Benjamin Franklin and Charles Moore.[73] In many cases, men were chosen as prospective members of these clubs and associations because of their status as members of an identifiable elite or because of their previous connections with other members. Charles Moore is a case in point.[74] He had political and family connections, as well as a professional profile as a doctor. He was asked to join a number of societies

71. Milcah Martha Moore to Hannah Moore [May 1784?], EWS.

72. For an analysis of the contribution of women to creating networks of association, see Nancy Tomes, "The Quaker Connection: Visiting Patterns Among Women in the Philadelphia Society of Friends, 1750–1800," in Michael Zuckerman, ed., *Friends and Neighbors: Group Life in America's First Plural Society* (Philadelphia: Temple University Press, 1982), 174–95.

73. See Carl Bridenbaugh, *Cities In Revolt: Urban Life in America, 1743–1776,* 2d ed. (New York: Capricorn Books, 1964), 411–16. On literary clubs, see David Shields, "Anglo-American Clubs: Their Wit, Their Heterodoxy, Their Sedition," *WMQ,* 3d ser. 51 (1994): 293–304; and "The Tuesday Club Writings and the Literature of Sociability," review essay in *EAL* 26 (1991): 276–90.

74. Bell, draft of biography of Charles Moore, Box 5, EWS, 2–3.

in the 1760s, although there is little record of his interest in any of them. He was chosen, for example, as secretary of the American Philosophical Society in early 1768, but there is no record he attended any meetings until 1771, when he was again chosen secretary. He never appeared at another meeting, perhaps for fear of another appointment.

For women, formal organization and the public presentation of intellectual interests was either a less attractive option or an impossibility given gendered assumptions about women's appropriate social roles. Particular women's intellects were highly praised, although often in terms that reinforced traditional ideas about the innate intellectual abilities of men as opposed to women's innate physicality. Elizabeth Graeme Fergusson's mother, for example, was celebrated by Benjamin Rush as possessing both "a masculine mind, with all those female charms and accomplishments which render a woman alike agreeable to both sexes."[75] Nevertheless, the impulse to create networks of association based on intellectual affinity, in addition to the traditional patterns of association among colonials based on family, religion, and politics, was as strong among women as it was among men.

Schools also played an important role in forming friendships among women, and in circulating the manuscript copies of verse by women authors. A number of small schools, supported by the Quakers, operated in colonial Philadelphia.[76] Teachers like Rebecca Birchall and Rebecca Jones, in the 1750s and the 1770s respectively, used the poems of Susanna Wright and Hannah Griffitts to help teach penmanship and writing. While printed books of miscellanies and other writings were also popular, students' surviving copybooks from these schools as well as other evidence from diaries suggests that these teachers relied on women poets they knew to supply selections for their students. Elizabeth Drinker, Hannah Callender, and other girls for example, attended Rebecca Birchall's school in the 1750s.[77] There

---

75. Benjamin Rush, "Mrs. Elizabeth Fergusson," originally printed in the *Port Folio*, reprinted in *Hazard's Register of Pennsylvania* 3, no. 24 (June 13, 1829): 394.

76. These schools were less formal than the school systems contemporary Americans find familiar. Students were not required to attend for a particular period, but enrolled for several months at a time. Boys and girls were generally schooled together until the late 1740s, when teachers like Anthony Benezet began to focus on teaching girls exclusively. See Rosenberg, "The Sub-textual Religion," 339–43.

77. Elaine F. Crane, ed. *The Diary of Elizabeth Drinker*, 3 vols. (Boston: Northeastern University Press, 1990), 1:99.

they copied many of the same kinds of writing that is represented in *Moore's Book*. They copied letters from Quaker luminaries and portions of Quaker meetings' epistles. They also copied poetry, including Susanna Wright's verse version of the letter from Henry VIII to Ann Boleyn (*MMMB* 3).[78] In the 1770s Drinker's daughter, Sarah Sandwith Drinker, and Catherine Haines took classes at the school of Rebecca Jones and her partner Hannah Catherall.[79] There they copied poems by Hannah Griffitts, most of them memorials.[80] Thus the writing of these women would circulate not only among families they knew through the Quaker Meeting, but also into the copybooks of younger girls they might not know individually. Schools provided an important institutional setting for the appreciation of women's writing, and an important place in which manuscripts, as opposed to printed materials, were circulated.

The connections among Wright, Griffitts, and Moore began as primarily religious, political, and familial and then developed according to mutual intellectual interests. Susanna Wright's family was long connected to the extended family of which Moore and Griffitts were members. The two families were political allies, as Wright's father and brother served in the Pennsylvania Assembly with Moore's and

78. In October 1758 Callender recorded six lines of the verse in her diary and then noted it was "S Wrights translation of Ann Bullens letter into verse." See Susan E. Klepp and Karin A. Wulf, eds., *The Diary of Hannah Callender, 1758–1788* (Philadelphia: University of Pennsylvania Press, forthcoming). For other examples from the 1750s and 1760s, see the copybooks of Mary Flower and Deborah Haines in QC.

79. Sarah Sandwith Drinker and Catherine Haines appear to have been schooled together quite regularly. The contents of their commonplace books for 1775, for example, are strikingly similar. See the commonplace book of Sarah Sandwith Drinker in the collection of the Library Company of Philadelphia at the HSP, and the commonplace book of Catherine Haines at the QC, HC. A rather peripatetic education was apparently common. Elizabeth Drinker's diary records details of Sarah's education, beginning in 1765 when she was just four years old. She attended "writing school" for the first time in 1772, and was enrolled for some time in the Rebecca Jones and Hannah Catherall school. In 1781, she and Haines were tutored together with several other young women by Charles Mifflin. See Crane, ed. *Diary of Elizabeth Drinker*, entries for April 18, 1765; April 22, 1772; July 20, 1774; and February 1, 1781.

80. These included the exchange between Griffitts and a male member of Susanna James' family, and the poem on the death of Margaret Mason. Sarah Sandwith Drinker's commonplace book (1775), HSP; Catherine Haines's commonplace book (1775), QC.

Griffitts' relatives, Isaac Norris Sr. and his son Isaac Norris Jr.[81] The
bond between the families was predicated on their Quaker roots and
their commitment to William Penn's vision for Pennsylvania.[82] The
families joined to fight off Maryland's claims to Pennsylvania terri-
tory located in close proximity to the Wright's settlement at Hempfield (just west of Lancaster), and to oppose the policies of William
Penn's son and successor as proprietor, Thomas Penn, a lapsed
Quaker.[83] An important bond developed among Susanna and James
Wright, her brother, and the generation of Norris siblings that included Elizabeth, Deborah, Isaac Jr., and Charles Norris. This second
generation of Quaker Pennsylvanians (although born in England, the
Wright children had emigrated to America with their parents) shared
a common understanding and a privileged position as children of politically powerful and economically secure parents. They inherited
both wealth and an assumed role in the leadership of the colony. Letters among this group emphasize the importance of their political
connections and mutual political interests.

Letters among this second generation of Wrights and Norrises also
reveal the role of literature in cementing their friendship.[84] As a dis-

81. Excellent accounts of the Assembly service of the Norrises and the Wrights, as
well as the best genealogical material on the Wright family to date, can be found in
Craig Horle, chief ed., *Lawmaking and Legislators in Pennsylvania, 1710–1756* (Philadelphia: University of Pennsylvania Press, forthcoming). I thank Craig Horle for an
advance look at the essays on John Wright Sr. and John Wright Jr., as well as information on James Wright gathered for the coming volume of *Lawmaking and Legislators*.

82. See Susanna Wright's reference to her ancenstral home in England, afterward
the home of Samuel Fothergill, *MMMB* 36.

83. For an account of the border dispute between Pennsylvania and Maryland, see
Tully, *William Penn's Legacy*, 6–11, 85–86. An elegantly presented treatment of the
growing antagonisms between Quakers and the Pennsylvania proprietors can be
found in Tully, *Forming American Politics*, 82–85, 258–67. For additional information on the Wrights' and Norrises' involvement in the dispute, see Horle, *Lawmaking
and Legislators*.

84. It is important to note that I distinguish here between the social or communal
nature and value of reading and writing, as opposed to the collective cultural or individual significance of these acts. Historians and literary scholars have looked to the
production and consumption of literature (printed and manuscript, highbrow and
popular) as evidence of broader cultural developments. Some look for the impact of
texts on individuals (as prescriptive literature), or vice-versa (as resistant readers). For
a useful analysis of the ways that scholars of both disciplines seek meaning in these
texts, see David D. Hall, "Readers and Reading in America: Historical and Critical
Perspectives," *Proceedings of the American Antiquarian Society* 103 (1992): 337–57.

play of their education, as well as a use for their education, exchanges of books and other printed materials formed a sort of circulating library. In sending favorite selections or in returning classic "must reads," a letter writer could also provide a commentary on his or her own experience of the literature. This exchange was not limited to printed books, however; the more intimate form of circulating literature was the manuscript. Copies of self-authored prose and poetry, copies of recently obtained and transcribed Quaker and political literature, or personal letters formed the core of this intimate epistolary salon. Not founded exclusively in the interests of furthering an appreciation of belles lettres or of creating political alliances along the French model, these epistolary exchanges reinforced already existing connections of status and affinity, and were constructed around an interest in religious and intellectual improvement.

Connections between Moore's and Griffitts's generation and the older generation of Wrights and Norrises were facilitated by the closeness of the two families and the special relationships among women within the group. Beyond familial friendships and political alliances, the first connections among women represented in the commonplace book were those between Hannah Griffitts and Susanna Wright. The two women had an important relationship in common: Wright's dear friend Elizabeth Norris, fellow spinster and mistress of Fairhill mansion, was also Hannah Griffitts's aunt and "parental friend" after the death of her own parents. They also had special interests and sympathies in common. Norris, Wright, and Griffitts were spinsters, and all three shared a conviction that marriage was not necessarily the highest calling for a Quaker woman. In possibly the most powerful piece of poetry produced by an eighteenth-century American woman, Wright praised Norris's ability to resist the gender hierarchy of secular marriage patterns, and praised celibacy as even superior to the equalitarian model of marriage that Quaker theology supported.[85] Wright celebrated Norris, whom "no Seducing Tales Can gain / To yield obedience, or to wear the Chain / But set a Queen & in your freedom reign."[86] Griffitts came to express similar senti-

---

85. "To Eliza Norris—at Fairhill" is discussed in detail in Karin Wulf, "'My Dear Liberty': Marriage, Spinsterhood and Conceptions of Female Autonomy in Eighteenth-Century Philadelphia," in Larry D. Eldridge, ed. *Women and Freedom in Early America* (New York University Press, 1996).
86. Susanna Wright, "To Eliza Norris—at Fairhill," LCP.

ments about the importance of personal liberty outside of marriage, some of which appear in *Moore's Book* ("To Sophronia," *MMMB* 39).

Hannah Griffitts came into this circle created by Norris and Wright through Charles Norris, Elizabeth's brother. No doubt already acquainted with Wright through her aunt, Griffitts reveled in the opportunity to exchange poetry with someone held in such high esteem by the elders of her own family as well as other Quaker luminaries. The Norris family took Hannah Griffitts and her sister to live with them at Fairhill in late 1751. Griffitts was then in her mid-twenties, her parents had died, and her brother had disgraced their family with outrageous financial and social behavior.[87] At a vulnerable time in her life, Griffitts went to Fairhill to have her emotional wounds nursed. She expressed herself in poetry from a young age, writing at Fairhill about the loss of parents, aspects of nature, and spiritual issues. In the spring of 1761 Charles Norris determined to cheer Griffitts with the possibility of a correspondence with Susanna Wright. Norris wrote directly to Wright, asking that she "judge for thy Self" the product of "Fidelia's muse," which had lately "met with such rebuffs, that it seems at present quite shagreend, how it may Revive I know not . . . sometimes merit lyes opress'd."[88] Griffitts responded to this enthusiastically, and immediately forwarded to Wright "some . . . rough scribles."[89]

An intense friendship between Wright and Griffitts seems to have flared and then faded in the early 1760s, but it is likely that the product of Griffitts's and Wright's poetical exchange during that period constitutes the majority of the Wright material found in *Moore's Book*. Moore noted that she copied the Wright pieces from manuscripts written in the author's handwriting, just as Griffitts copied others of Wright's poems with the same notation.[90] It is also possible

87. Isaac Griffitts drank to excess, causing his uncle Charles Norris to castigate him for his "DRUNKENESS, the most odious & distructive of all Vices." Griffitts also lost money assigned to his care as Sheriff of Philadelphia. See Karin Wulf, "A Marginal Independence: Unmarried Women in Colonial Philadelphia" (Ph.D. diss., Johns Hopkins University, Baltimore, 1993), 291–93.

88. Charles Norris to Susanna Wright, Philadelphia, April 2, 1761, 12:29, Logan Papers, HSP.

89. The development of this relationship and exchange is documented and more fully explored in Wulf, "A Marginal Independence," 299–303.

90. "To Eliza Norris—at Fairhill" is copied along with the following notation by Hannah Griffitts: "I Copied the above Lines, from a very torne Copy, In SW hand, Address'd to Elz Norris (but without any Date)" (LCP).

that Elizabeth Norris, elderly and living with Hannah Griffitts in Philadelphia during the 1770s, had a collection of Wright's poems to which she allowed her nieces access.

Connections among the other women, with the exception of the two cousins, Moore and Griffitts, are much less fully documented.[91] Moore and Griffitts wrote to one another regularly from the 1770s through Moore's death in 1817. They wrote of family news, the kinds of produce and dry goods available in their respective places of residence, and of course exchanging literature. One letter from Moore to Wright is extant, but the subject of that letter is dying fabric (a subject of great interest to Wright, who experimented with botany and raised silkworms near her home in Lancaster County). No direct connections between Wright and Fergusson, or Griffitts and Fergusson, can be documented.[92]

Moore's and the others' connection to Elizabeth Graeme Fergusson was a matter of socioeconomic status and geographical proximity. Fergusson, like the others, belonged to the colonial elite. Before the Revolution, however, her circle was composed primarily of Anglicans. Fergusson's mother was the stepdaughter of an early Pennsylvania governor, William Keith; her father, Dr. Thomas Graeme, was a royal official. Their country home, Graeme Park, was the site of numerous gatherings, particularly attracting young men studying at the College of Philadelphia.[93] Anglican clergymen Jacob Duché, Nathaniel Evans, and Richard Peters also formed an important part of the Graeme family's circle of friends.

William Franklin, the illegitimate but acknowledged son of Benjamin Franklin, was introduced into this circle in the mid-1750s.

91. An undated poem from Sarah Dillwyn to Milcah Marth Moore, addressed "Sally Hill to Miss Patsy Hill" from Wright's Ferry suggests that perhaps the Hills knew the Wright family. Because the elite Quaker circle was small, surely they would have known of them. See J. J. Smith, *Letters of Doctor Richard Hill*, 151–52.

92. A single letter from "H Griffitts" to Elizabeth Graeme Fergusson, in the Gratz Collection, HSP, has confused a number of scholars. The author of that letter was Hester Griffitts (also called "Hetty" and the "Amanda" of *Moore's Book*), Hannah Griffitts' cousin (daughter of her father's brother William Griffitts and his wife Abigail Griffitts).

93. See Martha C. Slotten, "Elizabeth Graeme Ferguson: A Poet in 'The Athens of North America,'" *PMHB* (1984): 259–88. Anne Ousterhout's forthcoming biography of Fergusson will be a welcome and sorely needed addition to the literature on women in colonial America. I am grateful for her comments and suggestions about Fergusson sources.

Franklin and young "Betsy" Graeme began a lively and committed courtship, exchanging letters and poetry.[94] They often courted long distance, as Franklin went to New York and then to London on business with his famous father. Time and distance ultimately ended the relationship, although its duration, passion, and unpleasant ending were formative for Fergusson and her family. Both parties' playful references to Franklin's tendency to allow months to pass between correspondences, as well as political tensions between the Franklins (who opposed the proprietary government) and the Graemes (who supported Pennsylvania proprietor Thomas Penn) escalated into a final, angry break in early 1759.[95] William Franklin's return to Philadelphia in late 1762 as the newly appointed, and recently married, Royal Governor of New Jersey caused Fergusson much anguish. She apparently confided all details of the relationship to her parents, who recommended she try to get away, before suffering confinement for a lengthy illness.[96] After a postponement of the voyage on account of this illness, she finally left for England, where she traveled for much of 1764 and 1765.

It is from the journal of this trip to England that the prose extracts in *Moore's Book* are derived. This journal received some fame later in the eighteenth century, when Benjamin Rush's published eulogy for Fergusson praised it as "a feast to all who read it."[97] It was also the topic of more immediate discussion, when, while still in England, Fergusson sent it to her friend Elizabeth Steadman. "I have perused your journal," Steadman wrote back, "and often have I wish'd to have per-

94. A number of these poems appear in Fergusson's commonplace book, "Poemata Juvenilia," kept between 1752 and 1772; LCP. A good account of the Franklin-Graeme courtship, particularly as it related to William Franklin's service for his father during the latter's attempts to negotiate with the proprietary government in London, is in Sheila Skemp, *William Franklin: Son of a Patriot, Servant of a King* (New York: Oxford University Press), 23–38.

95. Franklin's final, astonishingly long, and alternately plaintive and furious letter to Elizabeth Graeme, dated October 24, 1758, is in the Gratz Collection, HSP.

96. Letters from Ann and Thomas Graeme to their daughter express their sorrow at her discomfort over the situation as well as keen analyses of the awkwardness that Franklin's new position might entail. Franklin was also still friendly with members of the New Jersey and Pennsylvania elite who were also close to the Graeme family. See Ann Graeme to Elizabeth Graeme, December 3, 1762; and Thomas Graeme to Elizabeth Graeme, January 2, 1763; Gratz Collection, HSP.

97. Rush, "Mrs. Elizabeth Ferguson," 395 (see note 74, above).

took with you in those delightful scenes indeed I envy you the enjoyment . . . but as I cant enjoy it with you there I will by the help of immagination [enjoy it] here."[98]

How Fergusson's writings, including the journal, came to be included in Moore's commonplace book is not entirely clear. Exchanges of poetry among these women before the American Revolution followed several distinct patterns. School settings were an arena for the exchange and copying of manuscript writings. Elizabeth Graeme Fergusson's evening gatherings provided a forum for reading aloud from poetry or prose manuscripts. Another setting was the intense exchange established and conducted through family ties, such as that experienced by Wright and Griffitts, and by Elizabeth Graeme Fergusson with her own circle of friends. The connection between Fergusson and Moore represents a fourth kind of communication and exchange altogether. During and after the Revolution their families found themselves caught in the same kinds of troubling and complex situation, when the lines blurred between patriotism and loyalism, Quaker and Anglican, and when elites of different backgrounds all found themselves contending with the vicissitudes of warfare and political turmoil. During the war, Fergusson came to rely on members of Moore's and Griffitts's extended family for help, and Moore found herself with a neighbor in distress and in intellectual sympathy. No documentation exists to prove that Moore came into possession of Fergusson's journal and commonplace book during the Revolution, but because that is the period during which Moore copied the material, and the first period when we can document the connections between their families as especially strong, it is likely that this was when their acquaintance flowered.

The Revolutionary Context of Moore's Commonplace Book

The American Revolution plays a prominent role in Milcah Moore's commonplace book. While many pieces predate the Revolution, it

98. Elizabeth Steadman to Elizabeth Graeme, Philadelphia, March 9, 1765, Gratz Collection, HSP.

seems that Moore copied everything into her book during the war. None of the works are dated later than 1778, and much of the earliest material is mixed in with later pieces. Significant clusters of material are dated between 1764 and 1769 and from 1773 through 1776 and address the political events of those periods such as the nonimportation movements, British taxation of colonials, and the course of the Revolutionary War itself, including specific battles. Much of Hannah Griffitts's poetry in particular focused on politics and war.

While it was common for copyists to include material from a wide variety of sources representing a spectrum of dates, including literary magazines, the timing of Moore's copying activity is reflected in her choice of poetry and prose pieces as well as in the variety of authors whose work appears in the book. Moore chose works that appealed to her aesthetically, but which also represented a particular aspect of the Revolutionary War experience. Moore and her circle were mostly loyal to the Crown, or objected to the war because of Quaker pacifist principles, but they were by no means a politically homogeneous group. Two of Moore's (and Hannah Griffitts's) cousins were married to prominent, albeit moderate, Patriots, John Dickinson and Charles Thomson. Moore's sister Margaret Morris, however, harbored the ardent Loyalist Jonathan Odell in her New Jersey home to protect him from Patriots. Moore's commonplace book reflects this heterogeneity. Loyalist Odell appears as an author alongside disowned Quaker and radical Patriot Timothy Matlack. Representing an entirely different view, Hannah Griffitts's poetry espoused moderation and castigated extremism in any form. Thus the range of political opinions expressed in Moore's commonplace book, and the authors of those opinions, ranged from extreme patriotism to extreme loyalism.[99]

The American Revolution exposed fault lines in American society and politics, aggravating existing tensions in the colonies even as it addressed the intense disputes between England and America over the nature of the imperial relationship. In colonial Pennsylvania, political

99. The complexity of loyalism is treated in a number of works by Robert Calhoon. See especially Calhoun's *The Loyalists in Revolutionary America, 1760–1781* (New York: Harcourt, Brace Jovanovich, 1965); idem, *The Loyalist Perception and Other Essays* (Columbia: University of South Carolina Press, 1989); and Calhoun's introduction to a special issue of *Pennsylvania History* 62 (1995): 273–75. See also Anne M. Ousterhout, *A State Divided: Opposition in Pennsylvania to the American Revolution* (Westport: Greenwood Press, 1987).

disputes had often pitted the prominent and pacifist Quakers against other groups that favored armed conflict.[100] It was just this sort of dispute that had previously convinced most Quaker politicians to retreat from political life altogether in 1755–56, when pressure to answer the combined French and Indian threats with combat became too great. Rather than commit public funds to weapons or soldiers, a number of prominent Quaker politicians resigned from the Pennsylvania Assembly. Quakers did not completely relinquish their political control of William Penn's colony, but the values espoused by Quakerism, including pacifism, had much less political force.[101] Never completely submerged, the same problems resurfaced during the Revolution. While some Quakers sympathized with American grievances, particularly early in the crisis and especially on matters of trade, the Society of Friends adamantly opposed independence and war.

The Revolution, then, reinvigorated questions about the relationship between Quakers and governance. It also fueled conflicts between more "worldly" or "political" Quakers and those Quakers increasingly concerned with reform and spiritual renewal, which meant in many instances a renewed commitment to pacifism and zero tolerance for wartime activity. Beginning in earnest in the 1750s Quaker reformers had worried that Friends were losing their faith amidst the secular attractions of economic success and political power. The essential tenets of Quaker spiritualism and discipline were being disregarded. The same Quaker reformers who opposed slavery and moved the Society of Friends toward abolitionism also advocated increased discipline of members who married non-Quakers, or who violated Quaker marriage doctrine in other ways by, for example, marrying a cousin. The Revolution and the crises preceding it posed new concerns for these reformers. Could pacifist Quakers justly condone or participate in any activities leading to either combat or to the overthrow of government? In January 1775 Philadelphia Quakers pub-

---

100. The fullest treatment of the Quaker experience of the Revolution is in Arthur J. Mekeel, *The Relation of the Quakers to the American Revolution* (Washington: University Press of America, 1979). On the Quaker reform movement and its effect on Quaker engagement in politics before and during the war, see Marietta, *The Reformation of American Quakerism.*

101. On the resignation of high-profile Quakers from the Assembly and the continued, albeit much diminished, role of other Quakers in Pennsylvania politics, see Tully, *Forming American Politics*, 149–54 and 272–73.

lished a declaration "against every usurpation of power and authority, in opposition to the laws and government, and against all combinations, insurrections, conspiracies and illegal assemblies."[102] In September 1776 the Philadelphia Yearly Meeting, the largest Quaker group in America, created guidelines for Quaker conduct during the war. This included maintaining strict neutrality, refraining from voting or taking any oaths of loyalty to either side, refusing to serve in combat or to pay for a substitute, and refusing to pay taxes to support the war effort.[103] Milcah Moore's family confronted this problem directly upon learning that a nephew proposed to join the Continental army. Imploring him to reconsider, two uncles, three aunts, and a cousin signed a letter expressing worry that he "hath not considered its inconsistency with the religious principles of thy education and the wishes of thy nearest relations and best friends."[104] During the Revolution almost one thousand Pennsylvania Quakers were disowned by the Society of Friends for supporting the war by either directly bearing arms (the transgression of the majority of those disowned), paying taxes to the Revolutionary governments, serving in office, or taking oaths of allegiance.[105] Some of the disowned formed their own separatist meeting called the Free Quakers or the Fighting Quakers (see *MMMB* 114, by Timothy Matlack). Quakers, already a minority and already political outsiders, were now formally fragmented.[106]

102. Philadelphia Meeting for Suffering as quoted in Hugh Barbour and J. William Frost, *The Quakers* (Richmond, Ind.: Friends United Press, 1994), 140.

103. This set of guidelines is most clearly laid out in Barbour and Frost, *The Quakers*, 142–43. As they note, there was a great deal of variation in Quaker's payment of taxes. See Richard Bauman, *For the Reputation of Truth: Politics, Religion and Conflict Among the Pennsylvania Quakers, 1750–1800* (Baltimore: Johns Hopkins University Press, 1971).

104. Charles Moore to Samuel Preston Moore, Jr., Montgomery, Pennsylvania, June 2, 1777, in J. J. Smith, *Letters of Doctor Richard Hill*, 241–42.

105. The number of Pennsylvania Quakers disowned was 948. See Marietta, *The Reformation of American Quakerism*, 234.

106. Other issues divided Quakers. The most significant aspect of the mid-century reform movement, which also required that Milcah Martha Moore and Charles Moore be disowned for marrying close kin (contrary to Quaker teachings), was abolitionism. Quaker families were divided over the question of emancipating slaves. Some immediately supported the position that was eventually adopted by the Quaker Meeting, that all slaves immediately be manumitted, but others dragged their feet. Samuel Preston Moore, Milcah Moore's brother-in-law, was a very important member of the Quaker community for a long time, and was considered one of its leaders.

The Revolution created all kinds of hardships and anxieties for many Philadelphia Quakers. In Milcah Martha Moore's case, as for many Quakers, "loyalism" was the result of complicated negotiation among a common sense of obligation and attachment to England and the king, genuine aggrievement at British policies and particular British politicians, and a commitment to pacifism. Quakers were torn by their loyalties to the crown, to William Penn's "holy experiment," to friends on both sides of the conflict, and to their religious convictions. Moore's commonplace book reflects this sense of conflict and tension about the war and its combatants.

The political poetry in the commonplace book, written primarily by Hannah Griffitts, expresses this ambivalence most clearly. In the poems "The female Patriots" (*MMMB* 38) and "Beware the Ides of March" (*MMMB* 81), Griffitts lashed out at British politicians. Written seven years apart, in 1768 and 1775, Griffitts's two poems criticized the policy of taxing colonial consumption of British imports such as tea. "The female Patriots" was "Address'd to the Daughters of Liberty in America," a clear jab at the sometimes violent, self-appointed leaders of American protest, the Sons of Liberty. Griffitts called on women to navigate a course between the resistance efforts of the "degenerate" Sons and other men too "Suppinely" slow to act. Women should join the nonconsumption movement, finding substitutes or doing without the taxed items such as paper, paint, glass, and, of course, tea. "Stand firmly resolvd and bid Grenville to see," Griffitts exhorted, "that rather than Freedom, we'll part with our Tea." Seven years later Griffitts took another minister, Lord North, to task for yet another tax on tea. Her tone had changed little in the intervening years. In 1768 she encouraged American women to thwart George Grenville's policies. By 1775 she not only advocated nonconsumption but also warned that "Justice" would deal with "wicked North." Griffitts also implied that this plan might placate the Patriots already on the brink of violence.[107] Many Americans joined the nonconsumption and nonimportation movements, believing the British

---

But during the struggle over the abolitionism question, Samuel Moore apparently declined to manumit slaves and never participated in a Yearly Meeting (the formal annual meeting of Quakers) after 1756. See Jean R. Soderlund, *Quakers and Slavery: A Divided Spirit* (Princeton: Princeton University Press, 1985), 44.

107. Poem "Wrote on the Last Day of Feby. 1775" (*MMMB* 81).

tax policies to be a violation of the imperial relationship. Regulating trade through taxation was within the purview of the mother country, but taxation simply for raising money was well beyond it. Griffitts's views were hardly out of the mainstream; even the most loyal colonists questioned these policies. But for Quakers, the connection between pacifism and loyalism was particularly complicated. Sympathy and agreement with American grievances only added to the difficulty of Quakers' position.

In general, Quakers eschewed radicals and advocated policies of moderation, supporting those politicians on both sides of the Atlantic who pursued negotiated settlement as an alternative to independence and war. Griffitts's poetry expressed disgust at the rhetoric and actions of both radical Patriots and British politicians who refused to acknowledge the legitimacy of colonial complaints. In the late 1760s Griffitts warmly praised the eminent British politician William Pitt, claiming "Nations unborn shall praise thy patriot Name," for his support for the colonists' claims against Parliament during the Stamp Act crisis. Pitt opposed the Stamp Act, declaring that while Britain could regulate colonial trade and enact legislation taxing imports and exports for that purpose, only the colonists had the right to tax themselves for revenue. In 1775 Griffitts lauded the "patriotic Minority in both Houses of the British Parliament" (*MMMB* 80), members of which "nobly dar'd . . . pursue . . . The Rights of Justice, & support of Laws" and voted against further taxation of the colonists. Then in 1776 she excoriated Thomas Paine, the radical author of *Common Sense*. Published in early 1776, Paine's pamphlet had an immediate and inflammatory effect on the crisis. Paine argued that the Americans should declare their independence, not only because of Britain's actions during the 1760s and 1770s, but because the monarchy itself was a flawed institution. The concentration of power implicit in monarchy would inevitably lead to corrupt, unconstitutional actions such as those commercial and legal restrictions the Americans deplored. In "upon reading a Book entitled Common Sense" (*MMMB* 86), Griffitts denounced Paine as a "Snake beneath the Grass" and an ensnaring "Serpent." His arguments about monarchy and the concentration of power were specious, she countered, because "Sixty as well as one can tyrannize." Griffitts regretted that the voices of "moderate M[e]n" were drowned out by extremists like Paine.

Hannah Griffitts's political poetry is both artful and meaningful.

Milcah Martha Moore no doubt included many of Griffitts's poems in her commonplace book not only because they are quite good but also because they captured the sentiments of many Quakers. For Moore's and Griffitts's extended family, the political questions raised by the Revolution were especially acute. For close to eighty years after William Penn founded the colony in 1682, Quakers had constituted a ruling elite. Although many withdrew from politics in the mid-1750s, many families still had intimate connections to powerful politicians. Not all Quakers gave up public office, and large families that inter-married with other powerful, non-Quaker families found themselves politically and religiously opposed to policies advocated by dear relations. For example, Griffitts's young cousin, Mary Norris Dickinson, was married to moderate Patriot leader, John Dickinson.[108] Dickinson was so moderate, in fact, that when Paine and other radicals seized power in Pennsylvania in 1776, they turned out of office the elected Pennsylvania Assembly, including Dickinson. But he ultimately supported independence. The subject of politics, then, became quite delicate among the members of this large but close-knit family. Amidst the crises immediately preceding independence, Griffitts wrote to "Polly" Dickinson, thanking her for a gift of fruit and telling news of their aged aunt under Griffitts's care, but also to expressing her displeasure at recent acts of the Assembly. "I have Charity to believe they did for ye best in their opinion," she wrote, but "I am not alone in Thinking They have Push'd things to an Extremity."[109] When the Dickinsons followed much of the city's population and abandoned Philadelphia under the threat of a British approach and siege in late 1776, Griffitts worried. She worried about the safety of her cousin, and she also knew that their relationship could prove dangerous to the entire family. Some of John Dickinson's allies and enemies blamed his political reversals on his marriage to a Quaker, and some Quakers blamed Mary Norris Dickinson's "downfall" on her marriage to a non-Quaker.[110] These social and political difficulties took on new

108. Another niece, Hannah Harrison, married Patriot Charles Thomson.

109. Hannah Griffitts to Polly Dickinson, n.d. [1775], Logan Papers, HSP.

110. William Logan wrote to his brother-in-law John Smith about Mary Norris's marriage to Dickinson in 1770, noting, "I am greatly concerned for the example Polly has set by this her outgoing in marriage. I fear she has slipped from the top of the hill of the reputation she had gained in the Society and among her friends, and that it will be a long time before she gains it again, if ever" (quoted in Charles Stille, *Memoirs of*

urgency during wartime. "C. Thomson has taken his family to Baltimore," Griffitts wrote to Charles Moore, "& his neighbor gone—we know not where; nor how to Direct a Line to our Dear Sophia (I use this Name to Thee now, for Particular reasons, thee will guess at our, Judge, My Cousin, at our distress on this occassion)."[111]

Despite the Quaker Meeting's clear prohibition on revolutionary activities, and despite her loyalism, Griffitts, like many others, felt sympathy for the challenges that faced the American Patriots. Her close familial connection to avowed Patriots notwithstanding, Griffitts appreciated the ways that the crisis had forced partisans on both sides to make difficult choices. In late 1777 she penned "To Captain Charles Craige" (*MMMB* 122), which addressed these issues. An encomium to a Patriot soldier, this poem expressed deep regret at the "mean Distinctions [the] Times have made," serving to "break each sacred Tye, each social Band." In a letter to Milcah Martha Moore early in the uncertain winter of 1777, Griffitts revealed her ambivalent feelings about the two sides as she contemplated the potential arrival of British troops in Philadelphia. "If our Present accounts are true," she wrote, "its probable ye English Army will not Disturb us this winter, as . . . our forces have drive them back towards NYork." "How many Lives (if not souls) have been lost to procure this advantage," she asked, and "Who is to answer for this waste of Mankind[?]" While she identified the American troops as "our forces," in this same letter Griffitts also expressed her impatience with those Patriots who found the question of allegiance a simple one. "I yesterday rec'd a Long Letter from Sophronia [Hannah Thomson]," she reported, who was "Happy in a social society of sentiments alike, [where] 'Not one Tory suffer'd to breathe ye air of Baltimore.'"[112]

While presenting a portrait of the conflicting ties and sentiments that comprised loyalism, patriotism, and the gray areas between those

---

the *Historical Society of Pennsylvania* [Philadelphia: Historical Society of Pennsylvania, 1891–95], 13:317). See also John Dickinson's letter to an unnamed correspondent in August 1776, noting that his marriage to a Quaker heiress and his seeming sympathy with Quaker views or at least political views that Quakers could support, cost him support among other factions (quoted in Richard Ryerson, *The Revolution Has Now Begun: The Radical Committees of Philadelphia, 1765–1776* [Philadelphia: University of Pennsylvania, 1978], 245).

111. Hannah Griffitts to Charles Moore, Philadelphia, December 14, 1776, EWS.

112. Hannah Griffitts to [Milcah Martha Moore], [Philadelphia], January 8, 1777, EWS.

two political stances, Moore's book also represents a particular geo-graphical experience of the American Revolution. The mid-Atlantic states of Pennsylvania, New York, Delaware, and New Jersey were the site of some of the war's earliest and most dramatic campaigns. The battles at Lexington and Concord in April 1775 initiated a year of ac-tion concentrated in New England, and especially around Boston. In the summer of 1776 the Americans signed the Declaration of Inde-pendence, and the British began in earnest to fight a war, rather than a small insurrection, by sending General William Howe to occupy New York City. In the fall of 1776, Washington's and Howe's armies chased each other back and forth across the New York and New Jersey bor-ders. Early 1777 brought the war further south, first to Trenton and then to Princeton. The fall of 1777 found the primary theater shifted south again, this time to Philadelphia. On September 26, 1777, Howe's army marched into Philadelphia. They stayed—occupying the city, invading residents' homes, and inflating prices for food and fuel—until June the following year. During that time, while Philadel-phians either fled or lived in an occupied city, Washington's troops weathered a bitter winter at Valley Forge, and New Jerseyans experi-enced reversal after reversal of political fortunes. First the Patriots were in charge, then the Loyalists. France's intervention in the Amer-ican Revolution, the turning point for the Americans, also marked the end of major combat in the Delaware Valley. For the remainder of the war, except for problems with mutinous troops demanding long promised back pay, Philadelphians watched from the sidelines as southerners battled the British in Virginia and the Carolinas.

The counter-seizures of New York and Philadelphia and the move-ment of troops on both sides across the New Jersey countryside made Moore's family's Revolutionary War experience unpleasantly distinct. Unlike Americans living in other areas, Moore and her family experi-enced the war at home early and often. One immediate question they confronted was whether to remain within reach of either army, or to retreat to a safer place. The Moores left Philadelphia with many oth-ers who abandoned the city when British occupation seemed immi-nent, although Hannah Griffitts stayed behind with her sister Mary Griffitts and their aged aunt Elizabeth Norris. Invited to join the Moores, Griffitts explained that she would not quit the city. She was both practical and philosophical about this decision. "We are en-circled with fears & almost daily alarms," Griffitts wrote to Charles Moore, "& yet some doubt whether Howe will be here before spring." She also took solace in faith. "A secret Something seems to forbid our Leaving ye City—or shall I Rather say—we have more freedom to stay—we trust in the best counsel . . . Direction & Protection of Infinite Power Wisdom & Love."[113] Writing from her home on the Susquehanna River and starved for news, Susanna Wright could not believe that anyone would stay in the city. "Why would not every person who had it in their power, leave that devoted city, before those miscreants entered it[?]," she wondered. "I can in no way account for the conduct of Several Individuals, who might have come to places of more probable Security—but now have only to wish they had done it."[114] From the vantage point of south-central Pennsylvania, Philadelphia's perils no doubt seemed severe. Griffitts, however, was determined to stay. She had an elderly aunt and an ailing sister in her care, and perhaps moving them both was more daunting than the advancing British army. Having survived the Patriot mobs, Griffitts may have felt emboldened to face the British.

The threat to property was quite real from Patriots seeking to punish Loyalists, from the British seeking to punish Patriots, or from either side in search of provisions. Quakers were particularly vulnerable to such acts. Moore's sister and brother-in-law, Hannah Hill Moore and Samuel Preston Moore, suffered losses when a Patriot mob in Philadelphia ransacked the homes of suspected Loyalists. Writing to Milcah, Hannah Moore described "such a sceen . . . never before in this town & . . . I fear just the beginning of what we may expect."[115] From a neighbor's home the Moores watched while "the mob attacked our house . . . . breaking the windows that had no shutters & some shutters . . . . they came a second time to our houses & pounded with stones. . . . We thought all was over when P Lloyd came & told us they were determined to have our house down." In the end "we had only the lights over the door broke," Hannah Moore reported, but "its not to [be] told the damage that has been done to many F[rien]ds houses."[116]

On the other side, the British attacked and plundered country estates, including the original Norris mansion Fairhill, which by the

113. Hannah Griffitts to Charles Moore, Philadelphia, December 14, 1776, EWS.
114. Susanna Wright to Hannah Thomson, [Hempfield], December 11, 1777, Logan Collection, HSP.
115. Hannah Moore to Milcah Martha Moore, n.d. [1775], EWS.
116. Hannah Moore to Milcah Martha Moore, n.d. [1775], EWS.

time of the Revolution was the country home of John and Mary Norris Dickinson. British maps of the period identify Fairhill as belonging to the "patriot Dickinson."[117] With that kind of billing, it became a natural target. In 1777, Fairhill was attacked and burned. The library survived, due in part perhaps to the thick brick walls and its separation from the main house. Susanna Wright wrote to Hannah Thomson, another cousin of Moore, Griffitts and the Dickinsons, and the wife of Patriot leader Charles Thomson, expressing dismay at the passing of this icon of familial convivity. She complained that the British troops seemed to have no "spark of honor" but were instead

> a Banditte to plunder and Burn all they come across—I never can forgive their exploits at fairhill, & if the actors were in my power, they should be rewarded in an exemplary manner: when we heard of the sad fate of that once happy & Elegant residence, we were not only affected with sorrow but my sister & my self felt such emotions, as made us downright sick for some time—I cannot help recollecting I was upon the place before the house was finished, & spent some of the most agreable hours of my life in it, from time to time afterwards; I recall to my mind the agreable faces, & chearful conversations to be found there.[118]

Margaret Hill Morris and Sarah Hill Dillwyn, Milcah Moore's sisters, found themselves in the thick of things during the winter of 1776–77. Living at Green Bank on the Delaware River near Burlington, in the former home of the last Royal Governor of New Jersey, William Franklin, Morris, and Dillwyn experienced first hand the advances and retreats of the British and American troops.[119] Morris kept a diary for Moore, often recording in breathless prose the arrival of the competing armies and the quartering of the troops, her efforts to

117. See the map created by the British engineering corps in late 1777, identifying Fairhill as "Dickinson's a Post of the Rebels Burnt," reprinted in Martin P. Snyder, *City of Independence: Views of Philadelphia Before 1800* (New York: Praeger, 1975), 117.

118. Susanna Wright to Hannah Thomson, December 11, 1777, Logan Collection, HSP.

119. New Jersey's rapid swing between patriot and loyalist power is the topic of *MMMB* 57 and 104.

provide for her family as well as imposing soldiers in the neighborhood, and the complications that ensued when friends of either side
were sought by their respective enemies. Morris's journal opened on
December 6, 1776, the day before Washington crossed into Pennsylvania, after which the British pulled back temporarily into New York
leaving a force of Hessian soldiers in their employ to hold the British
line in New Jersey. Morris recorded the shifting presence of the
British-Hessian forces and the American troops, and the pressures
each brought to bear on the resident population. When the Hessians
arrived on December 11, they wanted a full report of any "persons in
Town in arms [or] any Arms, Ammunition, or other effects, belonging
to Persons that were in Arms against the King." Anything concealed
and subsequently discovered would be "given up to Pillage."[120] Loyalist Jonathan Odell served as interpreter for the Hessian comman-
dant, and by Morris's report managed to protect some Patriot property left to his care by friends. But Odell was not so lucky when the
pendulum swung again. Just two days later a Patriot "search was made
in & about the Town for Men distinguished by the name of Tories."[121]
Homes were searched. Morris's young son aggravated the situation by
watching the action through a spy glass, which attracted the attention
of the search party. They arrived at Morris's door demanding to be let
in. As she reported it, she "kept locking and unlocking [the door] that
I might get my ruffled face, a little composed" and, when she did open
the door, played dumb. "I put on a very simple look & cryed out,"
Morris remembered, "bless me I hope you are not Hessians—say
good men are you the Hessians? do we look like Hessian? asked one
of them rudely—indeed I dont know; Did you ever see a Hessian? no
never in my life but they *are men* & you are men & may be Hessians
for anything I know."[122] This ruse worked wonderfully well. She led
the searchers to the home of her absent neighbor where they looked
fruitlessly for "the tory—strange where could he be." As it turned
out, Morris's disingenuous exchange with the Patriots did save a
Tory—Jonathan Odell, closeted away in a secret, windowless attic
room outfitted for the occassion with an emergency warning bell.[123]

120. John W. Jackson, *Margaret Morris Her Journal* (Philadelphia: George S. Mac-
Manus Company, 1949), 43.
    121. Ibid., 47.
    122. Ibid., 48.
    123. Ibid., 47–49, 91–92, for the legend of the "auger hole" in the attic.

Having had enough excitement, Morris escorted Odell to a new safe house. In 1777 Odell escaped to New York where he served a number of Loyalist regiments as a minister. After the war he lived in a Loyalist settlement in New Brunswick.[124]

While Margaret Morris was facing down inquisitorial Patriots, Philadelphians were wondering when the British General Howe would turn his attention toward their city. It was widely rumored in December 1776 that Howe would occupy the city immediately, but in fact he did not arrive until almost ten months later. In the meantime both Quakers and Patriot leaders had staked out less tolerant positions. Quaker leaders and the Society of Friends Meeting strictly enforced the ban on any activity contributing to the war, while Patriot leaders and committees created ever harsher penalties for noncompliance and lack of cooperation with their Revolutionary War efforts. The presence of the Continental Congress in the city (the Congress stayed in Philadelphia from 1774 to late 1777 and again beginning in mid-1778) only exacerbated these problems. An example of the difficulties that ensued was the issuance of paper currency. The Continental Congress authorized the printing and circulation of paper money to finance the war. The Quaker printer hired by Congress to carry out the production of these notes had been disowned by the Quaker meeting. Subsequently, other Quakers refused to accept the notes as a legitimate form of payment. Quaker shops were closed by the Philadelphia Committee of Safety, and the anti-Quaker rhetoric of Patriot leaders intensified. After the Philadelphia Yearly Meeting of September 1776 issued an epistle delineating exactly how Quakers ought to resist aiding the Revolutionary cause, some Philadelphians pressed the Committee of Safety to prosecute Quaker leaders for treason. Thomas Paine charged that the Quakers were hypocritical ("continuously harping on the great sin of *our* bearing arms [while] the King of great Britain may lay waste the world") and that the Yearly Meeting epistle was intended to "promote sedition and treason and to encourage the enemy."[125] During the summer of 1777 problems worsened, as the newly radical Assembly passed laws mandating not only

---

124. See Cynthia Dubin Edelberg, *Jonathon Odell: Loyalist Poet of the American Revolution* (Durham: Duke University Press, 1987), 147–59.

125. Mekeel, *Relation of the Quakers*, 160–69; Thomas Paine in *The Crisis*, no. 2, as quoted in Mekeel, *Relation of the Quakers*, 165.

military service, but oaths of allegiance to the Revolutionary governments and renunciations of the king's authority. Quakers were fined, chased by mobs and jailed; their property was seized and their houses vandalized.[126]

By the time Howe capitalized on the advances he had made the previous winter and decided to take Philadelphia, Quakers' troubles with the Patriots had reached a crisis. The Continental Congress and the army watched and waited from inside a city full of Quakers while Howe spent the last part of the summer of 1777 seemingly just on the verge of striking at Philadelphia. From the Patriots' perspective, Quakers were clearly Loyalist and probably treacherous. The discovery of a detailed plan of the size and position of the American forces supposedly sent to the British by the obviously bogus "Quaker Yearly Meeting at Spanktown" convinced both political and military leaders of the seriousness of the Quaker threat. Congress resolved that Pennsylvania's Supreme Executive Council should take twelve leading Quakers into custody, along with any Meeting records of a political nature.

In September, 1777 these twelve Quakers and a handful of other suspected traitors to the Revolution were jailed, and then exiled to Winchester, Virginia. That same month General Howe and his British regulars finally moved to occupy Philadelphia. While the Quaker exiles in Virginia petitioned for their release, the Pennsylvania government withdrew to Lancaster and the Continental Congress moved to New York City. Over the wretched winter of 1777–78 Washington's troops at Valley Forge confronted Quaker farmers who would not willingly supply food for the army and the exiles at Winchester battled new charges. In occupied Philadelphia, the exiles' families and others organized petitions to Congress and the Pennsylvania Assembly. In early March 1778 two of the exiles died from ill health (and possibly the stress of their confinement), and in early April four of the exiles' wives travelled to Lancaster to plead with General Washington for their husbands' return. The issue was becoming an embarrassment for the Pennsylvania government and for the Congress, which worried that even their allies in independence would be put off by this long internment of a group that, while troublesome, had never been

126. Mekeel, *Relation of the Quakers*, 166–68.

proved threatening. Finally on April 29, Washington signed an order allowing the exiles to return to Philadelphia.[127]

This episode, the subject of Hannah Griffitts's poems (*MMMB* 123 and 124), occasioned tremendous agitation in a city already troubled by the residence of British troops.[128] The loss of America's premier city had been a tremendous blow to the Patriots, and as they left they tried to take much of value with them. Many printing presses, for example, were removed, and standard newspapers like the *Pennsylvania Gazette* were published from places like Lancaster and York for the duration of the British occupation.[129] With the help of Philadelphia Loyalists the British arrested and jailed close to five hundred American Patriots. Intermittent shortages of food, as well as the enforced quartering of British officers, made the occupation unpleasant. The behavior of the British troops and officers, on the other hand, seemed sometimes designed to irk those Quakers they might have thought most loyal. Many Quakers and others were displeased at the elaborate spectacle called the "Meschianza" that honored the departing General Howe (recalled to England and replaced by General Henry Clinton). Including a mock medieval tournament, dancing, feasting, fireworks, and boat rides on the Delaware, the event attracted many Philadelphia girls, dressed as Turkish maidens to complement the British officers dressed as knights.[130]

Milcah Moore's family, and that of Hannah Griffitts in particular, was again in the middle of the action. Not only were they and their family members intimately tied to the events, but they were geo-

---

127. Ibid., 173–88. The fullest account of the exiles can be found in Thomas Gilpin's edition of relevant documents, *Exiles in Virginia: With Observations on the Conduct of the Society of Friends During the Revolutionary War* (Philadelphia, 1848). Accounts of the expedition to Lancaster to plead for the exiles return can be found in the diary of Elizabeth Drinker, whose husband Henry was among the twelve Quaker leaders first arrested. See Crane, ed., *Diary of Elizabeth Drinker*, entry for April 25, 1778.

128. An excellent recent account of the reaction of Loyalist women (mostly Quaker and including Hannah Griffitts) to the events of the Revolution in Philadelphia is in Judith Van Buskirk, "They Didn't Join The Band: Disaffected Women in Revolutionary Philadelphia," *Pennsylvania History* 62 (Summer 1995): 306–25.

129. Harry M. Tinkcom, "The Revolutionary City," in Weigley, *Philadelphia: A 300-year History*, 134.

130. Tinkcom, "The Revolutionary City," 142.

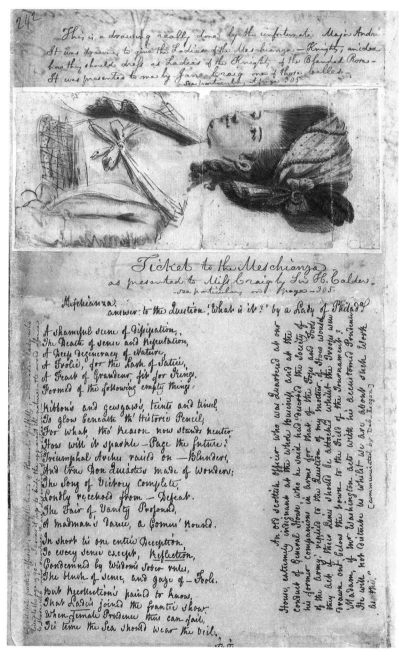

Fig. 4. A scrapbook for John Watson's famous early nineteenth-century history, the *Annals of Philadelphia*, paired Hannah Griffitts's satire on the Meschianza with a sketch of a woman's costume by principal organizer, "the unfortunate Major Andre." Watson noted that he was given a copy of Griffitts's poem by her niece, Deborah Norris Logan. Courtesy of the Library Company of Philadelphia.

graphically situated to receive an uncomfortably close view. The jailed Quakers, soon to be exiled, were first confined at the Free Mason's Lodge in Norris Alley on the same block where Griffitts lived with her sister and aunt. Moore and Griffitts were not only close friends with but also relatives of some of the exiles.[131] When General Howe arrived in late September 1777 he initially took up residence just north of the city at Stenton, the home of Griffitts's relations, fellow Quakers, and important politicians, the Logans. No one could ignore the Meschianza, and Griffitts responded with satirical verse calling it "a shameful scene of dissipation" and "a deep degeneracy of nature," deploring especially that "*Ladies* join'd the frantic show."[132]

Other Philadelphians or New Jerseyans who appear in *Milcah Martha Moore's Book*, either as authors or as the subjects of poetry or prose, were similarly caught up in the events of the late 1770s. In many ways their experiences demonstrate that, despite the harsh rhetoric and often violent or coercive efforts to enforce absolute allegiance to one side or another in the revolutionary contest, many people either contemporaneously or subsequently identified as Patriot or Loyalist in fact had friends and family on both sides of the aisle. For some this meant that even during and after the war their political loyalties were ambiguous and their actions subject to the exigencies of the moment. Elizabeth Graeme Fergusson was such a figure. The step-granddaughter of Pennsylvania Governor William Keith, daughter of respected Anglican doctor and sometime local officeholder Thomas Graeme, and forsaken fiancée of William Franklin, Elizabeth Graeme Fergusson had a colorful history of connections well before the start of the Revolution. During the war her close friendships with elite Anglicans and Quakers, her connections to

131. At least three of the original twelve, Israel, James, and John Pemberton, were related by blood and marriage to Moore's and Griffitts's extended family. Their second cousin Hannah Lloyd (granddaughter of Thomas Lloyd Jr.) married James Pemberton in 1751. The ties were even closer for John Dickinson's wife and Hannah Griffitts's cousin Mary Norris Dickinson. She was related to James Pemberton by marriage but also by blood. He was Sarah Logan Norris's (Mary's mother) cousin through her maternal line, the Reads. Pemberton gave Mary Norris a great deal of assistance after her father died and before she married Dickinson. He acted as her lawyer in a number of transactions. Mekeel, *Relation of the Quakers*, 186n; Wulf, "A Marginal Independence," chap. 7.

132. "Letters Addressed to John F. Watson on the Subject of his Annals of Philada," Am 30163, 1:29, HSP.

some highly placed Patriots, and her marriage to an avowed Tory (a Scotsman ten years her junior) complicated her efforts to remain in Pennsylvania and retain ownership of her property. A friend brought Henry Hugh Fergusson to Graeme Park in 1771, and just four months later he married its mistress. Their marriage remained a secret until Thomas Graeme died in 1772, and then both Fergussons lived together at Graeme Park until Henry Fergusson returned to England in September of 1775. Caught out by the changing tides of the war's progress, he finally returned to Philadelphia with Howe's army and was made Commissary of the Prisoners in the city. He fled again in the spring of 1778 (after being accused of treason by the Patriots), was reported to be in New York in the fall, and finally saw his wife for the last time at a friend's home in New Jersey in February 1779.[133]

When her husband fled Philadelphia in 1778, Elizabeth Graeme Fergusson's family home at Graeme Park was confiscated as Loyalist property. She was allowed to remain in the house, although some furniture was sold at auction.[134] While the war still raged, albeit after the focus of the fighting had shifted to the south, only an arrangement by the Supreme Court of Pennsylvania and then a special act of the Pennsylvania Assembly allowed her to retain possession of the house and land.[135] This crisis had caused Fergusson to call on the aid of a number of friends and acquaintances, some of whom were in no position to help her. In late 1779 John Dickinson had to remind Fergusson that his political fortunes were such that his intervention would be neither forthcoming nor effective. "If some circumstances were known to you," Dickinson reported, 'your good sense would immediately have perceived that you could hardly have asked the Intrposition of a person less likely to succeed." [136]

133. Slotten, "Elizabeth Graeme Fergusson," 265–67.

134. Some furniture and other property was sold as part of Henry Hugh Fergusson's confiscated estate, and Elizabeth Graeme Fergusson repurchased pieces worth over £55, including chairs, candlesticks, and "2 Red Sows and Pigs" (vendue receipt signed by George Smith, Agent, Philadelphia, October 15, 1778, Gratz Collection, HSP).

135. See *Statutes of Pennsylvania* 10 (1799–81), 281–82; petitions and correspondence, 1778-81, including a note in Elizabeth Graeme Fergusson's hand of "Gentlemen who Eerted their Influence in Behalf of Elizabeth Fergusson when her Estate was Confiscated And whose good offices she Remembers with Gratitude"; Gratz Collection, HSP.

136. John Dickinson to Elizabeth Fergusson, Philadelphia, September 8, 1779, Joseph Mickle Fox collection, bound with Henry Simpson, *Lives of Eminent Phila-*

During the Revolution, Fergusson's life intersected with Moore's and Griffitts's on a number of fronts. Moore's brother Henry Hill and John Dickinson were among those who tried to help Fergusson regain clear title to her property after the war, for example. But this is probably also the period when Moore and Fergusson became acquainted, or perhaps better acquainted. While most wealthy families maintained homes in the city and the two could have known each other before the war, during and after the war both women retired to country houses quite close together. During the war the Moores moved their permanent residence to Montgomery township in the northern part of Philadelphia County, next to Horsham township, the residence of Fergusson at Graeme Park. When Moore began her educational enterprises in the 1780s, opening a school and publishing a textbook, the *Miscellanies, Moral and Instructive*, Fergusson publicly supported both efforts.[137]

Afterward the two women continued to move in separate intellectual circles, Moore communicating extensively with her Quaker relatives including her sisters and Hannah Griffitts, and Fergusson concentrating on her relationships with other women who published poetry such as her old friend Annis Boudinot Stockton. Fergusson herself now published her poetry in magazines such as the *Columbian Magazine* and the *Pennsylvania Magazine*.[138] Fergusson also spent considerable time in copying her own works for others' amusement, and circulating her commonplace books and journals.

Moore's attention to publishing her collection of poetry by prominent British authors, the *Miscellanies*, and Fergusson's interests in publishing her own poetry in literary magazines demonstrate two post-Revolutionary phenomena. The first of these is the emerging dominance of printed material. After the war, printed literature was created and circulated in greater and greater numbers. Manuscript material would continue to play an essential role in circulating writing among an intimate audience of readers, but the the prevalence of

---

delphians Now Deceased (Philadelphia: William Brotherhead, 1859), 4: 310–11, in Rosenbach Museum and Library. For an explanation of the violence and anti-Toryism of 1779, and of the eventual re-establishment of political conservatives like Dickinson thereafter, see Tinkcom, "The Revolutionary City," 145–49.

137. Fergusson published a poem, "Lines on reading Martha Moore's Selections," in the *Colonial Magazine* in 1788. I am grateful to Anne Ousterhout for supplying this reference. Fergusson also contributed funds to Moore's school.

138. Slotten, "Elizabeth Graeme Fergusson," 267–68.

printed books in the growing number of girls' schools, for example, is evidence of the diminished role of the manuscript. While Hannah Griffitts's poetry could be used, copied, and circulated through small schools as well as among her close circle of friends and family before and during the war, after the war teachers including Milcah Martha Moore looked to printed textbooks.

The implications of this transition were profoundly gendered. A comparison of the material in Moore's and others' commonplace books and copybooks before the war suggests a wide range of topics and approaches. These were also dominated by women's writings. The *Miscellanies*, on the other hand, promoted a selection of writings by more men than women, and more English writers than Americans. In addition, the place that women's writings were now published, the new literary magazines for women in particular, emphasized a particular kind of domestic role for women. Even as women's education was celebrated and encouraged as never before, in the early Republic women's intellectual activity was understood to be part of their service to the new nation. Women would read, write, and be educated in order to more effectively raise good citizen-sons.[139] The era in which Susanna Wright, Hannah Griffitts, and Elizabeth Graeme Fergusson wrote prose and poetry, and in which Milcah Martha Moore collected, selected, and transcribed their words, was passing.

Milcah Martha Moore captured an exciting time in American history in her commonplace book. Written during the American Revolution, many of the poems reflect the highly charged political environment of the period. Clearly the political poetry is place- and time-specific. Hannah Griffitts's pithy commentaries on the British tea taxes, for example, give us a window into popular sentiments about the hardships and necessity of the boycotts. Although many of the poems are works in the timeless genres of memorials and friendship testimonials, they too are products of a specific time and place. It was a period of intense debate and difficult political reflection. It was also a period when young girls of the economic elite could expect to receive schooling, and in urban areas particularly, could get access to reading materials ranging from novels to literary magazines to newspapers. Thus the appearance of a varied and rich literary culture in the colonies included women. In Philadelphia, where Moore's family was

139. Although a number of historians and literary scholars have engaged in debate about the nature of this transition, and have modified some of Linda Kerber's argu-

based, the large population of Quakers was undergoing intense spiritual reexamination, as most of their members retreated from politics because of their pacifist ideals and were rethinking their role in the colony founded by Quaker William Penn as a "holy experiment" in religious pluralism. All of these issues and more are represented through the poetry and prose in *Moore's Book*.

The book also reveals some of the tensions surrounding these issues. The American Revolution provoked enormous debate about the nature of government, the relationship of America to England and the king, and the relationship of American Patriots to American Loyalists. Loyalism itself was complex, and experienced by the women in *Moore's Book* as a conflicting set of allegiances to family, friends, sovereign, home, and religion. Women's reading and writing was part of a shared culture for some, but a threatening, unfamiliar and insufficiently domesticated activity for others. Questions about women's appropriate social roles, including in marriage and in religious activity, appear in the poetry. Social issues like the abolition of slavery also mark *Moore's Book* as the product of a specific place and time.

Perhaps most important, in Moore's commonplace book modern readers find testimony to the significance of reading, writing, and intimate communication among a network of intellectual women in the mid- to late-eighteenth century. For the most part, historians and literary scholars have looked to the post-Revolutionary era, and particularly the early nineteenth century, as the era of American women's movement out of domestic and sacred literature and toward consumption of ever more widely available printed literature, especially novels.[140] In *Moore's Book* we see women writing and reading across a broad subject matter, with work represented from the late 1720s through the late 1770s. We see women's engagement with issues of politics, war, friendship, worship, and death. We see women's interest in and concern with communicating ideas and sentiments to other women. In short, we see women's engagement with the full range of issues that affected the course of their eighteenth-century lives.

---

ments, the most important statement on the subject is still her *Women of the Republic: Intellect and Ideology in Revolutionary America* (Chapel Hill: University of North Carolina Press, 1980).

140. Richard D. Brown, *Knowledge is Power: The Diffusion of Information in Early America, 1700–1865* (New York: Oxford University Press, 1989); Cathy N. Davidson, *Revolution and the Word: The Rise of the Novel in America* (New York: Oxford University Press, 1986).

READING MOORE'S BOOK

Manuscripts vs. Print Culture,
and the Development of
Early American Literature

Catherine La Courreye Blecki

Just as Milcah Martha Moore's commonplace book opens a window into the historical life of colonial and revolutionary America, it offers modern readers a unique perspective on the development of early American literature through a manuscript collection transcribed for sociable circles of writers and readers.[1] The selections that Milcah Martha Moore chose to copy give us an insight into literature, both documentary and imaginative, that her family and friends enjoyed writing and reading. Rather than being published in print, Moore's

---

1. One of the most valuable "recoveries" literary scholars have made in the late twentieth century is that manuscript circulation was a viable alternative to print publication from the sixteenth through the eighteenth centuries. For English literature, see Arthur Marotti, *Manuscript, Print, and the English Renaissance* (Ithaca: Cornell University Press, 1995); Harold Love, *Scribal Publication in Seventeenth-Century England* (Oxford: Clarendon Press, 1993); Mary Hobbs, *Early Seventeenth-Verse Miscellany* (Hants, Eng.: Scholar Press, 1992). For American literature, see Carla

Fig. 5.   Milcah Martha Moore's three commonplace books. Private collection.

commonplace book was compiled for a relatively small audience of family and friends who were affectionate, literate, and tolerant of many points of view. Many were Quakers (members of the Society of Friends), who already believed in the equality of men and women as persons in the spirit, so reading a collection of writing chiefly composed by women presented few barriers based on traditional ideas of gender.

Milcah Martha Moore compiled three unpublished manuscripts; perhaps, other works are unidentified or have been lost.[2] The three texts can be seen in Figure 5. The smallest (about 5 × 3 inches) is dated 1776 and was a gift to Moore from her sister Sarah Dillwyn. A place where Moore kept her prayers and personal reflections, this book was meant for a private audience. The large volume in the center (7 × 9 inches) contains Moore's transcriptions of Quaker testimonies,

---

Mulford, *'Only for the Eye of a Friend': The Poems of Annis Stockton Boudinot* (Charlottesville: University of Virginia, 1995); David S. Shields, "British-American Belles Lettres," in Sacvan Bercovitch, ed., *The Cambridge History of American Literature* (Cambridge: Cambridge University Press, 1994), 1:307–43. David Shields reports finding another manuscript by a compiler who deliberately collected writing by American colonial writers. See Shields, "The Manuscript in the World of Print, *Proceedings of the American Antiquarian Society* 102, pt. 2 (1993): 410.

2. For the first two volumes of Moore's commonplace books, the small books of prayers and reflections and the large book of Quaker testimony, see MS. 975A, QC. For the commonplace book that is now *Moore's Book*, see MS. 955, EWS.

with entries from the 1680s through the 1770s. These three manuscripts contrast with Moore's only published work, *Miscellanies, Moral and Instructive* (see Figures 6a and 6b). As its title indicates, this textbook has a didactic focus and contains a different selection of authors, most of whom were British male writers.[3]

It is the third unpublished manuscript collection that became the *Milcah Martha Moore's Book* included in this volume. By considering the literary tradition of commonplace books and miscellanies and looking at a few eighteenth-century examples, we may appreciate Moore's skill as a compiler of such a collection, undoubtedly her best artistic work. By comparing *Moore's Book* with the *Miscellanies*, we see the superior quality of the entries in *Moore's Book* and observe a few of the ambiguites of national identity and purpose that Moore reflects during this period. Finally, by placing *Moore's Book* in the context of eighteenth-century British and American literary aesthetics, we understand the ways in which this work is rooted in the experience of Moore and her friends as they lived in the Delaware Valley.

The type of collection that Moore developed draws from two related traditions of compiling transcribed material: the "commonplace book" and the "miscellany." As a type of collection, "commonplace" originates from the "classical notion," as Kenneth Lockridge explains, of *topoi*, which were "common places" or "common topics" that students of composition or oratory could memorize for future use in organizing and developing ideas for composition or speech. Aristotle may have been the first teacher to recommend this practice to his students of rhetoric and logic.[4] Revived in the Renaissance by Erasmus, the rhetorical/academic commonplace book was used as a tool of education. Erasmus designed a system of headings and subheadings by

3. The editions of the *Miscellanies* text that were printed in Philadelphia, Burlington, and London kept the same title. The editors have not seen copies of the texts printed in Dublin.

4. Kenneth Lockridge, *On the Sources of Patriarchal Rage: The Commonplace Books of William Byrd and Thomas Jefferson and the Gendering of Power in the Eighteenth Century* (New York: New York University Press, 1992), 1: "The genre [commonplace book] originates in the classical notion that one should memorize *topoi*, or places, past utterances in which telling rhetoric and moral knowledge were inseparably embodied. When memorized, *topoi* became literally places in the mind which could serve as weapons in future rhetorical struggles." See also *The Rhetoric of Aristotle*, ed. Lane Cooper (New York: Appleton, 1960), 15.

which students could organize their extrapolations from literature or other written material under such "common" themes as "the virtues and vices, love and hate, and so on."[5] This system made a significant impact on readers, especially on young boys and men who needed to organize their reading around common topics that they would use in orations and composition in school and later in their professional lives. John Milton's commonplace book (c. 1620), for example, has received fruitful attention from Ruth Mohl, as she has noted the headings of some of Milton's early transcriptions, "Moral Evil," "Of the Good Man," and "Of Courage," and traced his reading through to his use and transformation of this material in his political and religious tracts and *Paradise Lost.*[6]

In the late seventeenth-century, John Locke (1632–1704) modified the commonplace book in terms of organizing and indexing the transcriptions. Printed as part of his posthumous works, *A New Method of Common-Place Book*, Locke described his method for placing short titles in an alphabetical grid and following each transcription with a note about the author's name, the title of the book, the volume, and page number.[7] Locke's method was widely used in the eighteenth century. Moore's brother-in-law, George Dillwyn, for example, followed a modified version of Locke's method in his commonplace book.[8]

Whether a person followed the methodology of Erasmus, Locke, or modified them, organizing transcriptions in a commonplace book reveals a transcriber's habits of mind and emotion. The work that has been done on Thomas Jefferson's literary commonplace books

5. Peter Beale, "Notions in Garrison: The Seventeenth-Century Commonplace Book," in *New Ways of Looking at Old Texts*, 154 vols., Papers of the Renaissance English Text Society, 1985–1991, ed. W. Speed Hill (Binghamton, N.Y.: Medieval & Renaissance Text & Studies and Renaissance English Text Society), 107:137. Beale gives a thorough background on the development of commonplace books and miscellanies.

6. Ruth Mohl, *John Milton and His Commonplace Book* (New York: Ungar, 1969), 31. Mohl dates Milton's first entries from the time he entered St. Paul's school in 1620. Milton continued making entries throughout his adult life. After his sight began to fail around 1650, Milton used scribes. Mohl gives a thorough background for commonplace books in chap. 2.

7. John Locke, *The Works*, ed. John C. Attig, *A New Method of Making Common-Place Books* (Westport: Greenwood Press, 1985).

8. George Dillwyn, commonplace book, MS. 975, QC.

(c. 1762–63) is an excellent example. Two scholars have made separate and complementary discoveries: one traced Jefferson's use of literary extracts in his later political and literary works, and the other discovered that the material Jefferson transcribed between the ages of thirteen and twenty-one disclose his feelings about power and misogyny.[9]

A second tradition, the "miscellany," emphasized the enjoyment of collecting over the usefulness of the compilation for education or for some future need. Some compilers of miscellanies included what pleased them to remember in random order: their diaries, household accounts, copies of correspondence, and verses. Others preferred to keep miscellanies that were strictly literary. Called "verse" miscellanies, they were used to preserve satirical political or social verse, parodies, extempore verses, riddles, libels, or epigrams.[10]

Although Moore omits Erasmus's headings as well as Locke's method of citation and organization, her manuscripts reflect aspects of both the commonplace book and miscellany. Like the commonplace book, her manuscripts were frequently used for instructive purposes.[11] Like the miscellany, two of Moore's manuscripts are loosely organized. When she came to compile the manuscript known as *Milcah Martha Moore's Book*, she departed from the haphazard transcription and random organization typical in a miscellany, and added elements particularly her own, giving special attention to the accuracy of her transcription and the arrangement of the entries.

Moore's method of transcription sets her apart from other compilers of miscellanies.[12] Moore was writing for readers rather than for herself. Her very regular handwriting places each entry clearly and centrally on the page. This is particularly true of her transcription of

9. *Jefferson's Literary Commonplace Book*, ed. Douglas L. Wilson, Papers of Thomas Jefferson, 2d ser. (Princeton: Princeton University Press, 1989); and Lockridge, *On the Sources of Patriarchal Rage*, 69. See also Mohl, *John Milton and His Commonplace Book*, 31.

10. Beale, "Notions in Garrison," 132–47; and Marotti, *Manuscript, Print, and the English Renaissance*, 2–16.

11. See Karin Wulf's introductory essay, pages 30–31.

12. In addition to the three commonplace book manuscripts by Milcah Martha Moore, the primary commonplace books and miscellanies that were read and analyzed for this study include:

Haverford College Library, Haverford College, Haverford, Pa., MS. 975A: George Dillwyn (c. 1789–95), Catharine Haines (1775); MS. 975B: two anonymous commonplace books (probably by men), Martha Allinson Cooper (n.d.), Samuel Allinson

poetry. Each poem has obviously been written out with attention to the appearance it makes on the page, with brackets for triple rhymes, and flourishes before and after each entry. When she knew it, Moore placed the attribution and the date of composition or the date of her transcription before or after the entry. She often linked entries written by the same writer with a simple notation, "by the same."[13]

The commonplace book that Moore's cousin Hannah Griffitts compiled in 1776–78 offers a striking contrast. Griffitts was a working poet, who cared more about writing a poem or copying one that she wanted to remember than about its appearance on the page. Her book is a small paperbound volume, 4 × 6 inches in size. There are many indications that she was using the book to write out "rough" copies of poems as she was working on them. Her entries have lines crossed out and rewritten, and words inserted. A poem, "from Etna's point," that she copied, has a note written below the poem: "hasty Copy needs amendments & far below the Charming Discriptive original—." She followed this note with an "alteration," which is a variation of the last lines of the poem, but Griffitts still was not satisfied, and wrote "very rough Copy—" below it.[14] There are examples of "fair" copies written by Griffitts, but not in her commonplace book.[15]

Griffitts's cousin, Milcah Martha Moore, seemed to be have been the "professional" transcriber in the family. In preserving Susanna Wright's poetry, Moore drew attention to the care she took in finding the best text and transcribing it accurately. The memorandum after one of Wright's poems (*MMMB* 22) is unusual in commonplace books and miscellanies: "The foregoing poetical Pieces are copied from the Authors original Mss—I have a Copy of the last page with

(1761), Mary Flower (1757), Deborah Haines (c. 1753–54), Rebecca Jones (c.1786), Mary Shackleton Leadbeater (1780), Mary Margaret White (1787); MS. 955, Box 1, additions: Anonymous (but probably Deborah Morris, daughter of Margaret Hill Morris).

Library Company of Philadelphia, Philadelphia, Pa., MS. 005: Anonymous; MS. Am. 13668Q: Sarah Sandwith Drinker; MSS. Am. 0670, Am. 13298Q, Am. 12394Q: Elizabeth Graeme Fergusson; MS. Loudon Collection: Hannah Griffitts.

Folger Library, Washington, D.C., MSS. a. 162, 180, 184, 185, 258: Anonymous.

Henry E. Huntington Library, San Marino, Calif., MS. HM 164: Joseph Norris.

13. Her format looks very much like the one followed by R. and J. Dodsley, *A Collection of Poems* (London, 1750).

14. Hannah Griffitts, commonplace book, MS., Loudon papers, HSP, 35.

15. See the collection of Griffitts's poetry, LCP.

several Alterations as may probably be the Case with several, or all, the others—but as I had not any of them I chose to follow the Originals." In the case of the selections from the travel journal of Elizabeth Graeme Fergusson, it is impossible to say whether Moore's transcription is accurate because the original manuscript is lost. Hannah Griffitts frequently dated her poems and said whether she sent a "rough" or "fair" copy to a person, but in the case of her cousin Moore, she rarely said what she was sending.[16] A simple comparison of the two poems by Fergusson in *Moore's Book*, "The Invitation" (*MMMB* 89) and "A Paraphrase on Augers Prayer" (*MMMB* 90), with these same poems in Fergusson's commonplace book, *Poemata Juvenalia*, indicates that Moore was as accurate in transcribing Fergusson's poems as she was with the poems of Susanna Wright.[17] From the available evidence, I can confirm that Moore was a precise transcriber, which is an advantage for twentieth-century readers because some of the originals are lost.

Although we have evidence of Moore's ability as a transcriber, we have no direct evidence that she wrote poetry herself, except for a poem on the death of her husband, written in her own hand.[18] The record of attributions in *Moore's Book* does not show that Moore

16. Among the many letters that refer to poetry, we can document one poem, in particular, that was sent by Griffitts to Moore: "To the Memory of my Late Valuable friend Susanna Wright, who died, Decr. 1st. 1784." On March 22, 1785, Moore wrote to her sister, Mary Lamar, that "I suppose you have heard of the Death of Susa. Wright. Coz. H. Griffitts promis'd to give me a copy of Verses on the Occasion, maybe when I get them, [I] may send them to thee." On April 1, 1785, Griffitts wrote to Moore: "As I know thou rates my scribbles much beyond their value (I speak, as I think) I enclose the Lines on the Death of my Dear Mother's Friend, & mine, with some others of my vacant hours" (EWS). In the exchange of poems on Wright's 64th birthday (*MMMB* 24–26), Wright recalled when "Thy Mothers social Hour was mine" in her verse epistle to Fidelia (*MMMB* 26), but we are not certain that we have the exact copy of the poem Griffitts sent Moore. Griffitts' elegy on Susanna Wright's death is in her collection (LCP). See the Appendix, for a copy of the poem.

17. Elizabeth Graeme, *Poemata Juvenalia*, LCP. In other instances when we have two copies of the same poem or prose piece that came from a printed source, like Samuel Clarke's "A Dream on September 18th 1769" (*MMMB* 28), we can see again how conscientious Moore was in transcribing the words of the text while making some modifications in punctuation and other incidentals that are not "word specific." For example, in copying "A Dream" by hand, Moore used more abbreviations than Clark's printer.

18. For a copy of this poem, see Appendix.

wrote any poems or prose. Although some scholars have attributed "The female Patriots" (*MMMB* 38) to her, there is no evidence to suggest that she wrote it. In fact, evidence demonstrates Hannah Griffitts wrote it.[19]

Not only was Moore a precise transcriber, but also she carefully arranged the entries in *Moore's Book*. While she did not follow the organizational methods of Erasmus or Locke, neither did she follow the random order of the usual compiler of miscellanies. Instead, she seems to have developed a fluid organizational method, in which she places entries in sequence, frequently by author, sometimes by author and chronology, and sometimes by subject matter (Quaker history) or by theme (friendship). Some of the contents of the manuscript appear to be new items entered as Moore received them, and others are from material dating back many years, which she apparently held separately. Although Moore follows chronological order in some sections, she also feels free to break this pattern. For example, when she is preserving one of Griffitts's thematic sequences honoring Quakers,

19. Pattie Cowell may have been the first to attribute "The female Patriots" to Milcah Martha Moore. In *Women Poets in Pre-Revolutionary America, 1650–1775: An Anthology* (Troy, N.Y.: Whitston, 1981), Cowell wrote that Moore's papers were unavailable to her, so Whitfield J. Bell Jr. "read Moore's commonplace book and some of her letters in 1967. He recalled the existence of a number of verses in the commonplace book, some of them surely of Moore's composition because of their personal character" (pp. 273–74). Cowell chose the text of "The Female Patriot" from the published text in the *Pennsylvania Chronicle* 3 (December 18–25, 1769), because the variations between the manuscript published in the *WMQ*, 3d ser. 34 (1977): 307–8, "are substantial enough to suggest that the piece is of Moore's composition." She does not list the variations in the manuscript or show why one is more definitive than the other. The poem is also attributed to Moore in the Heath anthology (1994) of American literature.

The way Moore organized her attributions, however, identifies Griffitts as the author. The poem previous to "The female Patriots" (*MMMB* 38) is "The Disappointment" (*MMMB* 37) attributed by Moore to "Fidelia" (Hannah Griffitts). The next poem is "The female Patriots," written "by the same." Given Moore's pattern of stating the author of a poem once, followed by other poems by the same author, identified only with the phrase, "by the same," we conclude that "The female Patriots" is by Hannah Griffitts. Furthermore, a comparison of the satiric content and style of the poem with other satires by Griffitts in the collection convince us that the poem is by Griffitts. As we noted in the Preface, we found only one poem that is conclusively Milcah Martha Moore's ("On the Death of my Husband, Dr. Chas. Moore" [EWS; see also Appendix]).

Moore places a poem celebrating Samuel Fothergill's return to England, June 4, 1756 (*MMMB* 84), between two elegies of Quaker women from 1775 (*MMMB* 83 and 85). Moore also appears to use juxtaposition of entries to make a point: the above sequence honoring good and devout Quakers follows two satires, one on Thomas Paine and one on informers (*MMMB* 86 and 87). By this sequence of five poems, Moore seems to suggest an ironic point for the reader to ponder: while the "good" have left for another world, the "bad" or "malicious" are still actively (and dangerously) present in colonial America. This juxtaposition of entries occurs a second time, but not so closely together with the elegy and acrostic on Hannah Hill (the matriarch of Moore's family), dated 1726, followed by two undated poems, and then by another satire on Thomas Paine, "A Few Paragraphs in the Crisis," dated April 1777 (*MMMB* 112, 113, and 116). The sense of contrasting values, for war or peace, is reinforced as the reader turns to the next poem, "Peace" (*MMMB* 117). By breaking chronology and juxtaposing entries, Moore leaves the reader with thematic issues that go beyond single poems.

Moore groups authors, genres, and themes in four informal sections. The first entries (*MMMB* 1–26) have an authorial and thematic unity as they preserve the work of Susanna Wright and celebrate the social and poetic relationship between Wright, the mentor, and Hannah Griffitts, the novice poet. It concludes with an exchange of poems in honor of Susanna Wright's sixty-fourth birthday. The next three entries (*MMMB* 27–29), written by anonymous or pseudonymous writers, form a transition to the broader themes in the manuscript: the political, religious, and elegiac.

The poems in the second section (*MMMB* 30–47) again reveal Moore's preservation of a body of work, the poetry of Hannah Griffitts. Except for the two poems that conclude the section, all of the poems are arranged in chronological order. Over half of the poems celebrate or commemorate the family and friends of Griffitts. Several poems express Griffitts' thinking on women's roles, social and political.

The third section of twenty-four entries (*MMMB* 48–70) seems to have little in common with the previous group because none of the entries is written by Griffitts, and all but two of the entries are in prose. Several selections are notable for themes that open up religious and social issues to voices outside Moore's family. In this way,

Moore's selections reflect the "noisy" diversity of opinion that is one characteristic of American identity: Patrick Henry on slavery (*MMMB* 51), Benjamin Franklin on his "religion" of good works (*MMMB* 59), and M. Morris on the philosophical versus the domestic wife (*MMMB* 64). Appropriately, Moore placed Elizabeth Graeme's travel journal (*MMMB* 58) in this section.[20] A number of entries concern the Society of Friends, with the focus on the travelling ministry and death of Samuel Fothergill; this section includes a letter on his death by Susanna Wright (*MMMB* 65, 66, and 67). A brief "Address of the Committee of Inspection to the Assembly against Independency May 1776" (*MMMB* 70) concludes this group of entries in the spirit of Quaker pacifism.

The last section (*MMMB* 71–126) contains a prose essay by Hannah Griffitts (*MMMB* 114) and poems by several poets, including Elizabeth Graeme Fergusson, Timothy Matlack, and Jonathan Odell (*MMMB* 89, 90, and 101–3). By far the greatest number of poems in this section are by Hannah Griffitts and from a crucial period of her career, 1774–78. With a few exceptions, many of the poems are dated and in chronological sequence, so that the reader can see the tensions of the Quaker community, as expressed by Griffitts, as the colonists are drawn into the Revolutionary War. There is a second exchange between Griffitts and Wright, over the tax on tea (*MMMB* 81 and 82). In contrast with the second section of the manuscript, which contains several entries by Franklin without any negative poems about him, Moore transcribes in this section Griffitts's satires on Thomas Paine (*MMMB* 86 and 116), Benjamin Franklin (*MMMB* 105), and David Rittenhouse (*MMMB* 88), who was considering supporting the Patriots.

In this brief summary, we can see Moore's principles of selection and arrangement: first, to preserve Wright's and Griffitts's work, and second, as she added letters from Franklin, Henry, and others, to include writers outside of her immediate circle of family and friends. As she continued to copy her entries, she not only observed her original purpose, but also deepened its significance by expanding the context for reading women's writing, generating dialogue between entries as she broke chronology and used juxtaposition to suggest comparison

---

20. See Wulf's introductory essay, pages 36–37.

between entries. In this way, Moore's arrangement of the selections in this manuscript implicitly reflects the national dialogue of the 1760s and 1780s, and American's emerging sense of literary and cultural identity.

There is no better way to appreciate the excellence and significance of this manuscript than by comparing it to her only published work, *Miscellanies, Moral and Instructive* (1787–1829). The freedom of selection and organization demonstrated in *Moore's Book* is significantly lacking in her other printed work. Instead of offering different political and social points of view, entries in the *Miscellanies* are didactic statements on religious duties, work habits, and ideal behavior for young men and women. The authors are either anonymous or British, more are men than women.

The source of the *Miscellanies* in her childhood instruction may account for some of the differences. Moore recollected the way she began her earliest transcriptions:

> I remember our dear mother and sister used to make me write some little piece of prose or poetry every day, and as I knew it would please them, I continued it for many years after I grew up. I suppose many hundreds of the "Miscellanies" were selected by them for me to copy, when I was a child, and afterwards given me by my elder sister.[21]

By the 1760s or 1770s, some of these transcriptions must been bound into a manuscript book and circulated among her family. In an undated letter written during the Revolutionary War, Sarah (Hill) Dillwyn wrote that she would return the book to Moore and that she has "found it a very pleasant companion, and part with it unwillingly."[22]

When *Miscellanies* was published in 1787, it became a popular textbook, printed and reprinted at least eight times in various places: Philadelphia, Pennsylvania; Burlington, New Jersey; London, and Dublin.[23] A brief comparison of the two collections, however, demonstrates that *Moore's Book* is her true literary and cultural success be-

21. Letter from Sarah Dillwyn to J. Phillips, London, 1797, in J. J. Smith, *Letters of Doctor Richard Hill*, 288–89.

22. Undated letter of Sarah Dillwyn to Milcah Martha Moore, J. J. Smith, *Letters of Doctor Richard Hill*, 203–4.

23. See Preface, note 10.

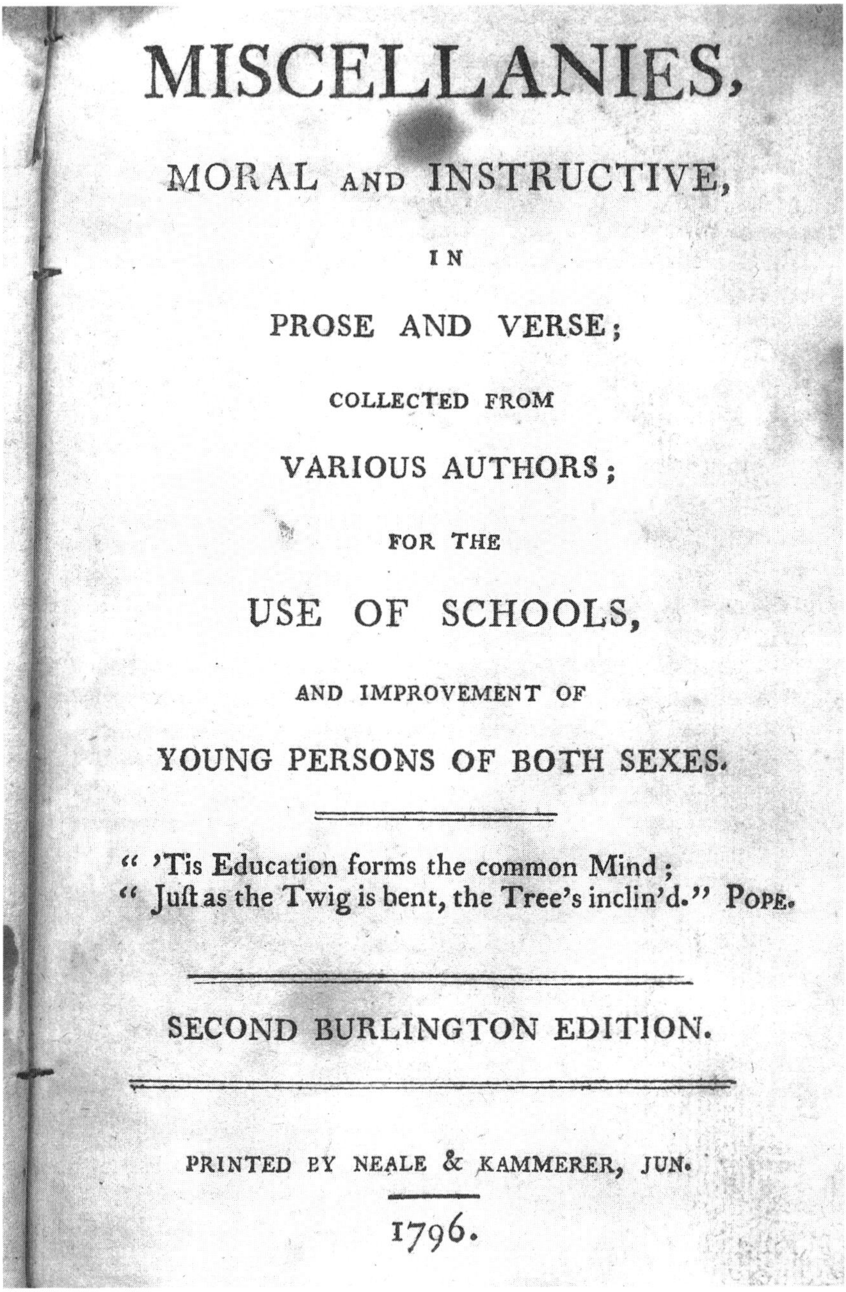

MISCELLANIES,

MORAL AND INSTRUCTIVE,

IN

PROSE AND VERSE;

COLLECTED FROM

VARIOUS AUTHORS;

FOR THE

USE OF SCHOOLS,

AND IMPROVEMENT OF

YOUNG PERSONS OF BOTH SEXES.

" 'Tis Education forms the common Mind;
" Juſt as the Twig is bent, the Tree's inclin'd." POPE.

SECOND BURLINGTON EDITION.

PRINTED BY NEALE & KAMMERER, JUN.

1796.

Fig. 6a.   Title page from *Miscellanies, Moral and Instructive*. Private collection.

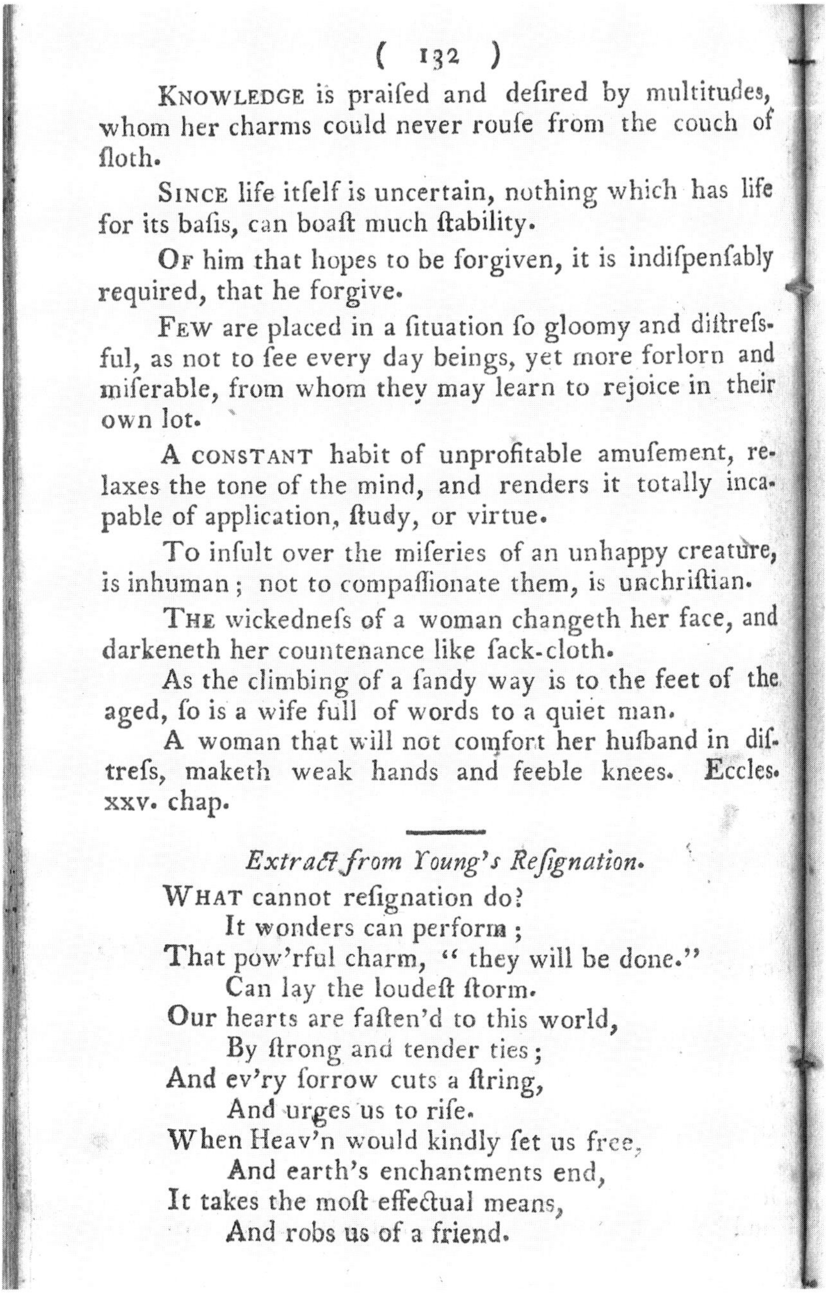

KNOWLEDGE is praifed and defired by multitudes, whom her charms could never roufe from the couch of floth.

SINCE life itfelf is uncertain, nothing which has life for its bafis, can boaft much ftability.

OF him that hopes to be forgiven, it is indifpenfably required, that he forgive.

FEW are placed in a fituation fo gloomy and diftrefsful, as not to fee every day beings, yet more forlorn and miferable, from whom they may learn to rejoice in their own lot.

A CONSTANT habit of unprofitable amufement, relaxes the tone of the mind, and renders it totally incapable of application, ftudy, or virtue.

To infult over the miferies of an unhappy creature, is inhuman; not to compaffionate them, is unchriftian.

THE wickednefs of a woman changeth her face, and darkeneth her countenance like fack-cloth.

As the climbing of a fandy way is to the feet of the aged, fo is a wife full of words to a quiet man.

A woman that will not comfort her hufband in diftrefs, maketh weak hands and feeble knees. Eccles. xxv. chap.

———

Extract from Young's Refignation.

WHAT cannot refignation do?
    It wonders can perform;
That pow'rful charm, " they will be done."
    Can lay the loudeft ftorm.
Our hearts are faften'd to this world,
    By ftrong and tender ties;
And ev'ry forrow cuts a ftring,
    And urges us to rife.
When Heav'n would kindly fet us free,
    And earth's enchantments end,
It takes the moft effectual means,
    And robs us of a friend.

Fig. 6b.   Selection from *Miscellanies, Moral and Instructive*. Private collection.

cause she, as editor and transcriber, preserved a significant body of work by American writers (chiefly women) and included material that reflects diverse issues of concern to American colonists. Whereas we can clearly see Moore's active editorial role in *Moore's Book* by her careful transcription and selection of entries, complete with attribution and dates when she knew them, Moore's role as editor of the *Miscellanies* is passive and even self-effacing. Although she signs her name on the frontispiece of *Moore's Book*, she never signs her name to the text of the *Miscellanies*. Rather than identifying herself as the editor in the preface, she refers to herself as "she" or "a person." When she writes "Editor" after the preface, she does not identify herself as the editor. Her tone at times sounds apologetic: "It gives some concern to the compiler, that she neglected to distinguish the different parts, with the names of their authors, at the time they were selected, as it is not now in her power to supply the omissions."[24]

Moore is more assertive when she explains her motives for publication. The education of youth is "a point of great importance," but "the want of proper books for the use of schools" is a general complaint. To improve the "understandings and morals" and "instructively amuse the vacant hours of young people," as well as to make teaching "more agreeable employment," she has agreed to offer "the following Miscellaneous Compilation."[25] If the reading material rep-

---

24. Preface to Moore's *Miscellanies, Moral and Instructive*, 2d Burlington ed. (n.p., 1796). Moore may be playing the conventional role of a woman who is presenting her work to be printed. As Mulford suggests, "some of the women who did write for those outside the home or beyond their usual network . . . adopted a formulaic subterfuge of apology in order to make it possible to present their writings publicly" (Carla Mulford, "Political Poetics: Annis Boudinot Stockton and Middle Atlantic Women's Culture" *New Jersey History* 111 [Spring-Summer 1993]: 71). Moore may also be genuinely apologetic about the omission of attributions since she was so conscientious about this matter in her other commonplace books.

25. Preface, Moore's *Miscellanies*, 2d Burlington ed. Moore's handwritten preface (MS. 955, QC) is almost the same as the written preface, with slight differences in phraseology. The printed preface has an addition, which is very much in keeping with Moore's desire to report exactly what she has done to the text: "The editor has thought it necessary to remark, that a few verbal alterations have been made in some of the extracts, the better to adapt them to the use of the present design; but as the sentiments and tenor of the original pieces are not thereby materially changed, it is hoped this freedom will be excused by their respective authors, to whom not the least injury or offence has been intended."

licates Moore's childhood education, it is not surprising that the selections include many British writers, whose work was easily available in print: Matthew Prior, Richard Steele and Joseph Addison (selections from *The Tatler* and *The Spectator*), Alexander Pope, and Edward Young. Women are represented by a few entries: Letitia Pilkington, Elizabeth Carter, and Hannah Moore. There are many more anonymous entries than attributed ones. Perhaps these selections are what Moore thought young people should be reading, while the entries in *Moore's Book* reflect her adult tastes and interests.

The relationship between the format and layout of the physical book and its contents also offer a contrast with *Moore's Book*. Once she submitted her work to a publisher, some of the decisions about the size of the *Miscellanies* and the arrangement of the selections probably were made by the publisher. The first edition published by Joseph James in Philadelphia (1787), and the Second Burlington edition, printed by Neale & Kammerer, Jr. (1796) are both bound volumes, 6½ inches by 4¼ inches, a useful size for a textbook. Rather than arranging the entries in some kind of order, Moore and/or her publisher seem to have mixed authors, genres, and topics. The placement of entries on the page probably was left up to the publisher. The entries of both editions are crowded together; selections of prose, for example, are barely separated with a line of space. Sometimes four selections are grouped together with a short bar dividing the prose group from the poem that follows. Poems are often extracts, without titles, and a bar or white space to separate them, so it is difficult, at first, to tell where one poem ends and another begins. In the Second Burlington edition, a poem on woman's duty begins on page 23 ("As some fair vi'let, loveliest of the glade,") and seems to stop in the middle of page 24, where another poem praising God begins: "Hail Power Eternal, infinite, immense." In short, there is little sense of the integrity of the prose or poetic piece, either as an extract or as a whole piece. The textbook, no doubt, needed to be inexpensive for schools to buy, but the contrast between the utilitarian nature of the printed text and the artistry of the manuscript, which is the source of *Moore's Book*, could not be clearer.

In contrast to the various points of views represented in *Moore's Book*, the tone and style of the *Miscellanies* are didactic. The anonymous writer of "A Morning Hymn," for example, prays that "This day thy fav'ring hand be nigh," but if "Affliction, should thy love intend, / As vice or folly's cure, / Patient to gain that gracious end, / May I the means endure" (p. 5, ll. 13, 20–24).[26] This poem is followed on page 6 by a series of four paragraphs; one of them begins: "To love an enemy, is the distinguished characteristic of a religion which is not of man but of God. . . . " The last prose entry is brief enough to quote in full: "Recreation after business is allowable; but he that follows his pleasures instead of his business, shall in little time have no business to follow.[27] The rest of the text has many entries similar in subject and tone.[28]

Not only is the text didactic, but also it is patriarchial in its attitude toward women. In contrast with *Moore's Book*, which offers different perspectives on gender roles, the *Miscellanies* simply present the domestic woman. This anonymous poem, for example, describes the demeanor and duties of the domestic woman:

> So woman born to dignify retreat,
> Unknown to flourish, and unseen, be great;
> To give domestic life its sweetest charm,
> With softness, polish, and with virtue warm;
> Fearful of fame, unwilling to be known,
> Should seek but Heaven's applauses and her own;
> No censures dread but those which crimes impart,
> The censures of a self-condemning Heart.[29]   (ll. 6–13)

This traditional woman is different from the many women we meet in *Moore's Book* from the pious wife, Margaret Mason, who had a "social Mind," and was a "Neighbour, Friend" as well as a "Parent & the

26. These and the following selections are from the Second Burlington edition, 1796. The first edition (1787) is in too fragile a condition to be handled, so my examples are from the Second Burlington, which is basically a reprint of the first edition with some slight modifications in placement and arrangement of entries. Although Moore did not match the selections with the authors who wrote them, one of the publishers, J. Crukshank (Philadelphia, 1793), was able to identify some of the authors with a number of entries.

27. These selections are from the Second Burlington edition (1796), p. 6.

28. J. Crukshank (Philadelphia, 1793) added some attributions to his edition: the prose on this page to the *Rambler*, the *Adventurer*, and Fuller's *Rule of Life*. The poem is by Elizabeth Carter. No dates or page numbers are given to verify these identifications.

29. *Miscellanies*, 2d Burlington ed., 24.

Wife" (*MMMB* 83, ll. 17, 24), to the Quaker ministers, like Sarah
Morris, who spoke "the powerful Language of her Tongue, / In soft
Persuasion, tho in Reasoning strong"(*MMMB* 85, ll. 33–34). Although the advice for women's behavior is only a small part the *Miscellanies*, Moore's attitude toward women seems to have changed from
the way she thought about them in her earlier manuscript (c. 1760–
78). Perhaps, she along with her society, was developing more specifically gendered attitudes toward women.[30]

Milcah Martha Moore was proud enough of the *Miscellanies* to give
a copy of the first edition to the Library Company of Philadelphia,
and Elizabeth Graeme Fergusson published a poem to celebrate the
collection.[31] Two references in the letters of Hannah Griffitts to Moore
are more cryptic. On June 20, 1797, Griffitts made a passing reference
to the *Miscellanies*: "—should be pleas'd to see the Miscellanies Thou
mention'd, having, I think, perus'd both the others." The next month,
August 28, 1797, Griffitts wrote, "I rec'd the Book safe, & as it bears
the well known mark, of the Instructive Compiler I should wish to
purchase one, if the valuable author can spare it."[32] Griffitts calls
Moore an "Instructive Compiler," alluding perhaps to the book's design to instruct young people. From the number of editions that were
printed, and the amount of money that went into Moore's school,
Miscellanies was a commercial and, perhaps, pedagogical success.[33]

Moore's Book, however, represents a different kind of literary and
cultural success because it reflects Americans' appreciation of their
own poetry and prose. It also preserves the literary friendships among
Moore's circle, especially between Wright and Griffitts, in their exchange of poetry, and commentary on each other's poems. As Karin
Wulf notes in her introduction, Fergusson probably shared her jour-

30. See pages 55–56, for the historical context of women's education and publication in the new republic.

31. "Lines by a Friend, on reading Mrs. M. Moore's printed and unprinted extracts
for the use of Schools," attributed to Elizabeth Graeme Fergusson, *The Columbian
Magazine* 2 (1788): 305. See the Appendix for a copy of this poem. The editors are
grateful to Professor Anne M. Ousterhout, Michigan State University, for assistance
with this note. Her biography of Elizabeth Graeme Fergusson is forthcoming.

32. Hannah Griffitts to Milcah Martha Moore, [Philadelphia], June 20, 1797, and
August 28, 1797 (MS. 955, QC).

33. Milcah Martha Moore, account book, papers regarding her school at Montgomery County, Pa. (MS. 955, QC).

nal with Moore during the American Revolution, when Anglican and Quaker elites found themselves contending with some of the same political misunderstanding and upheaval. Some of the pieces of *Moore's Book* are either interesting as literature or as documents of a specific time and place, and thus deserve our study.

Milcah Martha Moore's Book and Eighteenth-Century Literature

Although the entries in *Moore's Book* span the eighteenth century—from its earliest dated poem, 1704, to its latest, 1788—many of them reflect overlapping aesthetic tastes of eighteenth-century British and American literature, and Quaker attitudes toward literature. Opposed to the extravagances of witty metaphors ("metaphysical conceits") associated with poets like Donne and Cleveland, the Royal Society and some of its members, like John Dryden, approved a style that was clear and vigorous, one that demonstrated a poet's judgment over his unruly fancy.[34] William Penn's preface to *The Written Gospel Labors of John Whitehead* (1703) set out literary principles for the Society of Friends that were similiar in attitude. Penn cautioned Quakers against using "the Learning of the Schools," and an ornamental or "polished Stile" in their writing.[35] Frederick B. Tolles summarized the cumulative changes: "The Quaker theory of literary expression was clearly a part of the pervasive counter-baroque movement in the aesthetic of the seventeenth century, and it as rooted in the Quaker religious vision of Truth in its austere simplicity."[36] The new style of simplicity, for non-Quakers and Quakers, aimed to teach and delight the common reader.

---

34. George Watson has a valuable compilation of Dryden's statements on this subject in "To Roger, Earl of Orrey." in *Of Dramatic Poesy and other Critical Essays*, vol. 1, *Everyman* (London: Dent, 1962), 8n.

35. William Penn, quoted in Luella M. Wright, *The Literary Life of the Early Friends: 1650–1725* (New York: Columbia University Press, 1932), chap. 5, esp. 64, 68, 71.

36. Frederick B. Tolles, "'Of the Best Sort but Plain': The Quaker Esthetic," *American Quarterly* 9 (1959): 488.

These theories affected the style of the poets and writers in Moore's collection. In practice, when judgment controlled fancy, the poet paid attention to the rhetoric of the poetic line, using parallelism and antithesis and other rhetorical devices, rather than relying on elaborate figurative language. Writers aimed for clarity of expression. They were also aware of the appropriate poetic diction for a particular genre or type of literature: "low" vocabulary for satire, a "high" one for the epic. In descriptive or occasional verse, it was in keeping with poetic decorum to allude to the classical gods and goddesses, to use personification or appropriate metaphor or rhetorical schemes such as periphrasis (substituting a phrase or several words for one word): "winged tribe" for birds and "lowing herd" for cattle. The effect of this poetic practice was to develop a type of poetry that had a general, nonspecific quality to the poem, which is the ideal if poets wish to reach "general human nature," that is, what is common to the well-being of human society.[37]

Another eighteenth-century practice that may not be familiar to twentieth-century readers is the way writers identified themselves by the use of initials or pseudonyms. The three major contributors to *Moore's Book* varied in the way they projected themselves as writers. Susanna Wright did not use a pseudonym; she signed her name as "Susanna Wright," "Susa. Wright," "S. Wright," or with her initials, "S.W." A woman who lived on the frontier of western Pennsylvania, she did not want to mimic cosmopolitan fashions, literary or otherwise. She used the same signatures in the letters that she wrote to prominent intellectuals in Philadelphia, such as Isaac Norris II, James Logan, Charles Norris, and Benjamin Franklin, or to the women in the Hill family. The poems in *Moore's Book* are attributed to "S. Wright" or to "S. W."[38]

On the other hand, with her salon at Graeme Park Elizabeth Graeme was a part of the literary elite of Philadelphia. A pseudonym was a convention, particularly used by elite literary women both to

---

37. There are many sources for this summary of poetic diction in the eighteenth century, but one of earliest and best is Geoffrey Tillotson's "Eighteenth-century Poetic Diction," *Essays and Studies by Members of the English Association, 1939* 25 (1940): 50–80; reprinted in James L. Clifford, ed., *Eighteenth-Century English Literature: Modern Essays in Criticism* (New York: Oxford University Press, 1959), 212–32.

38. We were not permitted to see Susanna Wright's original manuscripts in the Wrights's Ferry Archive, Columbia, Pa., because of their fragile condition.

modestly conceal their personal identity and to reveal it to a small circle of friends. Fergusson used the pseudonym "Laura," when she wrote poems and when she wrote letters to her friends. The pseudonym could act as a code between friends; for example, when Fergusson and Annis Boudinot Stockton addressed each other as "Laura" and "Emilia" in poems and letters.[39]

Moore identified Fergusson by her given name, her married name, or her pseudonym. Because Fergusson did not want her travel journal published, Moore simply used Fergusson's unmarried initials, "E. G.," in her attribution. Moore inscribed the two poems by Fergusson, which are placed one after the other in the manuscript, with both Fergusson's married name and her pseudonym (*MMMB* 89 and 90).[40] Although there are many writers with pseudonyms in the collection, Moore only identifies one other poet by both birth name and pseudonym: "Amanda" or Hetty Griffitts, one of Hannah Griffitts' nieces. Perhaps neither woman was well-known by Moore's audience by their pseudonyms so she used both names to identify them.[41]

"Fidelia," the pseudonym of Moore's cousin Hannah Griffitts, is the one most frequently encountered in text. Both her given name and her penname must have been well known to Moore's audience since she was, practically speaking, the poet for the Quaker community in Philadelphia during this period. Although Griffitts never explained why she chose this name, to a Quaker poet "Fidelia" must have religious associations with faith and faithfulness. When Griffitts was ten years old, she consecrated her muse to God, promising "no trifling themes."[42] For as long as she was able to write, she wrote elegies for parents of dead children and for the friends and leaders of the Quaker

39. Mulford, '*Only for the Eye of a Friend*,' letters 23, 42, 56, and poems from Annis Boudinot Stockton to Laura, entry numbers: 10, 11, 18, 35. This kind of exchange typified the elite circle of friends that surrounded "the matchless Orinda," Katherine Phillips, in mid-seventeenth century England. See Marilyn L. Williamson, *Raising Their Voices: British Women Writers, 1650–1750* (Detroit: Wayne State University Press, 1990), 72.

40. Fergusson herself signed these early poems with her pseudonym, "Laura," in her commonplace book, *Poemata Juvenilia*, entry numbers 9 and 46, LCP.

41. For the historical context of these networks of associations among women writers, see pages 29–35.

42. Hannah Griffitts, no. 7422.F3, LCP.

community, satires defending the values of the Society of Friends, and occasional poems welcoming travelling ministers.

Griffitts appears to have developed a pattern in using her pseudonym. She signed herself "Fidelia" when she sent a "fair" copy of a poem. (Many of the rough copies of these poems, which she kept for her own use, are identified by her initials, "H. G." or with her distinctive flourish.) She did not use her pseudonym to sign personal letters to friends like Milcah Martha Moore. She either signed her full name or her initials with accompanying flourish—the same flourish she used to "sign" her rough or hasty copies.[43] It appears, then, that Griffitts used "Fidelia" when she wished to project her identity as a poet: a writer who was faithful to her vocation, to the values and beliefs of her Quaker faith, and to the social bond that she felt with her community.

Poetry in *Moore's Book*

There are many examples of popular poetic genres of the day in *Moore's Book*: religious and meditational poetry, elegies, verse epistles, satires, and occasional poems—some written "extempore." Although the pastoral was a popular poetic genre, especially for women, *Moore's Book* contains only a few, and these are simple "invitations" to retreat from the city, a common eighteenth-century theme.

Moore reflects the interests of her writers, the audience, and herself in the way she favors one type of poetry over another. The fact that she prefers poetry over prose reveals another aesthetic taste she held in common with other eighteenth-century anthologists. The concentration of women's poetry in her manuscript makes her collection different from her own published work and from other published anthologies, American or British. In fact, Moore's manuscript is evidence that in the pre-Revolutionary colonial world, poetry was a medium that brought women together in mutual support for writing. Many of the claims that Cathy Davidson makes about fiction in the

43. Hannah Griffitts, no. 7422.F72, LCP.

new Republic occurred earlier in poetry. Davidson argues that fiction, particularly sentimental fiction, was the medium that educated women and validated their world:

> Other forms of literature in the new Republic also specifically addressed the woman reader, most notably a wealth of advice literature often penned by clergymen. But this literature usually referred women more to the kitchen and the nursery than to the study or the library. Only in fiction would the average early woman reader encounter a version of her world existing for her sake, and, more important, only in the sentimental novel would her reading about this world be itself validated. . . . women readers encountered women characters whose opinions mattered. Numerous sentimental novels . . . took time out from the main seduction plot to show women discussing politics, law, philosophy and history—those same arenas of discourse from which the woman reader was often excluded.[44]

Davidson's research in the early sentimental novel does not take into account the activity of the manuscript world, especially during the 1760s and 1780s, which overlaps her study. Our research into the commonplace books, copybooks, and miscellanies of eighteenth-century colonial Pennsylvania reveal that, aside from the Bible, poetry was the primary medium for educating women to read and write, followed by short prose pieces, letters, and for Quakers, personal testimonies. Women's manuscripts show that they frequently question and answer traditional ideas of women's roles and, as the political and historical entries in *Moore's Book* reveal, women were already discoursing on these topics in writing before the sentimental novel appeared.[45] The poetry in *Moore's Book*—whether it be religious, elegaic, epistolary, or light verse—reflects women's discussion of the issues that engaged them intellectually and emotionally and affected

---

44. Cathy Davidson, *Revolution and the Word: The Rise of the Novel in America* (New York: Oxford University Press, 1986), 123.

45. See Donald D. Hall, "Readers and Reading in America: Historical and Critical Perspectives," *Proceedings of the American Antiquarian Society* 103 (1993): 335: "The historical evidence on which she [Davidson] relies may be more problematic than she allows, beginning with the fact that female literacy was already at a high level in the northern states a half century before the novels became available." See Hall, "Readers and Reading in America," 341 n. 9, for a series of studies on this point.

their understanding of their identity as eighteenth-century American women.

Although modern Americans are rarely interested in religious poetry and elegies, the readers of Moore's Book especially appreciated this type of lyric. Most eighteenth-century people, including Wright, Griffitts, and Fergusson, viewed life as a time of "probation," that is, "as a time of testing and training the will rather than of complete moral achievement." It is a process "in which temptation plays an essential part."[46] The relationship of God and humankind, and consequently the right relationship between people in society and between good and evil within human beings are issues of concern to the writers in *Moore's Book*. The Bible was often a part of their religious meditations: "How many Friends have tried to settle themselves by remembering favorite poems or verses from the Bible?" asks one contemporary Quaker writer.[47] This question must have run through Wright's and Griffitts's minds because so many of their poems begin with biblical verses.

Wright's religious meditations are outstanding. As Hannah Griffitts noted in the elegy she wrote about Wright, she had "striking sense and energy of mind"[48] that inquired into universal theological questions about life, death, and immortality, and she accepted no easy answers. Her poetry can be usefully compared with two of her contemporaries, the British poet Elizabeth Singer Rowe (1674–1737) and the American poet and popular preacher, Samuel Davies (1723–61). Significantly, both of these poets published their poetry, which indicates, at the very least, that they sought an audience. Samuel Davies, the dissenting minister, is more aggressive in using the "Divine Art of Poetry" to teach religion and virtue.[49] Rowe's editor, Madeleine Forell Marshall, places her works with those those poets who focus on Divine Love, and thus whose purpose was "'pathetick' or affective, to

---

46. See Frances Shields, "Probation" in *Encyclopedia of Religion and Ethics*, ed. James Hastings (New York: Scribner, 1928), vol. 10.

47. Mary Hoxie Jones, *Quaker Poets Past & Present* (Wallingford, Pa.: Pendle Hill, 1975), 5.

48. Hannah Griffitts, "To the Memory of My Late Valuable Friend Susanna Wright," LCP.

49. Samuel Davies, "Preface," *Miscellaneious Poems, Chiefly on Divine Subjects* (Williamsburg, Va., 1751): "The Divine Art of poetry might be made peculiarly subsurvient to the interests of Religion and Virtue" (vi).

move the reader, frequently and literally, to devotion." In "Soliloquy IV," for example, Rowe "imagines the missionary power of religion to reform the world and restore paradise."[50] The content of Rowe's poetry is quite different from Wright's because Rowe is a poet who focuses her theological devotion on divine and human love.

Wright's religious poetry is different in purpose from both Davies's and Rowe's. She does not have a devotional or missionary purpose for her poetry. Wright appears to have written for herself; her poems reflect her own inquiries into the meaning of the soul, its ability to know God. The content of Rowe's poetry, then, is also different from Wright's because Rowe focuses her theological attention on divine and human love. Wright and Davies, however, are both concerned about the role of reason in knowing God. A brief comparison of the way they express this theme demonstrates their different abilities as poets.

Wright unites meaning with form as she conveys her urgent and restless search for truth by repetition and unexpected pauses (*caesurae*) in the middle of lines in the untitled poem (*MMMB* 9), which begins:

> What Means yet unattempted can I try
> To still this anxious Searcher in my Breast
> These fond Enquiries—whence had I a Being?
> What am I now?—what shall I be hereafter?   (ll. 1–4)

Though she knows the answer in part, it does not satisfy her:

> I owe this Being to one powerful Cause,
> But what thou art I cannot comprehend,
> Or learn thy incommunicable Name.—
> I search & fain would gain some happy Knowledge
> Fain would I gain some faint Idea of thee
> Invisible, almighty, uncreated.—   (ll. 5–10)

Her simple diction belies the complexity of metrical variation within the blank verse lines, and the subtle repetitive effects of "fain/fain/faint" add passionate insistence to her desire to know God, even if she

---

50. Madeleine Forell Marshall, "Critical Essay," *The Poetry of Elizabeth Singer Rowe (1674-1737), Studies in Women and Religion* 25 (Lewiston, N.Y.: Mellen, 1987), 21, 61.

only gains a "faint Idea" of "this Being" who created her. The problem is compounded by the limitations of her human nature:

> With Knowledge just enough to guess at Error,
> But not enough to fix unerroring Truth—
> In this Perplexity of Thought I am lost,
> While tyrant Passions sway me here & there.
> Just God! this is not sure my only End.   (ll. 19–23)

The antithetical repetition of "Error" and "unerroring" precisely expresses the problem in such a search, while the last line, with its initial spondaic "Just God!" gives voice to the exasperation of the inquirer. Although Wright incisively argues her case, the last line of the poem demonstrates that passionate search has yielded no final results: "But oh!—'tis this Futurity confounds me" (l. 51).

Samuel Davies also searches for knowledge of God. In couplets, he explores:

> The Powers of immaterial Essences,
> And puzzling intellectual Mysteries;
> The Properties of Matter and its Laws,
> And each Phaenomenon from unseen Cause.[51]

He too finds frustration, but his is based on "insinuating Sorrows" that "pervade / The knowing Heart, and contemplative Head. / This curious Itch is never satisfy'd." In spite of this feeling, he submits to God's "heav'nly Plan," and "Tir'd of my fruitless Searches, here I rest, / With this Discovry pleas'd, content and blest."[52] Davies lists what he is exploring in conventional diction without subtle use of meter and rhyme. Wright's questions demonstrate her active speculation; her diction is more compelling, and it is given weight and emphasis by her effective use of poetic meter and form.

Some of Wright's religious poetry is based directly on a biblical scene. Her imaginative reconstructions of biblical events are captivating in the way she uses rhetoric and imagery to suggest, for example,

---

51. Samuel Davies, "Solomon," *Miscellaneous Poems, Chiefly on Divine Subjects*, 11.

52. Davies, "Solomon," 14.

the plight of Jonah, the prophet who fled from God's service in a boat, only to be thrown overboard when his disobedience was discovered. Wright describes his plight in her meditation on Jonah 2 (*MMMB* 2):

> Aghast he plung'd amidst the broken Wave,
> The living Tomb yawn'd dreadful to receive,
> He enter'd & in solid Darkness lay,
> The unweildy Monster roll'd his Bulk away,—
> Down to the Bottom of the boundless Flood
> He bore the Rebel from his angry God;
> Through shining Plains & coral Groves he pass'd
> Thro' groupes of Beauties all around him cast;
> But what avail'd, the Seer imprison'd lay,
> Secluded every chearful Beam of Day;
> 'Till after thrice collected Nights of Pain,
> Has cleans'd his Soul from her rebellious Stain,
> He landed on his native World again.   (ll. 20–32)

While the description keeps chiefly keeps to the poetic diction admired by both neoclassical and Quaker writers, Wright also uses oxymoron, "living Tomb," and irony, "the Seer . . ./ Secluded from every chearful Beam of Day." In another entry, she contemplates the thoughts of the exiled Adam, who found relief in work (*MMMB* 7). Wright's poetry derives much of its poetic power from two sources: her theological speculative mind and the Bible. Her religious meditations dramatize her passionate search for theological truth about the nature of God, the soul, and immortality. In other religious poetry, she ponders biblical verses and scenes, thoughtfully turning them over in her mind and heart, drawing out their meaning and significance for her—and her readers. Her religious poetry explores and expresses her poetic identity through her dialogue between God and herself.

There are many other religious poems in the *Moore's Book*, including Griffitts's paraphrases of the Bible and the Lord's Prayer as well as poems with a Christian theme, such as "The Christian Philosopher," (*MMMB* 97) and "Heaven the Christian's Home" (*MMMB* 124). In comparison with Wright, Griffitts's religious poetry is more ethical than speculative or imaginative in nature. When Griffitts combines descriptions of nature or natural phenomenon with divine praise as she does in "The Winter Prospect" (*MMMB* 41) or "Wrote in a violent Storm" (*MMMB* 43), her poetry approaches the lyric intensity of Anne Bradstreet's "Contemplations."[53]

The other dominant topic in the literature of Moore's Book is mortality. Even the most casual perusal of the table of contents will reveal that a major topic is death, memorialized in poetry and prose. Of the 126 entries, about 30 are solemn statements of the death of kings, queens, Quaker ministers, the young and the old, and expressed in elegies, epitaphs, letters, and one newspaper obituary. As Griffitts reminds the mourners of William Morris Jr. (*MMMB* 36), the husband of Margaret Hill Morris, Moore's sister, their lot in life is "to prepare to dye"; thus, "No longer trust to Times precarious Hand, / Nor build thy Hopes, upon the washing Sand" (ll. 53–54). Such direct statements, even with simple metaphors ("upon the washing Sand") are a long way from the "sympathy" cards that twentieth-century readers may send to grieving friends or relatives, yet both expressions spring from the same desire to comfort the bereaved. People in the eighteenth century often expressed human loss more formally, through elegies. Journalists also wrote obituaries, such as the one on Dr. Fothergill in the *Leeds Mercury* (*MMMB* 66) and people, like Susanna Wright, wrote personal letters: both elegiac forms common to the twentieth century. As pervasive as death was, however, it was not always treated solemnly. Moore also includes Franklin's "mock-epitaph" (*MMMB* 60), a "female" contributor's "The Death of a Fox" (*MMMB* 69), and Griffitts's satire on "On the Death & Character of a late english Nobleman" (*MMMB* 77).

As literature, the elegy lends itself to conventional diction and imagery since the occasion and the subject dictate the rhetorical strategies of the poem—praise, lamentation, and consolation.[54] Even the meter—the heroic couplet, or in the mid-eighteenth century, the heroic quatrain, used by Thomas Gray in his "Elegy Written in a Country Church-Yard" (1751)—is prescribed. Griffitts wrote so many elegies

53. Anne Bradstreet, *The Works of Anne Bradstreet*, ed. Jeannine Hensley (Cambridge, Mass.: Belknap-Harvard University Press, 1967), 204–14.

54. "Elegy" in *The New Princeton Handbook of Poetic Terms*, ed. T. V. F. Brogan (Princeton: Princeton University Press, 1994). For a brief history of the elegy as a genre and a mode, see Morton W. Bloomfield, "The Elegy and the Elegiac Mode: Praise and Alienation," *Renaissance Genres: Essays on Theory, History, and Interpretation*, ed. Barbara Kiefer Lewalski (Cambridge, Mass.: Harvard University Press, 1986): 147–57.

that she developed a "standard" elegiac form with common diction. Depending on the nature and occasion of the person's death, she often began by stating the deceased relationship to the mourners and the community. She praised the dead for the person's afflictions and virtues. With the words, "Hail favor'd Soul," she imagines the dead person, newly arrived "in the land of Canaan," "in the sweet climes of Liberty and Love." Finally, she turns to the mourners and asks them to wipe away the natural tears "for the dear & fond Connection" broken, to submit to Heaven, and to follow the virtuous path of the beloved dead.[55]

Wright and Griffitts occasionally departed or modified the conventional epitaph or elegy when the death involved close family and friends. Wright's brief epitaph "On the Death of two infant Nephews" (*MMMB* 18) mentions their early deaths, "Unknowing what they were,—or were to be" (l. 3). The question echoes her search for her own identity in her religious poetry. The only consolation is expressed in a hyperbole, the "ten thousand troubles" that they might have had before "They must have mix'd with kindred Clay at last" (l. 10), a stoic rather than Christian consolation. On the death of Sally Norris (*MMMB* 46), Griffitts departed from her usual couplet line to use the heroic quatrain of Gray's "Elegy Written in a Country Church-Yard." Instead of the usual lament, praise, and consolation, Griffitts's elegy dwells on lamentation for the dead girl, her mourning sister, and herself. She does not use her favorite poetic diction, "hail favor'd soul," or imagine Sally Norris in heaven, though the penultimate quatrain prays that "the kind Hand of Goodness" shall "Give you in Peace . . . / Beyond the Tyrants seperating Pow'r" (ll. 54–56). The last quatrain is reserved to comfort the sister and dear friend of Griffitts, Mary Norris. Although elegies and epitaphs are frequently conventional, and thus consoling for their public sympathy for the mourner, students of history and literature can begin to understand the eighteenth-century experience of death by reading these poems.

Griffitts breaks from the conventional elegy for another type of memorial when she confronts a politically serious theme, the deaths of American soldiers in the first sustained battle of the American Revolution, which the Americans lost. Entitled "The sympathetic

55. See, for example, *MMMB* 83. For a parallel section on death, and the role of Griffitts' elegies in consoling the family and friends of the diseased, see pages 19–20, 28n.

Scene—wrote August 31st 1776—occasioned by the unnatural Contest at Long Island August 27th & 28th" (*MMMB* 100), this poem is a formal memorial written in blank verse. Griffitts' imagines her soul retiring "to share my neighbors' Grief / Give Sigh for Sigh, & mingle Tears with Tears" (ll. 8–9). Unlike her position in other elegies, she does not presume to speak words of consolation to those whose fathers or brothers have died because "Words are vain, the Powers of Harmony / Are useless here, ev'n Friendships soothing Voice / Has lost its Calm, in Woundings like to yours" (ll. 17–19). Thus, she turns consolation over to heaven, and in another departure from her conventional elegies, she condemns those who caused such suffering:

> —But you, whose mad Ambition lawless Grasp
> Of proud Dominion & tyrannic Power
> Have spread the Flames of War around the Shores
> Where Peace once smil'd & social Union dwelt;
> How will you stand, the retributive Hour
> Or bear the Close of dread Decision's Voice.   (ll. 27–32)

Her rhetorical strategy, turning from lamentation and praise to blame, and then back to the scene of the suffering wounded soldiers, is a classic elegiac one. In her role as "kindred Muse," Griffitts' closes with a prayer that "contending Brethren" will speak Peace, and "Friends again in her soft Bands unite" (ll. 78 and 80). Although Griffitts opposed the war, she could sympathize with the wounded and dead as well as their families.

Ironically, Griffitts had another sad occasion in which to use this memorial, modified to fit different circumstances when she commemorated the deaths of the Quakers John Roberts and Abraham Carlisle on November 4, 1778, both of whom were hung by the Americans for their alleged collaboration with the British when they occupied Philadelphia. Since Griffitts used much of the same structure and diction, the two poems form set-pieces, reflecting suffering and death of Patriots and Quakers during the Revolutionary War. The most significant difference between the two poems is that Griffitts blames "Brutal Law," instead of "Brutal War," for the deaths of Roberts and Carlisle and the suffering of the Quaker community. There are other additions and modifications that make an interesting study of the two poems (see Appendix, for a copy of this poem). The elegies of Griffitts and

Wright demonstrate a variety of poetic expression, from the conventional, to the personal, to the communal. Their poems were frequently effective in consoling the mourners, and they give us an insight into the common human experience that we share with these eighteenth-century colonists.

Another significant genre in *Moore's Book* is the poetic epistle or letter—one is a formal verse epistle and two are exchanges of poetry that include the simple epistle combined with an occasional poem on Wright's birthday and, in a second exchange, combined with two satires (*MMMB* 24–26, 81, and 82). The verse epistle is a formal genre modeled on the Ovid's *Heroides* (first century A.D.).[56] The genre offers a useful contrast with poetry on death because it is based on the stories of legendary women who wrote to lovers who had rejected them. Thus, the subject matter is distant from the poet, which allows a degree of personal expression and dramatic license that the elegiac poet does not have. Wright's verse epistle, "Anna Boylens Letter to King Henry the 8th" (*MMMB* 3), expresses a theme that is found in other entries in *Moore's Book*, the desire of a woman to speak for herself.[57] The theme of the poem is an early statement of Wright's personal belief that if "Reason Govern, all the mighty frame / And Reason rules, in every one, the same / No Right, has man, His Equal, to Controul."[58] In *MMMB* 3, Anne Boleyn describes the injustice of a husband's power over his wife, for "What Innocence unaided & oppress'd / Could do, I've done but who can Pow'r resist" (ll. 72–73). Boleyn charges King Henry VIII with injustice done to her and her child, whom he "sternly casts . . . from his knee" (l. 30). Such a husband and a father can expect retribution:

> Yet think, o! think what Crimes will wound yr. Soul,
> When your dim Eyes in search of Slumber rowl,
> When Lamps burn blue & guilty Tapers fade,
> As by your bridal Bed I glide a ghastly Shade,
> While sanguine Streams from purple Fountains drain

56. "Verse Epistle" in *The New Princeton Handbook of Poetic Terms*. For an interesting commentary on the eighteenth-century verse epistle, see William C. Dowling, *The Epistolary Moment: The Poetics of the Eighteenth-Century Verse Epistle* (Princeton: Princeton University Press, 1991).

57. See, for example, *MMMB* 38 and 39.

58. "To Eliza Norris" (ll. 15–17), in Griffitts collection, LCP.

And all around the gay Apartment stain,
From conscious Guilt will these Illusions Rise,
And haunt your Steps & fill your watching Eyes,
For ever raising Tumults in your Breast,
But fear me not for I shall be at Rest.   (ll. 52–61)

This passage is a good example of the way the neo-classical poet can use general language ("sanguine Streams from purple Fountains") and rhetorical devices like repetition and alliteration to vividly "inspire" the imagination of the reader to see a scene without recourse to figures of speech that are difficult to understand. Wright transforms the neoclassical verse into a dramatic soliloquy of a wife condemning a husband's abuse of power. In her early twenties, Wright questioned the hierarchy of power in gender relationships. The poem, which was copied by Moore's neice, Deborah Morris, and by Hannah Callendar, had an effect on the younger generation of Moore's family and friends, and thus opened up the issue of gender relationships and identity to their questioning minds.[59]

There are other verse epistles that do not follow the classical tradition, but instead are letters written in verse addressed to a particular person. One of the notable features of *Moore's Book* is an exchange of verse letters and poems between Wright and Griffitts. Moore's transcription of the two exchanges of poems and commentary provides concrete evidence that women supported each other's writing. Scholars, working in this field, have commented on the "literary correspondence" between women, especially Elizabeth Graeme Fergusson and Annis Boudinot Stockton, and the subsequent "network of female literary communication" that resulted.[60] There are two exchanges of poems between Wright and Griffitts in *Moore's Book*. The first exchange of the two celebrates Wright's sixty-fourth birthday in 1761 (*MMMB* 24–26). The second was occasioned by Griffitts's two satires on British

---

59. Although the manuscript is not identified by name, the handwriting and other poems in the collection identify Deborah Morris as the compiler. (Morris commonplace book, ms. 955, QC); on Hannah Callendar's diary, see page 122n.

60. See Shields, "British-American Belles Lettres," 339. Carla Mulford examined the copybooks of Fergusson and Stockton. On the basis of letters that each woman wrote the other as well as notes in the copybooks, Mulford considers that it is probable the two women left their unpublished manuscript books as "late-in-life" gifts to each other. See her '*Only for the Eye of a Friend*,' 42.

taxation of tea (1775) (*MMMB* 81 and 82) with Wright's prose commentary (see *MMMB* 82). The placement of the exchange in Moore's commonplace book is a deliberate one: the birthday poem and response are in the first section, in which Wright is the main poet; the second occurs in the third section in which Griffitts is the main poet.

It is not surprising that the theme of Wright's "My own Birth Day" (*MMMB* 24) is a somber one. The biblical epigraph prepares us for a sober look at aging: "Few & evil have the Days & Years of my Life been" from Genesis 47:9. It is the patriarch Jacob's answer to Pharaoh's question: "How old are you?" Although Jacob has just been reunited with his lost son Joseph and given food and land by Pharaoh during a time of famine, he seems caught up in his long-suffering life that still "has not attained unto the days of the years of the life of my fathers in the days of their pilgrimage" (Genesis 47:9). In *Moore's Book*, four of the poems before this one have been elegies for people who were Wrights' family and friends. Nine have been religious meditations on life, death, and immortality. The "Birth Day" poem explores the question: Why continue to live when our days are few—and "evil," that is, full of suffering, and short: "Where's the Amount?—a Shadow & a Span" (l. 12). The poem explores the tension between Wright's human desire to see her dead friends and family once again and her desire to live, resigned to God's will. It concludes:

> Rest then my Soul—in these Appointments rest,
>   And down the Steep of Age pursue they Way,
> With humble Hope, & Faith unfailing blest,
>   The mortal shall surpass the natal Day.   (ll. 45–48)

Griffitts as "Fidelia" wrote a comment in the margin of the copy she sent to Moore, "Soft moving language, deep Reflection strong / Compose thy pow'rful Harmony of Song."[61]

At the time Griffitts responded to Wright's poem, she was thirty-four years old, and only beginning the exchange of letters and poems with Wright, which continued through 1765.[62] The fact that their

---

61. Neither of the copies of Wright's birthday poem in Griffitts's handwriting have this added comment, so perhaps this note was attached to a special copy sent to Moore. See Griffitts Collection, poems from 1761–68, LCP.

62. See pages 34–35.

friendship is new may explain Griffitts's laudatory tone, since she is now the beneficiary of Wright's advice on writing poetry. Appropriately, she responds to Wright's poem in a simple verse epistle (*MMMB* 25), using the same rhythm and form as Wright's "Birth Day" poem. Although she recognizes Wright's somber theme, she sees her poetry "smoothing" the "awful Passage of Decay":

> Amidst these Cares that crow'd the human Throng,
>> Serenely glows Venera's evening Ray,
> She wakes her Lyre to Harmony of Song,
>> And smooths the awful Passage of Decay.   (ll. 9–12)

Griffitts softens the vision of Wright's age by calling her "Venera," referring to the evening star, and in the next stanza as "sweet Philomel," the nightingale. When death will come, she prays that "Heaven propitious gild thy future Way" (l. 25), and imagines her body unfolded on the "Athenial Plains" of Greece while her soul joins the "the enraptur'd Throng" (ll. 30–31) in heaven. Though the sentiment does not match the seriousness of Wright's poem, Griffitts's epistle shows that she knows the formal techniques of poetry and is trying to respond to Wright's feelings about age.

Wright's verse epistle (*MMMB* 26) answering Griffitts's poem shifts the rhythm but keeps the form, as she compliments the younger poet for her "soft seraphic Strains" (l. 5), and praises her "Faith [in] Evidence of Things not seen" (l. 13) in an echo of Paul's letter to the Hebrews (11:1). Wright remembers a better time in her life when "Thy Mother's social Hour was mine, / As kindred Minds allied" (ll. 31–32). Appropriately, as Mary Norris Griffitts (1674–1750) had befriended the young Susanna Wright, Wright befriends Mary Griffitts's daughter. Several years later, after Susanna Wright's death, Griffitts closes their friendship with an acknowledgment of this exchange of poetry. Griffitts's elegy on Wright's death ends with the last line of Wright's birthday poem: "The mortal shall surpass the natal Day." [63]

---

63. Griffitts was deliberately repeating the last line of Wright's birthday poem. In the copy of the elegy in her own handwriting, she noted: "See a peice, she wrote on her own Birthday, which Closes with the above last line" (Griffitts Collection, LCP; also Appendix).

The second exchange is different from the format of the first. Both poems (*MMMB* 81 and 82) are satires written by Griffitts with a prose commentary added by Susanna Wright. The times are different. Politics, not age and mortality, is now the topic. Griffitts's two companion poems react to the Tea Act of 1773. In "Wrote on the last Day of Feby. 1775. Beware the Ides of March" (*MMMB* 81), Griffitts, using her usual pseudonym, "Fidelia," is supportive of the colonial opposition to the tax, but her tone is Quaker in attitude. Griffitts lightly links the soothsayer's hint to Julius Caesar with her later hint to the "Ladies":

> Then for the Sake of Freedom's Name
>   (Since British Wisdom scorns repealing)
> Come sacrifise to Patriot Fame,
>   And give up Tea by way of healing.
> This done within ourselves retreat
>   The industrious Arts of Life to follow
> Let the proud Nabobs storm & fret,
>   They cannot force our Throats to swallow.   (ll. 9–16)

Moore transcribes the companion poem, "The Ladies Lamentation over an empty Cannister" (*MMMB* 82), on the next page, so that the two poems face each other, just as they reflect two different attitudes toward the tea tax. Moore attributes the second poem to Griffitts, noting that it is "by the same," although the poem is signed "Europa," rather than the usual "Fidelia." Since the poem takes the opposite position from the one "Fidelia" takes, one in favor of drinking tea in spite of "all their Malice, noise & Bluster" (l. 20), the change in pseudonyms is appropriate. In the right margin of "The Ladies Lamentation" is Susanna Wright's prose commentary. Wright stays within Griffitts' lightly satiric attitude by asking "generous" gentlemen to consider: "[D]oes not this, largely partake of that Sp[iri]t. of D[e]spotism, so loudly complain'd of in America?" With a nicely ironic turn, she promises hyperbolically "never to taste one drop of what has pd. the Duty, but for such as has not, I must venture to use it as the Mohometans do Wine, not openly but in a manner to elude scandal & not to give offense."

The exchange of poems and commentaries between Wright and Griffitts in *Moore's Book* are significant literary and historical documents. They are the concluding evidence that women read and commented on each others' poetry, and thus helped each other develop their poetic identity. They also demonstrate that women discussed significant ideas of personal and political concern.

The exchange of poetry suggests a related group of poems in *Moore's Book*: those that reflect the sociable world of Moore and her family. Friendship, a theme especially among women, is the topic of five poems by Wright and Griffitts.[64] The theme of friendship is also found in poems such as Elizabeth Graeme Fergusson's "The Invitation" (*MMMB* 89), and in her letter to Betsy Stedman in her travel journal. Friendship fares better than love between the sexes in Moore's collection probably because two of the main contributors were single women, who were not on the "marriage market."[65] Although Moore's marriage was a happy one, she did not write original poetry, except for the poem on the death of her husband. Elizabeth Graeme Fergusson's marriage was, in part, a victim of the Revolutionary War. There is only one poem celebrating love and marriage, "An "Epithalamiun on the Marriage of E. D. with F. B–d" (*MMMB* 52). The unattributed "A Letter of Farewell from a Gent to a young Woman"(*MMMB* 47) shows only the grief of unrequited love.

On the other hand, Susanna Wright's question in "On Friendship" (*MMMB* 22) states a theme that is reiterated over and over again in poems on friendship: "What's life, unless a Friend the Measure fill? / Tasteless its Good—unsufferable its Ill" (ll. 54–55). The only poem that varies in theme is Wright's poem (*MMMB* 21) "To a Friend.—On some Misunderstanding." The opening metaphor is simple and disarming in its hyperbolic sincerity: she, like the physician facing a desperate illness, will try "Both likely & unlikely Means" (l. 3). Unsuccessful in every other way, "I've chose / To be a Jest in Rhyme as well as Prose" (ll. 14–15). With her "artless verse," she argues that defects are a part of being human, and that human fault lies with Adam, whom she wittily accuses: "Weak was his Reason, & his Will was strong" (l. 29). As a result of Adam's fall: "We cannot love or censure as we ought, / Unless we had a more extensive Thought" (ll. 40–41).

---

64. Wright: "To a Friend.—On some Misunderstanding" (*MMMB* 21) and "On Friendship" (*MMMB* 22); Griffitts: "An Essay on Friendship" (*MMMB* 1), "Primitive Friendship described" (*MMMB* 96), and "Steady Friendship" (*MMMB* 108).

65. See biographies of Susanna Wright and Hannah Griffitts in the Preface, pages xvi–xvii, and Karin Wulf's discussion of them, pages 34–35.

She closes with an implicit call to harmony between friends by contrasting those who are never happy in their friendships: "Still judging, still condemning, still the same / Still blaming, still creating Work for Blame" (ll. 50–51). Wright's stands out among the many poems on friendship for admitting that problems arise between friends and for her witty and poetic solutions to the problem.

In addition to the many religious, elegaic, epistolary poems in Moore's collection, there are also some lively and interesting extempore poetry and light verse. Griffitts especially enjoys writing this type of poetry. As she told Moore in a letter dated the first of April 1785, she writes because "this employ often Amuses my mind, & is I hope, an Innocent one—I am more free to entertain the muse—when in humour for her company—for I study not—This is very perceivable in my compositions,—however if my friends can condesend to receive pleasure from the perusal of them—the [ye] obligation is—on my side," [66] "Extempore," without planning, was a challenge to her wit and skill with verse, as in "Wrote extempore on Tea" (*MMMB* 115):

> Blest Leaf whose aromatic Gales dispence,
> To Men, Politeness & to Ladies Sense
> Gay Wit, Good-Nature, circulate with thee,
> Doctors & Misers, only rail at Tea.   (ll. 1–4)

Others in Moore's circle also liked the intellectual pleasure of a "satiric squib" extempore, at members of the family and friends. Henry Hill, Moore's brother, for example, was a wine merchant who equipped his grand home on Fourth Street with many fine furnishings, including "large Panes of Glass," according to the author "P. D. L." (*MMMB* 50).

> Happy the Man with such a Treasure,
> Whose greatest Pain's his greatest Pleasure;
> Stoics who do not fear the Devil,
> Assure us Pain is not an Evil,

---

66. Griffitts to Moore, [Philadelphia], April 1785, QC. Griffitts is being modest in the letter because her commonplace book and many rough drafts show that she sometimes took great care with her poetry.

> They boast a Negative at best
> But thou with Panes art truly blest.   (ll. 1–6)

G. D. (probably George Dillwyn) responded on the same page with an extempore verse: "What strange delusion must possess his pate / When bliss increases as his pains are great!" These witty exercises do not make great poetry, but they show us that the writers who see life as a "probation" and who are very aware of mortality, also have a witty sense of play.

Some of the "sociable" poetry of Griffitts expresses her thinking on women's roles and thus contributes to the debate over women's identity. Several poems in the second section of *Moore's Book* offer a variety of perspectives and poetic methods. The first, "The Disappointment" (*MMMB* 37), is a light narrative in tetrameter couplets about four maidens who wanted to take a ride to view the Schuykull, but could not because "Floods of Rain" interrupt their plans: "Day, after Day, the Torrent run, / And seem'd each Morn, as just begun" (ll. 28–30). The rapid movement of the tetrameter couplets ironically contrasts with the maidens who cannot move, and who, confined to their home, become sick or fretful. The following poem, "The female Patriots" (*MMMB* 38) presents a more militant perspective on women's roles. This satire in heroic couplets celebrates "the Daughters of Liberty in America," who act by economic boycott in refusing to buy "taxables." Instead, she recommends using what they have: "Sylvania's gay Meadows, can richly afford, / To pamper our Fancy, or furnish our Board" (ll. 15–16). Thus, the female patriots "point out their Duty to men" (l. 32). Again, though Griffitts is assertive in tone, her recommendation is in keeping with Quaker nonviolence. The third poem in the sequence returns to a lighter tone as Griffitts explains why she remains unmarried "To Sophronia" (*MMMB* 39):

> The Men, (as a Friend) I prefer, I esteem,
>   And love them as well as I ought
> But to fix all my Happiness, solely in Him
>   Was never my Wish or my Thought,   (ll. 9–12)

With hyperbolic undercutting, Griffitts says she "is not frighted by Giants," as she explains in a note; that is, "the Satyrical Sneers thrown on the single Life." While the poem presents her reasons for remaining single, she urges others to "go marry—as soon as you please" (l. 15).[67] The tolerance of Griffitts's attitude in these poems is a clear contrast to the her satire against immoral women, "On reading the Adventurer World &et[c]." (*MMMB* 99). The poem reveals that Griffitts has been doing some close reading of British periodicals, *The Rambler*, the *Adventurer*, and *The World*, where women were often a target for satire and moral instructions in essays and narratives. Griffitts seems to take what she reads for truth as she castigates the British female for allowing "gross Indecency yr. Honour stain."

> Will Gaming teach you Passions to controul
> Soften your Eye & harmonize your Soul?
> Or will you dare in this licentious Age
> To form yr. decent Manners by the Stage?   (ll. 9–12)

She uses her satiric muse to confront such morals: "Believe the Muse (& trust the Mirror true) / The Satyr's levell'd & the Laugh at you" (ll. 21–22). The poem ends by urging the British woman to listen to these "instructive Lines," so they can "stand yr. Species Glory Pride & Boast" (l. 62). While her satiric muse is in good form, I think Griffitts was enjoying herself in writing this poem. She often told Moore that she wrote to fill "vacant hours"; this poem shows her wit, but she has no immediate audience to persuade, as she did in the biting satires over issues and people in the Revolutionary War.

Whether in satires on political issues or in lighter social poetry, Griffitts delighted in making witty observations on the political and social scene. The role of women was an on-going topic of discussion

---

67. Griffitts's witty and tolerant perspective on the issue of the married versus the single life is reflected in an undated letter to Milcah Martha Moore. In a comment on a book that she was returning, Griffitts makes the observation that "the woman, who Lives Discontentedly single, & freting her Life away, because she could not 'catch' the Man she set her little heart upon & angry—with those, who succeded Better than Herself, is not an amiable Character—& there are many of you weded ones, who I believe, are Placed in your 'Proper' Sphere—for shining, I sincerely wish you increase of Happiness in it—without envying you, one atom of it; everyone is not fitted for the single Life—nor was I ever Moulded, for the weded one. To sustain the Character of an old maid, with Propriety, & that true Dignity, arising from virtue (& not Pride) is a Respectable one" (Philadelphia, MS., EWS).

in the eighteenth century. Wright's poem on "Anna Boylen"(*MMMB* 3) and Griffitts's poetry and satire offer some significant additions to this discussion, as does M. Morris' letter.[68]

Prose in *Moore's Book*

Although there are only twelve prose selections in *Moore's Book*, some of them are the best in the book, as documents for literary history as well as imaginative literature. Most of the prose entries are letters, which is appropriate for an age of letter-writing. They add breadth to Moore's collection by bringing other worlds to her circle of family and friends and by adding another type of discourse to the discussion of public issues in poetry. Some letters follow the conventions of the genre, and others mix with other prose genres. Elizabeth Grame Fergusson's travel journal, for example, is partly a letter to one of her best friends, Elizabeth ("Betsy") Stedman. The formulaic features of the familiar letter, with its salutation, conversational structure, and "complimentary close" are the frame for the Scriblerian parody of the memoir and digression on the philosophical versus the domestic woman in M. Morris' "Letter" (*MMMB* 64). When Moore selected letters, she chose both secular and religious examples. Both types were meant not only to be read by a particular correspondent, as ours usually are today, but also to be shared with others. Benjamin Franklin's letter to Joseph Huey (*MMMB* 59), for example, was often copied and even printed.[69]

Two unusual prose pieces for a twentieth-century audience are apocalyptic warnings. Both Samuel Clarke Jr.'s "A Dream on September 18th 1769" (*MMMB* 27) and Hannah Griffitts's "The Review of past & present Times in Pennsylvania" (June 1776) (*MMMB* 91), return to an earlier style of religious rhetoric. Clarke combines the dream vision with a jeremiad condemning New England for its ingratitude for God's protection from the enemy (the French) and from earthquakes. He prophecies that unnamed dire consequences will

---

68. For discussion of Griffitts's political satires, see pages 41–46.

69. See Leonard Labaree, ed. *The Papers of Benjamin Franklin*, 31 vols. (New Haven: Yale University Press, 1959–), 4:503–6.

happen to New Englanders, which will come from the troubles in Old England as well as from the personal sinfulness of the people of New England: "Death is at the Door, and our Sins crying for Vengeance: How do you intend to escape?"[70] Clarke's words struck a strong chord in Moore because she wrote out the "Dream" in her own handwriting into the commonplace book of her brother-in-law George Dilllwyn, who was a Quaker minister and believed in the prophetic power of dreams because he had them himself.[71]

Hannah Griffitts's language contrasts with Clarke's, but the message is the same. In the "Review of past & present Times" (*MMMB* 91) Griffitts uses seventeenth-century Quaker incantatory prose, with its repetition and clusters of biblical imagery.[72] A third-generation Quaker in America, Griffitts describes the early Quakers who used peaceful means in their relationships with the Indians and people of other religious groups. This is in contrast with the present generation who have lost their liberties: "the fair Plant of Freedom is withered to its Root" because they have "sounded the Alarm of War, in the City of Peace, & banished the 'Law of Kindness' from the 'Land of Love'." The last line of the "Review" warns Pennsylvanians to "return to the Lord yr. Leader & seek for Strength from the God of your Fathers." Both of these prose pieces attest to the common feeling among many Americans that the Revolutionary War was a time of testing, and thus a crucial time in the formation of their national identity.

Two selections of prose in *Moore's Book* are outstanding for their imaginative content and sophisticated style: the extracts from the "lost" travel journal of Elizabeth Graeme (before she became "Fergusson") (*MMMB* 58) and "A Copy of a Letter from M[.] Morris" (*MMMB* 64). The travel journal, as Dr. Benjamin Rush noted, reflects Fergusson's "happy talents for observation, reflection, and composition." The brief biography by Rush, which was published in *The Port*

---

70. Samuel Clarke, "A Short Relation Concerning a Dream" (Boston, 1769), 10.

71. See George Dillwyn, commonplace book, MS. 975, QC. Inserted into the commonplace book is a typescript of "George Dillwyn's Dream related in Dublin 1785," which describes a dream he had before the Revolutionary War. For further information, we look forward to a forthcoming Ph.D. dissertation by Carla Gerona, "Stairways to Heaven: The Authority of Dreams in American Quaker Culture, 1681–1829," Johns Hopkins University, Baltimore.

72. See Jackson I. Cope, "Seventeenth-Century Quaker Style," *Publication of the Modern Language Association* 71 (1956): 729.

Folio (June 1809) describes her reception in Philadelphia upon her return from England:

> She was visited by numerous circle of friends. . . . She soon discovered by the streams of information she poured upon her friends, that she had been 'all eye, all ear, and all grasp' during her visit to Great-Britain. The Journal she kept of her travels was a feast to all who read it. Manners and characters in an old and highly civilized country, contrasted with those to which she had been accustomed in our own, accompanied with many curious facts and anecdotes, were the component parts of this interesting manuscript. Her modesty alone prevented its being made public.[73]

Luckily for us, Milcah Martha Moore was given a chance to transcribe some of Fergusson's extracts.[74]

Part of the acuity of Fergusson's observation and the spontaneity of some of her reflections may have occurred because she was writing to an audience. She knew her friends would like to know about her experience, especially her long-time friend, "Betsy" Stedman, to whom she inserts a letter into her journal, dated May 31, 1765. This excerpt of the travel journal begins with the subtitle that Moore or Fergusson gave it, "Upon leaving England." Fergusson depicts her friendship with "Betsy" in the most intimate way, as she remembers their conversations "as we have sat at the Door of Graeme park, strolled on the Terrass or watched the Moon[,] that friend to Contemplation, how happy have we been there, & how happy may we be again."

The journal demonstrates Fergusson's reading as well as her values. In the letter to Betsy Stedman, she shares some lines from Edward Young, taken from memory, and then she begins to contemplate her future. Both the poem and the accompanying reflection reveal her values: her friends in Philadelphia, good health, and a clear conscience—and friends. The repetition emphasizes the value she places on friendship. As she shares her intimate musings about her future life, her style meanders with her thoughts. Even though she is twenty-seven

73. Benjamin Rush, "Elizabeth Graeme Fergusson," *The Port Folio* 1 (June 1809): 523.

74. For the relationship between Fergusson and Moore, and the background on this journal, see pages 36–37.

Fig. 7. Engraving of Elizabeth Graeme Fergusson. Courtesy,
Historical Society of Pennsylvania.

years old and unmarried, it is noteworthy that she does not include a
man in her future. Men enter the picture only as she considers how
time is important for happiness and that women may have more time
than "the noble Lordly Creature Man, whose Heart must glow, &
Head toil for his Country for you know some Author says ['] A
Woman's Glory is to shine unknown[']". Significantly, gender relationships were only worth a passing reflection. Although Graeme
placed the date at this point in the journal, she continues to write
to Betsy, perhaps the next day. She considers the subject of "love"
but again prefers friendship, especially friendship expressed through
letters, as she wittily considers "poor Eloisa," "with just Religion

enough to torture her, but not enough to vanquish her Passions." The passing allusion to one of the most popular verse epistles of the time, Pope's "Eloisa to Abelard" (1717), again shows Fergusson's depth of reading. From Graeme's letter to Betsy Stedman, we can see how important friendship, especially shared through reading and writing, was to her.

For the twentieth-century reader, the journal gives a supurb glimpse into the eighteenth-century world of the elite and literate, as Graeme reflects on her reading, politics, and the manners of the English. Her descriptions of the two gardens she visits, Dr. Fothergill's, which he was just beginning to design, and Mr. Goldney's, which he was just completing, show her ability to compose a vivid, well-organized essay, seemingly without effort. Graeme is masterful in her ability to capture eighteenth-century England from the point of view of a sophisticated provincial.

In contrast, her discursive poem to Dr. Fothergill may seem "rambling" to a twentieth-century reader. Although Elizabeth Graeme excelled in prose, she loved poetry—as her journal, her many commonplace books, and her unpublished translations of Fénelon's epic *Telemachus* and the Psalms all testify. Her discursive poem to Dr. Fothergill is more than a poem to her doctor; it is a versified letter to a person who was both a doctor and a friend. Thus, the poem expresses her ideas on the theme of health and happiness.

Fergusson was in poor health when she came to England, and as we read in her journal: "Health I look on to be the Basis on which we found all earthly Blessings," but as she reveals in the poem to Dr. Fothergill (*MMMB* 58), "Tho' England's Pleasures open to me lay / Pain barr'd my Entrance & forbad the Way" (ll. 90–91). The fluent couplets seem to come easy to her, as she versifies her thoughts on the role of health in happiness. The poem reveals a sophisticated understanding of the role of both "alternative" methods of healing through herbs as well as through the scientific knowledge of doctors. To achieve the life she wishes to live, she considers the relationship between physical and psychological health: "I wish to lead a calm & tranquil Life / Distant from Bustle & noisy Strife" (ll. 100–101). She'll foregoe "rich dress'd Viands" and "strain'd Passions (ll. 104–5), for a quiet "moon light Walk . . . on the Green" (l. 108). Significantly, for a person who knows the poetic diction of the pastoral poem, she drops the typical pastoral bird, the nightingale (or "Philomel," in poetic diction), for the simple "Mock-bird" who would "chaunt his rural Song" (l. 111). After her solitary walk, she combines the pleasures of Milton's "L'Allegro" with his "Il Penseroso" when she includes the happy group of her family, "a social Band," around a winter fire, where "much we'll talk & think of british Ground, / More temp'rate Climes you & yr. Friends enjoy" (ll. 121–22). She includes Fothergill and her travel in Britain in her future thoughts. When she is alone, Fergusson, unknowingly speaking for many of the women in *Moore's Book*, will turn to "The Book, the Work, the Pen can all employ / The vacant Moment to some peaceful Joy" (ll. 118–19). The last lines of the poem are foreboding, as she contemplates death—and the loneliness of the survivor. As she took the boat for Philadelphia in 1765, she knew her mother and sister were dead, but within ten years, she was the sole survivor of her immediate family. Even marriage with Henry Fergusson did not ensure her a "social Band" around a winter fire. As the Revolutionary War divided families, it also divided her from her Tory husband who returned to England. Her journal reflections were uncannily prescient. Through the hardships of the Revolutionary War and its aftermath, she continued to rely on her friends: Betsy Stedman, Dr. Rush, Annis Boudinot Stockton, and after the war, Moore's brother, Henry Hill, and Milcah Martha Moore.

The "Copy of a Letter from M[.] Morris" (*MMMB* 64) is an anomaly in *Moore's Book*. So far, we have not been able to confirm a family connection for the letter or find another copy in colonial newspapers or magazines that Moore's family read, or a transcription in a commonplace book from a printed collection, English or American.[75] Another difficulty is that date of the letter (1755) is incorrect based on internal evidence.[76]

In spite of our ignorance about the author, we can still discuss the letter's literary merits. One of the most sophisticated selections in the collection, it is a parody, that is, an appreciative imitation of the *Memoirs of Martinus Scriblerus*, a work of parody itself, written by the

75. The editors could not positively identify M. Morris. The satiric bite of the style is different from the prose style of Moore's sister, Margaret Hill Morris, or the M. Morris who Moore speculates wrote "Reflections on the Death of several valuable Friends" (*MMMB* 111).

76. The letter must have been written or printed around 1765. See the annotations for *MMMB* 64.

club of "Scriblerians," Pope, Swift, Arbuthnot, Gay, and Robert Hartley, the Earl of Oxford.[77] Although Morris's "Letter" is dense with literary and political allusion, the letter format, with its formulaic structure, makes it more accessible to the reader, at least at first glance. The two main topics of the letter are its parody of memoirs and its burlesque of the "battle of the sexes." Calling herself the sister of Martinus Scriblerus, she (the persona) proposes to write a memoir, but in spite of all her "reasons" to do so, she digresses from her "history" into a debate with her married friend, Kendall, over the "philosophical" versus the "domestic" woman.

M. Morris, the speaker, begins the parody of memoir-writing with ironic inversion. She admits, but quickly hides, her motives (and those of memoir-writers), envy and vanity. With a barrage of arguments, questions, allusions to sundry "great" and "would-be-greats" who have written memoirs, she turns to the example of her mentors, Pope and Swift,

> when they suffer'd the Minutes of their Lives to descend to Posterity, & justified the Importance of Man to himself, by giving to distinguished a Place in their works to the renowned Memoirs of P. P. Clk. of the Parish;— in Emulation, therefore, . . . I introduce the Memoirs of M. M. Spinster of this Parish.[78]

Morris's memoir is also undercut by lively digressions, particularly one on "the battle of the sexes." Her friend Kendall provokes her into a defense of the "philosophical woman" as a potential marriage partner over the "domestic" woman. Her proof that the philosophical woman can handle all things is to exalt the ridiculous, to place her whole defense of women on their method of handling a crisis in cookery: a burst pudding in the pot. In a dazzling recitation of scientific processes, much of it questionably accurate or useful, the author un-

77. For the "Background of the Club," see Charles Kerby-Miller, ed., *The Memoirs of the Extraordinary Life, Works, and Discoveries of Martinus Scriblerus* (Oxford: Oxford University Press, 1988), 2–22.

78. Pope wrote the "Memoirs of P. P., Clerk of This Parish" (1727), a mock-memoir. See Rosemary Cowler, ed., *The Prose Works of Alexander Pope* (Hamden, Conn.: Archon-The Shoe String Press, 1986), 2:99–129.

dermines the role of science in solving the "philosophical" wife's problem.

The domestic wife fares no better. Her orderly kitchen and sweet management become total confusion. In a display of verbal virtuosity, M. Morris describes the domestic woman discovering her pudding is burst:

> down drops the Ladle—up goes her hands—. . . raves at Betty—boxes the Scullion—kicks the Dog from the Fire—[who runs away, and in the process] oversets some of the Children—they are set a squalling—the affrighted Husband leaves the House, & begs a quiet Dinner of his Neighbours.

Returning to the parody of the *Memoir*, the author realizes "this also is a Digression from my History," but promising more of her "surprising Memoirs," she, following the forms of good letter-writing, concludes "with love & good Will to your Household, Docr. & Sally Young." The "Letter" appropriately includes the place, "Settle," and the date, "Jany 2d. 1755." The letter from M. Morris is one of the fascinating puzzles in Moore's Book.

Although we may understand it as a parody of the Scriblerian papers with a mock memoir and a digression on the philosophical versus the domestic woman, we may be overlooking an entire level of meaning. If there is a "real" as opposed to a "fictional" M. Morris, there may be a literal level of interpretation that we are missing—an added irony, for example. The literal allusions to contemporary figures suggest that there is more here to research and to interpret.

In discussions of early American literature it not unusual to hear that early America had no literature of its own. One scholar quotes William Cullen Bryant's opinion of the published writing of early Americans: "It was their highest ambition to attain a certain lofty, measured, declamatory manner. . . . The imagination is confined to one trodden circle, doomed to the chains of a perpetual mannerism, and condemned to tinkle the same eternal tune with its fetters."[79] The

---

79. William Cullen Bryant, quoted by John McWilliams, in "Poetry in the Early Republic," *Columbia Literary History of the United States*, ed. Emory Elliott (New York: Columbia University Press, 1988), 156.

same scholar generalizes that "little in the poetry of the American Revolutionary era . . . is indigenously American[;] few images are evocative rather than didactic, and even fewer lines are poetry rather than verse."[80] Neither the nineteenth-century poet nor the twentieth-century scholar have taken into account the many unpublished manuscripts of poetry. Certainly, neither of them knew about Milcah Martha Moore's remarkable manuscript.

Reading *Milcah Martha Moore's Book* opens up a different America to modern readers, one in which manuscripts were as important as sources for reading and writing as printed matter. *Moore's Book* is place- and time-specific: the Delaware Valley in the period before and during the Revolutionary War. Moore's writers and readers enjoyed documentary literature (letters, apocalyptic dreams, elegies of friends and family, travel journals), as well as imaginative literature (lyrics, meditations, verse epistles, prose parody), whether it was carefully composed or extemporaneous. Paradoxically, because *Moore's Book* is so rooted in the literary tastes of her elite Quaker circle, it transcends its age and speaks to modern readers. The writers that Moore copied wrote for each others' interest, consolation, and amusement; they did not expect to be remembered. They debated the issues that concerned them. When Moore transcribed their feelings about slavery, religion, friendship, the boycott on tea, the female Patriot, and the married versus the single life, she offered readers a unique insight into the contradictions and ambiguities of this revolutionary period in American life. For students of literature, the poetry and prose in *Moore's Book* is often written in language that is passionate, sincere, witty, and thoughtful—language that deserves discussion and analysis. The styles of diction and rhetoric are often difficult to understand or tedious by our aesthetic tastes, but these differences offer modern readers the unique perspective of the past.

Much of the value of the manuscript lies in Moore's ability as a transcriber. She wrote for readers, not just for herself, so she was careful to copy poems and letters clearly and accurately. Her memorandum on Wright's poetry (*MMMB* 23), for example, indicates that she respected the writer's text by searching for the "original" versions of the poems and transcribing them accurately. The organization of the entries reveals her purpose of preserving the work of three women

80. Williams, "Poetry in the Early Republic," 156.

writers who were significant in their time, but who are lost or unknown to most modern readers: Susanna Wright, Hannah Griffitts,
Elizabeth Graeme Fergusson. Her juxtaposition of entries in some
places in the manuscript suggests her desire to provoke discussion
over the leading issues of the day: the role of women and, most typi-
cally for America in the 1760s and 1770s, the issue of peace or war. Although the quality of their poetry and prose varies, there are many
writers, particularly Wright, Griffitts, Fergusson, and the mysterious
"M. Morris," who show their imagination was not "confined to one
trodden circle," as William Cullen Bryant described the work of early
American writers.

Milcah Martha Moore herself was obviously a prolific reader.
Sadly, all available evidence indicates that she did not continue transcribing the work of women writers or American writers. The comparison of *Moore's Book*, compiled in the 1770s, with the publication
of the *Miscellanies* in 1787 demonstrates that characterizing the nature
of early American literature is not simple. Ironically, Bryant's remark
best describes the poetry and prose (chiefly written by British men) in
the *Miscellanies*. Didactic in purpose, the literature in this textbook is
rarely evocative or lively, whether documentary or imaginative. The
writers do not inspire debate over personal or national identity. Students who used this collection were encouraged to follow standard
male and female gender roles, be diligent in their work and religious
practices, and imitate British culture.

After the Revolutionary War, the role of literature changed. Did the
new republic's desire for cohesion and unity stifle writers' creativity,
expecially women's? What happened to the debate over American
identity? More research needs to be done to clarify the shift in perspective from manuscript to print culture during the last decades of
eighteenth-century America. More research needs to be done to discover what women wrote before print culture became dominant. For
now, Moore has another audience—one she probably never expected:
modern readers who will be puzzled, surprised, and often pleased
in their discovery of the diverse voices that Milcah Martha Moore
preserved.

CONTENTS OF
Milcah Martha Moore's Book

MILCAH MARTHA MOORE'S BOOK

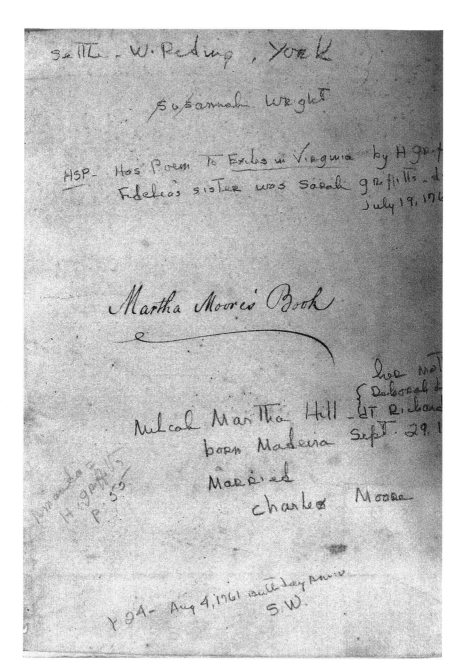

Fig. 8. Title Page from *Milcah Martha Moore's Book*. Courtesy, Haverford College
Library, Haverford, Pennsylvania. Quaker Collection.

1   An Essay on Friendship

The Friend requires, & friendship does demand,
At least th' attempt from my inferior Hand.
The Heart shall dictate & the Pen rehearse
And keep the Subject flowing with the Verse,
While I describe the social Joys we find   5
In Hearts cemented & the friendly Mind,
The strong Affection & the watchful Care,
The feeling Pity & the ardent Pray'r.
I paint the mutual Love, the melting Eye
And all the Beauties of the tender Tye.—   10
—Friendship, my Friend's an Union of the Soul
Expands its Flames & spread's throughout the whole.
The greatest Blessing we enjoy below,
From this pure Stream untainted Pleasures flow,
So fix'd this Friendship & so firm its Love,   15
'Tis only rival'd by the bless'd above,
Nor is it in the Pow'r of Death to end
Or seperate us from a virtuous Friend,
Keep but the sacred Bond forever fast,
'Till Death shall strike & Nature breathe her last   20
Then in her Glory, she shall brighter shine,
And all their Friendship will be quite divine,
But such the Nature of this tender Joy,
Reserve will wound it & distrust destroy
A cool Indiff'rence poison all the Name,   25
Damp the kind warmth & chill the vital Flame.
Let those who choose a bosom Friend on Earth
Judge before Friendship, then confide 'till Death—
To keep it lasting, thus the Centre be,
A noble unaffected Piety.   30
The other Virtues, here may claim a Place
This is the chief & this alone the Base,
The Bond to strengthen, it requires we find,
Similitude of Passions & of Mind,
Alike in Tempers, as alike in Love,   35
Mutual their Faith & Confidence improve
By simpathetic Tenderness are known

And feel each others Sorrows like their own,
Kind to their Failings, to their Virtues Just
With watchful Care they guard the sacred trust,   40
A feeling Heart, a sympathizing Soul
Can with a friend in all their Griefs condole
Joy when they Joy, & when they sorrow, mourn
Sighs to their Sighs, & Tears to theirs return,
In Silence weep, & bear the tender Part,   45
That wounds the Soul & melts the bleeding Heart,
For oh! in every Grief their Friend has known,
It strikes as deep & pains them as their own,
"In those dear Bonds of mutual Union ty'd,
"No Time can break, nor distant Lands divide."   50
When the calm Sea, with prosp'rous Gales is blest
They feel the Pleasure, & the Joy can taste
Nor is it only then they help to share
But in more adverse Scenes their Suff'rings bear,
In those dark times they heighten & improve   55
The cordial Drop which doubleth their Love
Brightens each Joy, & lessens every Fear,
T[o] increase their Pity & increase their Care,
Each Woe they feel,—in ev'ry Grief they grieve
Relief they offer—tho' they can't relieve,   60
On ev'ry Call with fond Concern attend,
And hand the Cordial to the fainting Friend.
When Storms arise & raging Tempests roll
Firm as the Centre, steady as the Pole,
Is such a Friend.—   65
For if sincere, (when once the Knot is ty'd)
No little Pett[1] can e'er the Bond divide
No Storms dissolve it, nor no Passions guide
No jealous Envy can disturb them here,
They love their Friend & can that Friend prefer,   70
With faithful Love each Virtue they reveal
With tender Care, each failing they conceal.
A friend will ever turn the brightest Side

---

1. **Pett**: "Offence at one's treatment; to sulk" (*Oxford English Dictionary*, hereafter *OED*).

And strive to lessen Faults they cannot hide,
Allow for frailty in a human Mind   75
And shew that Mercy which they hope to find,
If ever smiling Pleasure is their Guest
"And sweet Sensations chear the languid Breast
"No Pleasure they can taste, no Joy prefer,
" 'Till the fond Partner of their Soul is there,   80
"T'would loose the relish quite & be unknown
"If it was only felt & shar'd by one,
"And 'till they meet, 'till each the Friend has seen
" 'Tis all a painful Vacancy within"
When o'er past Scenes the wand'ring Mind does rove   85
They mourn their Absence, & recall their Love,
Bless the dear Hour & point the happy Day
When in sweet Converse past the Time away,
Instructive all—their Sorrows they reveal
Impart their Joys, or their Experience tell,   90
Their dearest Thoughts on each they can depend,
Securely trusting in their bosom Friend,
For by their Love, they e'er their Joys increase,
And by their Pity make their Sorrows less,
And such the Nature of this heav'nly Flame,   95
Their Joys, their Dangers, & their Hopes the same,
True friends we find in Union of the Soul
Are like the constant Needle to the Pole
And ever fixing there, whose guiding Ray
Directs the Trav'ler in the dubious Way,   100
Such are the Joys of Friendship, thus it chears
The social Breast, & all the darkness clears,
And when they meet what Pleasures do attend,
The sweet refreshings of a bosom Friend,
For what's contained in each others Breast   105
They find, or make it a sufficient Guest
Nor wish for more, most happy when alone,
For the dear Part'ner of their Soul is one,—
If diff'rence in Opinions ever rise
They speak their Sentiments without Disguise,   110
All open, gen'rous, unreserv'd & free,
With noble Truth & firm Sincerity

Reveal their inmost Thoughts, impart the whole
And open all the Treasures of the Soul,
And with that Freedom which becomes a friend,   115
Reprove the wrong, as well as do commend,
Try to convince, & 'tis with friendship heard,
Where they are right or where thro' failing err'd
And readier they will own the point they've mist
Than in awell known—Error to persist,   120
Or hold th' unfriendly Argument too long
Stiff in Opinion obstinately wrong
But still they mind when they a friend reprove,
To do it with the tenderness of Love,
Keep in their Minds this ever healing Charm   125
Cool in their tempers but in friendship warm.
And when the seperating Hour shall come,
That calls the Creature to its heav'nly Home,
When the grim Tyrant shoots the fatal Dart
When Life shall cease, & dearest Friends shall part,   130
How hard to bear, how sharp the Pangs we feel
Nor Balms can cure, nor Time itself can heal
Hard, but it must be done, it must be borne
When the dear half, is from our Bosom Torne
And leaves the other but to grieve & mourn,   135
    How deep the Gulf where all our Joys are drown'd
How vast the stroke is, & how large the Wound,
Each Scene we view encreases but our Grief
Adds to our Anguish, & forbids Relief,
When we recall the Virtues of the Dead   140
(The happy Moments now for ever fled,)
How the dear Partner lessen'd ev'ry Fear,
Calm'd ev'ry Woe, & sweeten'd every Care,
And bade us hope, when sinking in Despair,
On ev'ry Call did their Assistance lend   145
And prov'd themselves the firm unshaken Friend
Ah! these sweet Bonds of Friendship stronger bind,
Engage th' Affections & unite the Mind,
Beyond the tyes of Nature, they who've known,
Two friendly Souls made intimately one,   150
It['s] these can well express, & these can tell
How deep the Wounds, how sharp the Pangs they feel

They like the Turtle,[2] know not how to wed
Now the dear Part'ner of their Soul is fled.—
    As Good does sometimes out of Evil spring   155
We may from Grief this Consolation bring,
Raise our Dependence from this dusty Ball
And place it on the great Original,
Secure our Bliss above the starry Sphere
Where dwells the Centre of our Hopes, & lasting
    Comforts are.   160

Fidelia

2 *A Meditation* by S. Wright

For as Jonah was 3 Days & 3 Nights in the Whales Belly, so shall the Son of
Man be 3 Days & 3 Nights in the Heart of the Earth. [Matthew 12:40]

Where shall I this unfathom'd Secret find
Of what thou art? O my mysterious Mind,
Where learn what Crimes committed heretofore,
Exact a Course of Punishments so sore
In present Ills & one great Risque of more?   5
Would Heaven all wise, all Merciful & just
Have chang'd this intellectual Soul to Dust
If she no State of Pre existance knew?
If all these Ills were not her righteous Due?
Not one small Movement of herself she knows,   10
Involv'd in Darkness & oppress'd with Woes,
Whoes Weight our vain Inquietudes increase,
Strangers alike to Knowledge & to Peace,
'Till the full Expiation overpast,
(By Means in Heavens eternal Volume wrote   15
Surpassing all Extent of human Thought)
Peace, Light & Knowledge may be gain'd at last,

2. **Turtle**: "Affection for (another), like a turtle-dove for its mate" (*OED*).

So when the Prophet[3] his Obedience fled,
And the directed Lot mark'd his devoted Head
Aghast he plung'd amidst the broken Wave,   20
The living Tomb yawn'd dreadful to receive,
He enter'd & in solid Darkness lay,
The unweildy Monster roll'd his Bulk away,—
Down to the Bottom of the boundless Flood
He bore the Rebel from his angry God;   25
Through shining Plains & coral Groves he pass'd
Thro' groupes of Beauties all around him cast;
But what avail'd, the Seer imprison'd lay,
Secluded every chearful Beam of Day;
'Till after thrice collected Nights of Pain   30
Had cleans'd his Soul from her rebellious Stain,
He landed on his native World again.
Shadow & Type[4] of him who long foretold,—Gen. 3
Consol'd the patriarchal Sires of old,
Whose Day by Faith enraptur'd Abraham saw,   35
Completion of the Prophets & the Law,
With boundless Grace & unexampled Love
He left the Heaven of Heavens all Heights above,
Except the Throne supreme———

   3. the Prophet: "God commanded Jonah (1:1–2) to warn Nineveh in Assyria of
its great evil. Jonah, however, fled, boarding a ship to Tarshish that God then assailed
with a storm. The sailors called upon their gods and desperately cast lots to learn who
was responsbile for the divine wrath. Jonah, slumbering in the hold, was singled out.
He instructed the crew to cast him overboard, which, once done, quieted the sea. . . .
God then appointed a great fish to swallow Jonah. Inside the fish, Jonah burst into
prayer, expressing partly lament, partly thanksgiving for God's . . . deliverance. The
fish then vomited Jonah alive onto dry land (Jonah 2) . . . . The work was interpreted
allegorically by Jewish and Christian readers. . . . In Matt. 12:39–41, Jonah 2 is cited
to prefigure Jesus' death and resurrection" (1:1–2). See "Jonah" in Stephen Neill,
John Goodwin, and Arthur Dowle, eds., *Modern Reader's Dictionary of the Bible*
(New York: Association Press, 1966).
   4. Shadow & Type: This expression refers to a "method of Biblical exegesis or interpretation in which persons, events, or things of the OT [Old Testament] are interpreted as being foreshadowings or prototypes, of persons, events, or things in the NT
[New Testament]" (Richard N. Soulen, *Handbook of Biblical Criticism*, 2d ed. [At-
lanta: John Knox Press, 1981], 209). For example, Adam (the first man) foreshadows
Christ (the "new man"), who would, by his redemption of Adam's fall, give humanity a new beginning. This promise is recounted in Genesis 3, the reference Wright
placed in the margin of this line.

On this dark Orb a Veil of Flesh to wear,   40
And ev'ry Woe of human Nature bear,
Beneath the Weight of Heavens dread Wrath to groan
To expiate Transgression not his own,—
For the lost Tribes of Adams erring Race,
To gain Probation[5] & an Hour of Grace,   45
Fulfill'd the hard Conditions of his Birth,
And took his Lot with all the Sons of Earth;
'Till three long Days, & 3 long Nights past o'er,
The mighty Sufferer must endure no more,
First born of them who from the Dead shall rise   50
He all triumphant sought his regal Skies.—
    Lost & confounded in the amazing Plan
A God! subjected to this Reptile Man
For his wild Passions & unguarded Fall
Great Sacrifice! was offer'd once for all,   55
A Sacrifice sufficient full & great
For Crimes of any pre-existant Date,
When those of this frail Life are added to their Weight.

S. Wright

3   Anna Boylens[6] Letter[7] to King Henry the 8th. by the same. *1720*

From anxious Thoughts of every future Ill
From these lone Walls which Death & Terror fill,
To you great Sir! a loyal Wife from hence,

---

5. **Probation**: "Goodness is not forced upon us; we make it our own by willing identification of our will with the good. Hence probation implies freedom, power to 'choose the good and refuse the evil.'" See Frances Shields, "Probation" in *Encyclopedia of Religion and Ethics*, ed. James Hastings (New York: Scribners, 1928), vol. 10.

6. **Anna Boylens**: Anne Boleyn married Henry VIII in 1533. When Anne, like her predecessor, Catherine of Aragon, failed to produce a male heir, Henry accused her of adultery and had her beheaded in 1536. Their daughter Elizabeth I, the infant referred to in this poem, ruled England from 1558–1603.

7. **Letter**: The "letter" is a verse epistle, a conventional genre derived from Ovid's *Heroides*. Many such letters are from legendary women to absent husbands or lovers.

Writes to assert her injur'd Innocence.
To you, who on a Throne supremely great   5
Look down & guide the partial Hand of Fate,
Who rais'd your Subject to a royal Bride,
To the imperial Purples gaudy Pride
And glowing Gems around these Temples ty'd,
You glowing Gems your dazling Rays rebate   10
And fade thou purple, at thy wearers Fate,
To grandeur rais'd, to Misery cast down
And mourn my sad acquaintance with a Crown,
My Life & Fame must join the Sacrifice
The last alone all peaceful Thought denies,   15
Renews My Anguish & oe'rflows my Eyes.
For Life & Crown with Patience I forego,
There's no such Charm in filling Thrones below

Pope's epistle "Eloise to Abelard," published in 1717, was a popular eighteenth-century example of this kind of poem (see "Alexander Pope" in *Oxford Companion to English Literature*, 5th ed., ed. Margaret Drabble [Oxford: Oxford University Press, 1985], hereafter *OCEL*, 5th).

The American Quaker Hannah Callender noted in her diary for "1758, 10th mo." that she "read in the *Spectator* Ann Bullen's letter to Harry 8th, who I make no doubt will in her own words be confinced of his misstake." She quotes the following passage from Wright's poem:

> When Bones sepulcred leave there narrow rooms,
> And hostile Things rise tumbling from there tomb,
> When nor your heart nor mine can bye conceal'd,
> But every secret motive stands reveal'd,
> Stands full reveal'd that God and Man may see,
> How fate has err'd, and you have Injured me

The Diary of Hannah Callender, 1758–1788, ed. Susan E. Klepp and Karin A. Wulf (Philadelphia: University of Pennsylvania Press, forthcoming).

In *The Spectator* for Thursday, June 5, 1712, Joseph Addison reprinted a letter written by Anne Boleyn to Henry VIII, along with this prefatory remark: "I do not remember to have seen any Ancient or Modern Story more affecting than a Letter of *Ann* of *Bologne*, Wife to King *Henry* the Eighth, and Mother to Queen *Elizabeth*, which is still extant in the *Cotton* Library, as written by her own Hand. . . . One sees in it the Expostulations of a slighted Lover, the Resentments of an injured Woman, and the Sorrows of an imprisoned Queen" (*The Spectator*, ed. Donald F. Bond [Oxford: Clarendon Press, 1965], 3:487). For further discussion of Hannah Callendar, her circle of friends, and their reading, see Karin Wulf's introductory essay, "*Milcah Martha Moore's Book*: Documenting Culture and Connection in the Revolutionary Era," pages 30–31.

My Name alone, 'tis Anna Boylens Name
With whose low Station & unspotted Fame   20
All innocent & happy Days I'd seen,
This harmless Name exalted to a Queen
Is handed infamous to future Times
Loaded with Falshoods, blacken'd o'er with Crimes
Y[ou]r. infant Daughter her sad Part must bear,   25
And with her Mother's Heart her Suff'ring share,
Poor lovely Offspring of a wretched Bed
What are thy hapless Mother's Crimes that shed
This baleful Influence on thy harmless Head?
Thy Father sternly casts thee from his knee,   30
Whilst each licentious Tongue that rails at me
Points o'er thy opening Years with Infamy,
All Hopes on Earth with Patience I forego
But thee—poor Child left in a World of Woe
May thy dear Life in smoother Channels run   35
Secure from Ills thy Mother could not shun
All this is Pain, but nothing of Surprise
This Fall I look'd for from my fatal Rise,
From that unhappy Day, my Person pleas'd yr. Eyes.
Such slight Foundations never lasting prove   40
Where Fancy only lights the Torch of Love,
I see another Fair assume My Place
Who's in your Eyes what Anna Boylen was,
Beware triumphant Beauty how you shine
Those Charms, those Vows & ardours all were mine.   45
Look on me & beware for as you see,
What I am now, that you shall surely be,
But since my Death & nothing less will do
To bring you to the Bliss you have in View,
May bounteous Heaven the mighty Sin forgive   50
And not repay, the Injuries I receive,
Yet think, o! think what Crimes will wound yr. Soul,
When your dim Eyes in search of Slumber rowl,
When Lamps burn blue & guilty Tapers fade,
As by your bridal Bed I glide a ghastly Shade,   55
While sanguine Streams from purple Fountains drain
And all around the gay Apartment stain,
From conscious Guilt will these Illusions rise,

And haunt your Steps & fill your watching Eyes,
For ever raising Tumults in your Breast,   60
But fear me not for I shall be at Rest.
But at that Day when the last Trumpets Sound,
Shall reach the dead, & break their Sleep profound,
Bones long sepulchred burst their narrow Rooms
And hostile Kings rise trembling from their Tombs,   65
When nor your Heart, nor mine can lie conceal'd
But ev'ry secret Sin shall stand reveal'd,
Stand full reveal'd that God & Man may see,
How Fate has err'd, & you have injur'd me,
When, but alas all Arguments are vain   70
To bring your royal wand'ring Heart again
What Innocence unaided & oppress'd
Could do, I've done but who can Pow'r resist.
      I've but one Wish but one Request to make
Let not my Friends be Sufferers for my sake,   75
All Innocent, humane, & kindly good
May their dear Lives be ransom'd by my Blood,
For ev'ry one the Price I'd freely pay
So many Times could Life be drain'd away,
By what I once have been by what you are,   80
Happy & great,—by all yr. Joy & Care;
By all things sacred, all your Love forgive,
My Friends their harmless Crimes & let them live,
      Lo! on her bended Knees thus asks yr. Wife,
On terms, you see, she would not ask her Life,   85
With this I cease, to trouble your Repose,
A few short anxious Hours the stormy Scene will close.

4   [Untitled] by the same

—Now never more, you my auspicious Stars!
'Ill blame for Anguish, or a Life of Cares,
For Friends deserted, Fortune's Goods decay'd;
One happy Gift, has all those Wrongs o'er paid,
Rich in Possession, I despise my Fate,   5
Be but the joy as lasting as 'tis great,

But you too short, my slender Thread design
Ah, since so short—permit it to be fine!
Crowd yr. promiscuous Pleasures where you'll give
A length of years the Relish to outlive.   10
None but your chosen Blessings I desire,
And with so exquisite a Thought admire,
That winding up my Days, one step I rise,
To taste the Bliss of your imperial Skies.—*Extract Sept.*
  1st. 1721

5   [Untitled] by the same *July 24th 1722—Extract.*

—For they who've taken an extensive View,
Of all that Raphael or that Titian[8] drew,
With the same Fire, & the same Judgement,—Fraught,
As the immortal Workmanship was wrought,
Can they admire the cold & dull Design,   5
Of Pieces where no master touches shine,
Where all's unlabour'd, Light & Shade confus'd
The colouring artless, & the Strokes abus'd,
E'en the Design (tho' cold & dull at first)
By Accidents still alter'd for the worse,   10
And plac'd far from that advantageous Light
That gives to all a Tincture of its white,
—A transient View must tire the curious Eye
Which for Relief will pass regardless by,
And kindly let the Faults neglected dye.—   15

6   A Congratulation on Recovery from Sickness

When thro' this Land, impetuous Sickness ran,
And sacrific'd the brittle Life of Man,

8. **Raphael . . . Titian**: Italian Renaissance painters Raphael (1483–1520) and
Titian (c. 1487–1576).

When burning Syrius[9] like a Fury stood,
With purple Spots, & Arrows dipt in Blood,
And from his Magazine of Death & Pains   5
Shot scorching Fevers thro' our labouring Veins,
Then not a Life in sober Temperance spent
Warded the Blow, or hinder'd the Event,
But Infancy, & Youth, & bending Age
All sunk alike beneath the Conqueror's Rage,   10
Learning & Wit, & every powerful Charm,
Prov'd all too weak the Tyrant to disarm,
When thou my Frd. his Rage must undergo
'Till pale & faint, & sinking with the Blow
We saw—what every forward Fear cou'd show,   15
—Then what avails it, mortal Men to rise
'Till high exalted to their kindred Skies,
Their Souls impatient, every Day refine
'Till bright as their own native Heaven they shine,
If we so early must resign our Claim,   20
While they remount the Regions, whence they came,
It has been so, & must be so again
Tho' thus refin'd they are but Mortal Men,
For Addison & Garth[10] resign'd their Breath,
Nor can a worth more strong, repel the Arms of Death.   25
     But better News, these dark Reflections crost
That thou My Friend, regain'd the Health, thou'd lost,
In thy fair Consorts joys a Part we bear,
As in her Griefs, we had a real Share.—
     Late—So Brittannia saw the Sun arise   30

---

9. **Syrius**: The dog of Orion, "a mythical hunter of gigantic size and strength." Syrius is the brightest star in the constellation of Orion. References to Syrius as the "dog star" of summer go back to the *Illiad*. See "Orion" in Oskar Seyffert, ed., *Dictionary of Classical Antiquities*, rev. and ed. Henry Nettleship and J. E. Sandys (New York: World Publishing, 1969), p. 437.

10. **Addison & Garth**: Joseph Addison (1672–1719) was an English poet, essayist, and Whig politician. He was part of an elite circle of literati that included Jonathan Swift, and he was a regular contributor to the *Tatler* and *The Spectator*. Sir Samuel Garth (1661–1719) was a minor poet as well as a physician. See *Dictionary of National Biography*, ed. Leslie Stephen and Sidney Lee et al. (London: Oxford University Press, 1885–1900), hereafter *DNB*.

To bless the Earth & beautifie the Skies,
But as he shone in all his Strength of Light
Thick Shadows spread & veil'd him from their Sight,
And antient Night on mighty Wings uprose.
While silver Stars their feeble Lights disclose— 35
Each Beast of Prey, from out his Den appear'd,
And Birds of Night their screaming Voices rear'd
With Fear & Wonder every one drew nigh
To see such Omens threaten from on high,
But how their Hearts exulted, when they saw; 40
The Sun appear, & vanquish'd Shades withdraw,
'Till like himself, he shone again confest,
"With all his Arrows arm'd, in all his glory drest."—

[Susanna Wright]

7   On the Benefit of Labour. by the same

Adam from Paradise expell'd,
Was drove into a Locust Field,
Whose rich luxuriant Soils produce,
Nor Fruit, nor Plant, for human Use,
'Till clear'd by Toil, & till'd by Art 5
With Plenty chear'd his drooping Heart.—
—'Twas thus Relief our Father found
When sent to cultivate the Ground.
For God who knew what Man could bear,
Form'd not his Sentence too severe, 10
A Life of indolent Repose
Had been the Plan of greater Woes;
While tir'd with Ease too dearly bought,
He past the tedious Hours in Thought,
For Labour only causes Rest, 15
And calms the Tumults in the Breast.—
     More Leisure to revolve his Fate
Had added Sorrow to the Weight,
Of his unhappy fall'n State.—

While Memory drest the gaudy Scenes   20
Of Edens never fading Greens,
Of Trees that bloom without Decay,
Where Storms were silent—Zephyrs[11] play,
And Flowers their rifling sweets bestow,
On all the gentle Winds that blow,   25
With ev'ry Charm that crown'd the Place
Design'd for Adam & his Race:
Our Sire too weak for such a Stroke,
Had sunk beneath the heavy Yoke,
Had on his Breast the Sentence try'd,   30
Let out his tortur'd Soul & dy'd.—
But kindly to suspend his Doom
For sake of Ages yet to come,
A Life of Action was decreed,
And Labour must produce him Bread;   35
His Hands the artful Web prepare
To screen him from inclement Air,
And equal Pains a Tent provide
To turn the beating Storm aside.—
—These necessary Toils & Cares   40
For present Wants & future Tears,
Joyn'd to the Curse, a Blessing grow,
And lessen or divert our Woe.—*Octobr. 1728 Ext.*

8   [Untitled] by the same

—Thus whilst in Hope of better Days
    The present Moment flies,
And Fancy with Ill-fortune plays,
    The Fool deluded dies.—*Octobr. 1728 Ext.*

11. **Zephyrs**: "*Zephyrus*, in Greek mythology, the personification of the west wind." Thus, zephyrs are, by association, little breezes (*Oxford Companion to Classical Literature*, comp. Paul Harvey [Oxford: Clarendon Press, 1937], hereafter *OCCL*).

9   [Untitled]

Neither knoweth any Man the Father save the Son & he to whomsoever the
Son shall reveal him.—[Matthew 11:27] by the same

What Means yet unattempted can I try
To still this anxious Searcher in my Breast
These fond Enquiries—whence had I a Being?
What am I now?—what shall I be hereafter?—
I owe this Being to one powerful Cause,   5
But what thou art I cannot comprehend,
Or learn thy incommunicable Name.—
I search & fain would gain some happy Knowledge
Fain would I gain some faint Ideas of thee
Invisible, Almighty, uncreated.—   10
I am taught thy Temple is the Heart of Man:
But in this vain polluted Heart of mine,
Only a Consciousness of thee can dwell,
And that too weak.—O! strengthen thou who made me,
And placed me here upon a Stage of Wonders;   15
But to what End, 'tis thou who made me knows;
Sure to enjoy some fuller Good here after,
For here I'm toss'd upon a troubled Sea
With Knowledge just enough to guess at Error,
But not enough to fix unerring Truth—   20
In this Perplexity of Thought I am lost,
While tyrant Passions sway me here & there.
Just God! this is not sure my only End.—
—So in his shatter'd Bark the Sailor fares,
When cheating Calms & smiling summer Seas,   25
Have tempted far on the unfaithful Deep;—
Aghast! he sees the Tempest round him rage
Nor aught avail his Hopes nor aught his Art
So near to Death in the devouring Flood,
'Till pitying Powers above, rebuke the Storm,   30
And the directing Star shines full & clear;
Thou sov'reign Wisdom cast a gracious Ray
Of living Light on my benighted Soul.

Save the enquiring Fugitive from Ruin
And let me not transgress whilst I demand   35
What art thou, reasoning Principle within,
Thou something which I cannot comprehend.
I call thee Spirit, immaterial Being,
But tell me what is immaterial Being
And tell me what is Spirit—what thou art,   40
What e'er thou art reveal thee to thyself
What has thou been a thousand Ages past,
What shall thou be a thousand Ages hence?
What art thou now?—involv'd in Clouds & Tempests
Thou pants & labours for Eternity,—
Beneath a heavy Weight of finite Cares,   45
Though weary of Existance yet thou fears,
A falling into nothing—thus oppress'd,
With num'rous Cares, variety of Ills,
I bend beneath a Weight that is not lasting,   50
But oh!—'tis this Futurity confounds me.—

10   [Untitled]

So Man lieth down & riseth not, 'till the Heavens be no more, they shall not
awake nor be raised out of their Sleep.—[Job 14:2]
—And he said unto me, my Grace is sufficient for thee. [2 Cor. 12:9] by the
same

To live alone amidst the busy Scene,
Of busy Cares & hear thy God within,
Say by what Means from human Eyes conceal'd
Can those celestial Beauties be reveal'd
Which my chill'd Breast with potent Charms may fire   5
Calm & refine, prepare & then inspire?
For whiter Days to future Worlds I trust,
When this weak Frame shall moulder into Dust,
When my last Debt to Nature shall be paid,

And the soft Soul, rise in new Robes array'd;   10
Mean while with Patience, as our God commands,
I wait each kind Chastisement from his Hands,
Full well appris'd that Sorrow, Care & Pain,
Correct our Steps o'er Lifes uneven Plain,
Where Adams Sons in erring Paths have trod   15
Far from their Interest Duty & their God—
Hope to survive & patiently to bear,
The common Ills of Sorrow Pain & Care,
And more, shou'd more be sent—but where to find
The tranquil Bliss of an unruffled Mind   20
By what deep Art the Tempest to controul,
When Clouds of doubtful Reasonings crowd my Soul;
When the long Views in solemn Order spread,
Fill all my Breast with Wonder & with Dread,
How shall I plunge amidst the numerous Dead?   25
What, shall I be unbodied?—how & where?—
Instant—will those tremendous Scenes appear?
Or must I sleep unnumber'd Ages o'er?
'Till Nature sink & Time shall be no more?
Elude all Search, & each Enquiry fails   30
Though our first Parents curious Crime prevails.—
Then tell me O!—ye Messengers of Peace
(Your gospel Tydings of the World to come
Our Hope, our Rest, our long expected Home!)
What Angel Voice can charm the Soul to cease   35
Her fruitless Wanderings in a Path unknown,
Conceal'd from Man, & clear'd by Death alone.—
Since only Death these Mysteries can explore,
O! thou enquiring Mind, enquire no more—
But all too weak the vain Injunction proves,   40
From Thought to Thought incessantly she roves;
There neither Peace or Knowledge can attain,
Fruitless each Search & each Enquiry vain
She flies to thee O God!——
⠀⠀⠀⠀As Order calm'd Confusion's dreadful Storm,   45
When thy almighty Word call'd forth the Birth of Form,
And Chaos groan'd to see his Throne destroy'd,

Whilst Light came darting through the mighty Void,
So calm the Tempest labouring in my Soul,
Each View contract, each daring Search controul,   50
With Faith & Patience arm my wavering Breast
And let thy Grace conduct my Steps to rest.
  Then trembling Reason shall confess thy Pow'r
And low in Dust, lye prostrate, & adore,
Shall in thy Light her narrow Limits see,   55
And own that none art great & wise but Thee.—

11 On the Death of an Infant. by the same

I praise the Dead with undissembled Voice,
Who in that Sleep too deep for Dreams remain,
'Till happier, waking to immortal Joys,
  They find one Pleasure unallay'd with Pain.—

In Thoughts like these I vainly seek a Groan,   5
  Or Words of Woe to form the plaintive Song,
Death & the Grave have challeng'd as their own,
  The soft the sweet, the sprightly & the young.

If judging as the vulgar World, we mourn,
  To thee, dear Child, how many Tears are due?   10
From Life & Peace & Joy untimely Torne
  Thyself & each surrounding Object new.

But change the Scene————see the gay Colours fly—
  And true to Nature be the Portrait Just;
Shade it with Woe from the soft Infant Cry,   15
  'Till hoary Cares shall sink the Wretch in Dust.

Fair Innocence!—first & all envied State!
  Wisdom may err, & Virtue fall oppress'd;
But who untainted meet this Stroke of Fate,
  An Angel waffs them to eternal Rest.   20

So Flowers that open with the morning Sun,
    (As gay & fragrant as the Babe we mourn)
E'er to his Noon-Tide Height of Glory run,
    By wanton Hands from their fair Borders torne.

Of blasting Death endure the stern Command,   25
    And turn their gaudy Heads & droop & die,
Each fading Charm owns the Destroyers Hand,
    And closing Bells are thrown neglected by.

When Phoebus self, who ting'd their Leaves so gay,
    (E'er Ev'ning Falls or noxious Vapours rise,   30
To blast & darken the Remains of Day)
    Exhales their Souls into the painted Skies.—

For, I know that thou wilt bring me to Death & to the House appointed for all the living——[Job 30:23]
—For God created Man to be immortal & made him to be an Image of his own Eternity.——[Wisdom of Solomon 2:23]

12   A Meditation. by the same

I call to mind those Ages that are gone,
Whose fleeting Hours their Periods hurries on,
And well remember this precarious Breath,
Shall meet the Blast of all subduing Death,
Resolv'd to Dust this mouldering House of Clay,   5
Shall lie forgot, the Trifle of a Day;—
Then why so anxious by what unknown Doom,
I'm mark'd to fall this Victim to the Tomb;
All different Paths but to one Centre tend
On which Death waits us to our Journey's End   10
A frightful Spectre—or a gentle Friend:—
A welcome Visit to the Wretch he pays,
Lulls Pain to Sleep & ends his tedious Days;

But smiling Fortune in a bridal Dress
Chills with the Thought, & dreads his meagre Face   15
Thinks the calm Grave but comfortless & cold
A Lodging suited to the poor & old,
Exults in Manhood, fondly treads the Stage
Tearless, unconscious of Disease or Age;—
Fancy bewilder'd! can the Wretch forget,   20
To live is only running more in Debt,
A Debt all animated Beings owe,
'Till summon'd back to shady Realms below,
The hard Conditions of our Birth fulfill'd,
To which thro' strong Necessity we yield.—   25
'Tis one Release from all this World of Woes,
Here Care & Sorrow sink into Repose
And the last Scenes of human Action close.—
Then let no smiling Hours alure thee on
To childish Fears of what thou cannot shun   30
Or angry Fates urge thee to seek thy Doom,
From thy own Hand impatient of the Tomb,
An unknown Solace of that World to come:
But calmly wait the grand deciding Blow,
Of this kind Friend—or unrelenting Foe;   35
Nor the great Father of Mankind distrust,
But stand the Shock & mix with common Dust,
This Share of blended Elements resign,
Which have been once, & may again be thine;
Natures fix'd Laws inviolable stand,   40
The mighty Work of an unerring Hand,
And thou a Part of the stupendous Frame,
Art still to be, but whether still the same,
Or chang'd to what new Form, if reasoning Mind
Its Source to Matters purest Parts confin'd,   45
Or if (without Ideas) we believe
Our Souls shall immaterial Beings live,
Trust thou in God, who form'd them what they are,
Will still preserve them with paternal Care
Through Ages infinite they shall endure,   50
A Part of his Creation most secure.—*August 1735.*—

13   On Time. by the same

Since Moments past are as a Dream,
  A fleeting Evening Shade,
Which close like a divided Stream
  Like dying Tapers fade.—
Enjoy the Present & be bless'd,   5
  While yet they're in y[ou]r. Power,
Nor Place y[ou]r. Happiness or Rest,
  On any future Hour.
But know the Present will be gone
  And leave the Soul no more,   10
To feed its craving Wishes on,
  Than what you now deplore,
Enjoy the Present, but secure,
  The future as you go;
Alone the Future must endure   15
  A Happiness or Woe.
It will be present in its Time,
  But never can be pass'd
To an eternal Now you climb
  Which must forever last.   20

14   On the Death of a little Girl.—1735.—
by the same

The little Bird at break of Day,
  That charm'd us with its Song,
And fondly hopp'd from Spray to Spray,
  The Musick to prolong,
As Ev'ning came, ill fated fell,   5
  Struck by a Hand unseen,
Resign'd that Breath which pleas'd so well
  And flutter'd on the Green.
The Lambs that wont to bleat & play,
  And bask in Sunshine Air,   10

That danc'd the fleeting Hours away,
    And knew not Want or Care,
When Night her sable Curtain spread,
    Fell to the Wolf a Prey,
And here & there dispers'd & dead,   15
    The scatter'd Fragments lay.
The Blossoms which to vernal Air,
    Their fragrant Leaves unfold,
And deck the spreading Branches fair
    With Purple, White & Gold.   20
Diffuse their Sweets & Charm the Eye,
    And promise future Store,
Nipp'd by a Frost untimely dye,
    And shed Perfumes no more.—
'Twas thus the Poppet[12] ceas'd to breathe,   25
    The small Machine[13] stood still,
The little Lungs no longer heave
    Or Motion follows Will.
No more that flattering Voice we hear,
    Soft as the Linets Song,   30
Each idle Hour to sooth & chear,
    Which slowly rolls along.
That sprightly Action's past & gone,
    With all its tempting Play,
Sprightly as Lambs that tread the Lawn   35
    Along a Summers Day.
The Dawn of Reason we admir'd,
    As op'ning Blossoms fair,
Now to the silent Grave retir'd,
    Its Organs moulder there.   40
Flowers on thy Breast & round thy Head,

---

12. **Poppet**: "A small or dainty person. . . . Usually, in later use, a term of endearment, for a pretty child, or young woman: darling, pet." Poppet can also refer to "a human figure with jointed limbs, which can be moved by means of strings, or wires; . . . a marionette. Cf. 'puppet'" in *OED*.

13. **small Machine**: "Applied to the human and animal frame as a combination of several parts. . . . Now chiefly with metaphorical intention; as in Addison [1712] . . . in *The Spectator* No. 387, 2: 'Cheerfulness is . . . the best Promoter of Health. Repinings wear out the Machine insensibly'" (*OED*).

    With thee their Sweets resign,
Nipp'd from their tender Stalks & dead,
    Their Fate resembles thine.
Just as their Charms allure the Eye,   45
    And fragrant Leaves unfold,
Clos'd in eternal Night they lie,
    To mix with common Mould.
Thy harmless Soul releas'd from Earth,
    A Cherub sings above,   50
Immortal in a second Birth,
    By thy Redeemer's Love.

15   From the Athaliah of Racine.[14] —by the same

High Adoration & perpetual Pray'r
To thee whose Works ten Thousand Worlds declare!
Tho' back to an Infinity we run,
We find thy Empire fix'd e'er Time begun.
    And tho' our active Thought should roam,   5
    Ten thousand Ages yet to come,
    Ten thousand thousand Ages more
    Thy Throne unshaken as before
    Can never know a late Decay,
Tho' Time & all his Works shall pass away,   10
Tho' not a Track of where his Wheel had run,
Shall tell the wond'rous Race was e'er begun.—

16   On Death.—by the same

We know we once must dye, by sev'ral Ways
The same Decree has swept all Ages past,

   14. **Athaliah of Racine**: *Athalie* is the title of the last drama of Jean Racine (1639–99), from the biblical story of Ataliah (see 2 Kings 11:1–16). This poem is based on one of the choral odes.

Then oh! how vain to ask a Length of Days!
Each big with anxious Wonders of the last.
For the first Moment our frail Lives begun   5
Th' unalterable Period was ordain'd;
In vain would Man the righteous Sentence shun
No Art has ever one short Moment gain'd.
From a deceitful World to be remov'd,
From present Evils & from those to come,   10
From Objects too, too fading to be lov'd,
To the long Rest of an eternal Home.
With every blooming Virtue in its Spring,
Each Faculty full in its Strength & Prime,
Free from those Clouds, which Age & weakness bring,   15
O'er the declining Evening of our Time;
Will more than recompense the scanty Day
Allow'd us, our allotted Race to run,
Then who would strive, so rugged is the Way
A happy Period of their Toil to shun?   20
'Tis true, Amazement fills each Thought of Death,
'Tis not to be no more—'tis Fear—'tis Pain,
'Tis but a Step in yielding up our Breath;
From Life to Death—from Death to Life again.—*Finis*

17   *A Fragment.* by the same

"Sees infinite & in that Sight is lost"—*Prior's Solomon Book 1st.*[15]—

A second Thought on the Soul.—

—I contemplate thee Work of Art divine,
Thou glorious Being, subtle, strong, & pure

15. **Prior's Solomon Book 1st.**: Poet Matthew Prior (1664–1721), wrote "Solomon on the Vanity of the World" (1718), "a long soliloquy in heroic couplets on the same theme" (see *OCEL*, 5th, pp. 790–91). Wright quotes the line from the end of Prior's first book (line 759). See Matthew Prior, *The Literary Works of Matthew Prior*, 2 vols., ed. H. Bunker Wright and Monroe K. Spears (Oxford: Clarendon Press, 1959), 332.

That bears the fair Impression of a God!
So vastly high can thy Conceptions rise,
Thou takes the whole Creation at a View,   5
Grasps Worlds on Worlds, & ranges thro' them all;
To that vast boundless Space where Matter ends,
Passes the mighty Void, that separates
Invisible—and visible Abodes:
There forms Ideas of unnumber'd Hosts,   10
Which stand before the overflowing Light;
But far above where all Conceptions rise,
Beyond the utmost Stretch of human Thought
To an Infinity of Height, enthron'd
The great Creator—the first Cause of all,   15
Impenetrable sits—in vain we strive
To rise—for none shall see his Face & live.—

18   On the Death of two infant Nephews.[16] —
1736.—by the same

The darling Babes for whom these Tears we pay,
So early gone to join their kindred Clay,
Unknowing what they were,—or were to be,
With nervous Pangs, but with a Conscience free,
Have paid that Debt amidst the fatal Storm   5
Which Nature owes to animating Form.—
        Had they surviv'd unto a further Date,
Ten thousand Troubles might have crown'd their Fate;
And when the long revolving Train was past,
They must have mix'd with kindred Clay at last.   10

16. **infant Nephews**: These two nephews could be the children of either of Susanna Wright's two brothers, John and James, or of her two sisters, Patience and Elizabeth. It is most likely that they were the children of James Wright, with whom she was especially close. For help with the Wright family genealogy, the editors thank Craig Horle, chief editor of the *Lawmakers and Legislators in Pennsylvania: A Biographical Dictionary*, vol. 1 (Philadelphia: University of Pennsylvania Press, 1991).

19   [Untitled] by the same

—'Tis well there are new Worlds of Light in Store
For the oppress'd,—the wretched & the Poor,
For Sufferings all their rigid Fates ordain
Thro' many rolling years variety of Pain;
Thro' a false World, just to itself alone,   5
A World where Faith nor Gratitude are known,
Where Friendship's basely made a Trade—an Art,
That holds but while 'tis on the gaining Part.
—But hear & let your conscious Soul confess
The goods which God permits you to possess,   10
(Fatal Effects of human Happiness!)—
Make you forget you are no more than Man;
Amidst them all, yr. Life is but a Span.—
And I, whom now,—you as beneath you shun,
E'er ninety years their fleeting Course have run   15
Shall have as much as you of all your Store,
A quiet Tomb, & you can have no more.—
By Death, your Judgement rectified, you'll see
No odds betwixt your mighty self & me.
For all you of the late low World possest   20
And I with none of all her Treasures blest,
Then shall appear to your enlighten'd Eyes,
The only difference which must arise
Consists in this—in this & nothing more,
Of pious Works, who has the greatest Store   25
Of Justice, Temp'rance, Charity & Love,
Safe with their Heart, reposited above.

20   A Fragment. by the same

—So all Things are but alter'd, nothing dyes,
When Spirit to the World of Spirit flies,
Not useless long, the sever'd Body lies.—
Turn'd & o'er turn'd—mix'd in the common Mass,

Its Flowers shall grow or freshen into Grass,   5
The painted Beds & yellow Meads adorn,
Delight the Eye, & chear the op'ning Morn.—
    So from Corruption, Natures seeming Waste
New Charms shall rise, each yielding to the last,
'Till after num'rous different Changes past,   10
A Change to fix it evermore the same,
Comes rolling onwards in a Flood of Flame;
'Till melted Mountains, level with their Plains,
One mighty Mass of liquid Fire remains.
Each scatter'd Atom, shall no longer roam   15
But ev'ry Part fly to its proper Home,
'Till all refin'd & pass'd the searching Flame
Is fix'd & incorruptibly the same.
—If Souls must seek their kindred Clay again,
They thus refin'd, may rise immortal Men.—   20

Finis

21 To a Friend.—On some Misunderstanding by the same

When desp'rate Ills to such a Crisis rise,
As the Physicians utmost Art despise
Both likely & unlikely Means he tries.—
If after all his painful Labours past
He chance to find the happy Cure at last,   5
He sets it down the Sov'reign of his Skill
A future Med'cine for a future Ill.—
—Thy strange unkindness carried much too high
Has made me fondly every Method try,
To work a Cure, & every Dress essay—   10
The haughty—suppliant—serious & the gay
But as I fondly every Method try'd,
It mock'd my Hopes, & unsuccessful dy'd;

Uneasy still, another way I've chose
To be a Jest in Rhyme as well as Prose.   15
For if Resentment, Friendship must outlive
And injur'd Love forbids thee to forgive,
Be angry, be censorious, be severe,
Who feels the worst, has nothing more to fear.
But, if, as much I hope, yet scarce believe   20
This artless Verse may all my Fears deceive,
Thee—happy Muse!—I almost shall adore
Thee—but harmonious Folly heretofore,
But never now, harmonious Folly more!
Should every painful Ill of Life increase   25
I'd choose thy Charms to sooth'em all to Peace.
Think what was human Nature in its Bloom,
E'er Adam fell, or Death became his Doom.
Weak was his Reason, & his Will was strong,
Short were his Views of that eternal Wrong.   30
He fell not unappriz'd, his Fate he knew,
Yet on his Race, their long Destruction drew.—
     Where the collected Weakness finds a Place
Of that first Father of our helpless Race,
Whence must Perfection & fore knowledge rise   35
Which are requir'd, to be exactly wise;
For a Defect in every Thing beside
By a Defect in Knowledge is imply'd,
And this Defect can never be deny'd.—
We cannot love or censure as we ought,   40
Unless we had a more extensive Thought,
Of ev'ry Cause, the real Merit knew
Can say that this is false, & this is true.
Whoever human Nature better drest
Has never been impartial to his Breast   45
There num'rous Passions, num'rous Folly's reign,
A constant, long & solitary Train.
Our present Thoughts judge those already gone
And those to come will push the Contest on,
Still judging, still condemning, still the same   50
Still blaming, still creating Work for Blame.—

22   On Friendship. by the same

While I, too daring, such a Subject chuse,
As might demand an Angel for a Muse,
(For I these elevated Tasks pursue,
To write of Friendship & to write to you)
Do thou, oh! sov'reign Flame, each Thought controul,   5
And fill the vast Recesses of my Soul!
Thou can be sung, by no inferior Pow'r
As Music only Music can explore.—
      When the Creator did his Law unfold
By his distinguish'd Delegate[17] of old,   10
"I am"—he said, but what he was remain'd
Behind the Viel—not then to be explain'd;
But when this hallow'd Earth, Messiah trod
And Men beheld, the Actions of a God,
He condescended further to explain,   15
The Mystick Wonders of his peaceful Reign,—
Mankind, he with a clearer Prospect blest
And what he was the Deity exprest;
When his enlighten'd Servant from above
Inspir'd—declar'd that God himself was Love.—   20
—What Angels are, no Mortal can explore,
They mock the utmost Search of our enquiring Pow'r.
That they're possess'd of an unfading Bloom,
In human Form, our active Thoughts presume
There's the benevolent, the perfect Friend,   25
Thus far our weak Ideas comprehend,
But what's their Conversation, how convey'd
Thro' the bright Choirs which ask no Organs' aid,
Our Reason's Dumb, & our Enquiry vain
For Things of which we no Ideas gain   30
No human Understanding can attain,
But this we know—of the refin'd above,
Their most exalted Attribute is Love.—
      The Soul a Being—whether increate

17. **distinguish'd Delegate**: Refers to Moses; see Exodus 3:4.

(So justly worthy its eternal State)   35
A Part of him in whom we live & move,
Bright Essence of, Immensity of Love!
Which tho', a Time, its fetter'd in a Chain,
Shall be united to its Source again,
Or if it is created—'tis so fine   40
So free from Parts, so glorious, so divine;
Bears such exact Impressions of a God,
And form'd a Temple for his bright abode,
(That loving it, I part of God, adore
Or honour him in his creating Pow'r;)   45
Tho' its Original from Heaven it prove,
The highest Pitch it can attain to's Love,
And more we of this best of Passions know,
The more of Heaven's reveal'd to Men below.
    As Souls no Sexes have, I claim a Right   50
To love my Friend with that refin'd Delight
With all that Warmth, with all that pleasing Fire
A most harmonious Being can inspire.—
    What's Life, unless a Friend the Measure fill?
Tasteless its Good—unsufferable its Ill,   55
A Night of Shades, a ling'ring slow Disease,
A Course of Sorrows o'er unfaithful Seas,
But if a Friend, we're suffer'd to possess,
It colours all our Days with Happiness;
Improves the Relish of neglected Joys.   60
And ev'ry potent Ill of Life destroys;
Inspires—enlivens, now, e'en now, confest
The vast Idea fills my labouring Breast.
Be still, ye murmuring Thoughts! that dare complain
Forever dumb—there's no such Thing as Pain,   65
I'll lead you where eternal Pleasures reign!—
    To the still Grove where opening Buds declare
The genial Spring, in all its Beauty near;
Where Silence reigns, not in e'en the breathing Wind
Or creeping Streams—the close Retirement find.   70
    There thou, my Soul, thy secret self regard,
Thy Origin—thy Actions—thy Reward!
In an Existance, which shall never end,

All doubled in a kind & faithful Friend
This one good Thing, O! may I long possess!   75
In Lieu of all the World calls Happiness;
But if my Friends too dang'rous Blessings prove,
And I grow giddy with excess of Love,
Or if they change,—which too, too much I fear,
For Frailty is to human Nature, near,   80
How shall I stand a Tryal so severe?
When of my Friends, or of their Love, depriv'd,
I'll all resign—for long enough I've liv'd.
      But why this strange Emotion in my Breast
Why all this Passion, all this Care exprest?   85
For Things of which I may be dispossest.
'Twas Natures mighty Author gave the Soul
Desires beyond what Reason can controul,
Something with their full Bent, they must pursue
And while we keep created Good in View;   90
While from Lights great Original, we turn
Unsatisfied, our anxious Cravings mourn
But who can all Things visible despise,
And to this Source of Love & Beauty rise?
Their vitiated Sentiments refine,   95
And own no Passion but for Things divine,
In their capacious Souls shall know no void
No anxious Cravings mourn unsatisfied?
For he must all Things fill, who's infinite,
And all enlighten who created Light.   100
—The great Ideas, in such Throngs arise,
Fain would I speak, but weak Description dies.
Oh! thou supreme Director, Life & Light!
Before thee may my Ways be found upright!
What most of all I fear, Oh! grant I flee   105
Of loving the Creation, more than thee.—

Memorandum.—The foregoing poetical Pieces are copied from the
Authors original Mss—I have a Copy of the last pgs. with several
Alterations as may probably be the Case with several or all, the
others—but as I had not any of them I chose to follow the Originals

23   To the Memory of Charles Norris.[18] by the same.

When Woes unfeign'd the human Breast assail,
And Tears the first Resource of Sorrow fail,
The pensive Muse her soothing Aid extends,
To mourn thee! best of Men & best of Friends!
To mourn thee! late so blessing & so bless'd,   5
Thy Hopes all crown'd & every Wish possess'd;
Now vanish'd as a baseless Vision fled!
And thou art number'd with the silent dead;
Yet of thy Life & Worth, nor Time or Place,
Nor varying Scenes the Memory shall deface.—   10
     While Health was thine, prime Bliss beneath the Sky
Peace & Delight beam'd gently from thy Eye;
Thy placid Mien fair Image of thy Mind,
Where all was just, benevolent & Kind,
No more expressive of that heavenly Ray,   15
Is veild & shrouded from the Face of Day.
Thy Mind fair Image of those Seats above!
Serene Abodes of Harmony & Love,
Is now restor'd to its congenial Clime
Beyond the wild Viccissitudes of Time   20
Beyond the Grave, where human Sufferings cease,
And thy Remains rest in eternal Peace.—
     Your orphan children! & thou, widow'd Wife!
Balm of his Cares & Solace of his Life,
While Life was lent—our bleeding Hearts deplore,   25
The Husband & the Father now no more,
No more, with ever sympathetic Power,
To sooth the pain'd or gild the social Hour,
No more his infant Offspring to survey,
Meet their Caress & smile their Tears away;—   30

---

18. **Charles Norris**: And his widow, children, sisters, and friends. Charles Norris (1712–66) was a close friend of Susanna Wright and her brother James. Wright refers to Norris's widow, Mary Parker Norris, their four children, and his sisters, Elizabeth and Deborah Norris. The latter sister, a spinster, lived with Charles Norris as his housekeeper before and during his marriage. See Karin Wulf's introductory essay, pages 31–34, as well as her "A Marginal Independence": Unmarried Women in Colonial Philadelphia" (Ph.D. diss., Johns Hopkins University, Baltimore, 1993), chaps. 5 and 6.

One fatal Stroke dissolv'd these tender Tyes!—
But who shall say, Almighty & allwise!
Why was this Friend of Human Kind remov'd,
So amply bless'd, so honour'd, so belov'd,
When Thousands of thy Creatures, from their Birth,   35
Unbless'd, unblessing, still are found on Earth?
Presume not to enquire, or to repine,
For not our Will, Allwise! be done but thine.—
    You weeping Sisters! & each sorrowing Friend!
Who knew his Worth, & now lament his End,   40
Console your Minds, through Natures mournful Strife,
In calm reviews of that all blameless Life,
That stedfast Honour that unblemish'd Truth,
That Sanctity of Manners from his Youth,
Thro' Manhoods Prime, thro' the licentious Days   45
That Fear of God which guarded all his Ways,
Prepar'd him this tremendous Change to try,
Prepar'd—at the appointed Hour to die.—
    O Bliss! to be desir'd by all who live,
Beyond what Wealth, beyond what Things can give;   50
Nor Wealth nor Power one Terror can defeat,
Or gild the Gloom, or light the dark Retreat;
Virtue alone & all supporting Grace,
And Faith & Hope cou'd conquer in the Race,
The Prize of Immortality attain,   55
And bear him safe thro' Death to Life again.—

24   My own Birth Day.— August 4th 1761

Few & evil have the Days of the Years of my Life been.—
[Gen. 47:9]. by the same

Were few & Evil stil'd the Patriarchs Days,[19]
    Extended to a Length of Years unknown

19. **Patriarchs Days**: The ancestors of Israel, generally referring to Abraham, Isaac, Jacob, and Joseph (Gen. 12–50). "The godly race is marked by physical death, al-

In this luxurious Age whose swift Decays,
　　Allow to few so many as my own.
And what are they?—a Vision all the past,　　　　　　　5
　　A Bubble on the Waters shining Face,
What yet remain 'till the first transient Blast
　　Shall leave no more Remembrance of their Place.
　Still few & evil, as the Days of old,[20]
Are those allotted to the Race of Man,　　　　　　　　10
　　And three score Years in sounding Numbers told,
Where's the Amount?—a Shadow & a Span.—
　　Look back through this long Tide of rolling Years
Since early Reason gave Reflection Birth,
　　Recall each sad Occasion of thy Tears,　　　　　　15
Then say can Happiness be found on Earth?
　　Pass former Strokes—the recent only name!
A Brother[21] whom no healing Art could save,
　　In Life's full Prime unnerv'd his manly Frame
From wasting Pains took Refuge in the Grave.—　　　20
　　A Sister who long causeless Anguish knew,
A tender Parent & a patient Wife,
　　Calmly she bore the bitter Lot she drew,
And clos'd her Sorrows with her Close of Life.
　　A darling Child, all lovely, all admir'd,　　　　　25
Snatch'd from our Arms in Youths engaging Bloom
　　A Lazur[22] turn'd e'er his short Date expir'd,
And laid a piteous Object in the Tomb.
　　Your Memory from my Breast shall never stray
Should years to Patriarchal Age extend,　　　　　　30

---

though long-lived. The dirge 'and he died' tolls like a funeral bell throughout this chapter." Merrill F. Unger, *Unger's Bible Handbook* (Chicago: Moody Press, 1966), 46–47.

　　20. **Still few & evil . . .** : This line is at the top of a new page. When Moore turned the page, she inadvertently did not properly indent. She made a similar error again at line 33.

　　21. **A Brother**: Susanna Wright's brother James was elected to the Pennsylvania Assembly following the death of his father, who had also served in the legislature. James shared his sister's home until he died. His widow and children remained in her home. Wulf, "A Marginal Independence," 211–15.

　　22. **A Lazur**: "A poor and diseased person, usually one afflicted with a loathesome disease; esp. a leper" (*OED*).

Thro' Glooms of Night, thro' social Hours of Day
The starting Tear stands ready to descend.—
But tho' I mourn, not without Hope I mourn,[23]
    Dear kindred Shades! tho' all unknown yr. Place
Tho' to these Eyes you never must return,   35
    You're safe in the Infinitude of Space.—
One all disposing God who gave you Birth,
    That Life sustain'd which his good Pleasure gave,
Then cut you off from ev'ry Claim on Earth,
    Is the same guardian God beyond the Grave.   40
Tho' by impenetrable Darkness veil'd,
    Y[ou]r. separate State lies hid from mortal Sight,
The Saviour, Friend of Man, Messiah hail'd,
    Brought Life & Immortality to Light.
Rest then my Soul—in these Appointments rest,   45
    And down the Steep of Age pursue thy Way,
With humble Hope, & Faith unfailing blest,
    The mortal shall surpass the natal Day.

[Marginal note:]
Soft moving Language, deep Reflection strong
Compose thy pow'rful Harmony of Song. Fidelia

25   To Susa. Wright

On some Lines wrote by herself on her Birth-Day.

While Thousands mourn each pleasing Prospect past,
    And wintry Clouds obscure the vernal Clime,
By the rough Tempest or the noxious Blast,
    Fade in their Bloom or wither e'er their Prime.—
Or tiresome Length of Years with Surfeit days   5
    And feeble Age drags its attendant Train,
Damps every Relish of their former Joys,
    And wastes the expiring Lamp of Life in Pain.

23. Note that Moore forgot to indent when she turned the page.

Amidst these Cares that crow'd the human Throng,
　　Serenely glows Venera's[24] evening Ray,　　　　　　10
She wakes her Lyre to Harmony of Song,
　　And smooths the awful Passage of Decay.
So thro' the Grove the Songsters of the Night,
　　Sweet Philomel[25] attunes the echoing Plains,
While the pleas'd Traveller wrapt in soft Delight,　　　15
　　Attends the enchanting Music of her Strains.
Distinguish'd view in this superior Mind,
　　The Fire of Wit matur'd by ripening Age,
And striking Sense with soft Submission join'd.
　　Inspires Venera's animated Page.—　　　　　　　20
Thus down the Vale as feeble Nature treads,
　　Points to her Home & waits to be undrest,
Thy evening Star its gentle Influence sheds,
　　And glows serene, descending to its Rest.
Still Heaven propitious gild thy future Way,　　　　　25
　　With Hope unshaken & thy Faith secure,
Pour a full Lustre on thy setting Ray,
　　Soft be thy Passage & thy Entrance sure.—
And when unnerv'd the Hand, the Lyre unstrung,
　　And gentle Death unfolds the Athenial Plains,　　　30
Wing thy free Soul to join the enraptur'd Throng,
　　In Notes divine & high immortal Strains.—

Fidelia

26   S.W. to Fidelia. In answer to the foregoing.

Dear partial Maid, where shall I find,
　　One Spark of Fire divine,
To warm my dissipated Breast

---

24. **Venera's evening Ray**: From Latin Veneras(a) "of Venus, relating to [the goddess] Venus. . . . Charming or lovely" (*Cassell's New Latin Dictionary*, 1959). Griffitts could be referring to the planet Venus as the evening star.
25. **Sweet Philomel**: Conventional literary name for a nightingale, based on Philomela of Greek mythology (*OCCL*).

And make it glow like thine?
Where learn the soft seraphic Strains,   5
    Of thy enchanting Lay?
To charm our Cares, our Sorrows sooth,
    And steal our Souls away.
When ebbing Spirits languid flow,
    And Fancy's drooping Wing,   10
Unplum'd by Time no more can rise,
    To seek a second Spring,
The Evidence of Things not seen,
    Faiths bolder Pinions gain,
And gentle Hope unceasing smiles   15
    To soften human Pain.——
By these sustain'd the immortal Mind,
    Unconscious of Decay,
Feels all her Powers of Action strong
    Thro' Life's declining Day.   20
'Till that shall close in endless Shade,
    Each lenient Art engage
To temper Nature's rugged Cares,
    And smooth the Path of Age.
The social Hour, the enlighten'd Heart,   25
    That entertains & binds,
The endearing Intercourse of Friends,
    Bless'd with congenial Minds.
Such once—but long the Vision's past
    My Honour, Bliss & Pride!   30
Thy Mothers social Hour was mine,[26]
    As kindred Minds allied.
Such wou'd thou be, cou'd youth to Age,
    The engaging Hand extend;
Such wou'd I prize the tender Tye,   35
    And fondly call thee Friend.

S. Wright

26. **Thy Mother's social Hour**: Mary Norris Griffitts (1694–1750) was a contemporary of Wright. See Abbreviated Lloyd Genealogy, page 17.

27 On the Right Honble Willm. Pitt Esqr.[27]
by a Female.

Oh! that the Power of Eloquence was mine,
And flowing Language of the tuneful Nine,[28]
My Song shou'd emulate the Groecian Strain,
And in bold Verse parnassian[29] Heights atttain,
To sing thy Praise, who thus supports our Cause,   5
And rais'd us sinking by oppressive Laws:—
Thou Friend to Truth!—wise eloquent & just,
In thy impartial Care we fix our Trust,
Each Dupe of Faction but in vain contends,
While thou the Sons of Liberty[30] defends;   10
Inspir'd by Gratitude, these artless Lays
Wou'd fain express our Thanks & swell thy Praise;
But tho' they fail to paint thy deathless Fame,
Nations unborn shall bless thy patriot Name;
With one acclaim the Continent around,   15
Thy public Spirit gratefully resound:—
Thus may just Heaven such generous Care repay,
And grant, thee Health to chear thy future Day,
With Joys that worthy Minds alone can know,
And Virtue only on her Sons bestow,   20
Whose generous Hearts with Love of Freedom glow.—

Finis

27. **Willm. Pitt Esqr.:** William Pitt (1708–78), first earl of Chatham, was leader of the House of Commons from 1756 to 1761. During the Stamp Act crisis of 1765–66, he asserted that Parliament had no right to tax the colonies, an opinion warmly greeted in the colonies (*DNB*). See also Edmund S. Morgan and Helen M. Morgan, *The Stamp Act Crisis: Prologue to Revolution*, rev. ed. (New York: Macmillan, 1963), 334–35, 342–44.

28. **the tuneful Nine:** Nine muses are Greek deities of lyric poetry, comedy, tragedy, heroic poetry, music, dance, oratory, rhetoric, astronomy.

29. **Verse parnassian:** "Of or belonging to poetry, poetic" (*OED*).

30. **Sons of Liberty:** The Sons of Liberty were formed in a number of colonial port cities to oppose the Stamp Act. Their often violent protests against royal officials helped to bring about repeal of the Stamp Act in 1766. See Morgan and Morgan, *The Stamp Act Crisis*, 231–62.

28   A Dream[31] on September 18th 1769.

Being tired & very much worn out, & almost overcome by reason of a long & tedious Confinemt. I threw myself back upon my Bed, & fell into a Trance; & all at once I found myself in a strange Road, which was very much attended with many Evils, by Reason of its being frequented by wicked People that passed that Way.—I seemed to be in a Fright, my Flesh trembled the Hair of my Head stood upright, I heard nothing but a Voice saying, Woe be to mortal Man, for the End of all Flesh draws nigh: The Time is at hand, that is spoken of by the Angel in the Revelations which stood with one Foot on the Land & the other upon the Sea, & sware by him that liveth for ever & ever that Time should be no longer, to which another Voice said, Holy! holy! holy! just & true art thou O Lord! in all thy Ways, thou dost what is right in thyne own Eyes, for all Flesh is as Grass before thee,—Men have corrupted their Ways before the Lord,—for which Evil shall overspread the Land.—

I being in a great Surprize to think that I had got where no mortal Man was to be seen, only a Voice crying out, as I have told you: but all at once I heard nothing, my Fears abated, & my way seemed to be more pleasant to me, looking strait before me, I saw a Company of

31. **A Dream**: Written by Samuel Clarke, (Boston [1769]). See Charles Evans, *American Bibliography*, 14 vols. (Chicago: Privately printed, 1903–34). In "A Short Relation" after the "Dream," Samuel Clarke discusses the dream and the circumstances surrounding it: "Courteous Reader, my distress to you is unknown; for ever since the 18th of September last, which was my Birth Day for [illegible] Day I was 48 years of age, thirty of which I have been confined to my House, not so much as lifted my Hand to my Head, but how unworthy do I think myself to be favour'd with the least of God's mercies. O! What a poor maimed Creature am I that should make mention of the Name of the Lord (8)." He expresses sorrow for his sins: "Death is at the Door, and our Sins crying for Vengeance: How do you intend to escape? (10)" Clarke then returns to his dream: "As I was told in my Dream by that Old Man, that trouble would arise in *Old England*, which would be spread [illegible] *New*, gives me reason to think it will be so: But I don't pretend to say, but this I am bold [illegible] say, that God is about to bring great Calamaties upon the Land, and as my Distress leads me to these words, even to persuade all of those into whose Hands these lines may fall, to give themselves to God, to call upon him by earnest Prayer and Supplication" (10–11). We are grateful to Carla Gerona for assistance with this note. See Carla Gerona, "Stairways to Heaven: The Authority of Dreams in American Quaker Culture," forthcoming dissertation, Johns Hopkins University, Baltimore.

Men coming towards me, they seemed to be at a great Distance but making great haste towards me.—But beholding just by me, there sate a grave old Man, his Hair as white as Snow, with a grave Countenance, looking towards the East; with that I came up to him, & said, how do you Sir? he neither turned his Head to the right or to the left, but looked steady towards the East; with that my Fear came upon me, now I thought of my dying Hour, for which my Loins were filled with Pain,—Pangs took hold of me, as the Pangs of a Woman that travaileth, I am bowed down at the Thoughts of it, fearfulness hath affrighted me, for the Redemption of the Soul is prescious, for it endureth for ever—But taking Courage I spake to him again.—Pray Sir, tell me what is the meaning of that great Company that is coming towards us?—why, sd. he, (not turning his Head, but looking still towards the East) this great Company which you now see coming towards us is the fore runner of great Trouble that is coming upon New-England, With that I heard a Voice saying, "Watchman what of the Night! watchman what of the Night!" with that the old Man cried what of the Times? what of the Times?—then a Voice cried Midnight Midnight! Darkness is spreading itself over the Face of the whole Earth!—o! the Distress & Anguish that is coming upon New Engld. With that I cried what is the Matter?—what, sd. the old Man, are not yr. Eyes open, or cant you see?—are you without Understanding?— do but consider of God's Favours in Times past to N. England—how wonderful did God appear for the Deliverance of the Inhabitants of N. Engld.—when that vast Army & Fleet of Ships were sent by France for the Destruction of this People they arrived at Halifax[32] with hopes to make up their Fleet to destroy us, but God in a wonderful Manner, by his Providence wrought their Destruction, he destroyed their Army, & defeated their whole Fleet & sent them back, not suffering them to do us any harm, likewise since that, other Places have been destroyed by Earthquakes,[33] yet he preserved N. Engd.

---

32. **arrived at Halifax**: During the second half of 1757, the British navy concentrated portions of its fleet at Halifax to prepare for an assault on Louisburg and to prevent the French from fortifying that place. The French at first were able to stop these efforts, but ultimately failed. The British triumph over Louisburg in July 1758 was a turning point in the Seven Years' War. R. Earnest Dupuy and Trevor N. Dupuy, *The Encyclopedia of Military History*, 2d rev. ed. (New York: Harper, 1986), 706.

33. **destroyed by Earthquakes**: Earthquakes in New England in November 1755 provided fodder for debates about the state of the colonies' spiritual health. See

likewise subdued their Enemies before them.—God hath been wonderfully working out their Deliverance from Time to Time; but for all
these Things they have returned no thanks.—Pray Sir, said I, tell me
what you are looking at so steady?—why dont you see, sd. he what I
am looking at?—no Sir, I dont, well said he, I will tell you, I am looking at a blazing Star for such a strange one, was never seen before; the
blaze extending itself almost 6000 Miles, the blaze going before the
Star, hanging toward the West, which denotes great Troubles to arise
in old Engld. which shall spread themselves in New Engld. for the Inhabitants thereof, having grievously corrupted their Ways before the
Lord;—the People have cast off all Fear; no Truth, nor Justice in them,
for which the Earth mourns, & the Inhabitants thereof languish & die
out of it, such a Day scarce was ever known as is coming upon the
Earth.—By this time this great Company came up very near us, & as
I was looking upon them, they spread every Way at once,—There,
said the old Gent. don't you see how they spread every Way at
once,—well, says he, do you know the Meaning of it?—I do not said
I,—well said he, I will tell you: God will send forth his Judgements
upon the Earth, which shall spread themselves every Way at once, to
afflict the Childrn. of Men, because they have wickedly departed from
God; for which the Thunder bolts of God's Wrath hangs over their
Heads, ready to be poured out upon them, the Destruction God in-
tends to send upon the Earth, will come with Speed, even as the Star
was seen in the Evening, & since that to be seen at break of Day, &
was soon out of Sight; & as for the Company that you see, how soon
they spread themselves, so God will soon bring his judgements upon
you, in as much as the People of N. Engld have rejected the Council of
God, & foolishly departed from his Way, therefore shall a Curse go
forth which shall destroy the wicked from the Face of the Earth—I
turning myself about, by the side of a great Mountain, at which side
there was a a great Rock opened in which appeared to me a fine
Room, beautified to such a Degree, that no Eye could look upon it
without Admiration, but what surprized me most of all, there stood a
Man with his Hands & Eyes lifted up to Heaven, pleading with God
for N. Engld. his earnest Expressions would fill a Soul with Admira-

---

Jonathan Mayhew, *Practical Discourses Delivered on Occasion of the Earthquakes in
November, 1755[;] Wherin is particularly shown . . . The great Importance of Turning
our feet unto God's Testimonies* (Boston, 1760).

tion & Amazemt. crying Holy! holy! holy! Lord God, no Power is like thy Power, the Foundations of the Earth tremble at thy Voice, thy Dominion is an everlasting Dominion, & thy Days have no End.— Lord, for the sake of thy dear Son, the Lord Jesus Christ, remember thy Covenant with thy People of old, the Oath that thou swearedst to thy Servants.—Lord what is Man, that thou shouldst contend with him? O Lord spare thou the Inhabitant's of N. Engld. O! Lord let it repent thee of the Evil that thou art about to bring upon the People of N. Engld. O! New England, New Engd! hadst thou known in this thy Day the Things that belong to thy Peace, but now they are hid from thy Eyes.—with that the Rock shut up, & so I heard no more from him.—I then turned myself about not knowing what to do, or whither to go, for hearing nothing but the Destruction of my People on every Side, my Soul sunk almost within me, all that I could say, were these Words, when I am afraid I will put my Trust in the Lord; these Words I repeated very often; but at last spake the old Man,— Friend, said he, it is almost Day, I must be going; but before I depart, I must tell you, that you must return from whence you came, & declare to all yr. Friends, & Neighbours round about you, what you have seen & heard, & exhort all People, to a speedy preparation: let all, both young & old, bond & free, rich & poor, make their Request to God, for such a Time is coming that N. Engld. never saw, the Vials of Gods Wrath which are spoken of in the Revelations, will be poured out very soon upon the Earth, such sore Judgemts. & Calamities N. Engld. never saw before.—With that such bitter Lamentation was heard around me that wd. almost melt the Heart of a Stone; such lamentation & bitter cries, put me beyond myself: I stood amazed but I heard a Voice crying, how long, O Lord! how long shall thy Anger burn against thy People? how long shall these things be so?—I awoke & it was a Dream.—

29   Verses to the Memory of Rebecca Chapman.[34]—

From close Reflection on the human State
Its fears, disquiets & precarious Date,

34. **Rebecca Chapman**: The only Rebecca Chapman listed among Quakers in the early Delaware region was Rebecca Burr Chapman, reported married to James Chap-

This, only this, the sole Result appears
'Tis a rough Progress thro' a Vale of Tears
Where crowding Ills so thick o'er cast the Scene   5
Our languid Joys unheeded intervene
For lawless Passions Reason's voice suppress
And rule destructive of our Happiness.—
     Hence 'tis we mourn, hence Sorrow unreprov'd
For Pleasures past, or Intimates remov'd,   10
Else why (near Instance) why should I deplore
Your Loss o! Friend, when others weep no more?
Is't mean self love that with contracted View
Only laments her perish'd Joys in you?
Or Nature's weakness? or the dying Claim   15
Of sacred Friendships venerable Name?
     O Heav'n-born Virtue thee, 'tis thee sincere
Now sadly pours the tributary Tear
And wakes my Strains, which take departed Shade
As the last Proof of friendship undecay'd   20
Which strives to paint yr. Worth, long learn'd to prove
In near Relations & in distant tyes.—
Whether in private or in social Life
Whether as Parent, Sister, friend, or Wife,
In all which Duties (judg'd by strictest Laws)   25
You've well deserv'd & merited applause,
     But cease, O Muse, thy empty Lays controul
Far other Objects please her ravish'd Soul
Which now triumphant over Death & Pain
Inhabits Realms where only Pleasures reign,   30
Sharing the immortal Exstacies bestow'd
By the mild presence of a gracious God
And contemplates the Bliss of endless Day
Where Saints & Angels adoration pay
Midst whom she strives her bashful Voice to raise   35
In grateful Anthems to her Makers praise,
     When such her State, ev'n you who mourn her most,
(You who've a Parent, Wife & Sister lost)
Cease to complain, be every Sorrow o'er

man of the Burlington Meeting in 1771. Later that year she received a certificate to Richland Meeting in Pennsylvania (*DQB*).

Submit to Fate & learn to weep no more,   40
Reflecting thus, (whence Comfort must arise)
Heav'ns Dispensations are all just & wise
And the same Pow'r, who took this Blessing hence
For one recall'd, can many more dispence.—

Eugenio[35]

30 The grateful Receiver.[36]—July 30th. 1751—

To you (whose Motive was a noble End
The fatherless & friendless to defend,
That with a manly Courage stood for those,
Whose Friends were few, & numerous their Foes,
Sincere, impartial, not by Interest Sway'd,   5
No Gains you sought for, nor by Frowns dismay'd,
'Twas noble Pity touch'd yr. generous Breast
To aid the Orphan, succour the distrest,
And right the injur'd, far as in yr. Pow'r
Nor Heav'n requires—nor do we ask for more   10
Your manly Mind cou'd feel the Orphan's Grief.
And sought by ev'ry means to give Relief
Did (at our Call) yr. kind Assistance lend
Acted the Parent, & profess'd the Friend,
With prudent Courage soft Compassion join'd   15
(When both are blended, what a noble Mind)
And kindly undertook to plead the Cause
Of her that friendless, & that helpless was,
And now I offer what is justly due
My hearty Thanks & Gratitude to you   20

35. **Eugenio**: A literary pseudonym for a person whom the editors have not been able to positively identify.

36. **The greatful Receiver**: Content and date suggest that this poem was written for Isaac Norris, who welcomed Hannah Griffitts and her sister into his home after the death of their parents and their necessary removal from the home of their brother Isaac Griffitts. See Wulf, "A Marginal Independence," chap. 7, pp. 290–97.

For what you've done—& oh! may Heavn's Regard
That best of all Returns be your Reward,
If ever yours in such a State are laid,
Either to want or seek the Creatures aid,
If this shou'd be their Case, then may they find   25
A Friend as cordial, constant & as kind,
As we have found in you—but gracious Heav'n!
Forbid, that such a Lot, to them be giv'n.
When rolling years (as swift they haste away)
Brings on that last, & great decisive Day,   30
If in yr. Sphere, you've done the best you can
Perform'd yr. Duty both to God & Man
Nor all your Good in narrow Circles bind
That narrow Circle, a contracted Mind,
But at the Call of Grief assistance lend   35
The Orphans Parent & the Widow's Friend,
With feeling Care & soft Humanity
Have dry'd the falling Tear from Virtue's Eye
Have felt the Sorrow of the Soul distrest
And calm'd the Anguish of th' afflicted Breast   40
How fair yr. Lot—to Angels & to Men,
Earth shall approve, & Heaven will own you then
And 'till arrives this last distinguish'd Day
Accept from us, the grateful Thanks we pay
Which tho' a poor Return, its quite sincere   45
Wait to receive yr. greater Plaudit—There.—

Fidelia

31 To the Memory of Sarah Griffitts[37] who departed this Life July the 19th. 1764.—by the same.

From those sweet Shores, where human Suff'rings cease
Souls wake to Life,—& all to come is Peace,

37. **Sarah Griffitts:** Sarah Fitzwater Griffitts was the widow of Hannah Griffitts'
brother Isaac (d. 1755). Isaac disgraced the family through his public misbehavior. He

To Nature's Voice of mortal Love attend
My dear lost Sister & my constant Friend,
Accept the funeral Sigh,—the tender Tear   5
And grateful Tribute of a Heart sincere,
Our friendship claim'd, thy Mem'ry does demand
This fond Distinction from a Sisters Hand,
Whose Souls were once united as allied
Not Storms could break, nor shall the Grave divide   10
But as in Life thou did affection claim
In death, thy memory sacred shall remain.—
　　Thou late the Object of my warm Regard[38]

A like to each, the rugged Path below
Perplex'd with Thorns, & sabled deep in Woe,   15
(While wintry Clouds eclips'd our Summer Sun)
Our darlings lost, & our beloveds gone,
Thy fair Example—(midst Afflictions Night)
Pour'd its mild lustre with benignant Light,
In Affluence, humble, moderate, genrous kind   20
In adverse Waves, still patient & resign'd,—
Hail happy Soul, this stormy Scene is o'er
And the fierce Conflict shall be known no more,
No more the Voice of Langour shall complain
Nor fainting Nature sigh the Bed of Pain,   25
From Flesh releas'd, from all its Dangers free
My Friend exults in Immortality
Here thou shalt meet (in full celestial Bloom,)
Thy smiling Cherubs in their heav'nly Home,
Whom tyes of Nature once distinguish'd thine   30
And Life eternal shall again rejoin,
To thy fond Arms, thy angel Flock restore
Secure from Time, or Death's tyrannic Pow'r,

---

drank and may have abused his office of Philadelphia sheriff. He died with little or no money, and his widow renounced her claims to execute the estate, leaving that task to an uncle, William Griffitts. See Wulf, "A Marginal Independence," 243 and 290–93; and "Administration of the Estate of Isaac Griffitts," Book A 1755 #31, Philadelphia Department of Wills.

38. The space below may indicate that a line of poetry is missing from the hand-written manuscript.

Thus reunited—in this sweet abode,
Enjoy thy Darlings in your Father God.— 35
    And you who now with fond Affection mourn
And weep in her a Friend & Parent gone,
For such yr. Love & her maternal Care
Glow'd with Distinction & united near
Forbear to weep nor let us dare to shed, 40
Our human Passions o'er the happy dead,
Or can we wish our Friend shou'd still sustain
The stormy Passage & the Bed of Pain.
Still faint & feeble groan a Child of Earth,
And meet again the awful stroke of Death, 45
No—be our Love more perfect & refin'd
And join the Joy of her unbodied Mind
Hail the dear Victor on th' Immortal Shore,
Where Grief afflicts, nor Pain distresses more.
Then let her bright Example be our Care, 50
And as we lov'd the Friend—now follow her
Whose gentle Virtues shall survive the Tomb
And round her Memory shed a sweet Perfume.

Fidelia

32 On the Death of a Child. by the same.

(H. Harrison,[39] who died 19th of August 1764)

Hail happy Soul, the destin'd journeys run,
Thy Task compleated, & the Prize is won,
Thy Race is finish'd, & the Tribute made

---

39. **H. Harrison**: Hannah Harrison, daughter of Thomas and Francis Scull Harrison, granddaughter of Richard and Hannah Norris Harrison, was interred in the Friends Burial Ground in August 1764. She was twelve years old. The permit for her burial described her as "Hannah Harrison gr dau of Hannah," reinforcing her connection to the Norris family, and to Hannah Griffitts whose poem memorialized the

The Bond is cancell'd, & thy Debt is paid,
Thy Debt is paid to Nature & the Tomb,   5
And thou art safe at thy immortal Home
No more, thy gentle Spirit shall complain
The fierce Attacks of sharp conflicting Pain,
Whose Pain was Nature, & to Flesh confin'd
Nor knew the trembling Anguish of the Mind,   10
No guilty Pangs, its chilling Horrors spread,
Nor for that Guilt the conscious Tear was shed,
No Fears, or Doubts, to cloud th'etherial Road
And vail the Vision of her Father, God—
Safe, in his Arms, her spotless Spirit lay,   15
While Death advancing, seiz'd its destin'd Prey.
'Twas Peace within, sweet Innocence & calm,
And Nature only suffer'd in the Storm,
Secure in God, her Father & her Friend,
No further, could his boasted Power extend.   20
Without one Fear, she yielded up her Breath
And guiltless met the awful Stroke of Death,
Heaven spoke the little Captive her Release,
And clos'd a Life of Innocence & Peace.
Joyful she wing'd, to gain her native Home.   25
And left her Body for a spotless Tomb.
Can cruel Nature, thus itself prefer
Forbid such Happiness, & weep for her,
For her, superior (by this heavn'ly Birth)
To all the little royal Sons of Earth,   30
Secure from ev'ry Snare, & ev'ry Blast
The Struggle of her final Conflict past
With angel Guides, she wings th'immortal Road.
And shares the fulness of her Father God—
Exults in Freedom—joins the seraphs Throng   35
Unites in Praise—& learns the Cherubs Song.

---

dead child. See Charles Pemrose Keith, *The Norris Family* (Trenton: William Sharp, 1882), 6; Permits for interment in Friends' Burial Ground, Genealogical Society of Pennsylvania (GSP), Philadelphia, copied from original papers from the Arch Street Meeting House.

Then hail her Victor, to her native Home
Nor let yr. Tears defile her spotless Tomb.—

Fidelia

33   An Ode on Christmas Day 1765. by the same

For unto you is born this Day in the City of David a Saviour, which is Christ the Lord.— [Luke 2:11]. —

While others dedicate this Day
    To sensual Joy or frantic Mirth;
Let us awake the angelic Lay
    Sacred to our Emanuel's Birth.——
Hark! how the evangelic Seer   5
    Pierces the awful Rolls of Heaven
And wide th' enraptur'd Sounds declare
    To Man! lost Man! "A Son is given."
A Son, a Saviour! born to save,
    To heal from Sins polluting stain,   10
A conq'ring Victor o'er the Grave,
    And strong to break our captive chain.
Messiah! shall this Work perform,
    O'er Nature's deep aegyptian Night,
He bids the illustrious Day to dawn,   15
    Rich with the Beams of gospel Light
And when the Soul is humbled down
    By conscious Guilt (oppressive Load)
He wings the Eye of Faith to own
    The full Sufficiency of God.—   20
The sweet reviving Truth they see,
    For all the Race of Sinners lost—
And in this Rich Sufficiency,
    Fix deep their Trust & make their Boast.
The followers of the Lamb shall know,   25

The strength of his almighty Pow'r,
Arm'd as their Lord shall conqering go,
    And stand in fierce Temptations Hour.
In vain the Rage of Death & Hell,
    Against his ransom'd Church shall rise   30
Faith shall each fiery Dart repell
    And onward press to gain the Prize.
Alike all impotent & vain!
    Shall the proud Reasoners Doubt appear
While firm unshaken they sustain,   35
    The trembling Sceptics impious Sneer.
Not all the unbelieving Race,
    Arm'd with their Masters subtil Art
Shall quench the Power of sov'reign Grace,
    Messiah's gospel does impart   40
Nor Floods nor Storms, howe'er they prove,
    Nor Persecutions torturing Sword,
Nor Heights, nor Depths shall e'er remove,
    The true born Christian from his Lord.—
That these eternal Truths are seal'd,   45
    And past the Rolls of Time remain,
Come ye whose guilty Souls are heal'd
    Thro' Faith in our Emanuel slain
Stand forth confest in fullest View,
    And let the Infidel disown   50
The glorious Change enwrought in You
    By yr. victorious Lord alone.
A Change! which gives a feeble Worm,
    The Strength of an almighty Power
Triumphs in rough Afflictions Storm,   55
    And joys in Dissolution's Hour.
Thus thro' each Scene of Trial here,
    The Rock of God shall firm abide,
His gospel Light the Way shall clear,
    And his Salvation safely guide.   60
Even in the fainting Hour of Death,
    Fix'd on Omnipotence divine,
Distinguish'd from the Sons of Earth,

Shall these redeem'd of Zion shine.
    The Promise (now) the Prophet clears,   65
        Tho Nature drops amidst the Gloom,
The immortal Dawn of Heaven appears,
        And Glory gilds the wintry Tomb.
As, like their suff'ring Lord below,
        Patient the Conflict they sustain,   70
Like him shall these the Victory known,
        With him in Life eternal reign.
Oh! for this Gift with Blessings crown'd,
        Let Man his grateful Honours raise
Wide thro' Messiahs Courts resound   75
        The accepted Sacrifice of Praise.—

Fidelia

34   Part of the third Chapt. of Habbakuk[40] paraphrased by the same.

What tho' the Fig Tree blossom not, or shoot
    Her spreading Branches to the western Gale,
Tho' the rich Olive shall refuse her Fruit,
    And all the Labour of the vintage fail.
And tho' pale Famine dries the barren Field,   5
    Nor the kind Soil its former Blessings spare,
And Stalls no more the useful Herd shall yield,
    Nor sickly Folds produce their fleecy Care.
Yet in the Lord Jehovah will I trust,
    And in the God of my Salvation Joy,
He will support the pious & the Just,   10
    Tho' Famine rages, & the Sword destroy.—

---

40. **third Chapt. of Habbakuk**: Hab. 3:17–18 is Griffitts' paraphrase of the concluding prayer of Habakkuk. For another version of this same passage, see *MMMB* 76.

35   To the Memory of Eleanor Evans.[41]
by the same. 1765.

If the rich graces of a pious Mind,	
Enlarg'd, illuminated & refin'd,	
An humble walking through Life's narrow Road,	
A Soul devoted & resign'd to God,	
Distinguish'd Virtues of the Christian Name	5
And Life's Improvement, Love & Honour claim,	
Thy fair Example justly may demand	
The fond Memorial from the friendly Hand,	
And tho' thy humble Spirit wou'd disown	
The inscriptive Pride & monumental Stone,	10
In deeper Characters thy Name shall live	
Than sculptur'd Lines, or empty Titles give,	
The kindred Soul thy Virtue shall display,	
And point their Lecture to a future Day;	
Here lodg'd a Soul whose rich illumin'd View	15
The Centre gain'd & from the fulness drew,	
Where deep retir'd her active Soul could rise	
On Angel Pinions to her native Skies,	
And oft the humble Scholar wou'd resort	
To learn the Statutes of her Father's Court;	20
Returning Seasons tread the immortal Road,	
And paid the noblest Worship to her God.—	
The inward Temple of the human Breast	
Taught her the mystic Language of the blest,	
While Contemplation's deep exploring Eye	25
Reveal'd the Dawn of Immortality,	
Drew back the Veil & to her raptur'd Sight	

41. **Eleanor Evans**: Eleanor Ellis Evans (1685–1765) was born in Wales and immigrated to Pennsylvania with her parents. She married Quaker preacher John Evans. She was granted a certificate to Philadelphia Monthly Meeting in 1761, which may have been when she became acquainted with Griffitts. An "Ellen Evans" of Gwynedd Meeting, referred to as both "young" and "a worthy elder," corresponded with Samuel Fothergill and his wife (See John W. Jordan, *Colonial Families of Philadelphia* [New York: Lewis Publishing, 1911], 1468); William Wade Hinshaw, Encyclopedia of American Quaker Genealogy, vol. 2 (reprint, Baltimore Genealogy Publishing Company, 1969); *Friends' Library* 9:181; *The Friend* 15 [1840]: 399).

Gave a rich Glimpse of uncreated Light,
Unroll'd the Splendors of the World unknown,
And bid her claim the Glory as her own;   30
Thus while her Faith was fix'd on Things above,
Her Food was Knowledge, her Devotion Love,
Th'enlighten'd Soul in this divine Abode,
Pertook with Angels & convers'd with God;
To this illumin'd favour'd Soul conjoin'd   35
A solid judgement & entensive Mind,
Who nobly wore the fair attractive Grace,
A gen'rous Love to all the human Race;
Tho narrow Modes by partial Forms allied
Might kindred Souls in differing Names divide,   40
Where'er she saw the living Lustre glow,
She own'd her Union, for she knew no Foe,
Nor dar'd presumptive fathom Things divine
By the mean Measure of the Bigots Line,
More nobly wide her Soul extensive glow'd   45
Mankind her Brethren & her Father God.
Zealous the Christian Union to maintain
In the full Life & Lustre of its Name.
Within the Church she kept her proper Sphere.
And shone an honour'd useful Member there;   50
Tho' warm, her ardent Zeal wou'd oft aspire
A Christian Prudence curb'd the active Fire,
And humble Love & Charity sincere
Still bid the Flame its mildest Lustre wear;
Sedate in Judgement, in Affection warm,   55
A Friend to Order, not a Slave to Form;
Thus in the Church His firm fix'd Pillar stood
A bright Example and alive to God
Next to the fervour of Religion's Flame
She lov'd the warmth of Friendships tender Name,   60
In those soft Bonds of mutual Union ty'd
Not Time cou'd break nor distant Lands divide
No jealous Doubt remov'd the watchful-Care,
She lov'd her Friend & cou'd that Friend prefer,
With steady Faith the fond Engagement held,   65
She own'd it sacred & as such fulfill'd,

'Till years revolving her declining Day
Drew the long Shadow of the evening Ray,
Secure in Peace she view'd her setting Sun
Calm & serene, the Task of Life was done,   70
And with the Freedom of a guiltless Mind,
Firm in the Faith her Soul to God resign'd;
Heaven smil'd propitious on her latest Hour,
Disarm'd the Tyrant of his boasted Power,
In gentle Whispers of a soft Release.   75
Wing'd the freed Spirit to eternal Peace.
        Accept, dear Shade (tho' now enwrap'd above)
This Tribute of my Honour & my Love,
Who late in Life (howe'er unworthy) shar'd
Thy tender Friendship & thy warm Regard,   80
Who did our Sorrows as our Joys partake
And lov'd the Offspring for the Parents sake,
That darling Friend whose Loss I must deplore
Whilst a sad Tenant on the Mortal Shore,
Now in the fullest Bliss the Bond rejoin,   85
And be yr. Friendship perfect & divine
And while secure in this divine Abode,
You share the fulness of yr. Father God.
Thy Name shall live in full immortal Bloom,
A Victor over Nature and the Tomb.—   90

36   Wrote on the Death of Willm. Morris Junr.[42] Apl. 1766.—by the same

The Muse whose Tears for her own Grief can flow,
Friendship expands——to weep more distant Woe,
So form'd to Scenes afflictive all my Soul,
Swells the wide Wish, & Sorrows for the whole,
Oh! then can I unmov'd, behold this Stroke,   5

42. **Willm. Morris Junr.**: William Morris (1735–66), a Quaker merchant, was the husband of Milcah Moore's sister, Margaret Hill Morris (Jordan, *Colonial Families*, 77).

Which ev'ry smiling human Prospect broke,
Snatch'd from each fond Attachment here below,
And clos'd each flatt'ring Scene in funeral Woe,
So early taken in full Strength of Life
From the fond Parents, & the tender Wife.   10
From infant Tyes (that Cares with Comforts blend)
The sad Relative & the sorrowing Friend,
From all which Health, & Peace & Affluence give
Delusive smile, & make us wish to live,
From each, from all th'insatiate Hand of Death   15
Has veil'd in Darkness, & cut off from Earth,
Clos'd ev'ry Claim, dissolv'd each tender Tye,
Fond Nature's glow & Friendship's social Joy,
Oh! piercing Blow, to you who near allied
Saw yr. hopes fail, when the lov'd Object died.   20
(And when no more th'exerted Pow'r could save)
Resign'd with him yr. Prospects to the Grave,
I feel yr. Grief—& sympathetic share,
The Parents Anguish, & the Widow's Tear,
Who bend beneath the deep retir'd Distress,   25
Which Friendships cannot heal, nor Words express.
Was it for this you rear'd the infant Flow'r,
To breathe, to bloom, & wither in an Hour?
For this, did Hope on all yr. Labour smile,
Soothe ev'ry Pain, & soften ev'ry Toil,   30
For this, the fond unceasing Care bestow'd,
The Prospect gladen'd, & the Wishes glow'd,
To see yr. Charge resign his vernal Bloom,
And perish mid'st the Winter of the Tomb
May gracious Heaven who mark'd this Lot of Pain   35
Comfort the weeping Mourners, & sustain
Direct thro' all the deep afflictive Rod,
And wean'd from Creatures find their Rest in God.
Oh! Death, what Trophies, point thy conq'ring Arms,
O'er Nature's boasted Strength, & proudest Charms,   40
Thou strikes the fondest Grasp, the firmest Trust
And shakes our weak Foundation to the Dust,
Not the warm Sunshine of a prosp'rous State,
The Hope expanded & the Heart elate,

Can sooth thy Frown, or bribe thy hostile Pow'r   45
To spare the humble Pittance of an Hour,—
—And you, th' associates of his warm Regard,
Who oft, with him, the social Moments shar'd,
Now join your mutual Grief & sorrowing mourn
Th'obliging Friend & dear Relative gone,   50
View deep the Change, the active & the young
His Strength but Weakness, & his Nerves unstrung,
No longer trust to Times precarious Hand,
Nor build thy Hopes, upon the washing Sand,
The Task of Life is to prepare to dye   55
The Prize awarded—Immortality,
Then tread with cautious Steps the treach'rous Shore,
And strive to make thy future Heaven secure.
And tho' the humb'ling Lot of Death be thine
Thy bright Reversion shall eternal shine.—   60

37   The Disappointment. 1766. by the same.

Once on a memorable Day
As certain wise Historians say,
To view the Ridge on Schylkills [43] side,
Four Maidens join'd to take a Ride,
Two trusty Knights were to escort.   5
The Ladies from Millenium's Court,
While Footmen spruce brought up the Rear
To cut a Dash—in Livery Air,
(From Yorkshire one deriv'd his Grace
And Afric tawn'd the others Face)   10
The Nags with nicest Care were drest,
For Days—at one continued Feast,
At morn, at Noon, at Eve review'd.
To see, that well their Strength renew'd

43. the Ridge on Schylkills: The river forms the western boundary, and the Delaware River the eastern boundary, of Philadelphia's Center City. During the eighteenth-century, urban settlement did not yet reach the banks of the Schuylkill River.

And in Return for Care bestow'd   15
To trip the Ladies thro' the Road;
Thus, ready did the Nymphs appear
With tip-toe steps, & Will sincere,
The pleasing Jaunt, by one & more,
Was chatter'd often o'er & o'er,   20
The wish'd for Day, was fix'd at Even
To mount & take their Flight at Seven,
But oh! between the Cup & Lip,[44]
Reader behold, the mortal slip,
True, seven revolved round again   25
But clad in bursting Floods of Rain,
From sight, the chearful Sun withdrew,
Which darken'd all the Ladies View,
Day, after Day, the Torrent run,
And seem'd each Morn, as just begun   30
Too heavy, was this grevious Part,
To bear with philosophic Art,
(While Disappointment wou'd not leave her)
One got a Chill, & then a Fever,
The other found her Brain so thick   35
She deem'd it favour to be sick,
Another gentle Damsel, yet,
Wou'd (mildly) scold, or softly fret,
And loaded, with this Sorrow, double,
Thought she had ev'ry other Trouble,   40
The fourth, beneath the Stoic's Mien,
Disguis'd the disappointing Scene,
And as she could not jaunt away,
Wisely suppos'd it best to stay,
While sinking, thus, beneath their Cares   45
A sympathetic Friend of theirs,
To give the Mourners some Relief
And mitigate at least, the Grief,
This moral Recipe prescribing

---

44. **Cup & Lip**: "On the point of achievement," from the proverb: "There is many a slip 'twixt the cup and lip." Albert M. Hyamson, *A Dictionary of English Phrases* (London: Routledge, 1922).

For such Perplexities in riding,   50
   "Know all our Joy beneath the Skies
   "In flattering Expectation lies,
   "And Scenes of disappointing Woe
   "Are but a native Plant below
   "Let Trifles, then, ne'er break yr. Ease   55
   "Nor sigh, for little Strokes like these."

Fidelia

38   The female Patriots.[45] Address'd to the Daughters of Liberty in America. by the same 1768.—

Since the Men from a Party, or fear of a Frown,
Are kept by a Sugar-Plumb, quietly down.
Supinely asleep, & depriv'd of their Sight
Are strip'd of their Freedom, & rob'd of their Right.
If the Sons (so degenerate) the Blessing despise,   5
Let the Daughters of Liberty, nobly arise,
And tho' we've no Voice, but a negative here.
The use of the *Taxables, let us forebear,
(Then Merchants import till yr. Stores are all full
May the Buyers be few & yr. Traffick be dull.)   10
Stand firmly resolved & bid Grenville to see
That rather than Freedom, we'll part with our Tea
And well as we love the dear Draught when a dry,
As American Patriots,—our Taste we deny,
Sylvania's, gay Meadows, can richly afford,   15
To pamper our Fancy, or furnish our Board,

45. **The female Patriots**: This poem refers to American protest against a number of different British measures including George Grenville's tax on imported sugar products (1764), and Charles Townshend's tax on tea, paints, paper and glass (1767), which Moore transcribes in her note. Americans signed nonimportation agreements and championed domestic products, such as the "homespun" fabric Griffitts mentioned. For an overview of British colonial policies and American dissent, see R. C. Simmons, *The American Colonies: From Settlement to Independence* (New York: Norton, 1976), 294–332.

And Paper sufficient (at home) still we have,
To assure the Wise-acre, we will not sign Slave.
When this Homespun shall fail, to remonstrate our Grief
We can speak with the Tongue or scratch on a Leaf.   20
    Refuse all their Colours, tho richest of Dye,
The juice of a Berry—our Paint can supply,
To humour our Fancy—& as for our Houses,
They'll do without painting as well as our Spouses,
While to keep out the Cold of a keen winter Morn   25
We can screen the Northwest, with a well polish'd Horn,[46]
And trust me a Woman by honest Invention
Might give this State Doctor a Dose of Prevention.
Join mutual in this, & but small as it seems
We may Jostle a Grenville & puzzle his Schemes   30
But a motive more worthy our patriot Pen,
Thus acting—we point out their Duty to Men,
And should the bound Pensioners, tell us to hush
We can throw back the Satire by biding them blush.

[Marginal note:]
*Tea—Paper—Glass—& Paints.—

39 To Sophronia.[47] In answer to some Lines she directed to be wrote on my Fan. 1769.—by the same

I've neither Reserve or aversion to Man,
    (I assure you Sophronia in jingle)
But to keep my dear Liberty, long as I can,
    Is the Reason I chuse to live single,
My Sense, or the Want of it —free you may jest   5

46. **well-polish'd Horn**: "An article manufactured of horn; the side of a lantern" (*OED*), and, by analogy, perhaps a window to keep out the cold wind and let in some light.

47. **To Sophronia**: The name "Sophronia" does not seem to have a specific Greek association, but it was recognized as connoting an unmarried woman. Griffitts wrote at least one other poem "To Sophronia" on the subject of marriage ("The Maid's Husband," *Hazard's Register* 9 [January–July 1832]: 238); and an essayist in *Father Abraham's Almanack for 1772* [Philadelphia, 1771] expounded on the reasons why "the sagacious Sophronia remains unmarried."

And censure, dispise, or impeach,
But the Happiness center'd within my own Breast,
  Is luckily out of yr. reach.
The Men, (as a Friend) I prefer, I esteem,
  And love them as well as I ought   10
But to fix all my Happiness, solely in Him
  Was never my Wish or my Thought,
The cowardly Nymph, you so often reprove,
  Is not frighted by *Giants like these,
Leave me to enjoy the sweet Freedom I love   15
  And go marry—as soon as you please.

Fidelia

[Marginal note:]
*The satyrical Sneers thrown on the single Life.—

40 The Cits[48] Return from the Wilderness to the City 1770 by the same.—

Hail! once again, dear natal Seats
Ye plodding Cits, & slipp'ry Streets,
Better, a gentle fall, from you,
Than live excluded of the View,
Retir'd amidst the dismal Shades,   5
And Cows—& Chicks, & chattering Maids,
Who criticise with publick wonder,
Their undesigning Neighbour's blunder,
Blunders, in Cities, pass along,
Unnotic'd, with the blundering Throng,   10
But here, each little Slip is thrown
In public View—except their own.

48. **The Cits**: "Short for *citizen*; usually applied, more or less contemptuously, to a townsman or 'cockney' as distinguished from a countryman, or to a tradesman or shopkeeper as distinguished from a gentleman" (*OED*). This poem could reflect the Griffitts' sisters movement back and forth from Philadelphia, where they lived, to the country estate of the Norris's, Fairhill.

Ye criticising Dames adieu,
And fellow Cits—all hail to you!
The very Dust—on which you tread   15
I value—nearly with your Head,
Pardon the odd Compare, nor grumble
For should my hurrying gain a tumble,
I need not long deploring stand,
While Men are plenty, helps at hand.   20
But let us guard, midst all our blunder
To keep our brittle Heads asunder,
For should they strike, this frosty Weather,
'Twill silence all their Wit forever,
The very Smoak, yr. Chimnies lend   25
Are pleasing Prospects to yr. Friend,
But oh! the hurrying Crowds that beat
The broken Pavement of each Street,
Are Sights more fair than all the Plains
That dress the Songsters rural Strains,   30
Let them, to mount Parnassus⁴⁹ climb,
And with their Fiction swell their Rhyme,
Ye dear Realities of Life,
The happy Husband & his Wife,
The weeping Widower in his Sable   35
(Who eyes his second at the Table)
E'er for the first—his Tears are spent
If those kind drops were ever lent,—
And all the rest—who humbly wait
Their entrance to this blessed State,   40
I truly Joy, with you to meet
Tho' at the Risk of Head & Feet.

M.G.⁵⁰

49. **mount Parnassus**: "Name of a mountain in central Greece, anciently sacred to Apollo and the Muses; hence used allusively in reference to literature, especially poetry" (*OED*).

50. **M.G.** : Possibly Mary Griffitts, Hannah Griffitts's sister who lived with her. The initials placed at the end of the poem are ambiguous. This poem could be written by Mary Griffitts or to her by Hannah Griffitts.

41   The Winter Prospect. by the same.

Let Spleen & Faction, wrap in sable Gloom,
    The Face of Nature, in her wintry Sphere.
And lost to all her variegated Bloom,
    A lifeless Mass, a desart Waste appear.
The curious Frost-work, with resplendant Rays,   5
    In full Conviction prove the Charge untrue,
Creation, now in sparkling Pride displays,
    The illustrious Prospect to the amazing View.
Extensive, grand, one dazling Scene appears,
    Like Rocks of Diamond in their native Bed   10
The leafless Bough, a splendid Livery wears,
    Beneath our Feet, a glittring Carpet spread.
The glorious Orb of Day, in mildest Light
    Pours a full Lustre, twinkling o'er the Streams
Paints the gay Rain-Bow in each varying Sight,   15
    Rays meeting Rays, & mingling Beams with Beams.
Beneath the splendid Viel—the lofty Pine
    Bears its Fall Branches drest in verdant Pride
And humbler Shrubs—to swell the Prospect Join,
    In richer Tints, than Tyrian Purple[51] dyed.   20
Beyond poetic Fancy to express,
    Or mimic Art to paint the beautious Scene
While Nature, in her full illustrious Dress,
    Thus pours her Glory on the Eyes of Men.
What Praise, demands that Pow'r to whom is giv'n   25
    O'er Nature's Works, to swell this grand Display
Robe the rough Surface, like the Cape of Heav'n
    And add new Lustre to the Beams of Day.

51. **Tyrian Purple:** "In reference . . . to the purple or crimson dye anciently made at Tyre from certain molluscs" (*OED*).

42   To the Memory of Daniel Stanton,⁵² who exchanged this life for a better June the 28th. 1770. *by the same.*

Know ye [not] that there is a Prince & a great Man fallen in Isreal [2 Sam. 3:38]. —If I be not an Apostle to others yet doubtless I am to you for the Seal of my Apostleship are ye in the Lord.⁵³ [1 Cor. 9:2]

I need invoke no Fabled Muse to mourn
Or pour feign'd Sorrow o'er our Prophets Urn,
For oh! too deep my Soul partakes the Woe.
Our Zion feels on such a piercing Blow
Since in this Stroke a common Stroke is found,   5
A public Loss, as painful bleeding Wound,
For know this Day remov'd from Earths abode,
A Prince, a Priest, & Prophet to his God,
A faithful Lab'rer in his Master's Cause
A firm Asserter of Messiah's Laws   10
A steady Watchman careful to alarm
And rouse the Camp to Action & to arm,
To arm the Soul against its mortal Foe
Who well maintain'd the holy War below
Laid not his heav'nly Armour in the Dust   15
To soil its Beauty & contract a Rust,
But kept its Luster undefil'd & clean
A spotless Image of his Soul within

52. **Daniel Stanton**: Stanton (1708–70) was a Quaker minister who travelled in North America, the Caribbean, and Europe. He married Sarah Lloyd (d. 1748) in 1733. Elaine F. Crane, ed., *The Diary of Elizabeth Drinker: The Life Cycle of an Eighteenth-Century Woman* (Boston: Northeastern University Press, 1994), biographical directory. Stanton's journal and a testimony of his life were published in Philadelphia as early as 1772. Hannah Griffitts owned a copy of Stanton's memoirs in which she penned another version of this tribute.

53. **[1 Cor. 9:2]**: For conformity with the biblical text, "not" is added; in the verse from 1 Corinthians, the chapter number is changed from "19" to "9."

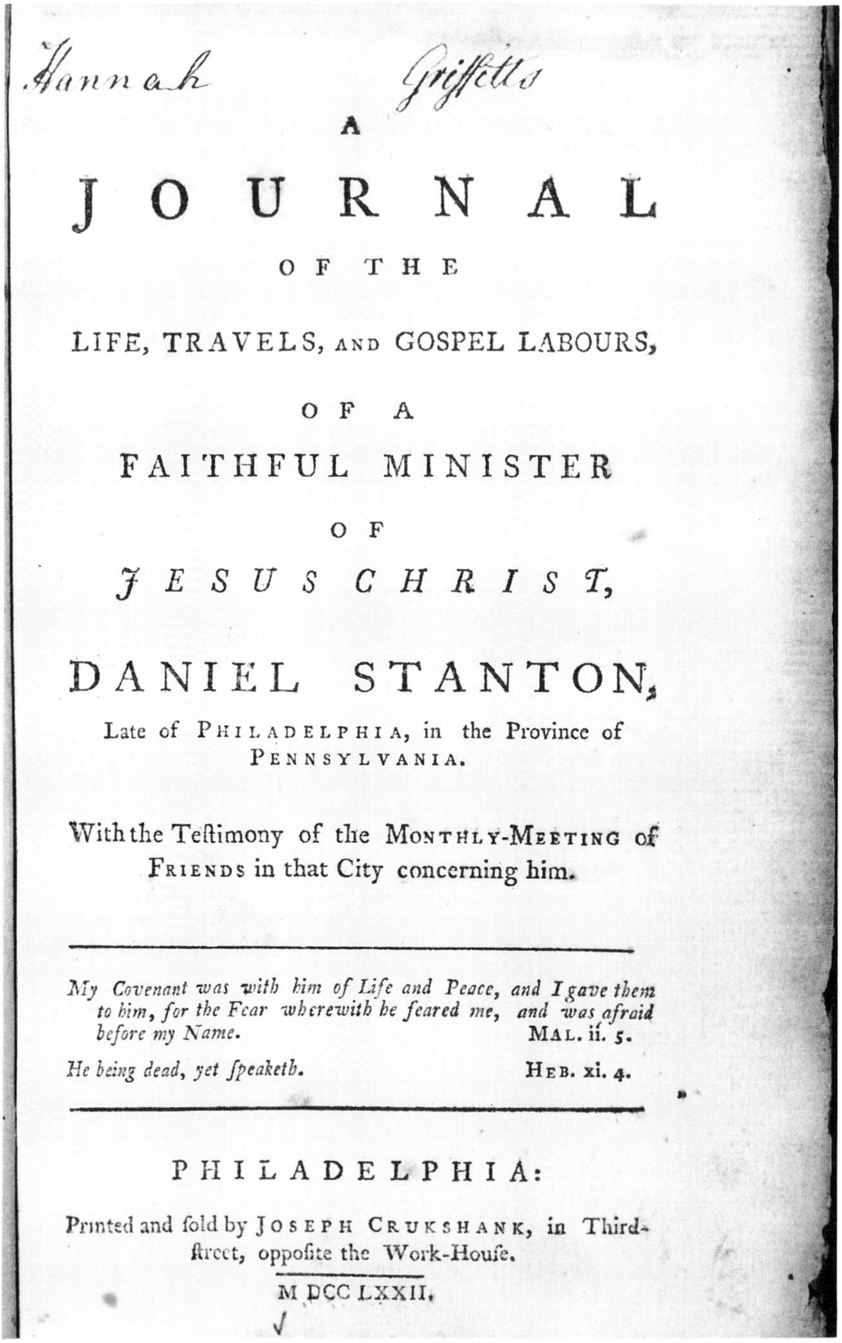

Hannah *Griffitts*

A

JOURNAL

OF THE

LIFE, TRAVELS, AND GOSPEL LABOURS,

OF A

FAITHFUL MINISTER

OF

JESUS CHRIST,

DANIEL STANTON,

Late of PHILADELPHIA, in the Province of
PENNSYLVANIA.

With the Teſtimony of the MONTHLY-MEETING of
FRIENDS in that City concerning him.

---

*My Covenant was with him of Life and Peace, and I gave them
to him, for the Fear wherewith he feared me, and was afraid
before my Name.* MAL. ii. 5.

He being dead, yet ſpeaketh. HEB. xi. 4.

PHILADELPHIA:

Printed and ſold by JOSEPH CRUKSHANK, in Third-
ſtreet, oppoſite the Work-Houſe.

M DCC LXXII.

√

Fig. 9a. Title page from Hannah Griffitts's personal copy of Daniel Stanton's memoirs. On the flyleaf, Griffitt's inscribed a version of her poem on the occasion of Stanton's death. Courtesy, Library Company of Philadelphia, Philadelphia, Pennsylvania.

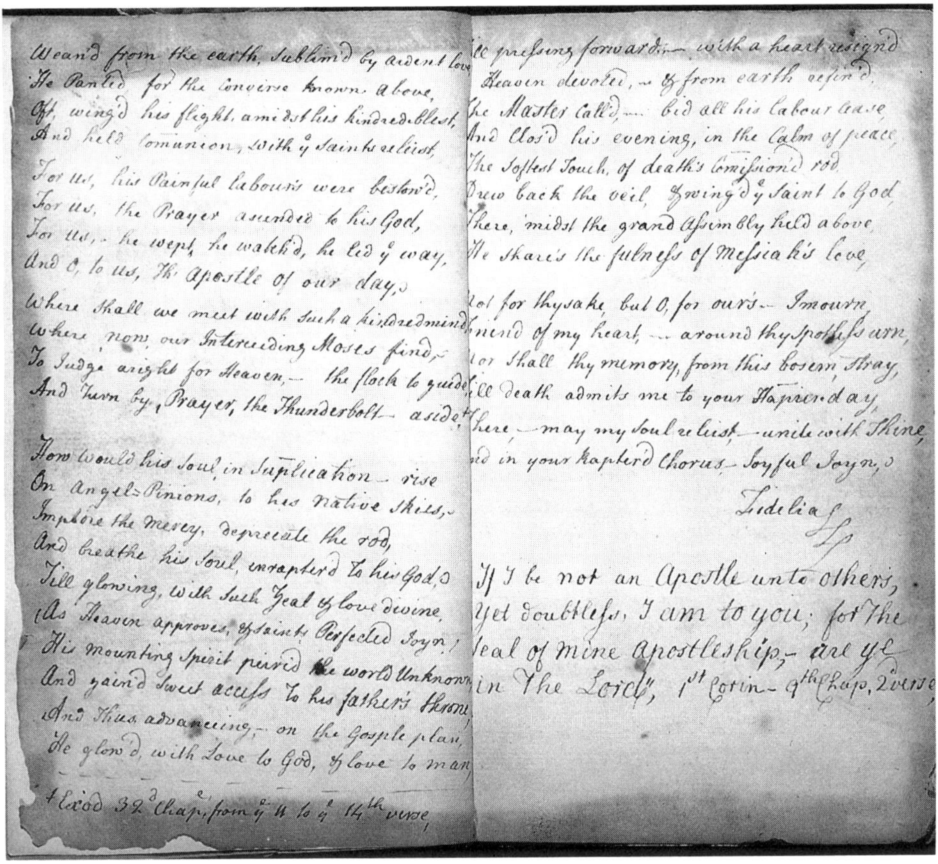

Fig. 9b. Selection from Hannah Griffitts's poem "To the Memory of Daniel Stanton" (*MMMB* 42). Courtesy, Library Company of Philadelphia, Philadelphia, Pennsylvania.

For few perhaps the Lot of Life endure
With Hearts less guilty, or with Hands more pure. 20
Anxious each Call of Duty to attend
A pow'rful Teacher & a christian Friend,
While with a cherubs Love, & Seraphs Zeal,
He sought to know & do his Masters Will
With Heav'n acceptance blest, his favour'd Mind 25

Grew daily more enlighten'd & refin'd
Wean'd from the Earth sublim'd by ardent Love,
He panted for the Converse known above,
Oft wing'd his flight amidst his kindred blest
And held Communion with the Saints releas'd,   30
For oh! in him conspicuously conjoin'd
The humble Christian, watchful & resign'd,
For us his painful Labours he bestow'd
For us the Prayer ascended to his God,
For us he wept he watch'd, he led the Way   35
And oh! to us, the Apostle of our Day,
Where shall we meet with such a kindred Mind
Where now, our interceeding Moses find,
To judge aright for Heaven, the Flock to guide
And turn by Prayer the Thunderbolt aside,   40
How would his Soul in Supplication rise
On Angel Pinions to his native Skies.
Implore the Mercy, deprecate the Rod
And breathe his Soul enraptur'd to his God
'Till glowing with such Zeal & Love divine   45
As Heaven approves & Saints perfected join,
His mounting Spirit pierc'd the World unknown,
And gain'd sweet Access to the Father's Throne.
And thus advancing on the Gospel Plan,
He glow'd with Love to God & Love to Man   50
Still pressing forward with a Heart resign'd
To Heaven devoted & from Earth refin'd
The Master call'd, bid all his Labour cease,
And clos'd his Ev'ning in the Calm of Peace,
The softest Touches of Deaths awful Rod,   55
Drew back the Veil & wing'd his Soul to God.
There 'midst the grand Assembly held above,
He shares the fulness of Messiah's Love.—
Not for thy Sake, but oh! for ours I mourn
Friend of my Heart around thy spotless Urn,   60
Nor shall thy Memory from my Bosom stray
'Till Death admits me to yr. happier Day
There may my Soul releas'd unite with thine
And in yr. raptur'd Chorus joyful join.—*Finis*

43   Wrote in a violent Storm, which, I think equall'd any, I ever heard, while writing,—but before I finished the Lines (a very short Time)—the Tempest fell, & there was scarce a Leaf moving when I left the Room.—1772.—by the same.

Let haughty Man with Fear adore
That awful sovereign Majesty
Who governs Nature, by his Pow'r
Supreme,—nor asketh leave to be.—

Happy for Man, his God shall guide   5
Who can, the alternate Change perform,
Bid Nature in a Calm subside
Or frown beneath the furious Storm.

Whose high stretch'd Arm when e'er he please
Can swell the Flood, beyond the Shore   10
Direct the vast Machine with Ease,
And hold the Reins of wild uproar

Hark! now the awful Charge is giv'n
The Winds rush forth—in Fury rise
Darken the blue Serene of Heaven   15
And dash their Billows to the Skies!

The boundless Reservoirs on high
United join the Floods below
The Deluge pours from Earth & Sky
A general dreadful overflow.   20

The Clash of Elements combine
To swell the aggravated Roar
'Till this almighty Voice divine
Shall bid the Tempest rage no more.

Soon as this awful Word was spoke   25
Submissive Nature, calm appears,

(The Power of all its Fury broke,)
An Infants smiling softness wears.

The Sun pours forth, his Beams of Light.
To bless the vegetative Race,   30
And the rich Canopy of Night
Expands in full illustrious Grace.

Th' amazing Change we see is thine
Who gave to Man the reasoning Soul,
But oh! how vast, beyond our Line,   35
Thou, that sustains the mighty whole.

Here fix thy Trust, tho' Nature shake,
And frighten'd feels her loosen'd Tye,
The Soul amidst the general Wreck,
Is safe; in God's Immensity.   40

Fidelia

44   The voluntary Retreat 1772.—*by the same*

Sweet are the Joys of calm sequester'd Life,
Far, from the vicious Luxuries of the great
The thirst of Grandeur, nor Ambition's Strife
Possess their Wishes, or the Heart date.

Not from the World, their Happiness they draw,   5
Or to its empty Vanities confin'd
Nor deify its Customs into Law
To warp the native Rectitude of Mind.

Strangers to every false delusive Art,
That from Religions Precepts dare entice   10
They hold the moral Empire of the Heart
And fly, the dark detested Paths of Vice.—

While far—from all the giddy Croud retir'd,
Above their fluttring Joys, or trifling Cares
They scorn the Liberty, by Guilt acquir'd,   15
Nor claim Distinction, from the Waste of years.

For better Views, the important Gift of Time,
To Man, probationary Man, was given,
To act regardful of the Life Divine,
And form a purer Candidate for Heaven.   20

The conscious Peace, which Innocence bestows
Th'illumin'd Virtue of a Mind serene,
Their Passions into Harmony compose,
And soften ev'ry rough afflictive Scene.

Nor with the Stoics Pride, or Cynic Sneer   25
Do they the Vanities of Life disclaim
They swell the generous Wish, the tender Tear
A social Tribute to their kindred Name.

This generous Warmth of Heart (extend[in]g wide)
To the meer Frailties of the human Mind   30
Extenuates the Fault they cannot hide
And gives that Mercy, which they hope to find.

To Sorrow's deep Distress, to suffering Pain,
The soothing Hand of Charity extend,
Nor let the Voice of Pity plead in vain   35
They give to human Misery a Friend.

To them, the Bigots narrow Tyes unknown,
They grasp the whole Creation in their Span,
No Modes offend, while Piety can own
The Name of Brethren, in the Name of Man.   40

Thus, safely lodg'd beneath the calm Retreat
They seek no Bliss,—or Bliss expect to find
But such as in the social Converse meet
By Virtue form'd & center'd in the Mind.

To Heav'n, sincere their firm allegiance held   45
Nor fix'd their joys or Hopes beneath the Sky,
To Man each Claim of social Life fulfill'd
They neither wish to live, nor fear to dye.

45   On the Death of King George the 2d.[54]—

1   See fair Britania clad in sable Woe
     Weeping the Interment of her royal Dust
     Bid the deep Sorrow unaffected flow
     Oer George the brave, the gen'rous & the Just.
2   Who rescued Britons from the papal Power,   5
     Secur'd their Freedom from the gallic Chain
     And thro' the Annals of the regal Hour
     Did well the Cause of Liberty maintain.
3   Tho' Heav'n propitious to our mutual Prayers
     Stretch'd the dear Blessing to a lengthen'd Date   10
     Gave us t'enjoy a Monarch full of years,
     Yet oh! too soon we mourn the Stroke of Fate.
4   Here on Sylvanias Shores the humble Maid,
     Far from the Influence of her Princes Eye,
     If not in public Pomp of Woe array'd   15
     Drops the warm Tear & joins a Nation's Sigh.
5   May Peace eternal watch thy royal Urn
     And Angels wait thee on th'immortal Shore,
     And while their Loss thy Son & People mourn,
     May he to us thy happy Reign restore.   20

Fidelia

54. **King George the 2d**: Was born in 1683, and ascended the throne in 1727 on the death of his father King George I. His reign was marked by a series of wars with other European powers both on the continent and in North America. Griffitts's reference to George's role in breaking the "gallic chain" probably refers to his actions, which helped defeat the French during the War of the Austrian Succession, at the Battle of Dettingen in June 1743. This was the last battle in which an Engish king took part. George II died October 25, 1760, leaving the throne of England to his grandson, George III. See F. J. C. Hearnshaw et al., *The Dictionary of English History*, new ed. (London: Cassell, 1928), 511–13.

46   To the Memory of Sally Norris[55] who died of the small Pox in the 23d. year of her Age. 1768. by the same

1   Dear lovely Maid in such a Stroke as thine
   Where fainting Nature sinks beneath the Rod
   How hard the painful Struggle to resign,
   Nor murmur at the chast'ning Hand of God.
2   Beyond Expression hard, where all the Powers   5
   Of Love & Friendship plead their tender Claim
   Where public Grief with us thy Loss deplores
   In Sighs laments, in Tears embalms thy Name.
3   Ah! what avails or Youth, or Wealth, or Fame
   Superior Worth—or Beauty's smiling Bloom   10
   On thy sweet Cheek the blasting Spoiler came
   And laid the spotless victim in the Tomb.
4   Cruel Disease that here couldst it point thy Dart
   And all the Pride of Nature thus deform
   Plunge the keen Dagger to our bleeding Heart   15
   And smile malignant midst the bursting Storm
5   Give Nature room—she must have leave to mourn
   At such a Call—in such a piercing Blow
   Snatch'd from our Side & from our Bosom torn
   And all our Hopes enwrap'd in sable Woe.   20
6   Deep from the sorrowing Eye, the mourning Mind
   Thy fair distinguish'd Virtues claim a Part
   Thy spotless Spirit, humble & resign'd
   Thy gentle Manners, Sanctity of Heart.
7   Tho' Beauty, Youth, & Affluence all conspir'd   25
   To tempt the Eye & turn thy Steps astray
   How oft thy Soul to nobler Views aspir'd,
   Breathe'd to thy God, & found the living Way.
8   The Hope within, which firm unshaken stood
   To guard thy Soul in Death's conflicting Hour   30
   That Hope serene press'd thro' the swelling Flood

55. **Sally Norris:** Sarah "Sally" Norris (1744–69) was the second daughter of Isaac Norris Jr. and Sarah Logan Norris. Sally died of smallpox, leaving her sister Mary grief-stricken. See Wulf, "A Marginal Independence," 243, 318–19; also Jordan, *Colonial Families*, 88.

Of Nature's Weakness with victorious Pow'r.
9　Thy Innocence no guilty Fears alarm
Nor trembling Doubts disturb thy Peace of Mind
Thou lean'd secure on Heavens unfailing Arm　　　　35
And bow'd submissive to his Will resign'd.
10　But oh! the firm indissoluble Tye
That bound thy Love to one congenial Heart
And trac'd the Anguish of a Sister's Eye,
Gave Death its Frown & edg'd his keenest Dart.　　40
11　Not for thyself, but oh! for her thou fear'd
And for her sake alone thou felt Distress
When even in Death the placid smile appear'd:
To sooth her Grief & make her Suffering less.
12　Ah! dear lamented Maid, we long must mourn,　　45
The bitter Cup which to our Lips is held
Long must we weep o'er thy distinguish'd Urn,
And humbly wish the Task of Life fulfill'd.
13　And when this trembling Hand—this feeling heart
On whom such painful Duty oft attends　　　　　　50
Shall fall—beneath the Tyrants ling'ring Dart
Oh may I meet my dear departed Friends.
14　Those bosom Friends the Shaft of Death destroy'd
But the kind Hand of Goodness shall restore,
Give you in Peace again to be enjoy'd　　　　　　55
Beyond the Tyrants seperating Pow'r.
15　Let this sweet Hope my fellow Mourner calm
Thy Weight of Anguish in this Flood of Grief
While Resignation sweetly soothing Balm
Shall heal the Wound, & gently breathe Relief.　　60

47　A Letter of Farewell from a Gent. to a young Woman whom he had long paid his Addresses to in vain.—

All Passions (as some Casuists opine)
Grow with their like, with their reverse decline—

Ambition, thus, but fans ambitions Fire,
And mild Affections, thro' Contempt, expire—
    The Instance follows—she who once cou'd move,   5
Within my Bosom every Source of Love;
Whose magic Face with Joy or Fear assaild,
My captive Heart, as Smiles or Frowns prevail'd;
The Influence of whose fascinating Eye,
Cou'd bid me hope, despair, even live or die—   10
Tho' still all-graceful—now no longer fires,
With jealous Rage, or melts with soft Desires—
For lost their Power—even Beauties still the same,
No more revive the extinguish'd Lovers Flame,
Who now unmov'd, surveys her Hoard of Charms,   15
Unmov'd, can hear them doom'd to other Arms,
Nor feels one Pang, nor breaths a secret Sigh,
Whether she Hymens social Fetters try,
Or unadmir'd live on to stale Virginity.—
    Learn here, coy Nymph! in this reverse of Things!   20
How short the Empire, which from Beauty springs:
Had but thy Breast with mutual Ardour beat,
Love yet had kept his abdicated Seat,
Still had thy Charms their wonted Force retain'd,
Still in my Soul unrival'd thou hadst reign'd,   25
And long e'er this, restrictive nuptial Bands,
As Choice our Hearts, had join'd our plighted Hands.
    Unhappy Sex!—Let this Example prove,
How close Indiff'rence follows slighted Love;
Repuls'd, how soon the offended God departs,   30
And stirs Rebellion in yr. Subjects Hearts,
Unless Complaisance fly to Beauty's Aid,
And fix the Conquests which her Charms have made.
    Adieu, my Fair!—& may a happier Fate
If more deserv'd, yr. future Lovers' wait: 35
For me kind Heaven some yielding Nymph ordain,
Who tho' less fair, has less Delight in Pain.—

48   The following Lines were wrote under H. Paytons Picture

Beauty how sweet, where unaffected Grace,
And modest Sense glows thro' the meaning Face,
Where the pleas'd Eye darts forth a Vestals Fire
And undesiring kindles up Desire,
The wanton Glance, may short-liv'd Passion move   5
But awful Virtue fixes solid Love.

49   On Happiness.—To N. S—U[56]

Oh! Happiness thou much desir'd Good,
So seldom found, so little understood,
Thy Pow'r resistless all the World obey,
And ev'ry beating Bosom owns thy Sway.
For thee, the Merchant quits the Bed of Ease   5
And tempts the Dangers of the wintry Seas,
In hopes that you, sweet Nymph, may come at last
And well reward him for his Labours past.
But oh! how vain are all his air built Schemes
Now Hopes still rise, & disappoint his Aims.   10
The Statesman anxious to acquire a Name,
Thinks to possess thee, in the breath of Fame,
Thro' the false Medium of Ambition sees
And at each step he rises hopes for Ease.
But still some higher step, that must be gain'd   15
Poisons the Sweets of all he has obtain'd,
Then say thou sweet Enslaver of the Mind
Thou fairy Dream, thou Being undefind,
Where may we hope, thy blest Abode to find?
Can Wealth which rules Mankind with tyrant Sway   20
With all its boasted Power procure thy stay?

---

56. **To N. S–U.**: The editors could not positively identify.

Can it relieve the sorrow smitten Heart,
Or from Infirmity bid Pain depart?
Alas! the Sons of Fortune, all will own
That Cares invade the softest Beds of Down,   25
Since then, not Wealth, with all its gaudy Train
Can the wish'd Lot of Happiness obtain,
Grant me ye Powers, that I may pass my Life,
Far from the madding Crowds of noisy Strife
In some lone Spot, where unrestrain'd by Art   30
Luxuriant Nature may her Charms impart
Far mov'd from Dissipations giddy Round,
For Happiness is there but seldom found,
Blest with a Wife, the Mistress of my breast
In whose fond Bosom all my Cares may rest,   35
Let her possess a tender feeling Mind
By sweetest Sensibility refin'd,
A Heart that can with sympathetic Glow
Partake a Brothers Joy, a Brothers Woe,
A Temper even & a Judgement clear,   40
Gentle as Zephyrs, & as Truth sincere,
Let Fortune then a Competence bestow,
Neither profusely great nor meanly low,
Enough to answer simple Natures ends,
And share our Blessings with some chosen Friends   45
From each years income will consign a Part,
To sooth the Sorrows of the suff'ring Heart
To wipe Affliction from the widow's Eye
Or feed the hungry Poor, that wander by,
And when our Store denies the Pow'r to give   50
We'll pity then the Wretch we can't relieve,
Thus cheaply blest, unknowing Care or Strife
With Delia[57] & my Friends I'd pass my Life
And if at length of Happiness I miss,
Foil'd in those Scenes of fondly fancied Bliss   55
With Grief I'll lay the dear Delusion down
And dying seek for her in Worlds unknown.

57. **Delia**: A literary pseudonym.

50   Wrote extempore[58] by P. D. L . . . y[59] on the Governors appearing much pleased with some new fashion'd large Panes of Glass he had got for his new House.

Happy the Man with such a Treasure,
Whose greatest Pain's his greatest Pleasure;
Stoics who do not fear the Devil,
Assure us Pain is not an Evil,
They boast a Negative at best   5
But thou with Panes art truly blest.
　　　What strange delusion must possess his pate
　　　When bliss increases as his pains are great!
　　　On read[in]g the foregoing by G. D.[60]

58. **extempore:** Extemporaneous. Extempore poems were expressions of eighteenth-century witty social verse. Other examples in this collection are *MMMB* 43, "Wrote in a violent Storm," and *MMMB* 115, "Wrote extempore on Tea." For further discussion of this type of poetry, see pages 94–95.

59. **P. D. L . . .y:** The editors could not positively identify.

60. **G. D.** : Possibly George Dillwyn (1738–1820), Moore's brother-in-law. She exchanged her commonplace book with him at least once to add *MMMB* 28, "A Dream," in her own handwriting. This satire may be George Dillwyn's amused observation as Henry Hill equipped his grand home in Fourth Street. In the late 1760s Hill corresponded with his sisters in London about the most fashionable furnishings, from the selection of seat covers and curtains to the placement of the tea tables and mirrors. They arranged to be sent to him at least a glass fanlight and a large mirror, and possibly more glass items. This display of fashion and wealth was not in keeping with the other family members' interests or means. The Dillwyns in particular never had much money and spent time in London amusedly aghast at the "fashionable" concerns of their English relations. See Mary Lamar to Henry Hill, London, n.d., and and Sarah Dillwyn's letters from England, both in Smith, *Letters of Doctor Richard Hill*, 197–98, 245–56.

51 A Letter from P. H. to R. P.[61]—Hanover Jany. 18th. 1773.

I take this opportunity to acknowledge the Rec[eip]t. of A. Benezets Book[62] against the Slave Trade, I thank you for it—It is not a little surprising that Christianity whose chief Excellence consists in softening the human Heart, in cherishing & improving its finer feelings, should encourage a Practice so totally repugnant to the first Impressions of right & wrong, what adds to the Wonder is, that this abominable Practice has been introduced in the most enlightened Ages.—Times that seem to have pretensions to boast of high Improvements in the Arts, Sciences & refined Morality, have brought into general Use, & guarded by many Laws; a species of Violence & Tyranny, which our more rude & barbarous, but more honest Ancestors detested.—Is it not amazing, that at a Time, when, the Rights of Humanity are defined and understood with Precision, in a Country above all others fond of Liberty, that in such an Age, & such a Country, we find Men, professing a Religion the most humane, mild, meek, gentle & generous, adopting a Principle as repugnant to humanity as it is inconsistant with the Bible, & destructive to Liberty.—Every thinking honest Man rejects it in Speculation, how few in Practice from conscientious Motives.—The World in general has denied yr. People a share of its Honours, but the wise will ascribe to you a just Tribute of virtuous Praise, for the Practice of a Train of Virtues

---

61. **P. H to R. P.** : Patrick Henry to Robert Pleasants. A copy of this letter, from Henry to the Virginia Quaker Pleasants, can be found in George S. Brookes, *Friend Anthony Benezet* (Philadelphia: University of Pennsylvania Press, 1937), 443–45.

62. **A. Benezets Book**: Anthony Benezet (1713–84) was a teacher and Quaker reformer. With other Quakers like John Woolman, Benezet campaigned for the abolition of slavery. He published a number of treatises on the subject, including *Some Historical Account of Guinea* (1772). Although his writings were purchased and read by many influential people in America and abroad, including the founder of Methodism, John Wesley, Benezet arranged to have his works sent to select figures including southerners Patrick Henry of Virginia and Henry Laurens of South Carolina. Benezet was the teacher of Milcah Martha Moore's brother-in-law, George Dillwyn, and his brother, William Dillwyn. The brothers corresponded with Benezet for many years, and assisted his work against slavery, particularly after they joined the Quaker ministry themselves. See Brookes, *Friend Anthony Benezet*, esp. 80–88, 276–77, 298–327, 425–26, and 443–45. See also Jean R. Soderlund, *Quakers and Slavery: A Divided Spirit* (Princeton: Princeton University Press, 1985).

among which yr. disagreement to Slavery will be principally ranked.—
I cannot but wish well to a People whose System immitates the Example of him whose Life was perfect.—And believe me, I shall honour the Quakers for their noble Effort to abolish Slavery. [I]t is equally calculated to promote Moral and political Good.—

Would any one believe that I am Master of Slaves of my own Purchase!—I am drawn along by the general Inconvenience of living without them, I will not, I cannot justify it[,] however culpable my Conduct, I will so far pay my Devoirs to Virtue as to own the excellence & Rectitude of her Precepts, & to lament my want of Conformity to them.—I believe a Time will come when an oppo.[rtunity] will be offered to abolish this lamentable Evil.—Every Thing we can do is to improve it, if it happens in our Day, if not, let us transmit to our Descendants together with our Slaves a Pity for their unhappy Lot, & an Abhorrence for Slavery. If we cannot reduce this wish'd for Reformation to Practice, let us treat the unhappy Victims with Lenity, it is the furthest advance we can make towards Justice.— [I]t is a Debt we owe to the Purity of our Religion, to shew that it is at variance with that Law which warrants Slavery[.]

Here is an Instance that silent Meetings (the Scoff of reverend Doctors) have done that, which learned & elaborate preaching could not effect, so much preferable are the genuine Dictates of Conscience & a steady Attention to its feelings above the teachings of those Men who pretend to have found a better Guide.—I exhort you to persevere in so worthy a Resolution, some of your People disagree, or at least are lukewarm in the Abolition of Slavery—many treat the Resolution of your Meeting with Redicule, & among those who throw Contempt on it, are Clergymen, whose surest Guard against both Redicule & Contempt is a certain Act of Assembly.—I know not where to stop, I could say many Things on this Subject, a serious Review of which gives a gloomy Prospect to future Times. Excuse this Scrawl & believe me with Esteem

Yr. hbl. Srvt.
Patrick Henry Junr.

52   An Epithalamium on the Marriage of E. D. with F. B—d.[63]

Why sleeps my Muse, arise, arise,
    And clad in all thy best Attire,
Attend this Day of nuptial Joys
    And with thee bring thy sounding Lyre.
       2
Attend the bright & solemn Throng,*   5
    That awes us while it gives Delight,
'Tis no dishonour to thy Song,
    To sing of the connubial Rite.
       3
Marriage in Eden first began,
    Ordain'd & bless'd by heav'nly Pow'rs;   10
The greatest Bliss attending Man,
    Unless the guilty Fault be ours:
       4
The force of Friendship all agree,
    In generous Tempers strongly binds,
For stronger will that Friendship be   15
    Where tenderest Love cements two Minds.
       5
But lo I see the happy Pair,
    With Hearts as well as Hands conjoin'd
Their Looks bespeak a pleasing fear,
    And solemn Joys possess the Mind.   20
       6
See how the Bridesgroom portly stands,
    A graceful Honesty & Truth,
Attention from all Eyes commands
    And adds a Lustre to his Youth.
       7
See, see the Bride serenely gay,   25
    And lovely as a Summers Sky;
When Phebus ushers in the Day,
    And not a cloud appears on high.

63. **Marriage of E. D. with F.B–d**: The editors could not positively identify.

8

Hymen, O! Hymen deign to come,
    And in resplendant Pomp appear;   30
If thou regards a hopeful Bloom,
    These Plants are worthy of the Care.

9

Let Love & Peace attend thy Train,
    With smiling Joys & sweet Delight
But banish Discord, banish Pain,   35
    Abhor'd forever from thy Sight.

10

Ye sacred Pow'rs of every Kind,
    Oh make this worthy Youth yr. Care
From Ills of Body & of Mind,
    O guard this charming lovely Fair.   40

11

Let them not know the Name of Strife
    And drive domestic Jarrs away;
That the whole Tenor of their Life
    May seem to them a nuptial Day.

[Marginal note:]
*The Marriage Assembly

53   On hearing J. Duchee[64] preach.

Could all like him the sacred Gospel preach,
And heav'nly Truths in heav'nly Language teach,

64. **J. Duchee**: Jacob Duché (1737–1798) graduated from the first class of the College of Philadelphia in 1757. He also studied at Cambridge. He was a minister at Philadelphia's Christ Church and St. Peter's and, although he openly disapproved of independence, was elected Chaplain of the Continental Congress in 1776. Then during Philadelphia's British occupation, he expressed Loyalist sentiments. Ultimately his property was confiscated by the Patriots, and he left for England. Duché was allowed to return to Philadelphia in 1792, where he died six years later. See Joseph Jackson, *Encyclopedia of Philadelphia* (Harrisburg: National Historical Assoc., 1931), 2:605–7. For the context of Duché's ministry among Philadelphia Anglicans, see Deborah Mathias Gough, *Christ Church Philadelphia: The Nation's Church*

Display the Scriptures in so clear a view,
And urge the Precepts by Example too,
No more the slighted Clergy would complain,   5
They labour'd for the good of Souls in vain;
Religion would in native Lustre shine,
The Priest & Office both esteem'd divine,
For when by him the Christian duty's Taught,
There is no leisure for a wandering Thought.   10
As from his Tongue the sweet Instruction flows,
Each ardent Mind in every Virtue grows.

54   A Poem on Christmas Day 1774.[65]
By Hetty Griffitts[66]

Forever hail! auspicious Morn,
On which the Son of God was born
    To save a sinful Race.
Devotion, Gratitude & Love,
Should every mortals Bosom move   5
    In ev'ry Heart take place.

---

in a Changing City (Philadelphia: University of Pennsylvania Press, 1995), chaps.
4–7. See pages 35–36, for a description of Duché's relationship with Elizabeth
Graeme Fergusson.

    65. **Christmas Day 1774**: In some places, especially in the Anglican south, Dutch
New York, and German Pennsylvania, Christmas was celebrated with church services
as well as more specifically ethnic and secular rituals such as the burning of yule logs.
Radical Protestants such as Puritans and Quakers resisted both kinds of celebrations,
and especially deplored the elaborate show of feasting and festivity which accompanied the arrival of December 25th. For the complexity of Quakers' relationship to the
historical figure of Jesus, see Hugh Barbour, *The Quakers in Puritan England* (New
Haven: Yale University Press, 1964), 145–47. On the reaction of Puritans to Christmas celebrations, see David D. Hall, *Worlds of Wonder, Days of Judgment: Popular
Religious Belief in Early New England* (Cambridge: Harvard University Press, 1989),
pp. 7, 216.

    66. **Hetty Griffitts**: Hester "Hetty" Griffitts was born in 1754 and married James
Montgomery in 1777. She was the daughter of William Griffitts, brother of Hannah
Griffitts' father Thomas, and Abigail Powell Griffitts. See Jordan, *Colonial Families of
Philadelphia*.

Fig. 10. Jacob Duché and Elizabeth Hopkins Duché, by T. S.
Duché. Courtesy, The Historical Society of Pennsylvania,
Philadelphia, Pennsylvania.

How vast the Debt to God we owe!
Who sent his only Son to know
    The bitter Pangs of Death,
And, from Perdition, Man to save   10
O'er Death to triumph & the Grave,
    He yielded up his Breath.
Yet not to Rulers of the Earth
Was first reveal'd the wond'rous Birth,
    But to the lowly Swains,   15
Who watch'd their fleecy Flocks by Night,
Sudden around the sacred Light

Illumin'd all the Plains.
Glory to God, good Will to Man
The Choir of Angels strait began   20
  With Melody divine;
Responsive Echo catch'd the Sound,
All Nature, struck with awe profound
  A list'ning Ear inclin'd.
To save from Misery & Woe,   25
The Race of Mortals here below,
  This Day a Saviour's born,
Nor regal Pomp or Splendors Grace
The holy Jesus dwelling place
  Nor Majesty adorn.   30

But, in a Manger you will find
The Friend & Saviour of Mankind,
  In swaddling Bands array'd,
Thus to th' astonish'd Swains they spoke
A Flood of Glory round them broke   35
  And strait to Heaven convey'd.—

Amanda[67]

55 [Untitled] By the same.

Come sweetly pleasing Solitude
Companion of the wise & good,
  Impart thy chearing Ray,
To guide my wand'ring footsteps, where,
Remote from hurry, Vice & Care   5
  Serene may glide each Day.

There, far from Splendor, Pomp & shew
Let me those lasting Pleasures know
  That from fair Virtue rise;

67. **Amanda**: Hetty Griffitts's pseudonym.

All other Joys, save hers, are vain   10
In Folly's gay fantastic Fane
    I ne'er will sacrifice.

O! lead me to some humble Cell
Where Innocence with Peace does dwell
    And rose-lipp'd sweet Content;   15
Their Smiles shall cheer the frugal Meal
And I shall greater Pleasure feel
    Than those on Wealth intent.

By gentle Riv'lets murmuring Streams,
Whilst Cynthia lends her silver Beams,   20
    To gild the devious Walk,
There with Monimia,[68] lovely Fair,
Friendship[']s soft Impulse may I share,
    Whilst of her Sweets we talk.

But say, Monimia, canst thou leave,   25
And for their Loss wilt thou not grieve,
    Of Life the Shew & Noise?
O yes! my friend, I know thy Heart
With empty Pleasure soon can part
    And its delusive Joys.—   30

Amanda

56 New Jail.[69] Philadelphia Jany. 1st. 1776.

Confinement hail!—in Honours justest Cause,
True to our King, our Country, & our Laws;
Opposing Anarchy, Sedition—Strife,

68. **Monimia**: Probably a pseudonym for one of Amanda's/Hetty Griffitts' women friends whose identity has not been discovered. The name itself derives from either the heroine of Otway's *The Orphan* (1680), or a character in Smollett's *Ferdinand Count Fathom* (1753) (*OCEL*, 5th).

69. **New Jail**: In response to pressure to support the patriot cause, Quakers issued an epistle from the fall 1776 Philadelphia Yearly Meeting urging Friends to maintain

And ev'ry other Bane of social Life,
These Colonies of british Freedom tir[']d,   5
Are by the Phrenzy of Distraction fir'd,
Surrounding Nations with Amazement view
The strange Infatuations they pursue,
Virtue in Tears deplores their Fate in vain,
And Satan smiles to see Disorder reign.   10
      The Days of Cromwell's puritannic Rage,
Return to curse, our more unhappy Age,
Rushing to Arms, they madly urge their Fate,
And levy War against their parent State,
      We Friends to Freedom, Government, & Laws   15
Are deem'd inimical unto their Cause,
In Vaults with Bars & iron Doors confin'd,
They hold our Persons, but cant rule the Mind,
Act now we cannot else we freely wou'd
But calmly suffer for our Countrys Good.   20
Success on Earth to Ill is sometimes giv'n
To brave Misfortune is the Gift of Heav'n,
What Man could do, we did, our Cause to serve,
We can't command Success—but we'll deserve.—*Finis*

57 M[r.] Hemp to M[r.] Skinner[70] on his Arrival on board the Dutchess of Gordon

Welcome! welcome! Brother Tory
    To this merry floating Place,
I came here a while before ye,
    Coming here is no Disgrace.

their commitment to pacifism. Friends had already experienced harassment, but the issuance of this epistle caused two New Jersey Friends, Mark Miller and Thomas Redman, to be jailed. Griffitts likens this situation to the persecution and jailing of Quakers under the Puritan Commonwealth (1649–58) of Oliver Cromwell. See Arthur J. Mekell, *The Relation of the Quakers to the American Revolution* (Lanham, Md.: University Press of America, 1979), 161–65; Barbour, *The Quakers in Puritan England*, 64, 62, 207.

70. **M[r]. Hemp to M[r]. Skinner**: Amidst the tumult of revolutionary New Jersey, many prominent families allied with the crown. Cordlandt Skinner was one of the

Freedom finds a safe Retreat here,   5
    On the Bosom of the Wave;
You, she now invites to meet her
    Welcome then, thou Tory brave!
As you serve, like us, the King, Sir,
    In a Hammock you must lay,   10
Better far, 'tis so to swing Sir,
    Than to swing another Way.
Tho' we've not dry Land to walk on,
    The Quarter-deck is smooth to tread,
Hear how fast, while we are talking   15
    Barrow[71] trips it o'er our Head.
Neptunes gallant Sons befriend us
    While at Anchor here we ride,
Britains wooden Walls defend us,
    Britain's Glory & her Pride.—   20

[Marginal note:]
*Barrow is Paymaster of the Kings Army.

58   A few Extracts from E. G.'s Journal.[72]—

Remarks—on the Passage from Phila:a. to Liverpool June 1764.

I could not help observing, that whatever way the Ship moved she appeared to be in the Centre of a Circle, for the Sea seems to be a perfect Circle, surrounded by the Clouds, that look as if they bent down at

proprietors of east New Jersey, the colony's Attorney General, Speaker of the Assembly, and a close advisor of Governor William Franklin. Skinner was forced to take refuge aboard a British man-of-war, the *Dutchess Gordon*, in January 1776 just hours before provincial soldiers raided his house to search for him. See Leonard Lundin, *Cockpit of the Revolution: The War for Independence in New Jersey* (Princeton: Princeton University Press, 1940), 46–47, 74–76, 120; Gregory Palmer, *Biographical Sketches of Loyalists of the American Revolution* (Westport: Meckler, 1984), 79; Frederick Ricord and W. M. Nelson, eds., *Documents Relating to the Colonial History of the State of New Jersey*, 21 vols. (Newark, 1886), 10:698–710.

    71. **Barrow**: The editors could not verify Moore's identification of this "Paymaster of the King's army."

    72. **E. G's Journal**: Moore transcribed "extracts" from Elizabeth Graeme's journal. The complete journal is still missing.

the Edges to join it, so that our own Eyes form the Horizon, & like Self-Love, we are always placing ourselves in the Middle, where all Things move round us.—I saw the Sun set clear, for the first Time, I was reading Priam's Petition to Achilles,[73] for the Body of Hector, I think my Eyes were engaged in one of the finest Sights in the Universe, & my Passions, interested in one of the most pathetic that History or Poetry can paint.—

At the York Races.

I was in the Balcony, with a Paper, the List of the Horses, in my Hand, a Gent. that stood by & had been chatting to another Lady, ask'd which Side I would bet, I told him that, that every one else was against, For the Race was not to the Swift nor the Battle to the Strong,[74]— we presently fell into a very free Conversation, on his Part a very sensible one, & told me he wished to lengthen the Time, but was under an Engagement to return to his Hermitage the next Morning, but desired I would meet him, at the Assembly Room in the Ev'ning, I told him I would be there, but questioned in such a Groupe whether I s[h]ould be found—He said he had some Interest in Apollo,[75] who would lend him his Torch on such an Occasion. This was no other than Yorick,[76] the celebrated Lawrence Sterne. Author of Tristram Shandy[.]

In Pomps or Joys the Palace or the Grot
My Country's Tears were never yet forgot;
My absent Parents rose before my Sight,
    And distant lay Contentment & Delight.
        9th Book of the Odyssy[77]

73. **Priam's Petition to Achilles:** *Iliad*, chap. 24 (ll.486–506).

74. **Battle to the Strong:** The allusion is to Ecclesiastes 9:11.

75. **Apollo:** "The god . . . of light" (*OCCL*).

76. **Yorick:** "The impulsive and argumentative parson" in *Tristram Shandy,* a novel by Lawrence Sterne (1713–68). "A good country pastor," Sterne was made famous by the publication of this novel in nine volumes (1759–67). In 1760, he moved into "Shandy Hall," probably the "Hermitage" to which he refers in this anecdote (*OCEL*, 5th).

77. **9th Book of the Odyssy:** Graeme quotes exactly from the nineth book of Pope's translation of the *Odyssey*.

My Lady Julianna Penn,[78] is among the few good Things that come up to the Character that is told of them.—She has strong good Sense, above Affectation, a most pleasing Manner that takes off the Distance of her Station, & at the same Time a conscious Dignity, that seems to arise more from the Goodness of her own Heart, than from any external Advantages, she has a great flow of Spirits, talks freely, & seems perfectly Mistress of all Subjects, yet with an Air of Humility, as if she was receiving instead of giving Information.

I cannot help classing my Books like my Friends, they all have their respective Merits, but I am not equally acquainted with them.—Doctor Young,[79] is a Friend in Affliction, that I could open my Heart to, Mrs. Rowe[80] flatters my Imagination, & takes Walks with me in a summer evening,—Mr. Addison[81] suits me in all Humours, Mr. Pope[82] I am a little afraid of, I think he knows so well the turnings of the human Heart, that he always sets me into an Examination.—Harvey[83] says the same Thing over & over so prettily, & I am persuaded

78. **Lady Julianna Penn**: Lady Juliana Fermor, daughter of the first Earl of Pomfret and an Anglican, married Thomas Penn on August 22, 1751, at St. George's Church, Hanover, thus ending Thomas Penn's association with Quakers. Lorett Treese, *A Storm Gathering: The Penn Family and the American Revolution* (University Park: The Pennsylvania State University Press, 1992), 17.

79. **Doctor Young**: Edward Young (1683–1765). Young's most celebrated poem, *The Complaint, or Night Thoughts on Life, Death and Immortality* (1742–45) "is a long and somewhat rambling meditation on life's vicissitudes, death, and immortality." Since Young includes references to his wife, his stepdaughter, and her husband, "a certain narrative and autobiographical interest is added to his evocation of 'delightful gloom' and the 'populous grave'" (See "Edward Young" and "Night Thoughts," in *OCEL*, 5th).

80. **Mrs. Rowe**: Elizabeth Rowe (1674–1737) was a poet, translator, and prose writer of letters. Her poems were included in a number of miscellanies. One of her books of letters, *Friendship in Death, in Letters from the Dead to the Living* (1728), was dedicated to Edward Young. See the headnote on "Elizabeth Rowe" in *Eighteenth-Century Women Poets*, ed. Roger Lonsdale (New York: Oxford University Press, 1990), 45–46. We are grateful to Professor Carla Mulford, Pennsylvania State University, for assistance with this note.

81. **Mr. Addison**: Joseph Addison (1672–1719), a distinguished classical scholar. "Between 1709 and 1711 he contributed a number of papers to Steele's *Tatler* and joined with him in the production of *The Spectator*" (*OCEL*, 5th).

82. **Mr. Pope**: Alexander Pope (1688–1744), major eighteenth-century poet, translator, editor, and prose writer (*OCEL*, 5th).

83. **Harvey**: Probably a reference to James Hervey (1714–58), rector of Weston-Favell, who was also a popular writer of *Meditations and Contemplations* (London

has so much Goodness of Soul, that I revere him, amid all his Prolixity, as for Mr. Richardson,[84] he is a perfect Proteus, ever assuming a new Form, but in all sensible.—

England like other places has its Sweets & Bitters—to be sure if you have an unlimited Taste for Pleasure, have Health & Fortune, here is the Place, but you must even then, have Moments of Doubt, whether that Indulgence of Desires, is consistant with Candidates & Probationers for Eternity, for my Part I think a moderate Fortune, Health, Peace of Mind, & agreable Connections, may be enjoyed in America—there it is I hope to spend my Days—If I have Health, I shall taste those Blessings, if not, Tranquility, & a Father & Mother's Bosom is the most fit to repose on.—

Doctor Fothergill[85] has that Knowledge of the World & sweet Humility, that makes the Company of a Man of Sense, with a good Heart, so very pleasing.—We pass'd thro' Islington, by Ham, & came to Upton in Essex, where the Docrs. Country House stands in a fine Plain,—the House is old, the Rooms very large, & most genteely furnished,—very pretty Tapestry, & the utmost neatness & Order, & attention in all the Servants, beyond what I almost ever met with.—

and Philadelphia, 1750). Volume 1 contains "Meditations among the Tombs," "Meditations on a Flower-Garden," and "A Descant on Creation." Volume 2 has "Contemplations on the Night," "Contemplations on the Starry Heavens," and "A Winter-Piece." A book plate of J. Logan (Jr.) is in the copy owned by the Library Company of Philadelphia.

84. **Mr. Richardson**: Samuel Richardson (1689–1761), novelist. Among his most famous is *Clarissa, or The History of a Young Lady*, an epistolary novel, published in London, 1747–48, in 7 vols. (*OCEL*).

85. **Doctor Fothergill**: John Fothergill (1712–80), was an English physician and eminent Quaker. Fothergill, who never married, lived with his sister Ann (1718–1802), who also never married. They had a home in London, and in 1762, Fothergill bought an estate at Upton in Essex, about five miles outside of London. There he created a botanical garden with thousands of specimens. Fothergill and his sister also founded and supervised the building of the Ackworth school, where the first pupils were admitted in 1779. Betsy C. Corner and Christopher C. Booth, eds., "Introduction," *Chain of Friendship: Selected Letters of Dr. John Fothergill of London, 1735–1780* (Cambridge: Belknap-Harvard University Press, 1971), 8, 102n, 241, 243n, 450n. See pages 36–37, for a brief discussion of Elizabeth Graeme Fergusson's trip to England, which included a visit with the Fothergills.

The House opens into the Garden which has on each Side of a large
gravel Walk, fine old high Hedges, that give a pleasing Solemnity to
the Place & when you are arrived at the Foot of the Garden, the
House at the end of the Walk is a pretty Object, being white, to termi-
nate the Eye at the End of the Vista; the Garden takes in 5 Acres, has
large green Walks & a fine Stream of Water, it is not perhaps, what
would be called here a fine Garden, but it is so full of flowering
Shrubs, Variety of Hedges, & so agreably diversified, that I think it a
pleasing Spot,—Altho' the Society the Docr. & his Sister are of, does
not admit of that kind of mechanical Politeness that shews itself in external Forms, yet true good Breeding, which arises from the goodness
of the Heart, & a kind Attention to the Wants of others—they in that
Light must ever be reckon'd, to be perfectly well bred, for they excell
in that.

—There was not so many Huzzas as one might expect from the
publick Appearance of so good a King, for by the unprejudiced Accounts of the most sensible People & those who know most of him, he
is a most amiable young Man.—It seems an Offence to some that he
enjoys the Sweets of domestic Life, they say he is too fond of his Wife
& Children, & leads too regular a Life, I suppose they want a Charles
the 2d. on the Throne, to make Mistresses of their Wives & Daughters, & furnish the Nation with a Race of royal illegitimate Children.—Because he turns all his Sense to good Purposes, many endeavour to represent him as a weak Man, but by the best Accounts he
is steady, sensible, pious & Calm.

───────ℓ─────────────

Upon leaving England

Perhaps if I had had high Health, Scenes of Pleasure & Disipation,
might have taken so far Possession of me as to make me regret leaving
a Country, where Pleasure in every Shape offers herself, yet not without Alloy, for there are many little Incidents, necessary to make even
what appears to be Joy, really so, & I am convinced many an Hour of
insipid Langour possesses the Mind that would wish to be thought
happy, this you & I have often talked over, as we have sat at the Door
of Graeme Park, strolled on the Terrass or watched the Moon that
friend to Contemplation, how happy have we been there, & how
happy may we be again—o! my Friend, keep yr. Heart open to be

Fig. 11. Elizabeth Graeme Fergusson's country home, Graeme Park. The house stands, and is open to visitors. Photo by Karin Wulf.

pleased with Nature & yr. own mind; which from all I ever saw of it, will present no Page, on which is not wrote Innocence & Truth—I would not flatter you, I really think it—Let me finish this Evening with some Lines from our favourite Young[86]

    "I envy none their Pageantry & Shew,

86. **Lines from our favourite Young**: These lines are quoted from Edward Young, *Love of Fame, the Universal Passion* (1725) taken from the First Satire:

> I envy none their pageantry and show;
> I envy none the gilding of their woe.
> Give me, indulgent gods! with mind serene,
> And guiltless heart, to range the sylvan Scene:
> No splendid poverty, no smiling care,
> No well-bred hate, or servile grandeur, there:
> There pleasing objects useful thoughts suggest:
> The sense is ravish'd, and the soul is blest:
> On every thorn delightful wisdom grows:
> In every rill a sweet instruction flows.

"I envy none the gilding of their Woe,
"Give me indulgent God with Mind serene
"A guiltless Heart, to range the sylvan Scene,
"Where rural Objects, useful Thoughts suggest
"The Soul is ravish'd & Senses blest,
"In every Bush some pleasing Lesson grows
"In every Brook some soft Instruction flows."—

I know not what my future State of life is to be, but was I to form a
Wish it should not be I think Extravagant. I am not particularly attached to any Spot, but while some dear Friends live, I hope it to be in
Philad[elphi]a. Health I look on to be the Basis on which we found all
earthly Blessings—A Conscience void of Offence as to gross Crimes
(for as to Faults & Foibles, no Life is unsullied with them), A Society
of Friends whose Actions are guided by Affection, Chearfulness, Pro-
bity & Good-sense—perhaps if I go any further, you will think me
unreasonable in Demands, but this writing diverts me, & I will go
on.—The Article of Climate I will give up, we must supply the De-
ficiencies of that by Contrivance, but then Fortune must be favour-
able to furnish a warm good House in the Winter, & airy pretty Gardens in the Summer—The Garden for many Reasons I cannot give
up, I do not wish for a Fortune that would not require Oeconomy, he
that saves in nothing is a mad man, he that saves in all Things a Fool—
every Person has some particular Taste to gratify which others whose
Turns do not lay the same way call Whims & Singularity, but the in-
dulging these Whims & Singularitys, frequently constitute the greatest Pleasure of our Lives, & while they incommode nobody, are not
to be restrained.—The Command of our Time is a pleasing Circum-
stance, but that depends so much on the Station we are placed in, that
I dare not make it a Preliminary, however, our Sex have a greater
Chance of obtaining it as the Publick has no Demands on us, it is the
noble Lordly Creature Man, whose Heart must glow, & Head toil for
his Country for you know some Author says A Woman's Glory is to
shine unknown
    As for the Pleasure of relieving the distressed, & all that—People as
frequently lose the Pleasure, as they obtain the Means, so that I shall

Edward Young, *The Poetical Works of Edward Young*, ed. John Mitford (London:
Bell, 1896), 2:67.

say nothing on that Score.—If you disapprove my Plan, write a better, in the mean Time I wish you all the above good Things.

31st of May 1765.

Let me add a Line or two of my own, for I am not in Love, & yet have experienced all the Pleasures that letters can possibly bestow from Affection.—

Poor Eloisa[87] had a Mind tore by disappointed Love, & you know, wasted her Bloom & Youth, in a gloomy Convent, with just Religion enough to torture her, but not enough to vanquish her Passions, so that she sustain'd a dreadful Conflict.

Can the fine Strokes express all Friendships Pow'r
And sooth the Anguish of the lonely Hour,
Can Stella's Soul[88] & Sentiment appear
O'er western Seas & raise the starting Tear?
Maternal Love can glow upon the Page   5
And all the Wisdom of experienc'd Age,
Honour, Religion, & each sov'reign Truth,
Advice & Caution, to each unguarded Youth
All this & more, can pow'rful Letters give,
And Paper may be almost said to live,   10
In Ovids Days[89] they thank great Cadmus Art[90]
Who did this Knowledge, to the World impart,
This did for Pagans, but a Christian Soul,
Must own the Deity inspir'd the whole.

87. **Poor Eloisa**: Graeme probably refers to "Eloisa" from the poem by Alexander Pope, published in 1717. "A heroic epistle, . . . Pope's version of the tragic love of Heloise and Abelard was highly popular; it portrays Heloise, in a Gothic seclusion of 'grots and caverns', still tormented by passionate love, unable to renounce for God the memory of 'unholy joy'" she had for the monk, Abelard (*OCEL*, 5th).

88. **Stella's Soul**: Another conventional pseudonym for a beautiful woman. The particular "Stella" in E. G.'s journal is probably Elizabeth Stedman, according to Martha C. Slotten, in "Elizabeth Graeme Ferguson: A Poet in 'The Athens of North America,'" *PMHB* 108 (1984), 296n.

89. **In Ovids Days**: Publius Ovidius Naso (43 B.C.–A.D. 17), Roman poet.

90. **Cadmus Art**: Cadmus's art (with the help of Athena) helped establish Thebes. "He was regarded as the inventor of agriculture, of working in bronze, and of civilization in general" (Seyffert, *Dictionary of Classical Antiquities*).

Lady Charlotte Finch,[91] & Lady Juliana Penn, called on me to go & breakfast with one Mr. Goldney[92] an eminent Quaker of an antient Family, his house is on Clifton Hill, about a Mile from the Hot-wells, & is allowed to be one of the finest Views in Engld.—we breakfasted with great Elegance & had a most genteel & hospitable Reception.— The Gent. was a particular frd. of Mr. Penns, a Batchelor & has two maiden Sisters, the polite Treatment that fell to my share, I know was owing to the Company I went with—but every Body that can, goes there, altho' it is made more difficult, as some low minded People stole some Shells out of a Grotto, that I am told without Dispute is the best in Engld. & many say not exceeded in Europe.— It is at the Foot of a beautiful green Walk, on each side of which, is a fine Hedge, the Grotto is 20 foot wide & 60 Long, the Roof supported by 4 Pillars which are covered with bristol Stones, bits of shining Rocks & petrified Spars, the Floor is a kind of Mosaic which appears to be finely veined & polished, but is only several Kinds of Clay mixed together & baked, but is so neatly inlaid, & well disposed that it has a fine Effect—there is a well Light let down from the Roof which is surrounded with Foliage & shell Flowers, this is the only Part that has the Appearance of Art in the whole——At one End is a Neptune in a reclining Posture who holds a large Pipe, thro' which the Water tumbles into a deep Cistern, made of Shells, & on each Side is a Shell of a monstrous Size brought from the East-Indies, that is scalloped & holds the drippings of the Water as it ouzes along—There is a Cavern that holds

91. **Lady Charlotte Finch**: Lady Finch hosted Elizabeth Graeme for some portion of her trip to England. She was the daughter of the Earl of Somerset and the wife of Heneage Finch, the Earl of Aylesford. Hubertis Cummings, *Richard Peters: Provincial Secretary and Cleric, 1704–1776* (Philadelphia: University of Pennsylvania Press, 1944), 278; Alan Valentine, *The British Establishment 1760–84* (Norman: University of Oklahoma Press, 1970), 1:317.

92. **Mr. Goldney**: Thomas Goldney III (1696–1768) was a third-generation Quaker who inherited money and property, and continued to increase his wealth through various ventures, including "a privateering voyage" to the South Seas, an iron works, and two banks. He occupied his leisure time with the creation and design of the unusual garden that Elizabeth Graeme described in her journal (*MMMB* 58). In 1737 he began his first major garden project, a grotto, that he built in stages; Elizabeth Graeme saw it when it was completed in 1764. The other projects—a terrace, a mock fortification, a rotunda with colonnade, and a tower—are all described in Goldney's personal garden diary. See P. K. Stembridge, *Goldney: A House and A Family* (Bristol: Burleigh Ltd., 1969).

a Lion large as the Life, that faces the Door & guards the Place—the Shells are so many—so proper for a Work of the Kind, & so beautiful that I thought it far exceeded Lord Tilney's at Wanstead, but that is vastly beautiful also.—Lady Charlotte Finch who has travelled over France & Italy, said it was the prettyest Thing she had ever seen.—After looking at this romantic Place, we went a considerable way thro' a Walk cut thro a Rock, & came into the open free Air, & a Prospect, of one of the finest Countrys imaginable.—Then we walked on a very delightful Terrass thrown up at an immense Expence & Labour, from which we returned to an octagon Building that is on the Point of the Hill, the Windows of this Building, are so disposed at the outside, to see a Camera Obscura,[93] of the whole Country & the Objects around—in the Garden is a pretty Piece of rural Painting, where the Sky is remarkably well done— there is a fine green House, & in the House a very fine Sett of english China on a Silver Tea Table, & two fine fruit Pieces done by a celebrated Hand.— We took our leave after a most agreable Morning.

Seeing fine Gardens in the Spring & Summer, ever was ranked among my capital Pleasures, it seems to be of that innocent Nature as occasions no Checks nor Reflections of a painful Kind upon the Recollection, & when the Mind feels that Chearfulness on rural Prospects that raise & enliven it,—it leads us to be thankful to the great Author of Nature, each one addressing him, under the Title of Jehovah, Jove or Lord.

And now let me conclude this Evening with almost dropping a few Tears, for the Loss the Christian, and Religious Part of the World sustain in the angelick Docr. Young,[94] who this Day I have heard is dead, & gave strict Orders all his Manuscripts & Papers should be burnt, You who admire & are conversant with his Writings know what a Soul he was blest with, but if the Soul is admitted to early Enjoyments of Bliss after Death I make no doubt, but he is now a glorified Saint in

93. **Camera Obscura**: "An instrument consisting of a darkened chamber or box, into which light is admitted through a double convex lens, forming an image of external objects on a surface of paper, glass, etc., placed at the focus of the lens" (*OED*).
94. **Docr. Young**: Edward Young died April 5, 1765 (*OCEL*, 5th).

Heaven, for sure by his Works, he fought the good Fight, he has finished his Course, & for him is laid up a Crown of Glory, for my Part I acknowledge myself, to be among the Number, that have been deeply touched with his Writings, & extracted many useful Sentiments from them, which if not sufficiently remembered, is owing to myself, not to the Writer who is admirable.

Peace be to his holy Spirit.

I spent this Day in reading a very beautiful eastern Tale—Almoran & Hamet,[95] where the steady Perseverance of Virtue in spite of the most alarming Appearances leads to Happiness—The eastern Stile when not filled too much with Bombast, & Rhapsody I ever admired, Truth at last flashes on the Soul, like the purest Rays of Light & by the Splendor & Brightness of its Illuminations drives & discovers Vice, in all its lurking Places & Obscurities & points out the Clue that unwinds the perplexing Labyrinth.—Yet my dear Betsy[96] as I am on the Subject, give me leave to drop a few Words as the Thing appears to me—I am wrong very probably in my Opinion.—The great End of the better kind of all these Works, is to vindicate the Ways of God to Men, who by a long Series of Calamities may think they are forgot or severely treated by the supreme Disposer of all Things, therefore by dwelling on Books of this Nature, if they are tolerably virtuous begin to think that the bright Side must appear tho' late, or their Lot is peculiarly hard, so far you will say Writings of this Kind prove a Consolation in Days of Gloom & Adversity, but should not all these Things be Transcripts of Life; & does not the World abound with modest Merit, & even sparkling Virtues, pining in Obscurity, while Pride & Insolence, vaunt it without Controul.—& this not for a transient Gleam, but from Year to Year, & Age to Age.—We are but too apt to

95. **Almoran & Hamet**: *Almoran & Hamet* (1761) is an exotic Oriental tale written by John Hawkesworth (1715–73). "Untrammelled by space or time, Almoran can change into any shape to pursue his strange, and often supernatural, adventures among magnificent heroes and base villains" (see "John Hawkesworth," in *OCEL*, 5th). "These tales enjoyed great popularity in the second half of the 18th and the early part of the 19th centuries" ("Oriental [or Eastern] novel [or tale]" in *OCEL*, 5th).

96. **Betsy**: Elizabeth Stedman, her friend. For additional information about Stedman's and Fergusson's correspondence during the latter's trip to England, see pages 36–37.

look on our own Misfortunes as Tryals, & our Neighbours as judgements—Self-love leads us to this unkind Distinction; but they whose
Lives are guided by that Religion which says we must love our Neighbour as ourself, are not to expect their Reward in this Life.—The amiable Author of Clarissa[97] in that uncomparable Novel, has pointed
out what I mean, & yet for that very Thing is his Work discom-
mended, & for the short lived Satisfaction of seeing the Hero & Heroine, at the End of a Book, with a fine House, a great many Children,
Friends & Servants, & wholly possessed of every good Thing, to obtain that as a Reward of their Merit is Nature strain'd & a Thousand
Circumstances turned from their proper Channel.——Will you forgive this tedious Digression?

I told my Doctor the other Day, that I feared my Friends would urge
me to use more Exercise & go more abroad than was consistant with
my Inclination, & I hoped he would not join in it, he told me that if I
would write down what I liked best, he would if possible subscribe to
it, this gave Rise to the latter Part of the following Copy of Verses.

To Doctor Fothergill.—

As Happiness must ever be our Aim,
By various Paths, we still pursue the same
We long for Pleasure & for Ease we sigh
And strain the Cords that draw the Object nigh.
Tho' Taste & Whim do oft, too oft prevail   5
And Arts refin'd pervert not trim the Scale,
Where Heav'n & Nature kindly meant to weigh,
With moral Rectitude each well spent Day,
While mild Humility that soft-ey'd Maid,
Views virtuous Actions, as if half afraid,   10
The very Thought, her Pupils could excell
Might stain the Lustre of their doing well
Internal Peace from different Causes flow,
Too deep the Subject to attempt to shew,
Howe'er Mankind thro' different Mediums see,   15
In this one Point I think they all agree,

---

97. **Author of Clarissa**: Samuel Richardson (1689–1761). See "Clarissa" in
OCEL, 5th, for a summary of the novel.

To draw, sweet Health, a pleasing Stream from thee.
As Soul & Body's for a Time confin'd,
'Till Heav'n permits the Knot to be disjoin'd;
Its but vain boasting, then, to talk of Bliss, 20
While this fine Frame feels—there is aught amiss.
The Stoics Tongue won't own the Force of Pain,
Too proud to yield, too Stubborn to complain,
From his first Maxims won[']t in Word depart,
And Doubly suffers for his Pride of Heart, 25
Tho' this great Evil can't be quite redrest,
I[t's] vastly soften'd in a Patient Breast,
Who prays of Heav'n to calm their gloomy Fears
And trust their Pray'rs will reach th'Almightys Ears.
In certain Herbs & Plants there lays a Power 30
To lull the Anguish of the painful Hour,
In Gums & Fossils was this Pow'r conceal'd,
'Till Chance, & Skill, & Time, this Pow'r reveal'd.
Deep Secrets yet may Nature have in Store,
But bless the present—humbly hope for more. 35
Most true her Bounties have been oft abus'd
And oft thro' Ignorance her Aid's misus'd.
For venal Gold, her Poisons dealt around,
And added Anguish to the aching Wound.
In ev'ry Age, in every Clime this wrong 40
Has damp'd th' Eulogy of Friendships Song,
Yet low Pretenders to each nobler Art
Serve but as Steps to mount the better Part.
Who rais'd, exalted, to a higher Sphere,
Not only heal, but drop the gen'rous Tear, 45
Their Heads may dictate, but their Hearts will feel
And mourn those Woes beyond their Pow'r to heal,
The Good & Modest, all unite in this
The bold Assumer thinks he ne'er can miss.
O Britain bless'd, for many Favours sent 50
Allow'd in Fame, by Europes in joint Consent,
To boast the Knowledge of the healing Tribe,
Where Skill with Virtue has been closely tied,
In Painting, Sculpture, & poetic Fire,
Your neighb'ring Nations may with Truth aspire 55

Fig. 12.   Dr. John Fothergill, by Gilbert Stuart. John Fothergill, a noted Quaker, was Elizabeth Graeme's physician in London. Courtesy, Pennsylvania Academy of Fine Arts, Philadelphia, Pennsylvania.

To struggle for the Laurel or the Palm;
Yet ev'n here you're far from proving Calm,
Let Naples boast the Pow'r of forming Stone,
Like Life born Features—this be all her own;
Let art drawn Pencils every Beauty trace,   60
And glowing Colours animate the Face
But Englands Sons more useful in their Skill
Can stop the Progress of destructive Ill,
The fine Anatomist can point the Way;
And find the Source where every Evil lay.   65

As some nice Florist marks the falling Show'r
That gives fresh Vigour to the drooping Flow'r,
Thro' ev'ry Tube or Channel views the Course
Where gently moving, or with active Force,
Thus Harvey[98] trac'd the Bloods meand'ring Stream   70
And saw thro' Natures fine wrought complex Scheme:
Untwin'd the Clue that veil'd the purple Tide
Explor'd those Views, no longer doom'd to hide,
Nor dy'd with him this Science so profound,
While Hunter[99] lives it falls not to the Ground;   75
The nice Contexture of the human Frame
But adds fresh Honour to his growing Fame.
Impartial Justice only waits the dead,
Then selfish Envy bends her drooping Head,
And all Mankind unite to praise those gone   80
Which living is with such reluctance done.
May Months & Years, in gentle Peace roll round,
Before that Justice to a Name is found;
Which to his Merit & his Skill they owe
My heart can dictate my Pen cant shew,   85
The first among Physicians may he shine.
As Friend as Brother I have shar'd his Time
Alone & Pensive & opprest with Pain
The starting Tear sometimes could scarce refrain.
Tho' England's Pleasures open to me lay   90
Pain barr'd my Entrance & forbad the Way.—
But Joy unmix'd is not our Fate below,
Still dash'd & sully'd from the Cup of Woe,
Lest I should cry from here, I can't depart
And Dissipation had usurp'd my Heart.   95
But let not here my Obligations end
But add to Favours of your grateful Friend;
Let me intreat Advice in distant Climes
Where Boreas[100] blusters, & where Phoebus shines,

98. **Harvey**: William Harvey (1578–1657), physician who discovered the circulation of the blood (*OCEL*, 5th).
99. **Hunter**: John Hunter (1728–93), Scottish biologist, physician, physiologist, surgeon, and Fellow of Royal Society, and his brother William Hunter (1718–83), Scottish anatomist, physician, and obsetrician (*DNB*).
100. **Boreas**: "The north wind" (*OCCL*).

I wish to lead a calm & tranquil Life 100
Distant from Bustle & a noisy Strife
Action & Exercise the World admire,
And call that best their Souls do most desire
No rich dress'd Viands shall my Health confound
Nor in strain'd Passions be my Senses drown'd 105
Nor very early would I meet the Dawn
While Dew drops glitter on the verdant Lawn;
A moon light Walk indulge me on the Green,
Or when the Sun makes ev'ry Shadow seen
In Forms gigantick, let me stroll along, 110
To hear the Mock-bird chaunt his rural Song
But when rough Winter with his Iron Hand,
Collects round crackling Fires a social Band;
I sit by that dear Pair unknown to you
Whose Souls can feel for Virtue all thats due 115
Let me remain nor rove abroad nor stray
Where Snows & Frosts point out the slipp'ry way.
The Book, the Work, the Pen can all employ
The vacant Moment to some peaceful Joy.
My Mentor too, shall join our little round, 120
And much we'll talk & think of british Ground,
More temp'rate Climes you & yr. Friends enjoy
No suns that scorch, nor Cold your Frames destroy,
    May ev'ry Pleasure to yr. Lot be join'd
You know the greatest of a virtuous Mind, 125
"As those we love, decay, we dye in Part
"String after String is sever'd from the Heart,
" 'Till loosen'd Life at last but breathing Clay,
"Without one Pang is glad to fall away.
"Unhappy he who latest feels the Blow, 130
"Whose Eyes have wept o'er ev'ry Friend laid low,
"Dragg'd ling'ring on from partial Death to Death,
"Still dying all he can resigns his Breath.["]
Londo. Pall Mall[101] July 3rd. 1765.

⟋⟍

101. **Londo. Pall Mall**: An exclusive street in London, actually an alley, where Nell Gwyn, the actress, lived in the Restoration period, and a century later Gainsborough (*OCEL*, 3d).

I hardly know what my Sensations were, when I went up the Ship side, a mixture of Pain & Pleasure, from my peculiar Situation,—I long to see you, & take all Pains to get at you, but here are People in Engld. that the Thoughts of never seeing again gives me some Pain—But my Duty & Inclination is to be with my dear Pappa, & you, & the Family, to taste the Sweets of domestic Life, as much as I can without my dear Mamma.—I have receiv'd not only Marks of Civility but real Friendship from People much my Superiors in Engld. & have receiv'd Advice, & made observations that if it is not my own Fault, may be of Service, to me throughout Life;—upon the whole, I like Engld. much, ev'ry Art & Science, every particular Mode of Life, People may indulge the Hobby Horse [102] to the utmost extent in, for the Number of People, create such a Variety of Pursuits, that London is the Mart for Knowledge & Pleasure, & Goodness & Virtue are by Individuals, as much practised there as any where. I love Engld. because my dear Mamma, was born in it, I love it because it has given Birth to so many great & good Men, whose Writings have helped to form our Education in America; & I love it because I have been treated with Humanity, Respect & Politeness. But I can be happy without the Prospect of ever seeing it again, I pretend not to object to the Ways of Providence[.] I hope to enjoy some Comforts yet at home, tho my Loss is too recent on my Mind, to figure Joy on our first Meeting[.]

Epitaph by E. G. on her Mother
Forgive great God, this one last filial Tear,
Indulge my Sorrow on a Theme so near,
This Earth born Strain indulge, that mourns the blest
And doubly mourns because they were the best,
Tho Truth remonstrates, Self-love will prevail,   5
And sink the Beam in Natures feeble Scale.
A God incarnate wept o'er Lazurus [103] dead,
Tho' Pow'r Divine recall'd his Soul when fled,
A poor frail Being weeps a Mother gone,

---

102. **Hobby Horse:** "A favourite pursuit or pastime" (*OED*).
103. **Lazurus:** Jesus wept over the dead Lazarus, brother of Martha and Mary (John 11:1–44).

The Tomb scarce clos'd before a Sister flown.   10
Each was a Guide, a Pattern, & a Friend,
She prays to join when fleeting Life shall end.

59 Copy of a Letter from B. F. to J. H.[104]

Sir/

I rec'd. yr. kind Letter of the 2nd Inst[ant]. & I am glad to hear you
increase in Strength, I hope you will continue mending 'till you re-
cover yr. former Health & firmness, let me know whether you still use
the cold Bath & what Effect it has.

   As to the Kindness you mention I wish it could have been of more
Service to you, but if it had, the only Thanks I should desire, is that
you would be always equally ready to serve any other Person that
may need yr. Assistance, & so let good Offices go round, for Mankind
are all of a Family.—For my own Part when I am employed in serving
others, I do not look upon myself as conferring Favours, but as paying Debts; In my Travels & since my Settlement I have received much
Kindness from Men to whom I shall never have an oppo[rtunity] of
making the least direct Return, & numberless Mercies from God who
is infinitely above being benefited by our Services; these Kindnesses
from Men I can only return on their fellow Men, & I can only shew
my Gratitude for these Mercies from God by a readiness to help his
other Childn. & my Brethren, for I do not think that Thanks and
Compliments tho' reapeated weekly can discharge our real Obligations to each other, & much less those to our Creator.—You will by
this see my Notions of good Works, & that I am far from expecting
Heaven by them, by Heaven we understand a State of Happiness,
infinite in Degree & eternal in Duration, I can do nothing to deserve
such Rewards. He that for giving a Draught of Water to a thirsty Person should expect to be paid with a good Plantation would be modest

104. **B. F. to J. H.**: This letter, sent from Benjamin Franklin to Joseph Huey, dated
June 6, 1753, was often copied and reprinted during the eighteenth century. There is
some controversey surrounding the identity of its recipient. For a copy of the letter, a
discussion of its history and efforts to identify Joseph Huey, see Labaree, *The Papers
of Benjamin Franklin*, 4:503–6.

in his Demands compared with those who think they deserve Heaven by the Good they can do on Earth; even the mixed Imperfect Pleasures we enjoy in this World are rather from Gods Goodness than our Merit, how much more so then the Happiness of Heaven, for my own Part, I have not the Vanity to think I deserve it, the Folly to expect, nor the Ambition to desire it, but content myself in submitting myself to the Will & disposal of him that made me who hath hitherto preserved me & blessed me, & in whose fatherly Goodness I may well confide, that he will never make me miserable & that even the Afflictions I may at any Time suffer, shall tend to my Benefit.—

The Faith you mention has doubtless its Use in the World, I do not desire to see it deminished nor would I lessen it in any Man, but I wish it was more productive of good Works, Works of Kindness, Charity[,] Mercy, & publick Spirit, not Holliday keeping, sermon reading, or having performed Church Ceremonies, or making long Prayers, filled with Flatteries & Compliments, despised even by wise Men, & much less capable of pleasing the Deity. The Worship of God is a Duty, the hearing or reading Sermons may be useful, but if a Man rests in hearing or praying as too many do, it is as if a Tree should value itself upon being watered & putting forth Leaves tho' it never produced any Fruit.

Your great Master thought much less of these outward Appearances & Professions, than many of his modern Disciples. He preferred the Doers of the Word to the meer hearers of it; the Son that seemingly refused to obey his Father & yet performed his Commands, to him that professed his Readiness & yet neglected the Work; the heretical tho' charitable Samaratin [105] to the uncharitable tho' sanctified Priest, & those who gave Food to the Hungry, Drink to the Thirsty, Raiment to the Naked, Entertainment to the Stranger & Relief to the Sick, tho' they never heard of his Name, he declares shall in the last Day be accepted, when those who cry Lord! Lord! who value themselves on their Faith tho' great enough to perform Miracles, but having neglected to perform good Works shall be rejected.

He professed that he came not to call the Righteous, but Sinners to Repentance, which implied his modest Opinion that there were in his Time some so good that they needed not to hear even him, but now a days we have scarce a little Parson who does not think it the Duty of every Man within his reach, to sit under his petty Ministration, & that

105. **charitable Samaratan**: The parable of the Good Samaritan, Luke 10:33ff.

whosoever omits them offends God, I wish to such more Humility and to you Sir more Health & Happiness

being yr. frd. and Hbl. Servt.
Benja. Franklin

60 [Epitaph]

The Body of
Ben Franklin, Printer,[106]
Like the Cover of an old Book,
Its Contents worn out,
And stript of its Lettering & gilding,
Lies here Food for the Worms,
Yet the Work shall not be lost,
For it will (as he believ'd) appear once more
In a new & more beautiful Edition,
Corrected & Amended
By the Author.
Was born Jun the 6th. 1706
Died 17

61 [Epitaph]

Josiah Franklin,
and
Abiah his Wife,[107]
lie here interred:—
They liv'd lovingly together in Wedlock
fifty five Year's

106. **Ben Franklin, Printer**: A number of these epitaphs, written by Franklin himself, exist in slightly different form. He gave a number of copies to friends, who passed them on. He may have written the first version in 1728. Labaree, *The Papers of Benjamin Franklin*, 1:109–11.

107. **Josiah Franklin and Abiah his Wife**: Benjamin Franklin composed this epitaph for a headstone that was placed in a Boston burial ground. A copy of it appeared

And without an Estate or any gainful Employment
By constant Labour & honest Industry
(with Gods Blessing)
Maintain'd a large Family comfortably,
And brought up thirteen Children & seven grand Children
Reputably:—
From this Instance Reader
Be encourag'd to Diligence in thy Calling
And distrust not Providence.
He was a pious & prudent Man
She a discreet & virtuous Woman!
Their youngest Son*
In filial Regard to their Memory
places this Stone.

J. F. born 1655 died 1744.
A. F. born 1667 died 1752.

[Marginal note:]
*Benja. Franklin

62   A Letter from the Countess of Huntingdon [108] to Ann Hyam, giving an Acct. of the late Queens Death.

I will not make any Apology, Dear Madam[,] for not having wrote
sooner, & I do assure you this is the first time I have taken Pen in hand

in *The New England Magazine of Knowledge and Pleasure* in 1758. A copy of the epitaph also appeared in Franklin's autobiography. Labaree, *The Papers of Benjamin Franklin*, 3:229–30.

108. **Countess of Huntington**: Selina Hastings, the Countess of Huntingdon (1701–91), was the daughter of the Earl of Ferrers and the wife of the Earl of Huntingdon. A convert to Methodism, she investigated various evangelical or dissenting religions throughout her life and founded various chapels and a seminary. She was a close friend and supporter of George Whitefield, to whom she left her property in America so that he could pursue his ambition of founding an orphans' home in Georgia. See George Crosfield, *Memoirs of the Life and Gospel Labours of Samuel Fothergill* (London: Charles Gilpin, 1843), 461; also, *DNB*.

since the Queens Illness, which lasted 12 Days, nine are now past since we lost the best Friend & Mistress that ever Servants had, yet all my Faculties seem benumbed as if seized with a Palsey, you that know what it is to feel can best judge, what one suffers with a broken Heart & a distracted Head, & how little one is capable of uttering, even Sorrow: from the first seizure I foresaw our Loss, & hardly ever felt one Gleam of Hope, & yet when the Stroke came, it found me unprepared, but not her that underwent it, she never from her first seisure had any Hopes of her Recovery, nor shew'd the least Fear of the Pains she endur'd or of the last closing Scene, her only Concern was for the Kings affliction, which certainly is as sincere & intense as ever human Nature sustained. The Arch-bishop who attended her constantly, told me he never saw a Behaviour equally glorious and Christian to hers, & that all she said to him, deserved to be printed. The first time he went, he express'd his Sorrow to see her so ill & her Pain so great, but she told him, tho' her Body suffered, she had a good Conscience, which spoke inexpressible Comfort to her & supported in the midst of all her Troubles.—About 2 hours before she died she called for the Duke who was in the Room with the King & Princesses, tho' she had a severe Fever, contracted by having sat up several Nights together, when he came to her Bedside she told him, she called him to give him her Blessing & upon it to charge him to be always dutiful to his Father, & never to listen to any one who might be wicked enough to insinuate that they could have seperate Interests, for if that were possible he would find more Comfort in haveing adhered to his Duty than in possessing all the Empires in the World; & added that whether he lived long or not, he would find no Thought worth his Care on a dying Bed, but how he had lived, & if he could then feel that he had acted the Part of a Man of Honour & Justice, & a Christian, it would give him Joy that he could feel but not describe.—she then ordered him to go to Bed, which he submitted to with great Reluctance.—After she had lain quiet some time, they ask'd her to take some Viper Broth, but she desired to have something to give her a little Spirit, they brought her some Palsey Drops in Mad[eir]a Wine, swallowing which put her into a Fit of Coughing & difficulty of drawing Breath for some Time—she then took leave of the Princesses one by one, and gave some particular Directions to each of them, last of all she took leave of the King & thanked him for all his Goodness to her in Terms the most moving imaginable & among other Things said.—"My poor Servants are under excessive Affliction, give me leave Sir, to recommend them to y[ou]r. Protection" when she had done speaking she bid one of the Bed-chamber Women take away the Candles that stood near the Bed, the King asked her if they offended her Eyes, she said, "No Sir, but I would spare you the Affliction of seeing me die."—she then laid quiet about a quarter of an Hour, at the End of which, she called to those in the Room (for the Bishop was gone) to read the recommendary Prayers, & desired them to pray for her, & read aloud that she might hear them, before it was finished she expired.—The King stay'd in the Room about half an Hour after & I believe has not known a Thought since but what tended in the strongest Manner to shew his tenderness & regard to her Memory.—His first Act was to confirm to all her Servants from the highest to the lowest, their respective Salaries for his Life.—The next was to look into her accounts of all her charitable Pensions which amounted to £13.000 per Year,—which he likewise confirmed, & not satisfied with that, he has ordered that we should all let him know the Names of those who received casual Relief through our Hands, that he may from Time to Time assist them.—This is the Behaviour of the Man that has been called false to her,—fickle in his Friendship, & avaritious.—He has ordered her Body to be embalmed as near as they can get any sight[109] into the Egyptian Manner at the Expence of between 5 & 600£—her Funeral is to be after the Manner of Queen Anne. Her whole Family attend their Days about, as if she was alive, the Lady of the Bed-chamber, Lord Chamberlain & Master of the Horse by Day; two maids of Honour, two Bed-Chamber Women, & an Equery, every Night.

63 A Letter from Queen Caroline[110] to her Children on the Death of the late King

My dear Children,

I write to you after a most troubled Night, with a dead King always before my Eyes, & he will never be out of my Thoughts I believe.—

109. **can get any sight**: as in "insight."

110. **Queen Caroline**: Caroline (1683–1737) was Queen of Great Britain and Ireland and the wife of King George II. Seven of her children lived to adulthood. She was active in politics and served as the King's regent during his absences abroad (*DNB*).

The King your Father cannot give you a greater Mark of his Love, & good Intentions he has for you, than in remembering you before he went to London.—I hope the death of yr. Grand-Father will be as a Lesson to you of the Instability of all human Grandeur, & that you will take Care to be always prepared to give an Account to the great God of all yr. Actions, when it pleases him to call you before him.—

Adieu my Dears,

Caroline.

June 15th. 1727.

64   Copy of a Letter from M[.] Morris[111]

I cannot help taking Notice, that my Aunt has been writing a Panegyrick upon Debby Wilson, & entirely overlooks me, which, I think not quite civil, & I propose, therefore, a slight sketch of myself, in order to spare her, or others the trouble: but, that I may not herein incur the censure of Vanity give me leave to observe, that if I am my own Biographer,[112] it is no more than several Heroes, Philosophers, Statesmen, & Bards have been before me; & as they wisely thought, so also think I, that 'tis the same Thing, nay, much more honest, than to employ an Hireling or Parasite to do it for us; in this Case, I refer myself to my frd. Kendall, a good Judge in these Matters—whether it would not have been of great Emolument to the present Times, had many illustrious Personages, who adorn both ancient & modern History, been constrained, a few Days before the setting of their Sun, to have drawn their own Portraits, proclaimed all their Transactions & their Motives—what unspeakable Benefit would have thence arisen to both Church and State?—I am delighted with the Thoughts of making such a Regulation among our great Folks, & the Worthies of the present & succeeding Ages.—As the scheme is intirely my own, I intend, upon proper encouragement to publish a Treatise on this Head, &

---

111. **M[.] Morris**: The editors have not been able to positively identify.

112. **Biographer**: *The New Cambridge Bibliography of English Literature,* ed. George Watson (Cambridge: Cambridge University Press, 1971), 2:1569–79. Over fifty biographies or memoirs were written during the eighteenth century in England.

also if my friends approve, to countermand Wilkes's writing[113] an Eulogium on Churchill,[114] candidly leaving him to stand or fall by his own Works, & that, instead of his drawing the Patriot, he puts the Pen into the hand of the glorious Pitt himself, immediately on hearing the Gout attacks his vital Parts.—I also propose, if agreable to my candid Critic, applying to my Brother, Martinus Scriblerus,[115] for an edict to confine Voltaire,[116] & entirely to deprive him of the use of Pen, Ink &

113. **Wilkes's writing**: John Wilkes (1727–97), English satirist and politician. His life was marked by controversy after controversy. A fine education and an early marriage to the straight-laced daughter of a wealthy grocer (from whom he quickly separated, although he continued to enjoy her money) allowed him access to politics and leisure. He served as high sheriff of Buckinghamshire, and then was elected Member of Parliament (MP) for Aylesbury. He also served as MP for Middlesex and sheriff of London and Middlesex. Wilkes began to write satirical political commentaries after becoming quickly disenchanted with various ministers, and eventually founded a political paper, *North Briton* (1762–63), with his friend, Charles Churchhill. For pieces in this paper as well as for privately publishing a scandalous essay called "An Essay on Woman," Wilkes's political enemies had him arrested for seditious libel. He was forced to leave England for France for a time in the 1760s and, on his return to England in 1768, he was committed to the king's bench prison, where he began a series of appeals to the House of Lords and petitions to the House of Commons. His legal problems, his appeals to invoke the privileges of an MP, and his eventual triumph made him a popular public figure in England and abroad (*DNB*).

114. **Eulogium on Churchill**: Charles Churchill (1731–64), like his friend Wilkes, was a renowned satirist. He also married and separated early, and had a short career as a clergyman. He published his first successful satirical poem, "Rosciad," in 1761. It was an instant success, which gained him notoriety and the friendship of a circle that included Wilkes. The two collaborated on *North Briton*, to which Churchill contributed a number of pieces. Churchill made Wilkes his literary executor. Apparently Wilkes made extravagant and unfulfilled promises to promote Churchill's memory (*DNB*).

115. **Martinus Scriblerus**: The fictitious Martinus Scriblerus, whose *Memoirs of the Extraordinary Life, Works and Discoveries* was first published by Pope in his *Works* (London, 1741). The "Memoirs" were written by the "club" of writers: Pope, Swift, Arbuthnot, Gay, and the Earl of Oxford. See "Martinus Scriblerus," in Charles Kerby-Miller, ed., *The Memoirs of the Extraordinary Life, Works, and Discoveries of Martinus Scriblerus* (Oxford: Oxford University Press, 1988).

116. **Voltaire**: "Pseudonym of Francois-Marie Arouet (1674–1778), French satirist, novelist, historian, poet, dramatist, polemicist, moralist, critic, and correspondent. Voltaire was the universal genius of the Enlightenment. Welcomed into the freethinking circles of Parisian society, he was committed to the Bastille for his satires in 1717–18, and again exiled to England in 1726–29" (*OCEL*, 5th). King Frederick II invited Voltaire to his court in 1743, but their relationship was a stormy one; Voltaire left "in haste" in 1753 after his interference in a quarrel between two noblemen an-

Paper, on the first notice of his Intention to write the History of the King of Prussia.—

Closing with so great a Name, it may now seem ridiculous to mention myself, but I have the Vanity to think, I am of as much Consequence to *some*, as the King of Prussia, & much more to myself— Pope & Swift were of the same Opinion, when they suffer'd the Minutes of their Lives to descend to Posterity, & justified the Importance of Man to himself, by giving so distinguished a Place in their works to the renowned Memoirs of P. P. Clk.[117] of the Parish;—in Emulation, therefore, of this eminent Character, I introduce the Memoirs of M. M. Spinster of this Parish.—It seems not material to me to enter into a detail of my Nativity,—Parentage, Shrewd Endowments & et[c].—for as much as the philosophical Birth, & scholastic Education, of my elder Bro[ther] the celebrated Martinus Scriblerus, renders a Repetition of this kind unnecessary. 'Tis sufficient to observe I have sojourned near 2 Months at Settle—that I'm a Damsel of a middle Stature, & ruddy Complexion, insomuch that it has been said, the Milk-maid looks not more blue in a frosty Morning than I do, neither has she a pleasanter Countenance when Collin[118] meets her in the Eventide, than I have, when all Things go well with me: Howbeit my Employment is working in divers Colours, & fine twined Woolen, & it is a Work of curious Device—of an exquisite cunning in the Art of the Needle: insomuch, that like Penelope[119] of old, I have not

gered the King. See "Voltaire," in *The New Columbia Encyclopedia*, ed. William H. Harris and Judith S. Levey (New York: Columbia University Press, 1975).

117. **Memoirs of P. P. Clk.**: Pope published the "Memoirs of P. P. Clerk of This Parish" (1727) in the second volume of the Swift-Pope *Miscellanies*. "Since the most discussed memoirs of the time were those of Bishop Burnet, the first volume of which had been published in 1724, it was assumed by Pope's enemies that a ridicule of [Burnet's] *History of His Own Time* was intended. Pope denied the accusation . . . but the idea of burlesquing such self-important writers of memoirs as the Bishop went back to [the Scriblerians] club days" (Kerby-Miller, *Memoirs*, 47–48. See also Pope, "Memoirs of P. P. Clerk of This Parish," in *The Prose Works of Alexander Pope*, ed. Rosemary Cowler (Hamden, Conn.: Archon-Shoestring Press, 1986), 2:100–28.

118. **Collin**: A literary name for a young man, particularly in songs and pastorals. There are several versions of a poem written from "Colin to Chloe," for example, that circulated in manuscript during the American Revolution. See Pemberton Papers at HSP (30:51–53), and a poem with this title in the Robinson Collection, Box 9, Newport Historical Society, Newport, R.I.

119. **Penelope**: In the *Odyssey*, Penelope, wife of Odysseus, put off suitors while waiting for her husband's return. She told them that she could not marry them until

list[e]ned, nor propose listening to any Suitors untill the same be finally accomplished; yet peradventure, should a young Man well favour'd, & of a goodly Aspect, draw near, I have not formed a positive Resolution on Penelope's Plan, for altho' it becomes us Virgins to deport ourselves soberly, & seem as it were, contented in this our State of Celibacy, yet, it is not unlawful to suffer our Eye, in a stated Degree, to glance over a consonant Form, & our Hearts a little to trepidate after supposed Merit, without being deemed Daughters of an airy Deportment—Moreover, from the earliest Acct. of Time, it has been judged not Good for Man to dwell alone,[120] & therefore for their own Sakes, it is a necessary Care & Duty incumbent on us Damsels to provide for them, & assign them proper & suitable Helpmates ever remembering in the Course of my benevolent Surveys to bestow the Treasure of my inestimable Self on some happy & lucky Individual, as a very suitable Partner.—This being only a Digression I proceed with my History. It has been concluded by the learned, that I have fallen away of late; that once in particular, I yielded to no entreaties of eating my Dinner—sat sullen & silent, so that it was suspected on all hands, that I was out of my right way of thinking, probably thro' the Communication between the Organs of Sense, & the *sensorium commune*[121] being obstructed;—It was judged that something hung heavier on me than my Cloaths, for I have frequently been observed to look steadily in the Fire—have not attended to Conversation—but have said no in the wrong Place; sure it is not ominous!—if I thought it was, so great is mine (like Bro[the]r Scriblerus's) aversion to Errors of Stile, that I possibly might, to avoid a second Mistake, be rash enough to say yes to the first Man that ask'd me; but dont inform my friend Kendall of this Menace, lest he frighten some timorous Adventurer; for it seems he scandalizes me with the Name of a Wit, & says things in my Face to this Effect,—that were he single, he would not have me, that I should make a bad Wife—be disputing against self evident Propositions, while the Jack[122] stands, & wrangling upon every new Hypothesis, with holes in my Stockings; &, like Jenny

---

she finished weaving a "tapestry" that she unravelled every night, so that the work was never finished (*OCEL,* 3d).

120. **Man to dwell alone**: Genesis 2:18.

121. *sensorium commune*: Translation, "common sense."

122. **the Jack**: "Variously applied to a serving-man or male attendant" (*OED*).

Bickerstaffe[123] of old, all snuffy, with a Mans dirty night-cap on, I should sit rocking the Cradle with one hand, & reading *Epictetus*[124] in the other, not once considering how necessary it is for each Sex & Station to qualify & ornament the Mind with philosophical Lessons, from this, or such like excellent Moralists: thereby dispelling the dark Clouds & thick benighted Mists of Passion, Ignorance, Error & Superstition; for what, pray, is the very exalted Character of a Pudding making Mortal in the Theory? Now, I'll endeavour to prove beyond a possibility of Dispute that *Philosophy* is not incompatible with *Cookery*, that a Woman, Mistress of the whole Cullinary Science, may, notwithstanding, be a very dangerous, as well as undesirable Companion—thus proving my Argument—A *Pudding* may be well compounded, have a proper Proportion of every necessary & relishing Ingredient, may to all Appearance, be well tied up, & safely committed to the Pot, but if, (as Accidents may happen to the best Pudding in the World) it should burst the Bag!—In this deplorable Case—what, but a Mind aided by the Light of Philosophy, supported by the Cordial of Ethicks, & soothed by the Anodyne of Metaphysics could bear with such an Event?—Now I, & all my Sisterhood (pardon the seeming Vanity, for Justice belongs to us as well as others) on this trying Occasion, endowed with philosophical Reflection & moral Reasoning, should probably, then & there, calmly descant on the rectitude & fitness of Things, & of the inviolable Laws of Nature, faithfully exerting their Influence according to the Will & Purpose of their Author.—Thus to Betty & the astonish'd Scullion—"You have, said I (sweetly smiling) accumulated the Pabulum[125] too hasty upon the Fire, & by that Means, raised such a brisk Vibration & coalition

123. **Jenny Bickerstaffe**: A fictional character, sister of Isaac Bickerstaff, invented by Sir Richard Steele (1672–1729) in a series of essays in *The Tatler* (1709–11). In number 75, Isaac Bickerstaff is asked to find a husband for his sister, whom he admits is "a wit . . . [who] instead of consulting her glass and her toilet for an hour and a half after her private devotions, sits with her nose full of snuff, and a man's night-cap on her head, reading plays and romances. Her wit she thinks her distinction: therefore knows nothing of the skill of dress, or making her person agreeable" (*The British Essayists*, ed. A. Chalmers [Boston: Little, Brown, 1850], 2:238–39).

124. *Epictetus*: A Stoic philosopher (A.D. 60–140).

125. **Pabulum**: The word has several levels of meaning. It derives from the Latin (*pabulum*) for "food, nourishment, fodder" and thus "anything taken in by an animal or plant to maintain life and growth; . . . Usually said of the 'food' of plants, or of animal organs or organisms; rarely in reference to higher animals." It is also "that which

among the ignited Particles thereof, which being communicated by
the aquamedia (for this it is but susceptible of, & can only convey a
certain Degree of heat, yet it will make a terrible Jumble in the Pot) to
the component heterogenious Particles of the Pudding, so as to extend their Bulk, & at the same Time rarify & disengage the latent Air,
whose elasticity overcoming the tenacity of the Bag, & the tying
thereof being too tight to give Way, a rupture in the weakest part of
the Cloth, constituting the said Bag, must happen of Course, & the
Contents, *qua data porta ruint*, will rush out where they can get
vent"——I shou'd take Care to advise my two almost petrified Disciples, that some Philosophers have entertained another Hypothesis
concerning Fire, as that Fire is *materia sui generis* or Matter of its own
kind, in opposition to others who have supposed it only a Mode of
Matter, or, in other Words, Matter ignited; further informing them,
that which ever Hypothesis we adopt (tho' for my part I incline to the
Latter) all culinary processes are solved with equal Ease, *mautatis mutandis*,[126] & this particular Phenomenon in Question, by which ever
Hypothesis we solve it, chiefly depends upon the elasticity of the Air,
& that Other which is supposed to be the Vehicle of Fire, both elec-
trick & cullinary: by this time my two Auditors would have a little re-
cover'd from their Surprize at so extraordinary a Catastrophe & we all
remain pleas'd & easy, as being convinced it was only a regular Consequence of natural Causes.—Now please to observe how yr. other
kind of Cooks behave on the like distressing Occasion.—She who is
term'd an excellent house-Wife & has been taught to think it the highest absurdity to venture out of the domestic Province—behold her in
a clean Apron, half round her, trotting about the Kitchen,—looking
after all Ends—Jack going,[127]—Eggs beating,—frizzling & frying—
bustle bustle—a Ladle in her hand,—her Face scorch'd & frowning—
fretting & fuming, that somebody has left the Print of their Heel on
the clean scour'd Parlour—Dinner ready to take up—she explores

---

supports or 'feeds' fire" and figuratively, "that which nourishes and sustains the mind
or soul; food for thought" (*OED*).

126. *mautatis mutandis*: A misspelling of *mutatis mutandis*: "The necessary
changes have been made."

127. **Jack going**: "A machine for turning the spit when roasting meat, either
wound up like a clock or actuated by the draught of heated air up a chimney; a
smoke-jack" (*OED*).

the Pot, & behold, (O cruel Fate!) the pudding Bag is burst!—down drops the Ladle—up goes her hands—she thought some dire Misfortune would befall 'em today, for two great Crows flapp'd at the Window—there's a Hobgoblin in the Pot, or else the Bag had a hole in it—raves at Betty—boxes the Scullion—kicks the Dog from the Fire—he throws down the dripping Pan, scalds himself, & runs away howling—oversets some of the Children—they are set a squalling—the affrighted Husband leaves the House, & begs a quiet Dinner of his Neighbours.—Tell fr[ien]d. Kendall I doubt not of his being a Proselyte to my Reasoning & therefore hope he'll make it his Business, by way of attonement, to recommend me & my pacific Sisterhood to the deserving of his Sex, & then I'll freely pardon him for past Declamation—This also is a Digression from my History: but as Time nor Paper will admit of my surprizing Memoirs, I shall conclude for the present, with love & good Will to your Houshold, Docr. & Sally Young

Settle Jany. 2d. 1755.   M[.] Morris

65   The following Letter was sent to Saml. Fothergill[128] by a Person who attended the yearly Meeting at Bristol in Engd.—

Dear Sir,   May 27th. 1764.

As you may have great Influence in establishing Things decent & orderly in your Society, I take the Liberty of troubling you with this Address—I have often attended silent Meetings, & came away greatly

128. **Saml. Fothergill**: Samuel Fothergill (1715–72), brother of Dr. John Fothergill, was an English Quaker. As a young man he was rebellious, but reformed and became recommitted to Quakerism, largely due to his marriage in 1738. His wife, Susanna Croudson, was a Quaker preacher fifteen years his senior. Fothergill frequently travelled to Quaker meetings in England and Scotland and to America in 1754, where he made many friends during a two-year stay. See *The Friend* 76 (1902): 60; also Corner and Booth, *Chain of Friendship*, 9.

edified, both from what I have felt myself & from the greatest Satisfaction I took in setting with so many Christian Philosophers (for
so I must esteem those who can sit two hours to improve, only from
the Operation of Divine Grace within) & indeed the Point I am concern'd about, is the great Want of Silence, too frequent after large
Meetings.—

After a few Words uttered by an excellent Woman yesterday after-
noon at Devonshire House, I was astonished—I was shock'd to hear
the universal babling after the Meeting broke up, I endeavour'd to account for it by many town Friends meeting their Country Friends after a years Absence, but this could not convince me, that the Clamour
was consistant with the Decorum expected from so still and quiet a
People.—If it is said that the House is only a House, and that after
Meeting it is as decent to talk in a meeting House as in the Streets
by the Way—to this I have no answer that can be satisfactory, to such
as esteem it only a proper Degree of Liberty, & if Custom has made
it inoffensive, I shall another Time only avoid the hearing of it, and
shall at all Times pray for the Prosperity of Mr. Fothergill and his
Friends.—

66   From the Leeds Mercury.—for June 1772.

On Monday the 15th Instant, died at Warrington in Lancashire, in
the 59th year of his Age, that valueable & much esteem'd Minister of
the Gospel, amongst the People called Quakers, Samuel Fothergill.—
His genuine & unaffected Eloquence, joined to the Pathos of his Discourses, signalized him amongst all Sorts of People; & in the Hearts of
many will be, the best & most lasting Monument of his Memory.—
He was no less remarkable for the catholic Generosity of his Mind, &
unity with all good People, of ev'ry Persuasion.—His Manner of De-
livery in Publick, was manly & pleasing, free from all Singularity of
Tone, & the disagreable Gutteral. In a Word, if the true Christian, &
the powerful Minister of the Gospel, join'd to a particular Tenderness,
for the Advancem[en]t. of true Religion amongst the young & rising
Generation, render the Memory of any one dear, the united Voice of
many will say, He was the Man.—One of that many, as a consolatory
Hint to his afflicted Friends desires to subjoin the following *Epitaph*

I heard a Voice from Heaven declare
That such forever blessed are,
Who die in Christ the living Lord,
Yea saith the Spirit & the Word
From all their Labours they shall rest
And find Repose in Jesu's Breast.—
[Rev. 14:13][129]

67   Extract of a Letter from S. Wright Sept. 22d. 1772.

We were surprized, & sensibly & deeply concerned to read in the Gazette, an acct. of the Death of our worthy Friend and distant Allie.[130] S. Fothergill, we are told he died at his own Home, which was the House in which my Father was born 105 years ago, & where his Parents lived & died:—after my grand Fathers death, the House was purchased by my grand-Mothers Bro[the]r who was Father to S. Fothergill's Wife, as I had past many of the happiest Days of my Life in it; those Days, unclouded by Care or Sorrow, which are quickly over, & can never return, & was intimately acquainted with every Part & cranny of it: he was pleas'd to describe all the alterations he had made, as he had in a manner rebuilt it, among other trifling Questions that I ask'd him, I enquired after a large old Clock that had been my G[o]d. Fathers, when my Father was a Child, & which stood in my Uncles Parlour when we left Engld. He answer'd it continued to go excellently well, after having measured Time to its several Own-ers for a 100 Years—& alas! it has now I presume, measur'd Time to himself to the latest Hour of his valuable Life. He moralized very seriously upon the Subject, as I ought to do upon this affecting Oc-casion, rather than relate these uninteresting Anecdotes of a House, & a Piece of its Furniture, but what could I say—such has been the

---

129. **[Rev. 14:13]:** a paraphrase of this Book of Revelation passage: "And I heard a voice from heaven saying unto me, Write, Blessed are the dead which die in the Lord from henceforth: Yea, saith the Spirit, that they may rest from their labours; and their works do follow them."

130. **distant Allie:** "united, joined. . . . by kindred or affinity" (*OED*).

Decree of divine Providence, & who shall presume to query—why
was it so.

68   The Bird of Passage.—upon leaving of Black-Point.

The Bird that strays from Clime to Clime
    Condemn'd by Fate to roam,
With mournful Note proclaims the Time
    He quits his transient Home.

He drooping sits within the Grove,   5
    'Till forc'd at length to fly
He leaves the soft Retreats of Love
    To brave a distant Sky

So I, a Slave to every Woe
    A tender Heart can feel,   10
Too soon from these fair Scenes must go
    Yet all my Pains conceal.—

But tho' with ling'ring Step forlorn,
    I different Realms explore
Each Wish on Fancy's Pinions borne   15
    Shall seek this happy Shore.

69   The Death of the Fox.— By a Female.

    The Fox from Covert unsecure,
Is rous'd & frighted by the Roar
Of Hounds, a wretched ghastly Clan,
That shame their Masters to a Man.
    O'er many a Hill he takes his Way,   5

Thro' many a Thicket seems to stray;
With horrid Speed the Gang pursue,
With horrid Yells delight the Crew,
 That rambling, roaring, ranting, tearing,
Kicking, spurring, cursing swearing,   10
Pursue the Chase with awkward Speed,
In Hopes to see a Reynard[131] bleed.
 The Victim trembling o'er the Plain,
By Turns across the Farmer's grain,
Extends his Course with Grief oppress'd,   15
In Hopes to find some Place of Rest;
 But all in vain:—The Gang draw near,
And with their yells increase his Fear;
Grim Horror darts from ev'ry Eye,
And threatens sad Destruction nigh: 20
 He falters, & the Dogs press on,
They seize him & the Jobb is done.
A Fox is kill'd by twenty Men;
That Fox, perhaps, had kill'd a Hen.
 A gallant Act no doubt is here: 25
All wicked Foxes ought to fear,
When twenty Dogs, & twenty Men,
Can kill a Fox that kill'd a Hen.—

70   [Untitled]

To forget Injuries, & to forgive those who have offended, is as con-
ducive to Happiness, as conformable to the Rules of Virtue; & we
make no doubt, the most salutary Events must result from Measures
form'd & conducted on such Principles.—Address of the Committee
of Inspection to the Assembly against Independancy[132] May 1776.—

131. **Reynard**: Conventional name given to a fox; it derives from the "Reynard the Fox" fables (*OCEL*, 3d).
132. **Assembly against Independancy**: In May 1776 the outlook was grim for those Pennsylvanians who opposed the colonies' independence from Great Britain. Despite

71   To a Relation on the Death of two Infants.

Sweet Babes releas'd from mortal Pain
Delusive Hope & anxious Care,
On Canaans' blest immortal Plain
In safety breathe yr. native Air.

Hail favour'd Babes, so soon remov'd   5
Just doom'd to touch this Scene of Woe,
Then lodg'd amidst the best belov'd
Where joys in full Perfection flow.

Where safe beneath yr. Fathers Hand
As Plants of his peculiar Care   10
Secure from ev'ry Blast you stand,
Which still endanger Virtue here.

Oh! Then not the Parents mind
With Murmur mourn at their Release
To Heaven's own Charge yr. Babes resign,   15
Shelter'd beneath his Smile of Peace.

To R. W.[133]   Fidelia

---

the popularity of recent radical publications advocating independence, such as *Common Sense*, on May 1st the ruling conservative party, which opposed independence, won victory in the Pennsylvania Assembly by a slim margin. The Continental Congress, however, responded by passing a resolution two weeks later that any governments operating under royal charter (such as Pennsylvania's) should be abolished. On May 20, 1776, the radical Committee of Inspection and Observation determined to inform the sitting Assembly that they would elect a new government. Under the guise of this authority, a constitutional convention was called for June. Griffitts' cousin by marriage, John Dickinson, led the conservatives. See Arthur J. Mekeel, *The Relation of Quakers to the American Revolution* (Washington, D.C.: University Press of America, 1979), chap. 9; Harry Tinkcom, "The Revolutionary City," in Russell F. Weigley, *Philadelphia: A 300-Year History* (New York: Norton, 1982), 124.

133. *R. W.*: Possibly Richard or Rachel Wells. Rachel was one of Moore's sisters, who had eleven children, four of whom died at birth or infancy. See Smith, *Letters of Doctor Richard Hill*, xlii–xliii.

72   On the Death of Sucky James [134] who departed this Life April 14th. 1774.

How transient, Friend, each human Bliss below,
    How false & feeble e'ry Mortal Trust
Or dash'd with Care, or veil'd in deeper Woe
    The Thorn our Pillow, & our Bed the Dust.
Life is a probationary State at best.   5
    To form the Spirit for a purer Air,
On Earth's bleak Coast, we at our Peril rest
    And Clouds eclipse the fairest Prospects here.
Come, feel this solemn disputed Truth,
    Come sympathetic view th'expiring Maid,   10
With Hope surrounded, in the Bloom of Youth,
    Of Friends possess'd—nor yet of Death afraid.
With each endearing Prospect, social Joy,
    The smile of Friendship, & the Voice of Love,
With all that binds more firm the mortal Tye,   15
    With all that can the Christian Hero prove,
Her guiltless Mind, with Innocence serene,
    Gave up each Blessing to the awful Rod;
Survey'd with Fortitude the closing Scene,
    Bow'd to the Stroke, & slept resign'd to God.   20
Adieu, dear Maid! While round thy spotless Urn
    The dear Smile of Friendship & the Voice of Love
Bending with Grief, thy early Exit mourn,
    Rest in thy Lot & share the Joys above.—
Hail, favour'd Soul!—with most peculiar Grace,   25
    (Could we the future as the past survey,)
So soon compleat thy Task, & run thy Race,

134. **Sucky James**: Susannah James (1757–74) was the daughter of Abel and Rebecca Chalkley James. Susannah James may have been the sister of Abel James, Henry Drinker's business partner and a successful, wealthy and prominent merchant in his own right. Susannah had several siblings, as mentioned in the poem. A man's response (calling himself "Florio") to Griffitts's elegy for Susannah James can be found in LCP manuscripts, entitled "To Fidelia, On her Verses, occasion'd by the Death of Susannah James." See Crane, *The Diary of Elizabeth Drinker*, biographical directory.

So early enter on immortal Day.
Nor let surviving Friends in Grief repine,
  Or view her favour'd Lot a chast'ning Rod.   30
The awful Call was perfect Love divine
  Unerring Wisdom & the Love of God.
But Nature claims & sympathy demands,
  The tender Tribute to her Mem'ry paid;
Around her Tomb, see—pensive Friendship stands, 35
  The sorrowing Matron, & the weeping Maid.
Each join the Fathers Sigh, the Mothers Woe,
  The Sister's Anguish & the Brother's Tear,
Grant Nature's Claim & Friendships' generous Glow
  From feeling Bosoms & from Hearts sincere.   40
Once more adieu!—safe in the Arms of God,
  Enjoy thy Rest, rest undisturb'd & pure
Shelter'd by Love, from ev'ry future Rod,
  Thy Warfare finish'd, & thy Heaven secure.
Then let not Friendships Voice, or Natures Claim 45
  Her smiling Virtues, or her early close,
Pierce the fond Mothers' tender Breast with Pain
  Awake the Parent & renew her Woes.—
Her end was favour'd with a Mind serene,
  With Christian Faith & Fortitude sustain'd,   50
(Escap'd each Danger of the future Scene)
  And by this Stroke her perfect Freedom gain'd.
Here fix thy Hopes!—secure from Floods of Woe,
  Thy Child is safe in Love & Life divine,
She clos'd in Peace th' important Race below   55
  And Angels hail—when Mortals dare repine.

Fidelia

73 The Query. March 1775

Have circling Suns the magic Pow'r
  To waste our Strength of Mind?
And is gay Fancy's sprightly Hour,

Alone to Youth confin'd?
Shall ev'ry Solace known below,   5
    With added Years decay?
Is Age, Infirmities, & Woe,
    Our fated Close of Day?
No—Heaven more kind, for Moments past
    In fancied Bliss of youth,   10
With solid Hope sustains the last
    And brighter Beams of Truth.
The Joys our vernal Years pursues
    In Expectation lye
But still the dear delusive Views   15
    From our Possession fly.
Let sage Experience, now decide
    The Claim of blooming Life
"One giddy scene of empty Pride
    Or guilty Passion's Strife."   20
What is it more, let Wisdom say
    (Or youth those Joys express)
What the bright Sun that gilds their Day
    "Than Flattery Charms & Dress."
The fairest Charms, by Poets sung,   25
    With Grief, or sickness fade,
And by the false & flattering Tongue,
    Are poison'd—& betray'd.
Or is it more—to Nature's Prime
    Is sense of Taste confin'd?   30
Which lost in swift revolving Time
    Leaves dark the vacant Mind.
Shall every Gift of gracious Heaven
    With years decline or cloy,
Has Age no Taste for Blessings given,   35
    No Relish to enjoy?
Is all their Portion ceaseless Toil
    Or groans of suffering Pain
Shall the gay Spring, in verdure smile,
    Or Friendship sooth in vain?   40
In vain, shall Natures sweets exhale,
    And bloom the fragrant Flowers

Nor vernal Sun, nor spicy Gale,
    Awake their torpid Powers.
Shall not the spangled Orbs above,   45
    One wishful Glow excite?
Nor the soft Musick of the Grove
    Their sickned Sense delight
No—Charms, nor Hope, nor Taste of Joys
    To evening Suns belong,   50
Nature a Blank, & Age destroys
    The Harmony of Song.
Thus, Life, to our discourag'd View,
    One dreary Waste appears,
And Clouds surround, & woes pursue   55
    The dark Decline of years.
'Tis Error all, by falshood fram'd
    Even Age enjoys its prize
By Virtue form'd, by Faith sustain'd,
    And by Experience wise,   60
Tho' lost each transient Charm of youth,
    Each fairy Vision past
Th' instructive Voice of sacred Truth,
    Is mostly prov'd at last.
From Age & Wisdom we obtain,   65
    A guide to point the Way,
To solace Care, to soften Pain
    And smooth a sure Decay.
From Age & Wisdom we may know,
    Our proper Bounds to scan   70
The estimate of Things below
    And Dignity of Man.
The Cares important, Hope divine
    (Which Wisdom's Son's pursue)
And far beyond the Change of Time   75
    They fix their boundless View.
They use each Blessing, as a Loan,
    From Heavens indulgent Hand,
Nor longer claim them as their own,
    Than God withholds—demand.   80
Renew'd by an immortal Birth,
    (Nor with Existance cloy'd)

Nature & Grace, & Life & Death
    Are best by Age enjoy'd.
Then be this Truth by all confess'd   85
    (Its Wisdom, worth the Cost)
"In Age, the Judgment, & the Taste,
    "Are rather chang'd than lost."
The Flight of Seasons as they run,
    Their Balm of Pleasure bring,   90
To them, glows bright the Summer Sun,
    And sweet perfume of Spring.
For Age like this, the Orbs above,
    In glorious Order roam,
'Till Death, the final Call of Love,   95
    Admits them to their Home.
There, freed from all the waste of years,
    Each wintry Season o'er,
Th' immortal Dawn of Heaven appears
    And Change is known no more.—   100

Fidelia

74   Social Love.—April 1775.

Where is that Love, benevolent & kind
Which warms the Breast, expands the Mind
And gladdens in the Welfare of the whole,
    Where the soft Pity for our kindred Race
    The gentle Harmony—the social Grace?   5
And all the generous Purposes of Soul.—

Ah! is it fled?—or why forsook the Breast
Where it was destin'd once to rest
To warm, & animate the human Span,
    The brutal Passions to controul,   10
    And by the finer feelings of the Soul,
To raise & dignify the Man.—

Shall then a Mortal suffer Grief or Pain
And Guilt, or Punishment of Guilt sustain?

Nor Man, his feeling Brother, take his Share   15
Shall not, soft Pity in that Bosom move
(Which Heaven design'd the Residence of Love)
And balm his Sorrows, with the tender Tear.

This one Distinction which we find,
Between the human & the brutal Mind,   20
"A soft & social sympathy of Heart"
    Where the wide Wish expansive glows
    Where Nature weeps o'er nature's Woes,
Shares in the Suffering, & sustains its part.

Leave to the fiercer Beasts of Prey,   25
To ravage torture & betray,
And rage, the Tyrants of the Wood,
    But oh! let kindred Men forbear
    Whose gentle Breasts, should feeling wear
And nobler Souls rejoice in Good.—   30

If once we strip the human Breast
Of this kind warmth, this social Guest
    Which Heaven a sacred Guard design'd,
We sink indeed, meer Clods of Earth
Degrade our Being, & our Birth,   35
    And fall below true Dignity of Mind.

Ah! Heaven forbid such Change should be
To break the Bands of Harmony,
    Which bid the Man, in social Union move
While suffering Nature must complain   40
Let sympathy, its Share sustain,
    'Till Souls cement, as Angels do—by Love.—

Fidelia

75   A moral Sonnet. 1775.

Behold the young Songster on Wing
    In the Pride of his Liberty gay,

He wafts on the Pinions of Spring,
    He sucks the Ambrosia of May.
"Ah! who is so happy as I"   5
    (Wou'd he say, cou'd his thoughts be express'd)
"I mount on the Breeze of the Sky
    "And enjoy the Delights of my Nest.
"On Freedom's wide Common I rove,
    "And scorn the restraints of the Cage,   10
"My Song can enliven the Grove,
    "My Plumage, shall Beauty engage."
Thus wing'd the sweet Warbler on high,
    With the Pride of the Season elate,
'Till mark'd by the murdering Eye   15
    A Gunner decided his Fate.
He drop'd in the Verdure of May
    (a Wreck on fair Liberty's Coast)
And fell to Destruction a Prey
    In the midst of his Glory & Boast.   20
Let youth learn a Caution from hence,
    Nor swell with the Pride of their Prime,
Let Virtue direct thee, & Sense,
    "For Death has the key of thy Time."—

Fidelia

76   Part of the third Chapt. of Hab[akkuk] [135]—

Tho' o'er the Fig-tree noxious Blasts prevail
The Olive perish, & the Vintage fail,
Tho' Earth, no more, her vital Influence shed,
Withdraw her Bounty, & deny us Bread,
Tho' sick'ning Herds, the crowded Stalls may hold   5
And dying Lambkins thin the fleecy Fold,
Tho' swords cut down the human Race on Earth

---

135. **third Chapt. of Hab[akkuk]**: This is Griffitts's second paraphrase on the third chapter of Habakkuk (3:17–18). See the first paraphrase, *MMMB* 34.

And Graves entomb the thoughtless Son's of Mirth
Amidst it all, a feeble Worm of Dust,
On thee Almighty, fix my stedfast Trust,   10
And in the God of my Salvation joy,
When Famine rages, & when Swords' destroy.

Fidelia

77   On the Death & Character of a late english Nobleman.[136] March 1775.

Now let the thirst of eastern Pomp attend
    And on this striking Lesson spare an Hour,
Of envy'd Greatness, here behold the End,
    And wild Ambition, mad with reach of Pow'r.
Aiming at Titles—& with Titles crown'd,   5
    Grasping at Wealth, & swell'd with Riches Boast,
Where was the Ballance of the Bliss he found?
    "A Tortur'd Conscience, & his Honour Lost."
Ah wretched grandeur, now unenvy'd lye
    No Bribe to blind, no Balm the Wound to heal,   10
While Justice points to Retribution nigh,
    And injur'd Millions make the dread Appeal.—
What can avail at his tremendous Bar,
    Who views the Heart amidst each winding Fold,
Can Fames loud Voice, the proud triumphal Car,   15
    *Golconda's Rock,[137] or Nigers Streams of Gold?
Ye real Shadows of an empty Sound,
    To him whose awful Ken the whole surveys,

    136. **a late english Nobleman**: Thomas Penn, proprietor of Pennsylvania, who died in March 1775. Penn's death left the proprietorship of Pennsylvania, already in doubt because of growing hostilities between Britian and her colonies, divided among members of the Penn family. Sources suggest that the news of Penn's death did not reach America until May, two months later, but Griffitts was probably pre-dating her memorial (*DNB*; Treese, *A Storm Gathering,* 144–45, and Appendix A).
    137. **Golconda's Rock**: "The old name of Hyderabad, formerly celebrated for its diamonds, a synonym for a mine of wealth" (*OCEL,* 3d).

Friend of the injur'd will that God be found,
    Who rules in Mercy, & with Justice Weighs.—   20

Fidelia

[Marginal note:]
*—Noted for the finest Diamonds of the E. Indias

78 To E. Robinson & M. Leaver[138] on their Return home from America. 1775.

Accept the ardent Wish sincere
    Which for your safety glows,
Oh! may the Masters watchful Care,
    His faithful Flock inclose.
May all these Showers refresh the Soil,   5
    Marks of divine Regard,
His Blessing crown yr. arduous Toil
    His Peace yr. sure Reward.
At his Command the raging Sea
    In peaceful Calm subside,   10
His Arm in every Danger be
    Your sure protecting Guide.
How e'er his Wisdom mark yr. Day,
    Or Clouds eclipse the Skies,
Still may his Smiles direct the Way   15
    And yield the fresh Supplies.
In dark Temptations various Forms
    Abide beneath his Love,
Nor heights, nor depths, nor Clouds or Storms
    Your stedfast Faith remove.—   20
Sure is yr. rock & shall abide,
    A firm unshaken Trust

138. **To E. Robinson & M. Leaver**: Elizabeth Robinson (1729–1804) and Mary Leaver (1720–89) were English Quakers who arrived in America in 1773 to visit Quakers and returned to England on May 1, 1775. See "An Account of Ministering Friends from Europe who visited America, 1656–1793," *Journal of the Friends Historical Society* 10 (1913): 120, 131.

When ev'ry feeble Hope beside
    Shall weaken into Dust.
O! may this guardian Pow'r divine,   25
    In Peace yr. Steps sustain
Those Gifts yr. Duty did resign
    His Love restore again.—

Fidelia

79 On reading Thomsons Seasons [139]

Thy Numbers soft with Harmony, & sweet
As thy own vernal Day, in Beauty blooms,
Nobly majestick—awfully sublime,[140]
As the full Glory, of thy Summer Sun,
And rich with flowing Treasure of the Nine,[141]   5
As bounteous Autumn, pours her Gifts on Man,
While keen thy Wit as Natures piercing Frost
Thy Theme, strikes awful, as her wintry Storm.—

Fidelia

80 The patriotic Minority in both Houses of the British Parliament.—1775.

Distinguish'd Patriots, the illustrious few
    Who brave stood forth, to aid fair Freedom's Cause,

139. **Thomsons Seasons**: James Thomson (1700–48) wrote *The Seasons* in the years 1726–30. This blank verse poem was "one of the most popular (and frequently reprinted and illustrated) of English poems. . . . [It] was immensely influential, offering both in style and subject a new departure from the urbanity of Pope and developing a highly distinctive manner the range of topographical poetry: Wordsworth recognized Thomson as the first poet since Milton to offer new images of 'external nature'" (*OCEL*, 5th).

140. **awfully sublime**: "Of things in nature and art: Affecting the mind with a sense of overwhelming grandeur or irresistible power" (*OED*). For more on "the sublime" as a philosophical and literary concept, see Longinus, *On the Sublime*" (1st or 2d century A.D.), in *OCCL*.

141. **the Nine**: The nine Muses, "the goddesses of literature and the arts" (*OCCL*).

And nobly dar'd midst venal Votes, pursue,
    The Rights of Justice, & support of Laws.
Those antient Laws which guarded Britons right   5
    And did to each, sweet Liberty extend,
(As Bulwarks firm against oppressive might)
    Which Hamden rose to aid, & you defend,
Tho' hearts corrupt,— the ministerial Frown,
    (Prelates deny'd *"the righteous Rule of Good")   10
The Rage of Power, & sanction of the Crown,
    Your nervous force of Eloquence withstood.
Fix'd is yr. sure Reward, a future Age,
    Shall mark yr. Names, with glowing Lustre bright
Record with Honour, thro' th' historic Page,   15
    "The Friends of Mankind, Liberty & Right."
And e'er this Date arrives—our western Coast,
    Oh thousand grateful Hearts inscribe yr. name,
Point to the World, "an injur'd Peoples Boast"
    And fix you, lasting on the Rolls of Fame.   20
Hail sacred Law of Liberty & Right
    Which Britons once had trembled to deface
And justice guarded from illegal Might,
    As the best Gift—to their succeeding Race.
Secure but this, & pleas'd the lab'ring Swain   25
    Can bear the scorching Sun, & fainting Toil
Whilst Liberty his native Rights maintain
    And bid him take the Produce of the Soil.—
Your brave *Dissent, applausive shall be heard,
    From western Climes—to Indias distant Shore,   30
By Patriot Virtue—honour'd & rever'd,
    " 'Till Justice, Laws & Freedom, are no more."
Your Names illustrious, tho' in Numbers few,
    (From midst yr. rash Compeers) [142] we place on high,
As faithful Guardians—to a Nation's View,   35
    As scatter'd Stars, in Brittain's clouded sky.—
O! may the patriot Freedom, you defend,
    From lawless Ravage & invasive Power,

---

142. **rash Compeers**: "A companion, associate, . . . used contemptuously, *obs.*" (*OED*).

Uninjur'd, to yr. latest Race descend,
   Smile on their first, & gild their final Hour.   40

Fidelia

[Marginal note:]
*[Matt. 7:12]
*The Lords Protest against all the illegal American Acts.—

81   Wrote on the last Day of Feby. 1775.[143]
Beware of the Ides of March[144]

Had Ceasar took this useful Hint
   E're to the senate House he enter'd,
Longer he might have liv'd to think
   Nor midst his cruel Murd'rers ventur'd.
Ladies this wiser Caution take,   5
   Trust not yr. Tea to *Marcus Brutus,
Our Draught he'll spoil our China break,
   And raise a Storm that will not suit us.
Then for the Sake of Freedom's Name
   (Since British Wisdom scorns repealing)   10
Come sacrifise to Patriot Fame,
   And give up Tea by way of healing.
This done within ourselves retreat
   The industrious Arts of Life to follow
Let the proud Nabobs storm & fret,   15
   They cannot force our Throats to swallow.

143. **last Day of Feby. 1775**: In late 1774, less hawkish members of the British Parliament attempted to reopen discussions with the Americans through Quaker intermediaries and Benjamin Franklin. These discussions went on into early 1775, but were scotched by Lord North and his allies who insisted on asserting British authority. Frustration at these negotiations caused Franklin to leave for America on March 2, 1775. See R. C. Simmons, *The American Colonies: From Settlement to Independence* (New York: Norton, 1976), 348; Robert Middlekauf, *The Glorious Cause: The American Revolution, 1763-1789* (Oxford: Oxford University Press, 1982), 264.
   144. **Ides of March**: In the Roman calendar, the 15th of March, or the "Ides of March was the day on which Julius Caesar was assassinated" (*OCEL*, 3d).

Tho' now the boistrous Surges rowl,
    Of wicked North's tempestuous Ocean,
Leave him for Justice to controul
    And strive to calm our own Commotion.   20
With us each prudent Caution meet,
    Against this blustering Son of Thunder,
And let our firm Resolve, defeat
    His Lordship's ministerial Blunder.—

Fidelia

[Marginal note:]
*Marcus Brutus was one of Caesars Murderers.

82   The Ladies Lamentation over an empty Cannister. by the Same

Whence all this hideous wild uproar,
I ne'er shall love the Congress more
'Twas they devis'd the evil Deed,
To kill this prescious Indian Weed,[145]
Come just Resentment guide my Pen,   5
And mark our mad Committee Men,
Pray what is Freedom, Right or Laws,
To such a vast important Cause?
Why all their Malice shewn to Tea
So near, so dear—belov'd by me,   10
Reviving Draught, when I am dry—
Tea I must have, or I shall dye,
Not all the Herbs our Gardens yield
Not all the Produce of the Field,

145. **Indian Weed:** The Tea Act of 1773 was designed to support the finanically ailing East India Tea Company. Although the tax on tea imported to the colonies was not raised through this legislation, it granted the East India Company a monopoly in the colonies. To the colonists, it served notice that their sustained opposition to taxation was secondary to the perceived needs of British government and finance. Thus, the Tea Act sparked massive protests and boycotting. See Middlekauff, *The Glorious Cause*, 221–27.

Wrote on ye last Day of Feby 1775. Beware of ye Ides of March

Had Cæsar took this useful Hint
  Ere to the senate House he enter'd,
Longer he might have liv'd to think
  Nor midst his cruel Murd'rers ventur'd.
Ladies this wiser Caution take,
  Trust not yr Tea to Marcus Brutus,*
Our Draught he'll spoil our China break,
  And raise a Storm that will not suit us.
Then for the Sake of Freedom's Name
  (Since British Wisdom scorns repealing)
Come sacrifise to Patriot Fame,
  And give up Tea by way of healing.
This done within ourselves retreat
  The industrious Arts of Life to follow
Let the proud Nabobs storm & fret,
  They cannot force our Throats to swallow.
Tho' now the boist'rous Surges rowl,
  Of wicked North's tempestuous Ocean,
Leave him for Justice to controul
  And strive to calm our own Commotions
With us each prudent Caution meet,
  Against this blustering Son of Thunder,
And let our firm Resolve, defeat
  His Lordship's ministerial Blunder.—

*Marcus Brutus one of ye Cæsars Murderers.

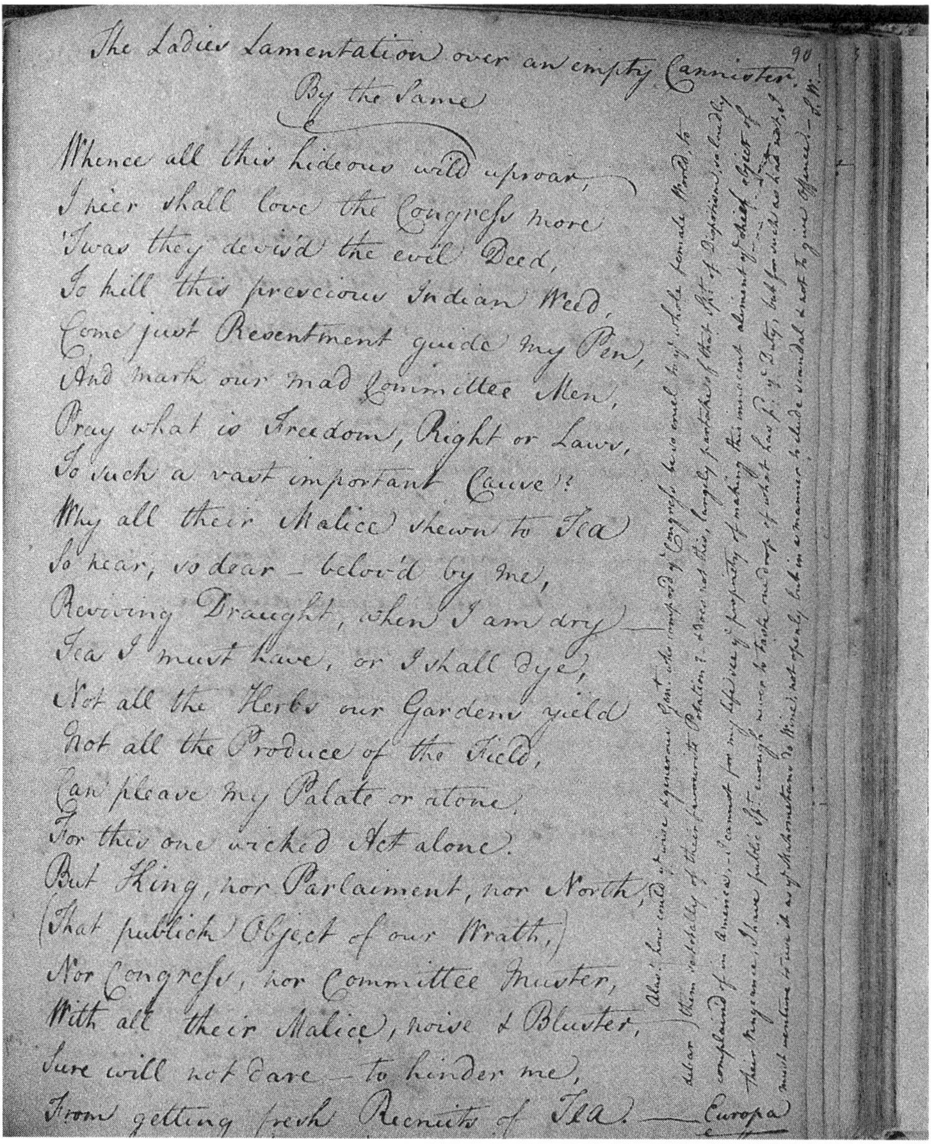

The Ladies Lamentation over an empty Cannister.
By the Same

Whence all this hideous wild uproar,
I ne'er shall love the Congress more
'Twas they devis'd the evil Deed,
To kill this precious Indian Weed,
Come just Resentment guide my Pen,
And mark our mad Committee Men,
Pray what is Freedom, Right or Laws,
To such a vast important Cause?
Why all their Malice shewn to Tea
So near, so dear — belov'd by me,
Reviving Draught, when I am dry —
Tea I must have, or I shall dye,
Not all the Herbs our Gardens yield
Not all the Produce of the Field,
Can please my Palate or atone,
For their one wicked Act alone.
But King, nor Parlaiment, nor North,
(That publick Object of our Wrath,)
Nor Congress, nor Committee Muster,
With all their Malice, noise & Bluster,
Sure will not dare — to hinder me,
From getting fresh Recruits of Tea — Europa

Figs. 13 a & b. Companion poems by Hannah Griffitts over the tax on tea
(*MMMB* 81 & 82), with Susanna Wright's prose commentary. Courtesy, Haverford
College Library, Haverford, Pennsylvania, Quaker Collection.

Can please my Palate or atone,   15
For this one wicked Act alone.
But King, nor Parlaiment, nor North,
(That publick Object of our Wrath,)
Nor Congress, nor Committee Muster,
With all their Malice, noise & Bluster,   20
Sure will not dare—to hinder me,
From getting fresh Recruits of Tea.—Europa [146]

[Marginal note:]
Alas! how could the wise & generous gent. who compos'd the Congress be so cruel to the whole female World, to debar them so totally
of their favourite Potation?—& does not this, largely partake of that
Sp[iri]t. of D[e]spotism, so loudly complain'd of in America,—I cannot for my Life see the propriety of making this innocent aliment the
chief object of their Vengeance, I have public sp[iri]t. enough never to
taste one drop of what has pd. the Duty, but for such as has not, I
must venture to use it as the Mahometans do Wine, not openly but in
a manner to elude scandal & not to give Offence.—S. W.—[147]

83   To the Memory of Margt. Mason [148] who died 29th. March 1775.

Delusive Life! what is the mighty Name
We load with Honours & enroll in Fame,
The Statesman, Patriot or victorious Sword,
Whose Desolations stile the Monsters Lord,
Or thro' the maze of Science range the Sky,   5
And trace the Planets with a Newtons Eye
What are ye all, a Vision, airy Name

146. **Europa**: Appears to be a pseudonym for Hannah Griffitts, since the poem
is written "by the same" person who "Wrote on the last Day of Feby 1775." For further discussion of this poem and the prose answer by Susanna Wright, see pages 92–93.

147. **S. W.**: Susanna Wright.

148. **Margt. Mason**: This may refer to the Margaret Mason who attended the wed-
ding of Thomas Walmsley and Agnes Mason at Fairhill Meeting in the Spring of 1768.
Abstracts of Minutes of the Byberry Monthly Metting, Genealogical Society of
Pennsylvania.

A Blast of Vapour, & a breath of Fame
Can this elude the Tyrants sov'reign Pow'r,
Or arm with Courage for the mortal Hour?   10
Can this the final Agony sustain,
The Pillow smooth, & ease the Bed of Pain?
Can this ensure our future Rest above
In the bright climes of Liberty & Love?
Ah no, departed Friend thy humbler Name,   15
Thy fair Example, & thy spotless Fame,
The gentle Virtues of thy social Mind
The Soul enlighten'd, & the Will resign'd
Shall meet thy Plaudit in the blest Abode
Where Saints enjoy the Vision of their God,   20
Who thro' the devious Path where thousands stray
Chose the best Part, & kept the narrow Way,
And midst each various Task of human Life
The Neighbour, Friend, the Parent & the Wife,
Thy gentle soft Benevolence of Mind   25
Left a fair Tract of pious Life behind,
Hail! favour'd Soul the happiest Voice of Peace
In softest Whispers sign'd thy swift Release,
And hush'd the Storm of Life in sweet Repose,
Bid all its Dangers end—& tryals close,   30
Favour'd Release, now wing thy joyful Way
To the bright Mansions of immortal Day,
The glorious Prize with kindred Spirits share,
Bliss unconceiv'd, unfelt, untasted here,
Where Souls are exil'd, Life a Tryal giv'n   35
To form the Spirit sanctified for Heav'n,
Probation ends, on Canaan's happy Shore
The Storm subsides, the wintry Season o'er,
And Tears for ever cease, & Change is known no more.—
No more shall thou thy Fathers absence mourn,   40
And vield in Darkness, sigh for his return,
No longer Conflict shall thy Soul sustain
Grow faint with Weakness or expire with Pain,
Secure from all, Heaven bid the Warfare cease
And clos'd thy Combat in the Smiles of Peace.   45
Ah! dear departed Friend enjoy the Prize,

Balm unembitter'd in thy native Skies,
'Till gracious Heaven, shall bid our Spirits join,
The draught of Bliss, the Song of Praise with thine,
Where holy Harmony, & perfect Love   50
In sacred Union bind the Ranks above
Where joy too high for Angel Tongues to paint,
Is the blest Portion of the embodied Saint.—
And you surviving Friends who bore the Stroke
Which thus yr. dear & fond Connection broke,   55
For you I feel, & sympathetic share
The Sigh of Sorrow, & the filial Tear,
I drank the bitter Cup & deeply know
The heart felt Anguish of this piercing blow,
Strive to submit beneath the Hand divine,   60
And Heaven will heal if Nature will resign,
Trace the fair Tract her pious steps have trod,
And claim a Parent in your Father God.—

Fidelia

84   To S. Fothergill on his leaving Philada. June 4th. 1756.

Since such the Will of that almighty Pow'r
That first commission'd for Sylvania's Shore,
To bid my Friend his painful Labours cease
Receive the Blessing & return in Peace,
Tho' hard to part, go with thy Sacred Guide   5
And under his parental Care abide
And in Return for all thy Love, receive
The warmest Wish the friendly Muse can give.
May Heaven propitious on thy Labours smile
And grant the Seed may meet a fruitful Soil,   10
Prosper the Work & give thy Words Success,
Guard all thy Steps & all thy Actions bless,
In Heights surround thee & in Depths sustain

Give every Good or sanctify each Pain,
Dispel each Doubt & ev'ry Darkness clear   15
Approve each Offering & accept each Pray'r,
Thus ev'ry Blessing to thy Lot be giv'n
And be thou still the constant Care of Heav'n
His guardian Eye o'er all thy Ways preside
Lead by his Love—& in his Councils guide   20
'Till Death commission'd shall dissolve thy Frame,
And thou assume a new immortal Name,
Awake in Life, & with an Angels Tongue,
Shall join the Church above in her triumphant Song.—

[Fidelia]¹⁴⁹

85   To the Memory of Sarah Morris ¹⁵⁰ who died at Philada. Octobr. 24th. 1775.

"Ye are they which have continued with me in my Temptations & I appoint unto you a Kingdom as my Father hath appointed unto me."—
[Luke 22:28–9]

When suffering Virtue from its Bands relees'd
Puts on the Victor, midst its kindred blest,
Hails the sweet Confines of th' immortal Shore
Where Sin shall wound, nor Pain afflict us more,
Where Frailty ends, where joy no Period knows   5

149. **[Fidelia]**: Although Moore seemingly forgot to attribute the poem to Hannah Griffitts, another copy of this poem is in her collection of poetry, LCP.

150. **Sarah Morris**: Sarah Morris (1704–75) was an eminent Quaker preacher. She chiefly ministered in her native city of Philadelphia, but traveled widely among Quaker meetings in Pennsylvania, New Jersey, New York, and Maryland. At the age of seventy she visited England. She was a member of an extensive family; her father married four times and had seventeen children. Sarah Morris's half-great-nephew (the grandson of her father and his first wife), William Morris, married Milcah Moore's sister Margaret. See Robert C. Moon, *The Morris Family of Philadelphia* (Philadelphia, 1898), 1:114–15 and 204–11; *Friends' Library*, 6:478–80.

But perfect Bliss shall each probation close,
Ah! shall the Tear of sorrowing Nature, shed,
Our human Weakness, o'er the favour'd dead,
What shall we mourn?—that exil'd Souls are free
In Life Divine & Heavens own Liberty,   10
Which oft the captive Spirit long'd to Taste,
Amidst the Perils of this desart Waste
Where Clouds & Storms our trembling Feet surround
The frailty weakens, & the Conflicts wound,
—No dear departed Friend we will not mourn   15
Or with our Tears defile thy peaceful Urn,
And while triumphant in Messiahs Rest
(In full performance of his Promise blest,)
Thy pious Labours shall survive thy Dust,
And glow amidst the Annals of the Just.   20
Zealous & faithful in her Master's Cause,
And form'd to teach Messiah's healing Laws,
Hark! the glad Voice by Heavens Command display'd
To point the Path—& feeble Pilgrim aid
To warn the Rash from Follys dang'rous Shore,   25
Direct the seeking, & the lost explore,
To cheer her fellow Travellers on the Way,
Revive their Hope & glad with Dawn of Day,
Ready to heal, & cautious to reprove
She touch'd the wounded with the Hand of Love.   30
Directed thus, by an enlighten'd Mind
The proper Portion, to each State assign'd
So flow'd the powerful Language of her Tongue,
In soft Persuasion, tho in Reasoning strong.—
Her noble Faith & generous Charity   35
(From Bigot Modes & Superstition free)
Fix'd her Foundation on the gospel Plan,
And grasp'd the whole Creation in her Span,
Nor dared presumptuous bar the heav'nly Road,
On Man her Brother to her Father God,   40
The Heart benevolent with Judgement join'd,
And easy Converse shew'd her generous Mind
Where christian Virtues did with Social blend,
And form'd th' Instructor in the chearful Friend,
—Hail! favour'd Soul, admitted to that Peace,   45

Which fears no Interruption or Decrease,
Where Souls are Victors, & the Storm no more,
Ruffles the Calm of Canaan's promis'd Shore,
Thro' Faiths Perspective, thus the Prospect clears
To happier Scenes beyond this Vale of Tears,   50
In Glory, robes frail Natures final Hour,
"Tho sown in Weakness, it is rais'd in Pow'r."
From Doubts remov'd, from ev'ry Danger free,
"The mortal puts on Immortality"
Where each fierce Conflict with the Foe is o'er,   55
Weakness shall cease & Change be known no more,
Where the glad Spirit in its native Clime
(Beyond each dark Vicissitude of Time)
Victorious soars above this earthly Clod,
And shares its Triumphs with the Sons of God.   60
—Oh! in these blissful Seats of Love divine
May we again the dear lost Friend rejoin,
In holy Union heav'nly Raptures raise,
And join our Chorus in their Song of Praise
And while but Pilgrims in this des[e]rt Road,   65
Patient submit to every Stroke from God.

Fidelia

86   Wrote by the same upon reading a Book entituled Common Sense.[151] Jany. 1776.

The Vizard drop'd, see Subtilty prevail,
Thro' ev'ry Page of this fallacious Tale,
Sylvania let it not unanswer'd pass,
But heed the well guess'd Snake beneath the Grass,
A deeper Wound at Freedom, ne'er was made,   5

151. **Common Sense**: A little more than a year after first arriving in America, Thomas Paine further inflamed the conflict between Great Britain and her colonies by publishing *Common Sense*. Contributing to a growing debate over independence versus reconciliation, Paine argued that common sense dictated Americans must declare their independence. The pamphlet was first published in Philadelphia in January of 1776. Over 100,000 copies were printed and it appeared in every colony (Middlekauff, *Glorious Cause*, 317–20).

Than by this Oliverian [152] is display'd.
Orders confounded,—Dignities thrown down,
Charters degraded equal with the Crown,
The impartial Press, most partially maintain'd
Freedom infring'd, & Conscience is restrain'd,   10
The moderate Man is held to publick View,
"The Friend of Tyranny & Foe to you,"
Deny'd the common Right to represent
Forbid to give his Reasons for Dissent,
Whilst base Informers—(Own'd a publick Pest)   15
Are round the Land encourag'd & caress'd
Our Representatives,—the Peoples Choice
Are held contemptuous by this daring Voice
Persons are seiz'd & Posts monopoliz'd
And all our Form of Government despis'd,—   20
—Then from this "Specimen of Rule" beware,
Behold the Serpent & avoid his Snare.
'Tis not in Names, our present Danger lyes
Sixty as well as one can tyrannize,
Ah! then awake Sylvania & beware,   25
The fatal Danger of this subtle Snare,
Hold fast yr. own, yr. charter'd Rights maintain
Nor let them weave the Snare into the Chain,
And whilst firm Union stands the British Foes,
Let not the native Hand yr. Date of Freedom close.—   30

87   To the Honble. Society of Informers.[153] by the same. *February 1776*

Tho' Work for the Merchant is sadly decay'd
And the Flame of Dissention grows warmer,
Still—open one notable Branch of our Trade,
The noble employ of Informer.
In the Days of an old fashion'd Virtue its true   5
(When Love warm'd the sociable Breast)

---

152. **Oliverian:** "A partisan or adherent of Oliver Cromwell"(*OED*).
153. **Society of Informers:** Griffitts's sly poem about the "informers" can be read as alluding either to Quakers or to Patriots. Each group was vigilant in enforcing ad-

Wherever this Monster appear'd to the View,
Even Goodness itself could detest.
But Talents & Times, & Manners & Men,
Are lost to this primitive Name*   10
Then gentle Informers come enter the Scene
And mount to the Temple of Fame.
Its the Run of the Tide, its a popular Cause,
(Nor the Candidate worse for his Crimes,)
Contrary its true to the known Christian Laws*   15
But this must give way to the Times.
You have little to do—only take special Care
That you always run opposite Right,
Search keenly for Foibles thy Neighbour may wear
Then nobly, expose them to sight.   20
The Reward will be sure, & the Kindness repaid
As thou shalt mete out to thy Brother,
In this Life full Honour attend on thy Trade
And the Ballance be clos'd in the other.

[Marginal note:]
*Virtues
*[Matt. 7:12, 18, 22]

88   The prophetick Muse: To David Rittenhouse Esqr.[154] by the same. May 1776.

Labour not in state Affairs
Keep Acquaintance with the Stars,

---

herence. The Patriot Committee of Inspection and Observation, beginning in December 1774 until its dissolution in September 1776, demanded cooperation with the goals of nonimportation, nonexportation, and nonconsumption. In 1775 the Quaker Yearly Meeting had adopted a strict code of nonparticipation in Revolutionary activities including office-holding and military activity. By the end of 1775, 163 Quakers had been disowned for such activity. See Tinkcom, "The Revolutionary City," 122, 131–32; Richard Bauman, *For the Reputation of Truth: Politics, Religion, and Conflict Among the Pennsylvania Quakers, 1750–1800* (Baltimore: Johns Hopkins University Press, 1971), 156–58.

154. **To David Rittenhouse Esqr.**: Rittenhouse (1732–1796) was a distinguished astronomer, engineer, mathematician, clockmaker, and member of the American

For there thy Genius lyes,
Science David is thy Line
Warp not Nature's great Design   5
    If thou to Fame would'st rise.—

Then follow learned Newton still,
Trust me, mischievous Machiavel* 155
    Thou'll find a dreary Coast
Where, damp'd the philosophic Fire,   10
Neglected Genius—will retire,
    And all thy Fame be lost.

Politicks will spoil the Man
Form'd for a more exalted Plan,
    Great Nature bade thee rise,   15
"To pour fair Science on our Age
"To shine amidst th' historic Page,
    And half unfold the Skies."

But if thou crush this great Design
And in the Politicians Line   20
    With wild Ambition soar,
Oblivion shall entomb thy Name
And from the Rolls of future Fame
    Thou'll fall to rise no more.—

[Marginal note:]
*A most subt[le] & dangerous Italian Politican.

Philosophical Society, who taught himself Newtonian physics. He organized American observation of "the Transit of Venus" across the face of the sun in 1769, using equipment of his own manufacture. See Brooke Hindle, *David Rittenhouse* (Princeton: Princeton University Press, 1964).

    155. **Machiavel**: "Machiavel" was a derogatory term deriving from Nicolo Machiavelli (1469–1527), who wrote *The Prince* (wr. 1513; pub. 1532), "a treatise on statecraft. . . . [Machiavelli] teaches that the lessons of the past (of Roman history in particular) should be applied to the present, and the acquisition and effective use of power may necessitate unethical methods not in themselves desirable." Griffitts uses

89   The Invitation. by E. Fergusson

Come dear Amanda,[156] prythee come,
    And share yr. Time with me,
The smiling Hours shall sweetly glide,
    From Noise & Scandal free.
Thro' lonely Walks, & shady Bowers,   5
    We may delighted rove,
Where no Intruders can invade,
    To ruffle gentle Love.
*Cupid shall guard us from all harm,
    And shew his faithful Care,   10
As we sit by some murmuring Rill
    And female Friendship share.
The Town with all its sprightly Charms,
    Was not ordain'd for me,
More lasting Happiness is found,   15
    Beneath a spreading Tree.
Here sweet Simplicity presides
    And glads the virtuous Heart,
And rural Elegance around
    Does Nature's Joy's impart.   20
Instruction glides in every Brook,
    To sentimental Minds,
Each Shrub conveys some virtuous Truth
    And earthly Bliss refines.—Laura[157]

[Marginal note:]
*A favorite Lap-Dog

---

the term in the derogatory tradition of the stage "Machiavel," who was characterized as a poisoner, politician, and revenger (*OCEL*, 5th).

    156. **Amanda**: Pseudonym for several different women in America during this period. Carla Mulford, in *'Only for the Eye of a Friend': The Poetry of Annis Boudinot Stockton* (Charlottsville: University of Virginia Press, 1995), notes that some "poetic names are used frequently, and there are no clear indications that anyone pseudonym refers exclusively to one person in the way that *Laura* stands for Elizabeth Graeme Fergusson or *Emeila* for Annis Stockton" (320). "Amanda" may be Hetty Griffitts who signs herself "Amanda" in 54, "A Poem on Christmas Day 1774."

    157. **Laura**: The pseudonym of Elizabeth Graeme Fergusson.

90 A Paraphrase on Agurs[158] Prayer [Prov. 30:7–9] by the same.

1

Two things, my God, my Soul of thee demands
And humbly begs them, from thy heavenly Hands,
O! gracious Lord! do not my Suit deny,
And these Desires permit, before I die.—

2

Remove far from me, Vanity & Lies,   5
And grant me needful Food for Life's supplies:
But let not Riches weigh my earthly Scale,
Nor Poverty's keen Blasts my Mind assail.

3

Lest I be full & say, who is the Lord?
By Wealth forgetful of his holy Word!   10
Or lest black Want, with all his gloomy Train,
Tempt me to steal, & take Gods name in vain.—

E Furguson

91 The Review of past & present Times in Pennsylvania. June 1776.

When the Almighty separated our Fathers from the Land of their Nativity, & gave the Possession of Strangers for their Inheritance, with
an high Hand he led them forth, & his Arm of Strength established
them;——his Mercy & Truth surrounded them, & his Goodness
flow'd as a refreshing Stream,—he brought them to the Wilderness,
he planted them in a desart Land, but the Angel of his Presence went
forth with them, & his Wisdom directed their Councils;—he spake &
the Wilderness became a fruitful Field, & the Des[e]rt bloom'd as a
well watered Garden, her Beauty shone as the Vales of Eden, & her

---

158. **Agurs**: A priestly "college" in the religion of Rome; they were "to take the
auspices and interpret them." By means of this ritual, Romans tried "to ascertain
whether the gods were favorable to an undertaking" (*OCCL*).

Verdure flowed as Streams in the South, the Excellency of her Name was spread abroad & the Glory of the Nations distinguished her, for the Lord alone was their Leader, & the most high their sure Defence, the destroying Sword was sheathed in the Land of Quiet, & the Desolations of War were unknown to the Children of Peace; by the "Bands of Love" they engaged the Natives, & the "Laws of Kindness" were their only Weapons, they took the Strangers into the Communion of Brethren, & with—mutual Faith held the Covenant of Friendship;— then did our Fathers establish Justice thro' the Land & executed Judgment in Uprightness, the Eye of Compassion was ever open, & the Hand of Mercy turned the Balance.—Her judges were distinguished as the Barriers of her Borders, & her Rulers stood as the Guardians of the People; their Hands were not polluted with Bribes, nor their Hearts corrupted by Ambition.—The Banners of Peace were erected as her Standard, & her Laws were supported on the "Rights of Justice"—the Voice of Complaint was not heard in her Borders, & the Violence of Oppression was exiled from the Land,—thus the Lord poured his Blessing on the Land, & his Favour upon the People, they worshipped before the Throne of the most high, & he smiled upon them as his peculiar Inheritance, untill our Fathers died in Peace, with the Covenant of their God sealed on their Spirits—they left the fair Possession to their Offspring, & the Fruit of their Labour to succeeding Generations,—they charged their Sons to worship the God of their Fathers nor lightly to esteem "the Lot of their Inheritance"— But they rejected their Council, nor kept the Word of their Lips in Remembrance, they departed from the Lord their Leader, & forgot the God of their Fathers, for they despised the "Lot of their Inheritance"—& shook the Foundation which their Fathers had established, they tore in Pieces the "Tree of Union" whose Root was supported on the "Rock of Virtue"— its Branches produced the fair "Fruit of Freedom" & the healing of its Balm was the "Strength of the People"—The Isles of Renown poured out their Thousands, & the Cities of antient Fame sent forth their Children; they sought the Shelter of its peaceful Covert & the Wing of its Shade gave sweet protection,—they sat them down in the Land of Safety, & the Vales of Innocence secured their Liberties, her Glory was the Envy or Admiration of the Nations, & the wretched fled to Pennsylvania as to the "Altar of Refuge"—Oh! ye degenerate Sons—go mourn for the Desolation you have brought upon yr. Fathers Inheritance, "to secure the

Shadow, you have lost the Substance" your Liberties are expiring, &
the fair Plant of Freedom is withered to its Root,—You have removed
it from its native Soil, you have relaxed the Bands of its Strength, &
the Shelter of its Wing is known no more—you have removed the
Standard of Justice from the Laws, & rent the Banners of Peace from
future Generations you have suffered the Hand of Oppression to bear
Rule in the Land, & the Paths of Desolation mark their Footsteps,
you have sounded the Alarm of War, in the City of Peace, & banished
the "Law of Kindness" from the "Land of Love" but the secret Sigh of
deep Distress will gain his Ear, "who sees in secret"—& the "Refuge
of the Helpless" will plead their Cause, the Day of Retribution hath
taken Wings, & the solemnity of Decision approacheth swiftly, Divine Justice will hold the Balance, "& the Measure they mete shall be
measured to them again."—Oh! ye degenerate Sons, go weep over the
Sepulchre of y[ou]r. Forefathers, for Confusion reigns in their peaceful City, & the Foot of Anarchy tramples upon the Statutes of Benevolence—But the Wisdom of Heaven presides not in yr. distracted
Councils, nor will the Blessings of the "God of yr. Fathers" attend yr.
Ways; you have pressed forward in yr. own Strength, you have rejected the Voice of Admonition, & your Weakness shall stand conspicuous to the View of the World, 'till you again return to the Lord
yr. Leader & seek for Strength from the God of your Fathers.

Fidelia

92   The Enquiry.

Where, Friend, beneath the glittering Stars,
That gild this spacious Round,
Amidst the various Tracts of Life
Shall Happiness be found?
— That Idol, which our Senses charms,   5
(Yet charms us to our cost)
Fair in our Expectation smiles,
But in Experience lost.
— Where shall the searcher safely seek,
Where sure the Prize to find,   10

In Nature's meer external Gifts
Or Graces of the Mind?
— Does it in Affluence or in Fame,
In Wit or Beauty dwell,
In the gay Glitter of a Court   15
Or midst the Hermits Cell,
— Does it reside, in frolic Mirth
Of Pleasure's giddy Dream?
In Ease of Indolence enjoy'd;
Or midst the busy Scene?   20
— Does it beneath the critic Page,
Of rugged Learning shroud?
Smile in the calm sequester'd Life,
Or revel with the Crowd?
— In vain, we ask, in vain we seek,   25
Still new Delusions rise,
'Till Reason's Voice direct our search
And Wisdom gain the Prize.
— To no peculiar Lot of Life
Is Happiness confin'd,   30
But in the self-approving Heart
And firm contented Mind.

Fidelia

93   By the same on reading Eliza. Carters Poems.[159]

Each pow'rful Charm that Language can inspire
Did once to thee sweet Harmonist belong
The genuine Christian, & the Poets Fire
Strike in thy Themes, & soften in thy Song

159. **Eliza. Carters Poems**: Elizabeth Carter (1717–1806), poet and translator. Rejecting several suitors, she seems to have made scholarship and poetry the main focus of her life. Her major project from 1749 was a translation from the Greek of Epictetus. When it was published in 1758, "with a list of subscribers which brought her al-

— By Wisdom taught, to scorn the vulgar Lyes,   5
    That can the giddy Crowd, from Duty draw,
    Alike cou'd thou their Smile or frown despise
    Nor deify their Customs into Law.
— To Reason's Rules, & nobler Views confin'd
    Ne'er cou'd thy Angel Soul descend so low   10
    Or waste thy Moments, or debase thy Mind
    On glittering Trifles of delusive Shew.
— Each meaner Thought in thy great Soul gave place
    The one grand Scheme of Heaven to comprehend,
    There from its first Existance, Being, trace   15
    Define its Nature, & explore its End.
— When disengag'd from philosophic Views,
    Thy Soul descending left its native Skies,
    The moral Lyre still wing'd th' immortal Muse,
    In Virtues Cause, & Friendship's mutual Tyes.   20
— A Genius form'd of such superior Mould
    Can ne'er by circling Suns, survive its Prime,
    In Heaven's own Annals thou shall live enroll'd
    Beyond the Blast of Death or Waste of Time.
— A Soul attun'd to Harmony like thine   25
    Shall now immortal (with th' illustrious Throng)
    Enraptur'd glow midst Worship all Divine
    And swell the Chorus of the Seraph's Song

94   The Lord's Prayer. by the same.

Father, whose Throne supreme is Heaven,
(Tho' not to Space or Bounds confin'd)

---

most £1000," she was "no longer dependent on her father. . . . Her new circle of friends, including William Pulteney, Earl of Bath, Lord Lyttleton, and Mrs. Montagu, persuaded her to collect her *Poems on Several Occasions* (1762; 4th edition by 1789). Other biographical material as well as two poems, "A Dialogue" between the mind and the body and "Ode to Wisdom" are in the anthology *Eighteenth-century Women Poets*, ed. Roger Lonsdale (Oxford: Oxford University Press, 1990), 165–71. *British Women Poets 1660–1800: An Anthology*, ed. Joyce Fullard (Troy, N.Y.: Whitston, 1990) includes "To —.Occasioned by an Ode Written by Mrs. Catherine Phillips" (see *MMMB* 114, and note 186). Among Griffitts's papers at LCP is a copy of Elizabeth Carter's poem "On a Watch."

To thee exalted Praise be given
The Chorus, by Creation join'd.

Thy Kingdom come,—extensive flow,   5
And Thousands taste redeeming Love,
Thy Will be done on Earth below,
As its perform'd by Saints above.

Supply our craving Wants, each Day
As thou in Wisdom sees most fit,   10
Pardon our Sins we humbly pray
As we our Neighbors Debts remit.

Save us when fierce Temptations rise,
Keep us from Sins Defilement free
The Sacrifice of Prayer & Praise   15
Father, belong alone to thee.

The Kingdom, Power & Glory thine,
From Age, to endless Age compleat,
While Seraphs wing the sacred Hymn,
Let Earth the loud Amen repeat.   20

Fidelia

95   A philosophic View of the World. by the same.

Now should the World in all its glitt'ring Glow,
To catch my Heart, or charm my Fancy, rise,
With all its Friendships, Equipage & Shew,
My Soul the giddy Phantom could despise.
— Not all the Wealth of India now could charm,   5
My Heart to trust the false deceitful Toy
Its Glare allure me, or its Friendships warm,
To quit Retirements philosophic Joy
— In happy Solitudes sequester'd Vale,
Above the World, or to that World unknown,   10

Content they steer beneath the humble Gale,
And claim the Right to call their Hours their own.
— Not idly fluttering, with the fluttering Crowd,
To catch a Smile, or share a transient Joy
(Such, for a Juno, clasp a fleeting Cloud)   15
Meer abject Slaves, to a deceitful Toy
— Shall Souls immortal, & of heavenly Birth,
So basely quit their sacred Liberty?
To draw their Hopes expectant from the Earth,
And to the Idol bow the suppliant Knee.   20
— How oft the envy'd Pride of gaudy Shew,
Is but an empty Shade & gay disguise,
To viel from View the throbbing Heart of Woe
And screen its "Want of Comfort" from our Eyes—
— See the grand Equipage adorn'd by Art,   25
In Pride conspicuous, & in Sculpture gay,
Ne'er would it swell the Envy of thy Heart,
Could thou its Owners Discontent survey.
— And what is Fame? she wakes the Morn of Praise
Inscribes with frantic Strains, the Heros' Bust   30
But e'er we meet the Sun's descending Rays,
The Voice of Faction, levels with the Dust.
— Then happy those, who free from all these Snares
The humble Virtues of Retirement crown,
Superior Joys the placid Bosom wears,   35
Nor courts the Smile, nor dreads the Idols Frown.—

Fidelia

96   Primitive Friendship described.—by the same

1   Where is the sacred Flame of Friendship fled,
The Balm of Life descended from above?
Or but in Fiction is each Passion dead
Of perfect Freedom, & united Love?—
2   Shall generous Souls, the mean disguisement wear,   5

Of sordid Bosoms—for a selfish End,
The stiff Reserve—the haughty distant Air,
And Affectation only of a Friend?
3 Where is that noble Liberty of Mind,   10
The undisguis'd Sincerity of Heart?
Which by no false Formalities confin'd
Are far above, the low designs of Art.
4 Where, the soft Confidence of Friendship's Flame?
Union of Thought, & mingling Soul with Soul.
In mutual Warmth unchangeably the same   15
Firm as the Centre, steady as the Pole.
5 "This tender Plant, breathes but in native Air,
"Reserve will wound it, & distrust destroy"
And sly Suspicion with its noxious Glare
Damp the kind Warmth & chill the vital Joy.   20
6 No sordid Bosom, with its selfish View
Can in true Friendship an Admittance find
More noble Sentiments must they pursue
Who claim this fond Engagement of the Mind.
7 Nor different Stations in the Lot of Life   25
Create a Difference, in this mutual Trust
Above the little Schemes of fretful Strife
The Glare of Eminence or glittering Dust.
8 Where Friendship reigns, with undivided Sway
There lurks no Fear, by Freedom to offend,   30
The generous Sentiment can each convey
With all the easy Dignity of Friend.
9 In Souls like these (& such as these alone)
Adorn the Bands of Liberty & Love
The tender Sympathy of Hearts are known   35
And the fond Cares which glow in Minds above.
10 In the strait Breast which cannot soar so high
Nor feel its soft & animating Flame,
The Virtues sicken, & the Graces die,
With ev'ry Motive to each social Claim.   40
11 Without this first of (mortal) Blessings given
To cheer the dark, & smooth the rugged Road
Joy is Delusion, Grief the Rod of Heaven
And Life itself, but one afflictive Load.—

97   The Christian Philosopher. by the same.

1   How far does Heaven admit the cautious Mind,
     ('Midst Cares perplexing & embitter'd Woe)
     To mitigate the Pain, Relief to find
     And draw Refreshment from the Streams below.
2   Know doubting Heart, each Comfort Man receives,   5
     Is sent from Heaven to cheer him, not to cloy,
     Then take with Gratitude, the Good he gives
     Adore the giver, & the Gift enjoy.
3   The good Man, thus, of conscious Peace possest
     Shall calm the Rigour of Affliction's Pow'r   10
     In Friendship's Bosom sooth his Cares to Rest
     And taste the Solace of the social Hour.
4   While Good & Evil still lye mingled here
     (From the same Root, the Thorn & fragrant Rose)
     With firm Philosophy encounter Care   15
     By Resignation soften deeper Woes.
5   Thro' ev'ry sad Vicissitude on Earth
     The Christian Hero will superior soar
     Nor let the Man disgrace his heav'nly Birth
     His kindred Angels, & his native Shore.   20
6   Life's rough Probation to the truly wise
     Is but a transient Passage, thro' the Road
     (Secure his rich Reversion in the Skies)
     He bears the Evil & enjoys the Good.
7   Ne'er sink his Spirits with depressive Cares   25
     Or silent Murmur sharpen every Rod
     A guiltless Smile, the chearful Christian wears
     He walks erect, & lives resign'd to God.—

98   [Untitled] Remember thy Creator in the Days of thy Youth. [Eccles. 12:1].

In the soft Season of thy blooming Hours,
     When the Nerves strengthen & the Pulse beats high,

Remember God! who gave the reasoning Pow'rs
    Supports thy Frame & can thy wants supply.
Secure his Favour, e'er the evil Day,   5
    With saddening Prospects swells the List of Woe
In which thy disappointed Hopes shall say
    "I draw no Comfort from the Streams below."
That Sun be dark, which round our vernal Sphere
    Rose in gay Vigour, an illustrious Morn,   10
And pale ey'd Cynthia [160] with the glittering Star
    No more our clouded Horizon adorn.
When feeble Age unnerves the fainting Frame;
    O'er ev'ry smiling Prospect draws the Veil;
When Pride connection with the Dust shall claim   15
    The Hero tremble & the Stoic fail.
The Glare of Life sink in Oblivion's Shade
    Tasteless remain or all forgotten lie
When from thy Cheek the transient Rose shall fade
    And the soft Sparkle languish in thine Eye.   20
When thou no more the festal Joys shall share,
    That charm the Relish of the jovial Throng
Nor Mirth, nor Musick strike thy deafen'd Ear
    Now clos'd to all the Harmony of Song.
When trembling Fears surround the mortal Coast,   25
    Straws to thy wasting Strength a Burden prove,
Desire shall languish, every Hope be lost
    And weeping Mourners point thy last Remove.
When the soft Cords of gay Delight are broke,
    And flowing Bowls no longer charm thy Taste   30
Enfeebled Nature waits the impending Stroke
    Tir'd with the Scene & sighs to be undress'd.
Now Dust shall to congenial Dust return
    The Soul to God who gave it Being rise,
Tho' Flesh revert Companion to the Worm   35
    Soul's claim immortal Kindred with the Skies.
Then seek thy God, with that first warmest Love,
    Which does to Vigour & to youth belong,

---

160. **Cynthia**: Another name for Diana. This epithet refers to her as the goddess of
the moon.

And he, that was thy Morning Star shall prove,
    Thy Noon-tide Glory, & thy Evening Song.   40

Fidelia

99   On reading the Adventurer World & et[c].[161] by the same.

Shall Virtue weeping call, shall Satyr[162] sneer,
And british Females still regardless hear?
Shall trifling Subjects thus yr. Sex disgrace,[163]
Each moral Tye & social Mark efface?
Shall deep Corruption, wear the Name of Joy[s]   5
And that be term'd Amuzement which destroys?

161. **Adventurer World & et[c]**: Periodicals. The *Adventurer* (1752–54), produced by John Hawkesworth, "with the considerable assistance of his friend Dr. Johnson and of J. Warton," was a bi-weekly successor to *The Rambler* (1750–52). *The World* (1753–56), produced by "Adam Fitz-Adam," was a weekly 'paper of entertainment,' owned by J. Dodsley, and edited by E. Moore. . . . Its contributors included Chesterfield, Horace Walpole, and Jenyns" (*OCEL*, 5th).

162. **Satyr**: Satyrs in Greek mythology were "represented as grotesque creatures, in the main of human form but with some part bestial, e.g. . . . the legs of a goat." They were characterized as "lustful and fond of revelry" (*OCCL*). Although the word is spelled "satyr," Griffitts could also be referring to "satire," "a work . . . that blends a censorious attitude with humor and wit for improving human institutions or humanity. Satirists attempt through laughter not so much to tear down as to inspire a remodeling. . . . The eighteenth-century in England became a period of *satire*; poetry, drama, essays, and criticism all took on the satirical manner at the hands of such writers as Dryden, Swift, Addison, Steele, Pope, and Fielding" (C. Hugh Holman and William Harmon, *A Handbook to Literature*, 6th ed. [New York: Macmillan, 1992]).

163. **Sex disgrace**: The "disgraces" and even "corruption" among British women noted in the poem seem to come from the pages of *The Rambler*, the *Adventurer*, and *The World*, where women were often a target for satire and moral instruction in essays and narratives. Of the three, *The World* took a lighter tone, ridiculing, for example, a country squire's wife for her taste in all things Chinese (no. 12). *The Adventurer* used the essay, such as "Scheme of a new memorandum-book for the use of the ladies" to satirize women's use of time for the "more important businesses of pleasure and amusement" (no. 23:133). Several issues are supposedly written by "fallen" women: "Fidelia" shares her autobiography, which includes a father who is a "free-thinker," a seducer named Sir George Freelove, and a rescuer, an elderly clergyman and his wife who give her new hope by teaching her about providence and redemption (nos. 77–79).

Shall gross Indecency yr. Honour stain
Or Forms fantastic prove yr. Judgement vain?
Will Gaming teach you Passions to controul
Soften your Eye & harmonize your Soul?   10
Or will you dare in this licentious Age
To form yr. decent Manners by the Stage?
While from each Pen th' instructive Shaft is hurl'd
The Adventurer, Rambler, even the speaking World,
Unite to heal the Breach your Folly made   15
And point the Path from whence you blindly stray'd,
Severe in Virtue or in Humour warm,
To improve yr. Morals & yr. Manners form,
And as they find repeated Labour vain,
Despise those Subjects that they can't reclaim: 20
Believe the Muse (& trust the Mirror true)
The Satyr's levell'd & the Laugh at you.
Degenerate Change! shall Men the Fault discern
And point the Folly where they ought to learn;—
Where now is fled that native Innocence,   25
The female Glory & our best Defence?
Where now that conscious Dignity refin'd
That checks the rude & awes the darkest Mind?
The Just Resentment & the Blush sincere
The Eye corrective, & the Heart severe?   30
Is Virtue now a Fiction of the Brain?
Is Female Honour but an empty Name?
Beneath the Notice of the gay polite
(Ties fit for vulgar Minds & Erro's Night)
Tenets like those may Epicurus[164] preach   35
And such the Sceptic Libertine[165] may Teach.—
But rise my Sex with just indignant Scorn
And the vile Reptile from yr. Presence spurn,

---

164. **Epicurus**: a Greek philosopher (c. 371–270 B.C.) who formed a school of philosophy that held "that pleasure (or absence of pain) is the only good, being the only good known to the senses. . . . The best pleasure . . . is a perfect harmony of body and mind, to be sought in plain living, and in virtue. . . . The English sense of the word 'Epicurean', i.e., 'devoted to refined and tasteful sensuous enjoyment' (*OED*), misrepresents the teaching of Epicurus" (*OCCL*).

165. **Sceptic Libertine**: "Skeptic" has both a philosophical and a popular meaning. Philosophically, a skeptic is "one who holds that there are no adequate grounds for

Nor suffer Vice tho' dignified to appear
Beneath yr. Influence, or yr. Notice share, 40
Fly far the infectious Herds as Beasts of Prey
They wait yr. Fall & flatter to betray,
Glory in Crimes of deep infernal Hue
And prove the Tempter & the Accuser too,
Not Birth nor Beauty, Wit nor Wealth can claim 45
The fair Distinction of unsullied Fame,
Be this yr. glorious Badge, yr. proudest Boast
And thus retrieve the female Honour lost,
Virtues immortal Flame inspire yr. Breast
Despise the trifle, & the Vice detest 50
The generous Act humane, the social Joy
And soft domestic Cares yr. Hours employ,
To Scenes important wing yr. active Powers
And be the glorious Task of Duty yours,
To form the moral Rectitude of Mind, 55
Manners severe & Modesty refin'd,
To glow in native Dignity & Grace,
And shine the Example of a guilty Race,
Let ev'ry Act the instructive Lines convey
And with improvement mark each circling Day 60
Thus may you still adorn Brittania's Coast
And stand yr. Species Glory Pride & Boast.

100 The sympathetic Scene[166]—wrote August 31st 1776—occasioned by the unnatural Contest at Long Island Augst. 27th. & 28th. by the same.

In the sad Chambers of retir'd Distress
The Scenes of speechless Woe, where Widows mourn

---

certainty as to the truth of any proposition whatever"; popularly, "one who maintains a doubting attitude." A "libertine" may be "one who holds loose or free opinions about religion; a free-thinker," or "one who follows his own inclinations or goes his own way," or "a man who is not restrained by moral law, esp. in his relations with the female sex; one who leads a dissolute, licentious life" (*OED*).

166. **The sympathetc Scene:** The Battle of Long Island was the first sustained battle of the American Revolution where organized American troops met British

The tender Husband lost,—where Orphans weep
Th' indulgent Friend & Father known no more,
Where the sad Sister faints beneath the Stroke   5
That rent th' associate Brother from her Heart,
Here clad in sympathetic sorrows Gloom
My Soul retires, to share my neighbors' Grief
Give Sigh for Sigh, & mingle Tears with Tears,
Or deeper still—beyond the gentle Power   10
Of Words to heal, or Tears to mitigate,
Deep in the awful Center of the Soul,
(Hid from the View of an unfeeling World)
And wrapt in solemn Silence of Distress
I still attend your melancholy Steps,   15
And say—the silent Tribute to yr. Woes.—
But Words are vain, the Powers of Harmony
Are useless here, ev'n Friendships soothing Voice
Has lost its Calm, in Woundings like to yours
Ah then from Heaven, from gracious Heaven alone   20
Look for the kind Relief, the healing Power
The Calm of Comfort, & sustaining Friend—
May he supply the soft cementing Bands
(Which brutal War, rent from yr. bleeding Hearts)
Direct yr. trembling Footsteps, & be found   25
The Husband, Father, & the Brother lost.
—But you, whose mad Ambition lawless Grasp
Of proud Dominion, & tyrannic Power
Have spread the Flames of War around the Shores
Where Peace once smil'd & social Union dwelt;   30
How will you stand, the retributive Hour
Or bear the Close of dread Decision's Voice,
When, as you mingled deep the Cup of Woe
For suffering Souls,—so well yr. Souls partake
The deeply mingled Cup of Woe again?—   35

regulars. The battle commenced August 26, 1776, when British General Howe ordered his troops to push Americans back to Brooklyn and ultimately off the island. The British were triumphant. By August 29th, General Washington's troops had been ferried to New York City. This was the beginning of the Americans' months-long retreat toward Philadelphia. See Ira D. Gruber, "America's First Battle: Long Island, 27 August 1776," in Charles E. Heller and William A. Stofft, eds., *America's First Battles, 1776–1965* (Lawrence: University Press of Kansas, 1986), 1–32.

You—have dissolv'd the tender Bands of Nature
And torne asunder (by the ruthless Hand
Of horrid War) the dear, the soft Connections
Which Heaven had join'd & blest, till you arose
The Scourge of Desolation on their Peace.—   40
To you, the Widow & the Orphan, look
With heart felt Anguish, as their Source of Woe
And in the Pang of Grief from you demand
The Husband, Father, & the Brother lost.
—But yet another Scene, the weeping Muse   45
Attends—with tender Sympathy of Heart
Go, view thy wounded Brother, in the Hour
Of keen Distress, & flesh corroding Pain,
Far—from the kind assistant kindred Hand
Or healing Friendship's soft consoling Voice.   50
Oh! pour the cordial Balm—the Balm of Love
And sympathetic Tears—into their Wounds,
Share in the Anguish of Reflections Hour
And feeling Pity sooth the Sufferers Groan,
Be ye, the Charge of ever gracious Heaven   55
How e'er by Man neglected,—Sons of Woe
May his kind Care yr. healing Safety prove
And may he meet you, here,—in Mercy meet
Upon the Bed of Languishment, & speak
The Voice of Peace & Pardon to yr. Souls,—   60
Oh may his strength sustain in the dread Hour
Of Pain & Dissolution—raise to Life
Or gracious fit you for th' unchanging Change⌐
So prays, yr. kindred Muse, who deeply shares
The painful Moments of yr. languid Hours,   65
And still the Image of yr. Woes remain,
With deep Impression not to be eras'd
From the sad sorrowing Bosom of yr. Friend.—
—How long, all gracious Heaven, shall kindred Man,
Break thro' the soft Cements thy Hand ordain'd   70
To join the whole, in gentlest Bands of Love,
Natures strong Tyes, & Friendship's Sympathies,
The generous Glow of Heart, the ardent Wish
For human Happiness, are broke & lost

In Wars devouring Rage, infernal Flame   75
(Unworthy of the Dignity of Man)
And kindled, from the dark Abodes below,
Oh! speak contending Brethren into Peace
Bid the sweet Cherub bless our weeping Shores
And Friends again in her soft Bands unite.—   80

101 Wrote by Docr. J. O.[167] on his Return from the Kings Chappel St. James's where he was ordained.—Jany. 4th 1767.—

'Tis done; —the solemn awful Scene is o'er!
My Heart, my Soul, my every Pow'r, adore
The dread Eternal, Father Son & Mind,
Author, Redeemer, Teacher of Mankind!
"Triune, unutterable," hallow'd Name,   5
O God, who wast, art, shalt be still the same!
O give my panting Soul, on Wings of Love,
Of Gratitude & Praise, to mount above
Unnumber'd Worlds & all created Things,
Up to thy awful Throne, thou King of Kings,   10
Thou great first, last, best, only Lord of all!
—And shall a Reptile of this Emmet-Ball,[168]
This rolling Particle of yesterday, shall I,
From this low Earth, look up to thee, most High,
Most wonderful great God! & call thee mine?   15
My Father & my Friend? O Love divine,
Ineffable, amazing!—Lo, a Race
Of guilty Rebels by an Act of Grace

167. **Docr. J. O.**: Jonathan Odell (1737–1818) was rector of St. Mary's Anglican church in Burlington. He was a loyalist and published verses in newspapers including Rivington's *Royal Gazette*. Milcah Moore's sister Margaret Morris hid Odell in her attic when he was sought by New Jersey Patriots (see page 38). Crane, *Diary of Elizabeth Drinker*, biographical directory; Amelia Mott Gummere, "Friends in Burlington," *PMHB* 8 (1884): 163–64.
168. **Emmet-Ball**: "Ant-hill" (*OED*).

Incomprehensible, redeem'd from Death,
And oh, redeem'd by him who gave us Breath!   20
By him releas'd from Vengeance due!—nay more,
By him restor'd to all we lost before!
By him (who died to wash our Guilt away!)
Made Heirs again of Heavn's eternal Day!
   Then let our grateful Transports humbly flow;   25
So dear a Claim 'twere impious to forego.
The Son himself has taught our infant-Cries
In filial Accents to ascend the Skies.
   Ye Sons of Men, obey the high behest;
Ask of your Father, & ye shall be blest!   30
Nor let ev'n me, tho' mean I am indeed,
Despair to find what I so greatly need.
   My Father & my God!—thy Grace impart
To raise my Soul & purify my Heart;
Dispel the Darkness that beclouds my Sight;   35
Save me from Error, lead me into Light,
That Light which breaks Time's fascinating Charm,
A Lamp to guide us & a Shield to arm,
A safe Conductor thro' the Wilds of Sense,
Against Temptation a secure Defence;   40
That Light which in the sacred Pages shines,
Informs the Mind & all the Man refines,
Gives holy Faith, fair Hope & boundless Love,
Subdues the World & plants our Bliss above!
For ah, without thy soul-enlight'ning Aid,   45
Vain are the solemn Vows my Heart has made!
But if thy Spirit deign my Steps to guide,
Unshaken shall I every Storm abide;
No Dangers shall dismay, no Ills defeat,
No Frailties tempt me to a base Retreat;   50
But, spurning Pleasure & unaw'd by Pain,
With Perseverance will I press to gain
A faithful Soldier's courage-purchas'd Prize,
My glorious Leader's Plaudit in the Skies.—
―― ―― ―― ―― ――
   Such are the Thoughts that, in my lab'ring Breast,   55

The Vows of yesterday have deep imprest;
Thus warmly felt, sincere & void of Art,
Be every future breathing of my Heart.—

Westminster Jany. 5th. 1767.
   The above Copy of Verses were, at the same Time, inclos'd in a Letter & sent as a small Token of filial Respect, to his spiritual Father, the
right Revd. the Lord Bishop of London.

102   Written in England on the Return of the 22nd. Regiment[169] after 8 years Service in N. America & the West Indies

From burning Sands, or frozen Plains,
   Where Victory led the Way,
Hail, ye returning small remains
   Of many a glorious Day!
Welcome, again, ye gallant Few,   5
   To breathe a native Air,
Enjoy the Praise to Merit due,
   And dear bought Laurels wear.
Let grateful Memory now retrace
   Your Pains, yr. Dangers past,   10
On Land oppos'd grim Battles' Face,
   At Sea the stormy Blast.
In eight revolving Years, alass!
   What Havock War has made,
A Tear shall swell one circling Glass   15

   169. **Return of the 22nd. Regiment**: A poem entitled "A Welcome Home to the
Twenty-Third Regiment: After the Peace of 1763" seems to be a duplicate of the
poem Moore transcribes, except for the regimental number. Winthrop Sargent attributes the poem to Dr. Jonathan Odell in *The Loyal Verses of Stansbury and Odell*,
Munsell's Historical Services, no. 6 (Albany, 1860), 106–8. Sargent adds, "The sub-
joined verses were doubtless addressed to the corps in which he had once served" as a
surgeon (106).

In Memory of the Dead.
"Farewel, thou much lamented Chief,
    And all ye Slain farewel;
Our Love & unabated Grief
    Let this Libation tell."   20
To every Frown of Fate resign'd
    They earn'd a deathless Fame,
For Glory bled, & left behind
    A sadly pleasing Name.
But while the Dead our Tears lament   25
    Their Loss while we bemoan,
Our Sorrows on ourselves are spent,
    The Grief is all our own.
On many a widely-distant Land,
    Or in the howling Deep,   30
Tho' now they seem, by Deaths cold Hand
    Sunk in eternal Sleep;
Tho' now they seem dissolv'd away
    And lost in gloomy Night,
Secluded from the chearful Day   35
    No more to see the Light,
Yet are they far from what they seem;
    Their Clay alone is cold;
The Soul, a warm aetherial Beam,
    No Pow'r of Death can hold.   40
This mortal Frame is but a Screen
    Between us & the Skies,
Death draws the Curtain, & the Scene
    Then opens on our Eyes.
'Tis we that dream, not they that sleep;   45
    Their hovering Spirits fly
Around you still, & on you keep
    A friendly watchful Eye.
And thus the Chief, who lately led
    Your Courage to the Field,   50
May still be fancied at yr. Head
    To warn you ne'er to yield.
Your lost Companions still may strive

With you each Toil to bear,
    May thus, in Fancy's Eye, survive,   55
        Your growing Fame to share.
With Joy & Triumph, then, review
        Your Toils & Dangers past;
Fill up the circling Glass anew
        And—welcome Home at last.—   60

103   Birth-Day Ode for a young Girl newly recover'd from a Fit of Illness. by the same

Life tho' sweet yet how uncertain,
    Held but by a fleeting Breath,
A slender Thread suspends the Curtain
    That viels approaching Death.
Death—he lately gave me Warning,   5
    But now his Warrant seems withdrawn,
Welcome then, this Birth-day Morning!
    O propitious prove the Dawn!
May the Life to me allotted,
    Whether long or short the Date   10
Prove oh gracious Heaven! unspotted,
    Fearless then I'll meet my Fate.
For the past forgive all Error,
    For the future guide my Youth,
Let not Hope, nor Joy, nor Terror   15
    Make me shun the Voice of Truth.
Ye from whom my Life descended,
    Teach, oh teach me how to pay;
The Debt of Infancy defended,
    Of Love & Care from Day to Day.   20
Teach my Heart, to prize the Beauty
    That alone can Time defy,
Charms that flow from Love & Duty,
    And gain Admission to the Sky.

104   [Untitled]

The New-Jersey State [170] by what I can hear.
Is condemn'd, as tyrannical, harsh & severe,
For so fast do they hold the terrific Rod,
As to punish, for winking, a Sign or a Nod,
But how kind these Reformers, how gentle their Sway.   5
While they leave us the Freedom to *think* & to *pray.*

Fidelia

[Marginal note:]
November 1776.

105   Inscription. [171] by the same

On a curious Chamber-Stove, in the Form of an Urn, contriv'd in
such a Manner as to make the Flame descend instead of rising from
the Fire.—
Invented by the celebrated B. F.—n.

Like a Newton sublimely he soar'd
To a Summit before unattain'd,
New Regions of Science explor'd

---

170. **New-Jersey State**: The people of New Jersey suffered from the movement of
American and British troops across New Jersey. The requirements for pledging loyalty to the Crown or to the independence movement were quite severe. Milcah
Moore's sister and Hannah Griffitts's cousin Margaret Hill Morris lived in New Jersey for much of the tumult of 1777 and 1778. See pages 47–49.

171. **Inscription**: Although Moore attributes this poem to Griffitts, the poem has
also been attributed to Jonathan Odell. It was first published under his name in the
Gentleman's Magazine and Historical Chronicle 47 (April 1777). Like other poems in
Moore's commonplace book, it probably circulated in manuscript. A "copy" of the
poem in Griffitts' handwriting is in the LCP's collection of Griffitts' poetry. She has
written "Copy" and the date, "Novr. 1776" next to the title of the poem. She also
adds a note to the word "defend" in the eighth line; " 'defend' was, I suppose intended
but I don't believe such Virtue was lodg'd in the man, or his Art."

And the Palm of Philosophy gain'd.
With a Spark that he caught from the Skies,   5
He display'd an unparallel'd Wonder,
And we saw with Delight & Surprize
That his Rod cou'd defend us from Thunder.
O! had he been wise to pursue
The Tract for his Talent design'd,   10
What a Tribute of Praise had been due,
To the Teacher & Friend of Mankind!
But, to covet political Fame
Was in him a degrading Ambition,
A Spark that from Lucifer came,   15
And kindled the Blaze of Sedition!
Let Candor, then write on his Urn,
Here lies the renowned Inventor,
Whose Flame to the Skies ought to burn,
But, inverted descends to the Centre!—   20

106 Written by R. R. May 4th. 1776.

What Notions of Happiness Mankind embrace,
As dependant on Riches, on Titles or Place,
On Beauty, Fame, Conquest, & I know not what,
It's all fiddle faddle[172]—she dwells in this cot.—

Here Freedom attends her with Humour & Ease,   5
The sociable Flow, the desire to please,
The Blossoms of Friendship untainted appear,
Here Spring reigns eternal, 'tis May all the Year.

From Tumult retir'd, from Faction & Strife,
These Moments improve as the Essence of Life,   10

---

172. **fiddle faddle**: "a 'fuss-pot', an habitual fusser" (*A Dictionary of Slang and Unconventional English*, 8th ed., by Eric Partridge and ed. Paul Beale, [New York: Macmillan, 1970]).

The Foes to all Order good Laws & Decorum,
Dare not enter here,—for here's the Sanctorum;[173]

Where Happiness, Virtue & Friendship reside,
The Temple shou'd be as the Universe wide,
I mean not to these narrow Walls to confine,   15
My Friend is their Priest, & his Heart is their Shrine.

107   Reflections on Human Happiness. by the same.

    Unthankful Man, perversely blind,
Calls Life unhappy, God unkind!
Our Being was bestow'd us, sure,
Not to enjoy it but endure.
    When foolish Envy pining sees   5
Those whom she deems the Sons of Ease,
The happy few, whose dazling State
Excites her jealousy & Hate,
How groundless her malignant Sighs!
How great her Error, when she cries,   10
"On these why lavish'd Joys denied
"By partial Heav'n to all beside?["]
Ah take—take but a nearer View
Of those you call the happy few;
Explore the vacant, joyless Breast;   15
And learn that they, who seem most blest,
Are destin'd still, by Heav'n, to bear
Of human Wretchedness their Share.
In this Mankind are all the same;
For Heav'n has mingled in our Frame   20
Such jarring elemental Fires,
Contending Passions & Desires,
That, still impell'd, the restless Mind
Labors, in vain alas! to find,
In some fond Wishes flattering Height,   25

173. **the Sanctorum**: "A shrine" (*OED*).

A full & permanent Delight.
But we no sooner gain the Prize,
Than all the promis'd Pleasure flies;
And other Wishes strait succeed
To urge again our fruitless Speed.   30
Bewilder'd in the breathless Chase
We still renew the giddy Race,
Thro' endless circling Mazes fly,
Pursue we know not what nor why,
Forget past Toils so ill repaid,   35
And, for a Substance, grasp—another Shade!
  Thus, ceaseless is our Toil & Pain,
And Disappointment all our Gain!
Thus Misery marks our mildest Fate!
We're form'd by Nature to create   40
Of fancied Wants substantial Ills;
While joy's fresh Blossom Passion kills!
  To stem the Tide we strive in vain;
We're born but to inherit Pain.
Let all that Earth & Seas afford   45
With Plenty crown our festive Board;
Let art her every Effort try,
With Art let bounteous Nature vie,
Let Health, Friends, every Thing we know,
Of fancied Happiness below,   50
Conspire to'anticipate our Will;
We're Men—& therefore wretched still!
Some Blank, some torturing Wish remains,
And every present Joy disdains.
  If such then be the Fate of those   55
Whose Cup with Plenty thus o'erflows,
What shall we deem their rigid Lot,
Who seem by Providence forgot?
Whom Want, Disease, & fruitless Care
Together hurry to Despair?   60
  To be was not our own Request;
Then why exist to be unblest!
What Benefit is Life, bestow'd
On such Conditions?—'Tis a Load,

A galling Load, which they, who dare   65
To cast it off, shou'd scorn to bear!
    By Folly led, betray'd by Pride,
Lorenzo [174] thus impatient cried;
Thus blindly dar'd, without Restraint,
To vent his blasphemous Complaint!   70
When lo!—All-gracious Heav'n! instead
Of Lightnings darted on his Head,
He saw, descending from above,
A radiant Messenger of Love!
Celestial Truth, divinely bright,   75
Array'd in flowing Robes of Light,
Down from her Father's awful Throne
Swift-gliding, all around him shone.
Her Hand a golden Sceptre bore,
Her Head a Crown of Glory wore,   80
In Majesty she stood confest,
And thus Lorenzo's conscious Heart addrest.
    Proud Foe to Truth & thy own Peace!
Thy senseless impious railing cease.
Thou breathing Particle of Dust,   85
Shall He, who by a Word, at first,
Gave Birth to countless Worlds, & still
Upholds Creation by his Will,
His Will omnipotent! shall He
Be scann'd, arraign'd, & judg'd by thee?   90
    To him who forms it, shall the Clay,
When wrought to shape, presume to say,
"Why hast thou made me thus?"—yet thou
Art not afraid to bend thy Brow,
To frown, to murmur & complain,   95
And treat thy Maker with Disdain!
    From nothing into Being brought,
Blest with the Godlike Pow'rs of Thought,
Reflection, Memory, Reason, Choice,
And Action ruled by Reason's Voice;   100
What Blessings these! & these are thine!

---

174. **Lorenzo**: A literary pseudonym or an unidentified historical person.

And canst thou still, o Man, repine?
Unthankful, still presume to vent
The Sighs of impious Discontent?
    But—Heav'n has kindled in thy Frame 105
An inextinguishable Flame,
A restless Avarice of Bliss,
Which all pursue, yet all must miss;
While Nature keeps alive the Fire
Of endless Hope, & warm Desire. 110
Thus fruitless Heav'n's best Gifts are found,
Because thy Wishes know no Bound!
    O fatal Blindness!—Rather thence
Let Reason draw this Inference:
Since God is not less good than wise, 115
Being, bestow'd unask'd, implies
The Gift was by the Giver meant
A Blessing, not a Punishment;
But, to desire, & not obtain,
Is but another Name for Pain, 120
A Malady without a Cure,
Which Man seems destin'd to endure;
Since then Man's Wishes ceaseless rise,
And nothing fully satisfies
Those boundless Wishes here below; 125
Heaven will some future Bliss bestow,
Some brighter Scene at last disclose
Of endless Joy & calm Repose.
    But then, alass! fond Man, beware!
Think not this happy Lot to share, 130
Unless, from Guilt unstain'd & free,
Thy Innocence support thy Plea.
If madly thou presume to sin
Against that Monitor within,
Of Right & Wrong that conscious Test 135
Which Nature plants in every Breast,
Groundless & vain thou must confess
Thy cancell'd Claim to Happiness.
    "Nature has giv'n thee Passions"—true;
And Reason to controul them too. 140

Thy Passions were by Heav'n design'd
To rouse thy Indolence of Mind,
To prompt thy Virtue, not seduce;
Thus Guilt remains without Excuse!
But—not without a Cure!—And this,   145
This Remedy secures thy Bliss!
Let Reason reassume her Sway,
Let Passion Reason's Voice obey;
To Heav'n's unerring Will resign'd,
Thy Tribute pay, a thankful Mind;   150
Subdue thy Discontent & Pride,
At aught bestow'd or aught denied;
Repent the past, offend no more,
And then with humble Trust, adore
That Love divine, which only can   155
Forgive & rescue guilty Man!
  Sweet smiling Peace from Heav'n descends,
And on these gracious Terms extends
Her olive Wand [175] to thee, to all
Who follow Truths inviting Call.   160
  Does human Frailty still impede
Thy prompt Obedience?—'Tis decreed,
Who does the best he can, to gain
The Prize of Virtue, shall obtain.
And this obtain'd shall crown at last,   165
With endless Bliss thy Labours past!
  Nor think thy present Fate severe;
Whatever be thy Portion here,
There is in Virtue still a Charm
To heighten Joy, or Grief disarm.   170
  Does Wealth enable thee to spare?
Let those who need it have a Share:
The Widow's gladden'd Heart shall sing,
The rescued Orphan round thee cling,
Neglected Genius, nurs'd by thee,   175
Confess the Hand that set it free,
And Thousands by thy Bounty fed,
Call down a Blessing on thy Head!

175. **Her olive Wand**: The olive branch, held by the personified Peace.

Nor let Disease, nor fruitless Care,
Nor Want, nor Death, create Despair! 180
    For, spight of all that Mortals know,
Of Good or Evil here below,
This middle State, at best, supplies
A Passage, only to the Skies:
And on this Passage let thy Lot 185
Be rough or smooth it matters not;
For, woud'st thou get with Comfort through,
Thou must this Maxim still pursue,
Let Hope look forward, & allow
"That Hope to be thy Blessing now." 190
    What woud'st thou more? what better Plan
Shall Heav'n adopt, to render Man
As blest as he wou'd wish to be?
Let Heav'n, for once, be taught by thee!
    Since Nature deviates from thy Will, 195
Perhaps thy less imperfect Skill
May shew what better Laws to make,
What wiser Course she ought to take!
Or, since unequal Providence
Gives thy less partial Eye offence, 200
Let thy superior Wisdom tell
Thy Maker how to govern well!
    Does Pride itself recoil & fly
From such an impious Thought?—o! why,
Why then, Lorenzo, dost thou still 205
Betray an unsubmitting Will?
    At length, be wise, renounce thy Pride,
And follow Truth, a faithful Guide.
God's Will presume not thou to blame;
Thro' Life be Virtue all thy Aim; 210
And then, whatever Ills befall,
The Grave shall make amends for all,
Shall land thee safe, upon that Shore,
Where Pain shall visit thee no more,
Where Fancy shall no more pursue 215
A painted Substance for a true,
But full, substantial, endless Joy
Thy growing Faculties employ!

Cease then thy unavailing Sighs,
And own that Man's true Wisdom lies   220
In Resignation to that Pow'r
Whose boundless Goodness, every Hour,
Unsought, unmerited, unpaid,
Sustains the Universe he made,
Directs for all what's wisest, best,   225
And, if they will, bids all be blest!
    The Goddess said, & took her Flight
Back to the Realms of uncreated Light.

108   Steady Friendship. Jany. 1777.

When Virtue feels the Strokes of Time,
    (For Time & Nature wounds)
Falls drooping from the vernal Prime,
    And Winter wide surrounds.

Friendship—with feeling Heart sincere,   5
    Wings to the Voice of Grief,
Takes in th' embitter'd Cup her Share
    Or fondly yeilds Relief;

She flies not when the Prospect fades,
    Of Season's gay & calm   10
Her Smiles revive the dreary Shades,
    And bring her healing Balm;

Mutual, sustains each Load below,
    And shares th' afflictive Part,
Kindly partakes in every Woe,   15
    And bears them on her Heart.

How e'er the gloomy Prospect pains,
    How e'er the Storms arise,
Still steady Friendship well maintains
    The sympathetic Tyes.   20

If Nature, thus is helpful made
 (With Weakness cloath'd & frail)
How much shall that superior Aid
 Of gracious Heav'n avail?

Whose Hand directs each Stroke of Time,   25
 Whose Eye each Step surveys,
"And will proportion Strength divine
 "To dark Affliction's Days;"

If with a steady Trust, we lean,
 On his almighty Pow'r   30
His Providence will intervene,
 And aid the trembling Hour

Faith, will sustain above the Flood,
 Or sanctify the Rod,
Produce from seeming Evil, Good,   35
 And lead us home to God!—

And those, who learn the sacred Art
 "Of Strength from Sorrows Spring,"
Draw healing Virtue from the Smart
 And Honey from the Sting   40

Fidelia

109 A Glance of Character. by the same.—

Pity or blame must sure betide the Man
 Whose hoary Age & Prudence ill agree
Who on the "Verge of Time" the Flame will fan,
 That loosens all the Bands of Unity.—
Is this,—the Wisdom of Example fair,   5
 (The only Boast of venerable Age,)
Caution! oh Muse his Juniors to beware
 Nor track his trimming Footsteps on the Stage.
The flattering Tongue of Science & of Fame,

The Noise of Genius loudly eccho'd round,   10
Is but the whist'ling of an empty Name,
   The Shade of Vanity, the breath of Sound.—
And can true Genius live upon the Wind,
   Is this, to Sons of Wisdom, solid Food?
No,—native Genius centers in the Mind   15
   And Wisdom seeks a more substantial Good.
Oft as the first, the second Childhood view,
   Now rais'd by Trifles, now depress'd by Fear,
Still with its own Importance pleas'd, pursue,
   An empty Shade, for Happiness sincere.   20
How different glows a wise instructive Age.
   The Wreath of Honour Glory & Renown
Shines with fresh Lustre thro' the exampled Page,
   Embalm their Memory, & their Labours crown.
While they exist, their Life a Blessing lent   25
   To all Mankind—the active useful Friend,
The good Man's final Close, a Tryal sent,
   And Virtue marks the Race, & crowns the End.
Judicious Age will shelter in the Shade,
   Of calm Retirement, walk of Wisdom's Vale,   30
Each Cause of Action in the Balance weigh'd
   They leave to youth the Current & the Gale,
Then trust me Friend, the wise & useful Man
   Is to the World a more extensive Good,
Than he who may the Depth of Science scan,   35
   Explor'd by few, by fewer understood;
Gentle the first,—as Sols refreshing Beams,[176]
   Still glowing warm, with steady Lustre bright,
The latter glaring as the Comet streams,
   We rather view with Horror than Delight.   40

110   On reading some pious Memorials of the Dead.

Let Man with all his philosophick Rules
The Glare of Learning, & the Pride of Schools,

---

176. **Sols refreshing Beams**: "Sol [is] the sun (personified)" (*OED*).

Taste all the Wisdom that the wise have writ
And all the empty Subtleties of Wit,
With curious Search explain great Nature's Laws,   5
And from th' Effect, explore the greater Cause,
Unfold the mystic Treasures of the Sky,
And range the Planets with a Newtons Eye,
Traverse with ceaseless Steps, the Wide Domain,
And stand distinguish'd, midst the Sons of Men,   10
How empty all & vain, if wanting Thee
Immortal Power—celestial Piety,
Trust of the Sinner, triumph of the Good.
Rest to the weary—to the hungry Food;
Robe to the Naked, Med'cine to the Faint   15
And glorious full Perfection of the Saint,
Our Strength in Weakness, thro' the Vale beneath
Our Light in Darkness, & our Life in Death.
Inspir'd by thee, these Antient Worthies trod
Virtue's strait Path & stood approv'd to God,   20
Thro' various suff'rings for the Faith endur'd
Unmov'd by Threat'nings nor by Smiles allur'd,
Bravely they stood, cou'd Loss & Pain despise,
Prest thro' th'unrighteous Throng, & won the Prize,
Thus they triumphant, baffled all the Force,   25
Of Earth & Hell to stop their heavenly Course,
While fix'd on thee, the Blessing they attain'd
The Battle finish'd, & the Victory gain'd,
Now in full Glory, shall thy Grace survey,
In unexhausted Light, & everlasting Day,   30
Nor shall these fair Memorials of the Just
Be lost in Silence, or corrupt to Dust,
But still to us, their bright Example shines
With teaching Lustre in these living Lines.
      Death soon o'er Man shall draw the final Veil   35
And Tongues shall cease, & human Knowledge fail,
Nature expire—in dark Confusion lost,
And all her fair & wond'rous Works be lost
But thou immortal, shall forever last
When Time is finish'd & its' Scenes are past.   40

Fidelia

111 Reflections on the Death of several valuable Friends lately remov'd from amongst us.—by a Female.—[177]

Whence, oh! my friend, that sadly pensive Sigh,
Whence these descending, sympathetick Tears?
Has thy firm Bosom met the adverse Shock
Or dost thou feel another's secret Woe?
    No—'tis a general universal Grief   5
That swells thy Bosom with augmenting Pangs,
Thou mourns for Sion—mourns the Churches Loss
Repeated Losses,—recently sustain'd
By the Removal of her valient Sons,
For who can view her stately Pillars gone,   10
(Those firm Supports of Virtues weighty Dome)
And not unite in tributary Tears?
No more—a Fothergill—with Truths bright Shield
Maintains the Dignity of Christian Zeal
No more he shines the Mirror of the Good;   15
The perfect Standard of accomplish'd Man,
What e'er of Great the Moralist can boast.
What e'er superior Grace Religion gives
In him portray'd, a finish'd Character.—
With what persuasive nervous Eloquence   20
His Lips have utter'd this endearing Call,
    "Ye rising Youth—ye Hope of future Times
    "You who have felt the Cords of heavn'ly Love,
    "To draw & disengage you from the World,
    "Keep near that quick'ning vivifying Power,   25
    "Which freed from Bondage Israel's favour'd Sons.
    "So shall you grow, to glad parental Care
    "And stand as Warriors, in defence of Truth
    "On you, th' important Cause must soon devolve

177. **by a Female**: When Moore transcribed this poem, she was not sure of the name of the author. At the end of the poem, she writes: "The above is supposed to be wrote by M. Morris, author of the Letter to a Clergyman." A later collector of Quaker testimonies and poems, William Armistead identifies the author (probably incorrectly) as Mary Barnard (afterward Dickenson) in *Select Miscellanies*, vol. 6 (London, 1851): 165–67. The stark contrast in styles suggests that this is not the same M. Morris as *MMMB* 64.

"O! be ye faithful, upright & sincere.["]—   30
— No more he speaks, his flowing Periods cease,
No more he lights Devotions sacred Flame;
No longer warms & aids th' ascending Soul
To scale the Altar whence his Virtue's flow'd,
For all proceeded from the Throne of Grace   35
His Light, his Love, his ardent Charity
Were but the Emanations of that Sun
Whose Rays diffusive are the Christians strength
His Bow, his Battle-ax & only Hope.
    Nor less rever'd the Memory of Hunt   40
That noble Veteran in his Master's Cause,
Who duteous left his Wife—his native Land
With every Pledge, that renders Life more dear
To purchase that best Gift—a peaceful Mind.
    You who with him have oft retir'd to sit   45
In inward Silence—awful & profound
Beneath the Shade of Sinais cloudy Top*
To wait the unfoldings of mysterious Love,
You only know—the deep & ardent Travail
Of his enlighten'd sympathetic Mind,   50
Whose fellow labouring lent a secret Strength
With yours uniting, raising Life & Light.
    And thou, Oh Woolman—venerable Seer,
Art highly worthy of the plaintive Lay,
In thee, th'astonish'd gazing World admir'd   55
What this degenerate Age can rarely boast
A faithful Follower of a suffering Lord,
'Twas thine the painful thorny Path to tread,
'Twas thine to bear a Saviour's dying Cross
Redeem'd from Earth, & Earths perplexing Cares   60
Redeem'd from lawful & unlawful self,
Thy Mind was tutor'd, fitted & prepar'd
To enjoy the highest priviledge of Man,
A near Communion with eternal Good,
A fellowship celestial while below,   65
The certain Earnest of immortal Bliss
His only Wish to hear & to obey
The sacred Mandates & supreme Decree,
Of him who calls to Purity & Peace.

Here stops my Pen this fainter Sketch forbear   70
Of what their retrospective Virtues preach,
Their bright Examples thus address Mankind.—
"Our painful arduous Warfare now is past
 "Our Minds releas'd from Earth's encumbr'ing Veil,
"Are gone to enjoy that Liberty they lov'd,   75
"That full Fruition of triumphant Joy
"For which we labour'd in our Militant State,
"Mourn not for us, the living claim y[ou]r. Tears,
"Weep for the Dead in Trespasses & Sin,
"Tread the same Steps that center'd us in Rest   80
"By good Example, call to the Supine
"The young encourage—animate the Weak,
"Comfort the Mourners—strengthen those who faint,
"That Sion thus may shake herself & shine,
"With the bright Lustre of her antient Days."   85

[Marginal notes:]
*[Exodus 19th Ch. 18 Ver.]
The above is supposed to be wrote by M. Morris, author of the Letter
to a Clergyman.

112   To the Memory of Hannah Hill.[178] (Consort to Richd. Hill) who departed this Life the 25th of 12 mo. 1726

As pious Matrons whose transcendant Worth,
Resplendent shines, are sacredly set forth,

178. **Hannah Hill**: Hannah Lloyd Hill (1666–1726) was Milcah Moore's great
aunt, sister of Moore's grandmother Deborah Lloyd Moore and wife of Richard Hill,
uncle of Moore's father Dr. Richard Hill. She was part of Philadelphia's early Quaker
elite and travelled as a Quaker minister. Her second husband, Richard Hill, served in
a variety of prominent political positions, including as a member of the Provincial
Council, Speaker of the Assembly, and Mayor of Philadelphia. Hannah Hill was remembered in a memorial by Eleanor Evans, the subject of *MMMB* 35. See also Jordan, *Colonial Families*; Frederick Tolles, *Meeting House and Counting House: The
Quaker Merchants of Colonial Philadelphia, 1682–1763* (New York: Norton, 1963),
17, 118–20; "Elinor Evan's Character of Hannah Hill," LCP.

In heavenly Order by the hallow'd Pen
Of some inspired holy Sons of Men,
As sacred Oracles do clear display,   5
Making their Glory shine like perfect Day;
So now a Saint who lived in these our Days
Whose meanest Gifts transcend our highest Praise,
Whose shining Virtues did her Worth proclaim,
Deserves a lasting Record of her Name,   10
By one who tho' not equally inspir'd,
Yet is with Love to Truths blest Preachers fir'd,
Like as an honest Israelite of old.[179]
As in the sacred Writings we are told,
Who for an holy peaceful Offering,   15
When he'd no Lamb two turtle Doves must bring.
For Want of these to speak without Offence,
My Offering shall be Truth with Innocence,
Believe it Friends my Offering has no Guile
Tho' it may be as small as one poor drop of Oil,   20
Thou mighty King; thou God that sits on high
Whose awful Nod commands the trembling Sky,
Refine my earthly Genius & inspire
Poor mourning Clay those Wonders to admire,
Which in our Sister and dear Friend were known,   25
Full fraught with Graces which were all her own.
Mourn oh ye Elders, drop a melting Tear
Lament ye Matrons her who was so dear,
Mourn all ye tender Virgins, every Youth
Whose spotless Souls bespangled are with Truth   30
Mourn antient Britons, let yr. Sighs proclaim
And sink more deep than Words have Pow'r to name
Let yr. grave Bards her shining Graces sing
And to her Honour, each an Offering bring,
And when their Souls are mov'd with soft Delight   35
Even then, & not till then begin to write;
Let breathing Numbers celebrate her Worth
Sweeter than precious Ointment pour'd forth
Bless'd be the Nation whence she had her Birth.

179. **honest Israelite of old**: Leviticus 12:7–8 prescribes that for ritual purification after birth, a poor couple could bring two turtledoves instead of lamb, which is what Joseph and Mary did in Luke 2:24.

Let other Females frequently relate   40
Her Graces—& those Graces imitate,
Let Babes unborn when they can speak their Sense
Declare her Virtues with due Reverence,
So holy, pure & peaceful was her Life,
A nursing Mother & most tender Wife,   45
Like Mary chusing still the better Part[180]
With every Christian Virtue of the Heart
Dove like she was full of Humility
Her left Hand Love, her right Hand Charity,
So kind to Strangers that she seem'd to be,   50
Of generous Virtues the Epitome
Bore others Sorrows simpathiz'd with those
Who wou'd the Anguish of their Hearts disclose,
Full of good Works in Heaven laid up much Store,
Gladly she gave her Substance to the Poor,   55
Too good to live on Earth—who can be more?
Her Heav'n-born Soul was purified from Sin
Like the Kings Daughter[181] glorious all within
Her Holiness of Heart did so declare
'Twas Christ that sway'd his kingly Sceptre there   60
With holy Tears of Joy she did proclain
The dazzling Wonders of her Saviour's Name
Her Soul enflam'd with Raptures from above
Her Testimonies breathing nought but Love,
'Twas Love to Soul's that royal Grace was given   65
To her—& Love's the very Soul of Heaven,
In powerful Sense of great Emanuels Name
She Seraph like darted a heavenly Flame
Such precious Emanations did impart
Which seiz'd & made a Captive of my Heart.   70
With Hermon's Dew & Israels holy Bread[182]

---

180. **Like Mary chusing still the better Part**: See Luke 10:38–42. This passage relates the story of Jesus' visit to Martha and Mary. Mary chose to sit at Jesus' feet to hear his words while "Martha was cumbered about much serving."

181. **Kings Daughter**: "Glorious all within" (Psalm 45:13).

182. **Hermon's Dew & Israels holy Bread**: Mt. Hermon, which is snow-covered even in summer, is the source of the Jordan river, and thus a significant source of Is-

Thro' her each panting hungry Soul was fed.[183]
Charm'd with the Musick of her heav'nly Tongue
More ravishing than Instrument well strung,
I've thought Heavens King did her dr. Soul prepare   75
To keep his Bounteous royal Treas'ry there.
Oh had I but the Pinions of a Dove
Or could I but dissolve in purest Love.
I'd mount on Wings of Faith & upwards flee
To have her blest her precious Company.   80
She was so meek so humble, truly wise,
As if she'd been an Angel in disguise.—

113   Acrostick[184] on Hannah Hill.

Hosannah now be given to Israel's King,
And let both Heav'n & Earth with Praises sing
No Thought imagines, nor can Tongue express
No Voice can tell one half of Hannahs Bliss
Arch Angels sing & Cherubs breathe Amen,   5
Hosannah's, Seraphs eccho back again,
Heav'n had her royal Heart when here below,
Inspir'd by Heaven for Christ decreed it so,
Let all Christ's Sheep & Lambs of each Degree,
Let all beg Christ to send more such as she.—   10

---

rael's water. "Holy Bread" refers to the manna in the desert that the Israelites ate on
their way through the wilderness, out of Egypt. See Exodus 16:13.

183. **Thro' her each panting hungry Soul was fed**: There are several allusions to
souls "panting" or hungering for the word of God: Psalm 42: "As the hart panteth after the water brooks, so panteth my soul after thee, O God"; Psalm 119:131: "I
opened my mouth, and panted: for I longed for thy commandments."

184. **Acrostick**: from the Greek ("at the tip of the verse"). "In an acrostic the first
letter of each line or stanza spells out either the alphabet . . . or a name–usually of the
author or the addressee (a patron, the beloved, a saint)" (*The New Princeton Handbook of Poetic Terms*, ed. T. V. F. Brogan [New Jersey: Princeton University Press,
1994]).

114   Verses on C. Payton[185] a Preacher among the People called Quakers.

Attend! attend a Message from on High,
Proclaims a Saviour, & a God that's nigh,
Lo Payton comes with heav'nly Sanction crown'd,
And spreads with Joy the welcome News around:
"Captive go free & thou O! Slave arise   5
"Shake off thy Chains & joyful mount the Skies,
"Lo thy Redeemer lives! arise & shine
"Confess the Power, the Energy divine,
"That thus could raise a poor dejected Slave
"From Satan's Power & from Destruction save,   10
"To Heaven with Saints a glorious Title give
"There with thy God in endless Joy to live."
Thro' Youth & Beauty, from their heav'nly Source,
These sacred Truths flow with redoubled Force
Cloath'd with resistless Eloquence around   15
An unknown Joy attends the pleasing Sound
Soft glow the flinty Hearts, the stubborn bend,
And Tears unfeign'd from Hypocrites descend,
Ev'n Atheists trembling, Deists wond'ring stand
Confess a God, confess a saving Hand.—   20
      Resign'd in Youth, she spends her early Days,
In Acts of Love that sound her Makers praise,
Wean'd from the World with all its pleasing Toys
Of low Enjoyments & of earthborn Joys,
Attentive only to that glorious Light   25
Whose piercing Rays illuminate the Night
And guide the Traveller in that narrow Way,
Which leads to Glory & eternal Day,

185. **Verses on C. Payton**: Catherine Peyton Phillips (1727–94), an English Quaker minister, traveled extensively in America. She arrived in 1754 with her companion Mary Peisley (later Neale), and they left in 1756 with Samuel Fothergill. In her journal of the trip Payton described being in Philadelphia during 1755, at which time Quakers in the colony were particularly distressed about war with the Indians. Catherine Peyton married William Phillips in 1772. See "An Account of Ministering Friends," 119; *The Friend* 55 (1882): 171; *Memoirs of the Life of Catherine Phillips* (London, 1797).

Thither she hastes inviting as she goes,
Her best lov'd Friends, & her inverterate Foes, 30
Yet but a little & behold her rise
With Joy triumphant to her native Skies!
Soaring on high as on an Eagles Wings
Her Maker's Praise ascending sweetly sings.—

T. Matlack [186]

115   Wrote extempore on Tea. by Fidelia

Blest Leaf whose aromatic Gales dispence,
To Men, Politeness, & to Ladies Sense
Gay Wit, Good-Nature, circulate with thee,
Doctors & Misers, only rail at Tea.

116   On reading a few Paragraphs in the Crisis April 1777

Paine, tho' thy Tongue may now run glibber,
Warm'd with thy independent Glow,
Thou art indeed, the boldest Fibber,
I ever knew or wish to know.
Here Page & Page,* ev'n num'rous Pages, 5
Are void of Breeding, Sense or Truth,
I hope thou dont receive thy Wages,
As Tutor to our rising Youth.
Of female Manners never scribble,
Nor with thy Rudeness wound our Ear, 10

---

186. *T. Matlack*: Timothy Matlack (1736–1829) was disowned by the Society of Friends in 1765 for military activity and became a member of the Free Quakers during the American Revolution. He served as a member of the Committee of Safety with radicals such as Thomas Paine, as a colonel during the war, as the clerk of the Continental Congress in 1776, and as a member of the U.S. Congress in 1780. Crane, ed. *Diary of Elizabeth Drinker*, biographical directory; Mekeel, *The Relation of the Quakers to the American Revolution*, 283–89.

How e'er thy trimming Pen may quibble,
The Delicate—is not thy Sphere;
And now to prove how false thy Stories
By Facts,—which wont admit a Doubt
Know there are conscientious Tories   15
And one poor Whig at least without
Wilt thou permit the Muse to mention,
A Whisper circulated round,
"Let Howe encrease the Scribblers Pension
"No more will Paine a Whig be found."—   20
For not from Principle, but Lucre,
He gains his Bread from out the Fire,
Let Court & Congress, both stand neuter,
And the poor Creature must expire.—*Finis*

[Marginal note:]
*citing the Pages.

117   Peace. August 1776.

Oh! for the gentle Voice of Peace to flow
With healing Virtue & cementing Power,
To charm a jarring World to rest, & warm,
With sweet Benignity the human Breast
The dark malignant Spirits banish far   5
Who break the soft Alliance, nature meant
In the kind Tyes, & social Ways of Men.
Revenge & Discord, with th' infernal Train
(That feed the Rage of War, amidst a Race
Form'd the high Offspring of the God of Peace   10
Bind to their dark Domains of hellish Hate.)
To rule oer ruin'd Natures like their own.
To link in Laws of Love the kindred Race
As Bretheren dear, as generous Friendship kind
With meek Allowance, judge a Being Frail,   15
"And watch for Good, & not for Evil spy,["]
As fellow Pilgrims, thro' Probations Path,
For others feel as for himself—& sooth

With lenient Hand the Wound of Sorrows Shaft
To smooth the Bed of Langour—& enlighten   20
The dreary Walk of rough Afflictions Vale,
At such a Scene seraphic Forms could joy
Share in the Bliss of renovated Nature,
Angels converse, & "God reside with Man."
    Passions, the Elements of Life would flow   25
In sweet Accordance to th' attemper'd Mind,
Of heav'nly Harmony, & mutual Love,
The Bands of Amity & Peace conjoin'd
In the soft Concord of a tender Union,
High Heaven would joy at Nature's holy Triumph,   30
And Man be found the guardian Friend of Man,
To watch with Angels round his Brother's Tent,
With equal kind Attention screen from Danger,
The soft Companion of his Exile here,
    Oh! glorious Change, no wild Destroyer found   35
Amidst the social Tyes of kindred Blood,
To stand "the Rival of the Brute" & prey
Upon his fellow-Trav'ler thro' the Road
No impious Hand to shew his Path with snares,
Or break the League of Natures solemn Peace;   40
Creation then would kindle into Love,
A blooming Eden smile, again renew'd
And Heaven & Earth, the Song of Joy attest
'Till by a soft Transition Man exchang'd
A short Probation for the Peace of God.—   45

Fidelia

118   The Vanity of Life.

   1
Fond Youth give o'er
And seek no more
(Below the Skies) for Happiness,
If Joys are thine

They soon decline   5
Our State admits no perfect Bliss.
    2
If thou hast Wealth
Content & Health
If Beauty triumphs in thine Eye
How soon appears   10
Concluding Years
And Hours on swiftest Pinions fly.
    3
If rising Fame
Adorns thy Name,
And smiling Wit thy sprightly Page   15
If Pleasure's stand
To court thy Hand
They lead to Life's concluding Stage.
    [4]
Thy youthful Prime
Revolving Time   20
Each rising & each setting Sun
Will wing thy Days
To run their Race
And bring thy final Period on.
    5
Thy blooming Hours   25
Thy sprightly Pow'rs
Will in succeeding years be lost
Thy Spring be gone
Thy Autumn come
And Winter shed its aged Frost.   30
    6
Thy evening Star
Will now appear
In this thy late declining Day,
The gayest Scene,
Nor garland green,   35
Will hide the melancholy Grey
    7
Now feeble Age
On every Page,

Is writ in our Infirmities,
With gentle Haste   40
Descending fast,
And fainting Nature sinks & dies.
　　　[8]
'Till quite undrest
With years opprest,
Their destin'd Period nearly run,   45
More faint displays
The feeble Rays,
The Shadows of their setting Sun.
　　　9
Then mighty Death
Demands thy Breath,   50
A Tribute to the silent Grave,
Distinction here
Will not appear,
Together lays the Base & Brave.
　　　10
Alas!—how poor   55
The trifling Store
Of all the gay Creation now,
The Monarch's Robe
The Miser's good
The Poets Bays or laurel'd Brow.   60

Fidelia

119　Wrote upon reading a curious physical Advertiz in the Evening Post[187] Augt. 1776.

Thy curious Advertisement Thomas
(Investigating thy Design)
Was wrote to draw our Money from us,
For the Support of thee & thine.

187. **Evening Post**: *The Pennsylvania Evening Post* was published tri-weekly, semi-weekly, and daily on an irregular basis from 1775 through 1784. During 1775 and 1776, it was published on Tuesday, Thursday, and Saturday by Benjamin Towne.

    2

Only to cure an autumn Fever,   5
Is no such Novelty we find,
Wouldst thou establish Fame forever,
Go cool the "Fever of the Mind."

    3

'Tis this which now malignant rages
'Tis this which does its thousands slay,   10
And what will be the final Wages,
For those who act the tragic Play?

    4

To expiate each publick Error
Unite to heal, & thus attone
Or haste (with thy Compeers* together)   15
Where thou art, "more belov'd & known."

Fidelia

[Marginal note:]
*tho. not a Master Builder he has been a journeyman in the Work of
Mischief.

120   A Riddle.[188] by the same.

As soon as Heavens creating Word,
    This mighty Change of Things began
I was appointed sovereign Lord,
    Over the new made Creature Man.
With him my Journey I begun,   5
    If Pleasure charm'd or Pain distress'd
With every rising setting Sun,
    Ordain'd to be his constant Guest.

On Thursday, August 29, 1776, a notice appeared addressed "to the Public," and
signed "T. Young." The subject of the notice was a medicinal cure for "autumnal
fevers" that Young claimed to possess. See Clarence S. Brigham, *History and Bibliography of American Newspapers, 1690–1820*, vol. 1 (Worcester, Mass.: American Antiquarian Society, 1947), 931–32; *Pennsylvania Evening Post*, vol. 2, no. 251, p. 429.

   188. **A Riddle**: Riddles have been poetic forms in Roman, Anglo-Saxon, and medieval poetry. See "Riddle" in Holman and Harmon, *A Handbook to Literature*, 6th
ed. (New York: Macmillan, 1992).

In deepest Darkness I am Light,
 And yet in Nature's fairest Day,   10
I'm all the Horrors of the Night
 Without one Beam or cheering Ray.
Courageous I the Coward make,
 And bid the trembling Hero fear,
And by my sov'reign Voice can shake   15
 The Prince, the Peasant & the Peer.
O'er Sea & Land supream I reign,
 The humble & the haughty Brow,
Acknowledge my superior Name,
 And unto me submissive bow.   20
The high, the low, the base, the brave,
 O'er all is my Dominion spread,
I rule the Monarch & the Slave
 The Patriots Gain; the Atheists Dread.
I'm black as Vice, as Virtue fair   25
 And am by both obey'd & lov'd
To each I'm a Companion dear
 And am by Heaven & Hell approv'd.—

121 Some Expressions of Saml. Fothergill[189] delivered to his Relations, at or near his close of Life 1772. attempted in Verse.

Hark the warm Accents of th'expiring Saint
And view the Hope—the dying Bed can paint
'Till rising with his favour'd Soul on high,
We hail the Hour & learn of him to die.

"Not Health or length of Days can we command   5
Dependant all, on Heavens disposing Hand,

189. **Some Expressions of Saml. Fothergill**: Prose excerpts of this testimony was circulated in manuscript form and later printed. It appears in manuscript in another commonplace book by Milcah Martha Moore (pp. 100–101), devoted only to Quaker writing, and in a commonplace book by Martha Cooper Allinson, 41–42. (MS. 975A, Haverford College, Pa.). William Armistead published them in his *Select Miscellanies*, vol. 2 (London, 1851), 250–51.

Descending now, my setting Sun decays
And draws the Shadows of its evening Rays,
But to my God resign'd, I bow my Head
Unerring Wisdom marks the Paths we tread.   10
One sweet Support remains with strengthning Pow'r
And bears me thro' the weak declining Hour,
And tho' the Tempest swell, the Surges beat
Th' unshaken Rock sustains my steady Feet
With earnest Zeal this living Blessing find,   15
And on its sacred Influence fix your Mind.—
         Tho' painful Nights & weary Days attend
My languid Couch, & point the awful End
In Patience kept, I feel the Hand divine
Sustain my Soul & to his Will resign,   20
Thro' Faith, the dreaded Sting of Death is lost
Nor Hell shall o'er my Soul, its Victory boast
Love, sacred Love shall from the Terror save
And in this Strength, I triumph o'er the Grave.
Each human Comfort we possess below   25
Are Gifts but lent & on Demand must go,
And tho' the Objects of our Love & Care,
Yet Disappointment is the Name they bear.
Did Heaven permit well pleas'd my Days to spend
And join the Service, which you now attend,   30
Where oft my Soul hath felt divine Regard
And with my Brethren in the Blessing shar'd;
But Heaven forbids—in sweet Remembrance join'd
We shall be present, in th' united Mind,
Our God best knows what is for each most fit   35
And to his sov'reign Wisdom I submit.
         Triumphant now, I soar beyond the Gloom
My raptur'd Spirit tastes the Bliss to come,
The glorious Prospect all my Soul employs
And wings my Faith to Life's immortal Joys   40
Oh! who would change, the favour'd State I know
For all the false delusive Glare below?
         Inform my Brethren, (whom the Bands of Love
Unite in Tyes which Death can ne'er remove)
That I shall joyful close as I have liv'd,   45
Firm on the Rock in whom we have believ'd,

With strong unshaken Faith I truly know,
We have not follow'd Fiction here below,
Devis'd the fabled Tale, deceitful trod,
But the pure Substance of the living God.   50
Let ev'ry Member of the Church below
A full Increase of sacred Virtue know,
Let Age grow strong,—the animating Fire
With active Zeal the Christian youth inspire,
Still Sion shall her glorious Guard possess   55
The Lord surrounds & will his Sion bless.
    If such the Master's Will, that now I go
And leave the Temple militant below,
Where in the Strength receiv'd I labour'd still
The humble Path of Duty to fulfill   60
The glorious Evidence of Faith I have,
My favour'd Spirit shall survive the Grave,
And to his Church triumphant joyful rise
Beyond the View of sublunary Skies,[190]
My Love the fervent Wish on each bestows   65
Whose Love to Jesus, as the Master glows.["]—

Fidelia

122 To Captain Charles Craige.[191] by the same

In these degenerate Days let Craige retain
The feeling Bosom, & the Heart humane,
Nor brutalize the Man, forget to glow,
At others Good or melt at others Woe,
But still at misery's Call the Hand extend   5

190. **sublunary Skies**: "Existing . . . beneath the moon; lying between the orbit of the moon and the earth; hence, subject to the moon's influence" (*OED*).

191. **To Captain Charles Craige**: There are at least two Captain Craiges in the historical record, and it is not clear which, if any, was the subject of Griffitts' poem. The *Pennsylvania Evening Post* carried a notice on August 1, 1776 that the "Congress privateer, Captain Craig, has taken and carried into Egg Harbor, a brig from Nevis. This prize is said to be worth near twenty thousand pounds." Charles Craig was a Captain in the Continental Dragoons in 1777, and was wounded at the battle of Brandywine.

And be to Virtue or to Man a Friend,
Despise the mean Distinctions Times have made
To swell Distress, & then refuse our Aid,
To break each sacred Tye, each social Band,
And in Affliction plunge the parent Land.   10
Be this the Son of Rapine's brutal Boast,
Where Nature's Glow is in the Warrior lost,
But Craige wou'd blush to merit such a Name,
Or at th' Expence of Virtue purchase Fame,
Then with firm Steps maintain fair Virtue's Cause   15
Nature support against inhuman Laws,
Still aid Distress, be to the Poor a Friend,
On every Call thy generous Hand extend
Still feeling Nature bend to Nature's Claim
And guard the Honour of the human Name,   20
In dark Afflictions Days (the Wane of Power)
Virtues Applause shall gild the dreary Hour,
The Hand of Friendship raise thy languid Head,
And smooth the Pillow of the dying Bed,
While fairer Fame shall to thy Memory glow   25
Than the proud warriors Ravage can bestow.

Decr. 20th. 1777.   Fidelia

123   To the Friends confined at Winchester in Virginia[192] by the same.

Reproach is oft the Christian's Lot to know,
Thro' dark Probations rugged Path below.

See Frances B. Heitman, *Historical Register of the Officers of the Continental Army During the War of the Revolution, April 1775 to December 1783* (Washington, D.C.: Rare Book Shop Publications, 1914) indicates that Craig did not rejoin the army, and died in 1782. A letter from Daniel Brodhead in December 1782 discusses the suicide of Captain Charles Craig over a disagreement with his father-in-law, Colonel Bird or Burd (possibly Benjamin Burd of Bedford Country). Gratz Collection, HSP.

    192. **Friends confined at Winchester in Virginia:** Quaker neutrality and/or loyalty was the source of a great deal of patriot animosity. Friends were persecuted by

His to endure the Worlds malignant Frown
And wear his Masters Cross as well as Crown.
This Lesson learn'd—he treads on exil'd Clime   5
Nor bounds his Prospects, by the Bounds of Time
Views human Life—A Passage—this the Road
That leads the Pilgrim to immortal Good
Beyond the Ken of Sense his Treasure lies
Safe in his bright reversionary Skies   10
But e'er the conquering Palm the Victors know
They first sustain the trying Lot below
So Jacobs Sons [193] amidst the desert Waste
With Want, with Weakness, & with Foes oppress'd
Experienc'd fresh supplies of needful Aid   15
When trembling Doubts bid human Prospects fade
From Egypts Yoke,[194] his chosen Flocks were freed
And thro' tremendous Ways did safely lead
What Beam of Hope could human Reason find
Fierce Floods before & Pharoah's Host behind   20
But Nature's God who still doth Nature guide
Commands the Sea whose awful Waves divide
And form'd the amazing Path for Israel's Host
Who walk'd secure where Egypts' Pride was lost
The enlighten'd Cloud prepar'd the unknown Way   25

---

the patriot government in a variety of ways, the most prominent example perhaps was the exile of Quaker leaders from Philadelphia to Winchester, Virginia, in the fall of 1777. The Continental Congress directed Pennsylvania's Supreme Executive Council to take into custody leading Quakers, along with any of their political papers. In September this group was exiled, and did not return to Philadelphia until late April of the following year. Mekeel, *Relation of Quakers to the Revolution,* chap. 10; Thomas Gilpin, ed., *Exiles in Virginia* (Philadelphia: n.p., 1848).

193. **Jacobs Sons:** The sons of the patriarch Jacob who wandered in the desert as nomads. During a seven-year faminine, they went to Egypt, whose graneries were full, thanks to their brother, Joseph, whom they thought they had killed years earlier. Joseph forgave them and took care of all their needs. Joseph tells his brothers: "Now therefore be not grieved, nor angry with yourselves, that ye sold me hither: for God did send me before you to preserve life. . . . to save your lives by a great deliverance" (Genesis 45:5–7). For the whole story, see Genesis 37–50.

194. **From Egypts Yoke:** The story of the Israelites' slavery in Egypt and miraculous liberation and departure from Egypt is told in Exodus 1–15. The next lines in the poem relate this story.

Guard of the Night & Leader of the Day
Whose sacred Care did o'er his Flocks preside
Their fainting Thirst the flinty Rocks supplied
With Angels Food,[195] their daily Hunger fed
And, there an Host of Foes in safety led   30
Mid'st Jordan Waves[196] his chosen Israel stood
And with his Covenants pass'd the awful Flood
Their Fears & Foes conducted by his Hand
They gain'd Possession of the promis'd Land
And thus may you the Sufferers of this Day   35
In Patience keep the Heaven-directed Way
'Till Love divine shall bid you joyful rise
To Friendship's Claim & Natures softer Ties,
'Till Strength renew'd in his unfailing Power
Pours healing Balm on Nature's weak'ning Hour   40
'Midst Floods & Foes direct the Pilgrims' Way
Thro' midnight Darkness as the blaze of Day
His sacred Presence in the Cloud be found
In Danger guard you, & in Depths surround
Nor Doubts your firm fix'd Confidence destroy   45
Sustain the Night, the Morning brings the Joy
Whose clearing Dawn we hail, that shall restore
The Friends of Virtue to their native Shore
Hiers of that Peace beyond the World to know
Whose Frowns cannot forbid nor flattering Smiles bestow.   50

Fidelia
Feb. 1778

---

195. **With Angels Food**: The "bread" that appeared as dew on the ground that fed the Israelites during their desert journey: "And the house of Israel called the name thereof Manna: and it was like coriander seed, white; and the taste of it was like wafers made with honey" (Exodus: 16:31).

196. **Mid'st Jordan's Waves**: After Moses delivered God's law and covenants to the people of Israel, he died, and God told Joshua: "Moses my servant is dead; now therefore arise, go over this Jordan, thou and all this people, unto the land which I do give to them. . . . " (Joshua 1:2).

124   Heaven the Christians Home. To a Friend. by the same

How ardent Rest the Christian Soul pursues,
Whose Steps have traed a long laborious Way,
How joyful Shore, the shipwreck'd Sailor views,
How pleas'd the Watchman hails the Dawn of Day.—
—Such cheering Prospect warms the Christian's Mind   5
Who oft in Conflict & in Peril stood,
When he the gentle Close of Life shall find,
"A sight of Shore & ebbing of the Flood."
—Hail blissful Clime where Tears forever cease
Heaven smiles applausive on the Journey run   10
Each Combat clos'd in everlasting Peace,
The Warfare finish'd & the Victory won.
—The enraptur'd Soul shall then its Freedom gain
(Which veil'd on Earth, a suffering Exile lyes)
With kindred Minds, Messiahs rest attain,   15
And glow immortal in their native Skies.
—Where the bright Beams of one unclouded Day
Pours a full Lustre round the ransom'd Race
Where Love divine its boundless Depths display
And God shines forth "the Glory of the Place."   20
—Where we shall see & know the great unknown
Adore his Power & in his Counsel move,
Join the pure Church, (once ransom'd as his own)
Dwell in his Light & triumph in his Love.
—Where Doubts no longer cloud th' enquiring Mind,   25
No more the Voice of Weakness shall complain,
Where Death the Tyrant all disarm'd we find
Nor Satan break our sacred Peace again.
—Hail glorious Period swift revolving Time
Perform thy Orders round these lower Spheres;   30
Wing the freed Spirit to its native Clime
And close our Conflict in this Vale of Tears.
—Admit us home, where Peace perpetual flows,
Where Love & Praise th' enraptur'd Powers employ
Where every Breast with holy Union glows,   35

And God th' eternal Center of their Joy
—The Christian thus (e'vn while a feeble Worm)
If mindful of his Origin from high,
Shall quell each Foe, shall triumph o'er each Storm
And the joynt Force of Sin & Death defy.   40
—Then Pilgrim, keep thy Faith devoid of Fear,
Higher thy Rock than all these Powers shall rise
'Till Love divine shall close the Conflict here
And seat thee Victor in thy native Skies.

125   To a Parent on the Death of a Child who died at Philada. 26th Apl. 1778. by the same

Lovely Infant well releas'd
Center'd in thy sacred Rest
Safe from ev'ry dangerous Snare,
That surrounds the Sons of Care,
Favour'd Child exempt from Pain   5
Or the Warfare to sustain
Life's rough Warfare on a Soil
Lost with Ease & won with Toil
All thy destin'd Task is o'er
Or Canaans promis'd Shore   10
There the lovely Plant shall rise,
And bloom in his immortal Skies,
Where no wintry Storms of Time,
Blast the Springs unfading Prime
Where no fierce Temptations roll   15
And cloud the Virtue of the Soul,—
He amidst the cherub Throng,
Shall join in the angelic Song,
And with Powers enlarg'd, refin'd
Grow exalted into Mind.—   20
     Cease my christian Friends to mourn
Round the smiling Cherubs Urn,
Favour'd is your Child to know
His Release from Scenes of Woe;

Scenes that not your fondest Care,   25
Could secure from Dangers here
Cease your Tears, & let him rise
To Heaven a spotless Sacrafice,
You e'er long the Babe shall join
And share with him in Bliss divine,   30
Where Joys enrich Canaans Shore
And Friends unite to part no more.
To S. E.[197]—

126   On the Death of Benjamin Trotter[198]
a Preacher among the People call'd Quakers.

If Sion may for earthly Losses mourn,
Or look with Sorrow on a Prophet's Urn,
She, guiltless, now may utter a Complaint,
In falling Tears, for this departed Saint.
  In love with Christ, he shone in Bloom of Youth,   5
A public living Minister of Truth,
Thro' Life 'till Death the narrow Passage* trod,
His Eye on Jesus, & his Trust in God,
Shunn'd ev'ry Act that brings a Christian Blame,
Lov'd ev'ry Virtue that adorns the Name.   10
  For one so lov'd so honour'd, & so dear,
Sion may pay the Tribute of a Tear;
But as she mourns, let her be sure to say,
The Lord who gave had Right to take away.—

[Marginal note:]
*Matt. 7th Chap. 14th Ver.

 197. **S. E.** : Unidentified.
 198. **Benjamin Trotter**: Benjamin Trotter (1699–1768) was a Philadelphia joiner and Quaker minister. Married to Mary Corker, he travelled for the ministry in Pennsylvania and New Jersey. He was a close friend of Daniel Stanton, and was memorialized by the Philadelphia Monthy Meeting when he died. See *The Friend* 35 (1861): 68; "Testimony of the Monthly Meeting Concerning Benjamin Trotter," *Friends Biography* 10: 129–32.

Appendix

1   On the Death of John Roberts and Abraham Carlisle Novr. 4, 1778

In the sad Chambers of retir'd distress
The scenes of speechless woe, where widow's mourn
The Tender Husband lost; where orphan's weep
The Indulgent father, and sustaining friend
Th' Indulgent friend & father known no more;
Where the sad sister, faints beneath the stroke
That rent th' associate Brother from her heart;
Here, clad in solemn sympathy of woe,
My soul retire's to share my neighbour's grief,
Give sigh for sigh; & mingle tears with tears;
Or deeper still; beyond the gentle power,
Of words to Heal; or tears to mitigate
Deeper in the awful Center of the soul,
(Hid from the view of an unfeeling world,)
And wrap'd in fellow feeling of Distress
I still attend your melancholy steps,
And pay the Tender Tribute to your woes;
But words are vain; the Powers of harmony
Are useless here; ev'n friendship's soothing voice
Has lost its balm; in woundings like to your's;
Oh then from Heaven, from gracious heaven alone
Look for the strength to stand; the healing power,
The Balm of Comfort; the sustaining friend;
May He supply those soft Cementing bands,
Which Brutal Laws rent from your bleeding hearts
Direct your trenbling footsteps, and be found,
The Husband, Father, & the Brother lost;

And you, the guiltless victims of the day
(Who to a Timid City's late reproach
And blush of its Inhabitants,) have fallen,
A Prey to Laws; Disgraceful to the man
Fallen, on the Cruel shores, that gave you birth
Fallen, on th' ungrateful shores, your father's plan'd
"On the firm Basis of true Liberty,["]
"The Laws of Justice; & the rights of man";
Long, shall your names, survive the brutal deed;

And fair, Transmitted down to better times
Stand the Reproach of our's; when Lawless power
And wealth, by Rapine gain'd; shall shroud its head
In Infamous oblivion; or be held
The warning, not example of mankind;

And you, whose mad ambition, Lawless grasp
Of Proud Dominion, and oppressive power
Have spread the flames of war around the shores
Where Peace once smiled & social union dwelt;
How will you stand the Retributive hour,
Or bear the Close of dread Decision's voice;
When, as you mingled deep the Cup of woe
For suffering souls; so will your souls partake
The deeply mingled Cup of woe again,
You have Dissolv'd the tender tyes of Nature,
And torn asunder, (by the barbarous hand
Of Cruel Laws) the Dear, the soft Connections
Which Heaven had Joynd & blest; till you arose
The sourge of Desolation on their peace;
To you, the widow & orphan look
With heartfelt anguish, as their source of woe,
And in the silent Pang, from you demand
The Tender Husband & the father lost;
Tho' here, the voice of nature breath'd in vain,
To Tig[e]rs fierce, and admantine rocks,
Or, hearts unfeeling, & as hard as theirs;
The day* will come, & wing'd with swift approach
When piercing deep, Armed in Tremendous power
The voice of God, & Conscience shall be heard
Oh, in "this day of Pleading," if His hand,
Mark you severe; as you, have other's mark'd,
How will your souls, sustain His dread Decision
Whose Laws are Justice; & whose words are truth[?]

Fidelia
[Library Company of Philadelphia]

[Marginal note:]
*[Matt. 18:23–35]

2   To the Memory of my Late Valuable friend Susanna Wright, who Died, Decr. 1st, 1784 (in the 88th Year of her Age)

Shall thou, whose gentle muse in softest strain
    Wept others sorrow, with a feeling breast
Ah shall Veneria, close her Lot of pain,
    Nor leave a muse, her Virtues to attest,

Not so; the muse once favor'd and belov'd
    Shall have her Mild Benignity of heart,
The soul that wish'd each human ill remov'd,
    The Hand, that every Comfort would impart,

And tho' with innate Powers superior blest,
    The striking sense and energy of mind
How Veil'd their Lustre, while her form express'd,
    The Humble; Courteous; Diffident; & Kind;

While o'er the "Tomb of Friendship," sorrow flow'd,
    In feeling grief; and deep reflextion strong,
How, with the theme; her gentle Bosom glow'd,
    How sweet, her Powerful Harmony of song.

For, genius, thus, Distinguish'd, and admir'd;
    Above Ambitions Low Contracted Care,
She walk'd with wisdom, in the "vale retir'd,"
    And left the world; its tinsel, & its glare;

Warm to the Tyes of nature & of love
    She own'd their Influence & Cementing power
(And in this sphere of Duty, fond to move,
    From them, the Pleasing; & the painful hour,

Did suffering wound; or Death remove the friend,
    She felt the anguish of its keenest Dart;
Did brighter fancy, the social-hour attend,
    She pour'd the Balm, Compassionately kind
On Human sufferings, with a healing hand,

Thus; thro' each Period, of a lengthen'd day,
　　(Fulfill'd the Tender Claim; the social tye,)
*"She kept the noiseless Tenor of her way,"
　　Yet sign'd for good; the world could not supply,

Till nature droop'd beneath the waste of years,
　　Panted for Life; and long'd to be undress'd;
A Life, beyond these sublunary spheres;
　　A Life; Distinguish'd by eternal rest;

Perfected thus, may thou, departed friend
　　The full fruition of thy bliss enjoy,
A Bliss, that fears no Change, decrease or end;
　　A portion, time nor death can ere destroy,

And while this Bosom, once to friendship dear,
　　In artless verse enbalms its kindred clay,
Center'd in God, releas'd from sorrowing care,
　　*"Thy mortal, shall surpass thy natal day[.]"
[rough copy, Library Company of Philadelphia]

[Marginal note:]
*Gray's Church-Yard
*See a peice she wrote on her own Birthday which closes with the
above last line.

3　Lines by a Friend, on reading Mrs. M. Moore's printed and unprinted extracts for the use of Schools

I rang'd one lovely morn,
　　Within a garden's bound;
And mark'd the rose, and mark'd the thorn,
　　And various objects round.

I spy'd an active busy Bee,
　　Fly nimbly from her cell;
She lit' on flower, on shrub, and tree
　　Where balmy odours dwell.

The modest snow-drop in the shade,
    And lilly of the vales;
Carnation streak'd, near which each maid,
    Her fainter charms bewails.

The rich Magnolia towering high,
    The wood-bine of the bower;
Industrious back the flutterer drives,
    And skims it through the air.

Thus has Melissa cull'd each sweet,
    From the informing page,
And brought an intellectual treat,
    For youth, and hoary age.

The bee from instinct and self-love,
    Her balmy store collects;
Superior aims Melissa move,
    A nobler view directs:

To draw the young by pleasing lays,
    To truth and honour's cause;
To paint religion's peaceful ways,
    And piety's pure laws:

Then hear, ye rising modest fair,
    Let not her aims be lost:
Aims, generous, kind, polite, sincere,
    Which time and labour cost.

But grateful read the nice mark'd lines,
    Where taste and judgment's shewn;
Where virtue all harmonious shines;
    And make her choice your own.

Montgomery County, May 28th 1788.
[Printed in *The Columbian Magazine* (1788): 350]

4   On the death of my husband, Dr. Chas. Moore Montgomery 8 mo: 1801

To thy cold Bosom take, oh parent Earth!
    All thou canst claim of "Heav'ns best Gift to me"
This better part from thee, great God had Birth
    And now returns to Happiness and Thee.

Who'eer than him on this Life's Stage could move
    With greater Wisdom, Piety and Care,
Whose Conduct more excite Esteem and Love,
    In all Connections whether far or near;

What Heart more touch'd by Sorrows plaintive Tale
    What Head more quick to think or Hand to ease,
And when Physicians Aid could naught avail
    Who more submissive to Divine Decrees?

But o'er his Grave while fond Affection bends
    And heartfelt Sorrow waits around his Bier
Forgive the Weakness of lamenting Friends,
    My God! forgive a Wife's empassion'd Tear.

[no signature]
[Edward Wanton Smith Collection, Haverford College, Haverford, Pa.]

SUGGESTED READINGS

Barbour, Hugh. *The Quakers in Puritan England*. New Haven: Yale University Press, 1964.

———, and J. William Frost. *The Quakers*. Richmond, Ind.: Friends United Press, 1994.

Bauman, Richard. *For the Reputation of Truth: Politics, Religion, and Conflict Among the Pennsylvania Quakers, 1750–1800*. Baltimore: Johns Hopkins University Press, 1971.

Beale, Peter. "Notions in Garrison: The Seventeenth-Century Commonplace Book." In *New Ways of Looking at Old Texts*, ed. W. Speed Hill, 131–47. Vol. 107 of *Papers of the Renaissance English Text Society 1985–1991*. Binghamton, N.Y.: Medieval & Renaissance Texts Studies, Renaissance Text Society, 1993.

Bloomfield, Morton W. "The Elegy and the Elegiac Mode: Praise and Alienation." In *Renaissance Genres: Essays on Theory, History, and Interpretation*, ed. Barbara Kiefer Lewalski. Cambridge, Mass.: Harvard University Press, 1986.

Bradstreet, Anne. *The Works of Anne Bradstreet*. Edited by Jeannine Hensley. Cambridge, Mass.: Belknap-Harvard University Press, 1967.

British Women Poets 1660–1800: An Anthology. Edited by Joyce Fullard. Troy, N.Y.: Whitston, 1990.

Brookes, George S. *Friend Anthony Benezet*. Philadelphia: University of Pennsylvania Press, 1937.

Butt, John. *The Mid-Eighteenth Century*. Vol. 9 of the *Oxford History of English Literature*. Oxford: Clarendon Press, 1979.

Butterfield, Lyman, ed. *Letters of Benjamin Rush*. Princeton: Princeton University Press, 1951.

Calhoon, Robert. *The Loyalists in Revolutionary America, 1760–1781*. New York: Harcourt, Brace Jovanovich, 1965.

———, ed. *The Loyalist Perception and Other Essays*. Columbia: University of South Carolina Press, 1989.

Corner, Betsy C., and Christopher C. Booth, eds. *Chain of Friendship: Selected Letters of Dr. John Fothergill of London, 1735–1780*. Cambridge: Belknap-Harvard University Press, 1971.

Cowell, Pattie, ed. *Women Poets in Pre-Revolutionary America, 1650–1775: An Anthology*. Troy, N.Y.: Whitston, 1981.

Crane, Elaine, ed. *The Diary of Elizabeth Drinker*. 3 vols. Boston: Northeastern University Press, 1993.

————. "The World of Elizabeth Drinker. *Pennsylvania Magazine of History and Biography* 107 (1983): 3–28.

Cummings, Hubertis. *Richard Peters: Provincial Secretary and Cleric, 1704–1776*. Philadelphia: University of Pennsylvania Press, 1944.

Davidson, Cathy. *Revolution and the Word: The Rise of the Novel in America*. New York: Oxford University Press, 1986.

Davis, Natalie Zemon, and Arlette Farge. *A History of Women: Renaissance and Enlightenment Paradoxes*. Cambridge: Belknap Harvard University Press, 1993.

Dobree, Bonamy. *English Literature in the Early Eighteenth Century: 1700–1740*. Vol. 7 of *Oxford History of English Literature*. Oxford: Clarendon Press, 1959.

Dowling, William C. *The Epistolary Moment: The Poetics of the Eighteenth-Century Verse Epistle*. Princeton: Princeton University Press, 1991.

Dryden, John. *Of Dramatic Poesy and Other Critcal Essays*. 2 vols. Edited by George Watson. London: Dent, 1962.

Eighteenth-Century Women Poets. Edited by Roger Lonsdale. New York: Oxford University Press, 1990.

Gilpin, Thomas, ed. *Exiles in Virginia: With Observations on the Conduct of the Society of Friends During the Revolutionary War*. Philadelphia, 1848.

Gough, Deborah Mathias. *Christ Church Philadelphia: The Nation's Church in a Changing City*. Philadelphia: University of Pennsylvania Press, 1995.

Grasso, Christopher. *Poetry and Ideology in Revolutionary Connecticut*. Athens: University of Georgia, 1990.

Hall, David D. "Readers and Reading in America: Historical and Critical Perspectives." *Proceedings of the American Antiquarian Society*. Vol. 103 (1993).

Harris, Sharon M., ed. *American Women Writers to 1800*. New York: Oxford University Press, 1996.

Hindle, Brooke. *David Rittenhouse*. Princeton: Princeton University Press, 1964.

Hobbs, Mary. *Early Seventeenth-Century Verse Miscellany*. Hants, England: Scholars Press, 1992.

Holman, C. Hugh and William Harmon. *A Handbook to Literature*. 6th ed. New York: Macmillan, 1992.

Hyamson, Albert M. *A Dictionary of English Phrases*. London: Routledge, 1922.

Jack, Ian. *Augustan Satire: Intention and Idiom in English Poetry, 1660–1750*. Oxford: Clarendon Press, 1952.

Jackson, John W. *Margaret Morris Her Journal*. Philadelphia: George S. MacManus Company, 1949.

James, Janet Wilson. *Women in American Religion*. Philadelphia: University of Pennsylvania Press, 1980.

Jones, Mary Hoxie. *Quaker Poets Past & Present*. Wallingford, Pa.: Pendle Hill, 1975.

Kerber, Linda K. *Women of the Republic: Intellect and Ideology in Revolutionary America*. Chapel Hill: University of North Carolina Press, 1980.

Kerby-Miller, Charles, ed. *The Memoirs of the Extraordinary Life, Works, and Discoveries of Martinus Scriblerus*. Oxford: Oxford University Press, 1988.

Klepp, Susan E. "Fragmented Knowledge: Questions in Regional Demographic History," *Proceedings of the American Philosophical Society* 133 (June 1989).

———. *"The Swift Progress of Population": A Documentary and Bibliographic Study of Philadelphia's Growth, 1642–1859.* Philadelphia: American Philosophical Society, 1991.

Labaree, Leonard, ed. *The Papers of Benjamin Franklin.* 31 vols. New Haven: Yale University Press, 1959– .

Lemay, J. A. Leo, ed. *A Calendar of American Poetry in the Colonial Newspapers and Magazines and in the Major English Magazines Through 1765.* Worcester, Conn.: Amercan Antiquarian Society, 1972.

Levy, Barry. *Quakers and the American Family: British Settlement in the Delaware Valley.* New York: Oxford University Press, 1988.

Lockridge, Kenneth. *On the Sources of Patriarchal Rage: The Commonplace Books of William Byrd and Thomas Jefferson and the Gendering of Power in the Eighteenth Century.* New York: New York University Press, 1992.

Lockwood, Thomas. *Post-Augustan Satire: Charles Churchill and Satirical Poetry, 1750–1800.* Seattle: University of Washington Press, 1979.

Love, Harold. *Scribal Publication in Seventeenth-Century England.* Oxford: Clarendon Press, 1993.

Lundin, Leonard. *Cockpit of the Revolution: The War for Independence in New Jersey.* Princeton: Princeton University Press, 1940.

Marietta, Jack D. *The Reformation of American Quakerism, 1748–1783.* Philadelphia: University of Pennsylvania Press, 1984.

Marotti, Arthur. *Manuscript, Print, and the English Renaissance.* Ithaca: Cornell University Press, 1995.

Mekeel, Arthur J. *The Relation of the Quakers to the American Revolutionary War.* Washington: University Press of America, 1979.

Middlekauff, Robert. *The Glorious Cause: The American Revolution, 1763–1789.* Oxford: Oxford University Press, 1982.

Mohl, Ruth. *John Milton and His Commonplace Book.* New York: Ungar, 1969.

Morgan, Edmund S. and Helen M. *The Stamp Act Crisis: Prologue to Revolution.* Revised edition. New York: Macmillan, 1963.

Mulford, Carla. *"Only for the Eye of a Friend": The Poems of Annis Boudinot Stockton.* Charlottesville: University of Virginia Press, 1995.

———. "Political Poetics: Annis Boudinot Stockton and Middle Atlantic Women's Culture." *New Jersey History* 111 (1993): 66–110.

Nash, Gary B. *The Urban Crucible: The Northern Seaports and the Origins of the American Revolution.* Abridged edition. Cambridge, Mass.: Harvard University Press, 1986.

Norton, Mary Beth. *Liberty's Daughters: The Revolutionary Experience of American Women, 1750–1800.* Boston: Little, Brown and Company, 1980.

Ousterhout, Anne M. *A State Divided: Opposition in Pennsylvania to the American Revolution.* Westport, Conn.: Greenwood Press, 1987.

Pope, Alexander. *The Complete Poetical Works of Alexander Pope.* Cambridge student's edition. Boston: Houghton, Mifflin & Company, 1931.

———. *The Prose Works of Alexander Pope.* Edited by Rosemary Cowler. Hamden, Conn.: Archon-The Shoestring Press, 1986.

Prior, Matthew. *The Literary Works of Matthew Prior*. 2 vols. Edited by H. Bunker Wright and Monroe K. Spears. Oxford: Clarendon Press, 1959.

Rosenberg, Nancy. "The Sub-textual Religion: Quakers, the Book, and Public Education in Philadelphia, 1682–1800." Ph.D. diss., University of Michigan, Ann Arbor, 1991.

Rowe, Elizabeth Singer. *The Poetry of Elizabeth Singer Rowe: 1674–1737*. Edited by Madeleine Forell Marshall. Lewiston, N.Y.: Edwin Mellen Press, 1987.

Ryerson, Richard. *The Revolution Has Now Begun: The Radical Committees of Philadelphia, 1765–1776*. Philadelphia: University of Pennsylvania Press, 1978.

Sargent, Winthrop, ed. *The Loyal Verses of Stansbury and Odell*. Albany: N.p., 1860.

Shea, Daniel B. "Beginnings to 1810." *Columbia Literary History of the United States*, 3–205. Gen. ed. Emory Elliott. New York: Columbia University Press, 1987.

Shields, David S. "British-American Belles Lettres." *The Cambridge History of American Literature*, 1:309–45. Gen. Ed. Sacvan Bercovitch. Cambridge: Cambridge University Press, 1994.

———. "The Manuscript in the World of Print." *Proceedings of the American Antiquarian Society* 102, pt. 2 (1993): 403–16.

———. *Oracles of Empire: Poetry, Politics, and Commerce in British America, 1690–1750*. Chicago: University of Chicago Press, 1990.

Skemp, Sheila. *William Franklin: Son of a Patriot, Servant of a King*. New York: Oxford University Press, 1990.

Slotten, Martha C. "Elizabeth Graeme Ferguson: A Poet in 'The Athens of North America.'" *Pennsylvania Magazine of History and Biography* 108 (1984): 259–88.

Smith, Billy. *The "Lower Sort": Philadelphia's Laboring People, 1750–1800*. Ithaca: Cornell University Press, 1990.

Smith, John J., ed. *Letters of Doctor Richard Hill and His Children*. Philadelphia, 1854.

Soderlund, Jean R. *Quakers and Slavery: A Divided Spirit*. Princeton: Princeton University Press, 1985.

———. "Women's Authority in Pennsylvania and New Jersey Quaker Meetings, 1680–1760." *William and Mary Quarterly* 44 (October 1987): 722–49.

Steele, Richard. *The British Essayists*. Edited by A. Chalmers. Vol. 2. Boston: Little Brown, 1850.

Thomas, Claudia N. *Alexander Pope and His Eighteenth-Century Women Readers*. Carbondale: Southern Illinois University Press, 1994.

Tillotson, Geoffrey. "Eighteenth-century Poetic Diction." *Eighteenth-Century English Literature: Modern Essays in Criticism*, 212–32. Edited by James L. Clifford. New York: Oxford University Press, 1959.

Tolles, Frederick. *Meeting House and Counting House: The Quaker Merchants of Colonial Philadelphia, 1682–1763*. New York: Norton, 1963.

———. "'Of the Best Sort but Plain': The Quaker Aesthetic." *American Quarterly* 9 (1959): 484–502.

Tomes, Nancy. "The Quaker Connection: Visiting Patterns among Women in the Philadelphia Society of Friends, 1750–1800." *Friends and Neighbors: Group*

Life in America's First Plural Society, 174–93. Edited by Michael Zuckerman. Philadelphia: Temple University Press, 1982.

Treese, Lorett. *A Storm Gathering: The Penn Family and the American Revolution.* University Park: Pennsylvania State University Press, 1992.

Tully, Allan. *Forming American Politics: Ideals, Interests and Institutions in Colonial New York and Pennsylvania.* Baltimore: Johns Hopkins University Press, 1977.

———. *William Penn's Legacy: Politics and Social Structure in Provincial Pennsylvania.* Baltimore: Johns Hopkins University Press, 1977.

Warner, Michael. *The Letters of the Republic: Publication and the Public Sphere in Eighteenth-Century America.* Cambridge: Harvard University Press, 1990.

Weigley, Russell F., ed. *Philadelphia: A 300-year History.* New York: W. W. Norton, 1982.

Williamson, Marilyn L. *Raising Their Voices: British Women Writers, 1650–1750.* Detroit: Wayne State University Press, 1990.

Wilson, Douglas L., ed. *Jefferson's Literary Commonplace Book.* Princeton: Princeton University Press, 1989.

Wister, Sarah. *The Journal and Occasional Writings of Sarah Wister.* Edited by Kathryn Zabelle Derounian. Rutherford: Fairleigh Dickinson University Press, 1987.

Wright, Luella M. *The Literary Life of the Early Friends: 1650–1725.* New York: Columbia University Press, 1932.

Wulf, Karin. "A Marginal Independence: Unmarried Women in Colonial Philadelphia." Ph.D diss., Johns Hopkins University, Baltimore, Maryland, 1993.

———. " 'My Dear Liberty': Marriage, Spinsterhood and Conceptions of Female Autonomy in Eighteenth-Century Philadelphia." In Larry D. Eldridge, ed. *Women and Freedom in Early America.* New York: New York University Press, 1996.

Young, Edward. *The Poetical Works of Edward Young.* London: Bell, 1896.

INDEX OF TITLES BY AUTHOR

Index of First Lines
of Poems

The number in parentheses indicates the *MMMB* entry number.

INDEX OF NAMES AND SUBJECTS